CYBER WARFARE

SECOND EDITION

CYBER WARFARE
Techniques, Tactics and Tools for Security Practitioners

SECOND EDITION

JASON ANDRESS

STEVE WINTERFELD

LILLIAN ABLON
Technical Editor

ELSEVIER

AMSTERDAM • BOSTON • HEIDELBERG • LONDON
NEW YORK • OXFORD • PARIS • SAN DIEGO
SAN FRANCISCO • SINGAPORE • SYDNEY • TOKYO
Syngress is an imprint of Elsevier

Acquiring Editor: *Chris Katsaropoulos*
Editorial Project Manager: *Benjamin Rearick*
Project Manager: *Punithavathy Govindaradjane*
Designer: *Mark Rogers*

Syngress is an imprint of Elsevier
225 Wyman Street, Waltham, MA 02451, USA

Library of Congress Cataloging-in-Publication Data
Andress, Jason.
  Cyber warfare : techniques, tactics and tools for security practitioners / Jason Andress, Steve
Winterfeld. – Second edition.
     pages cm
  Includes bibliographical references and index.
  ISBN 978-0-12-416672-1 (pbk.)
1. Information warfare–Handbooks, manuals, etc. 2. Computer networks–Security measures–
Handbooks, manuals, etc. I. Winterfeld, Steve. II. Title. III. Title: Cyberwarfare, techniques, tactics and
tools for security practitioners.
  U163.A64 2014
  355.3'43–dc23
                                                                        2013034031

British Library Cataloguing-in-Publication Data
A catalogue record for this book is available from the British Library

ISBN: 978-0-12-416672-1

Printed and bound in the United States of America
   16   17   18   10   9   8   7   6   5   4   3

For information on all Syngress publications, visit our website at *store.elsevier.com/Syngress*

Contents

Acknowledgments

We thank our families and friends for their guidance, support, and fortitude throughout this project. We dedicate this book to those in the security industry who are making the world a better place through efforts like Hackers for Charity (You may have seen their T-shirts—"i hack charities." For more information, go to http://hackersforcharity.org/). To those who are not we say—get engaged!

Foreword

WHY A BOOK ON CYBER WARFARE IS IMPORTANT

"...it's now clear this cyber threat is one of the most serious economic and national security challenges we face as a nation," Obama said, adding, *"...we're not as prepared as we should be, as a government or as a country"* [1].

According to the Director of National Intelligence James Clapper, "The cyber warfare threat facing the United States is increasing in scope and scale and its impact is difficult to overstate" [2]. A variety of educational institutions, both military and civilian, are grappling with the question, "What should we teach each and every one of our students about cybersecurity?" When these students take their places as leaders and officers in the defense of our country, they need to be aware of this persistent threat.

Today's threatscape is constantly changing, adapting to our countermeasures and continuing to successfully pursue various missions ranging from identity theft, to criminal and nation-based corporate espionage, and, in the case of a worm called Stuxnet, to sabotage. Only a decade ago we had kids attacking systems for the thrill of it; then it was criminals attacking identities. Now it appears to be more about social media, ideology, and insider threats. This book provides great graphics for the threatscape and challenges we are facing today.

In May, the Atlantic Wire reported China was winning the cyberwar, in part because they had accessed US physical war plans. Also last week Edward Snowden claimed the United States and Israel co-wrote the Stuxnet worm to damage the Iranian Nuclear program; today, we are still trying to figure out exactly how Stuxnet worked. And while WikiLeaks and Anonymous (the ideology-driven group intent on punishing organizations that did not support WikiLeaks) have been in the news of late, the theft of RSA two-factor authentication intellectual property is especially chilling. If access control fails, everything fails. Identity theft is so commonplace that it is no longer newsworthy. How many people in the United States have had their identity stolen? Many experts say all of them. There is just so much stolen data that the criminals have not yet figured out how to use them all. But they will. Criminal groups are hiring computer scientists to run their cyber-based scams and mine the results. The term *cyber warfare* is becoming part of discussions on national security. Cybersecurity is an issue that can impact us at the personal level as users of the Internet and at the national defense level as an advanced, persistent threat.

WHY SHOULD YOU READ THIS BOOK

Everyone needs to understand the risks to our information so that we can make an informed decision regarding the steps that we might take to secure it.

The Internet connection in your home that you use to talk to friends with Skype, play games, and send email may also be used to conduct crimes, undertake international espionage, and quite possibly fight a new kind of war.

This new Wild West of the Internet matters to each of us at both the personal and national levels. *Cyber Warfare* is focused more on the national level and what the Department of Defense (DoD) has done and is doing.

A week doesn't go by without a story of a cyber attack, hacker group causing a data breach or malcode spreading across the Internet. Cyber Warfare puts the threatscape into context by showing how the threat operates as well as how all the different stories relate to one another.

If you work with the US government, or want to know what the US government is doing to organize and respond to the cyber threat, *Cyber Warfare* lays it out in comprehensive detail. The authors will show you how cyber attacks and defense intersect with each of the classic warfighting domains of land (Army), sea (Navy), air (Air Force), space (Joint, with Air Force in the lead), and cyber (ubiquitous, with US Cyber Command [USCYBERCOM] just getting organized).

Cyber Warfare covers the doctrine being developed today and lays out the tactics, techniques, and procedures of Computer Network Operations (CNO) including attack, defend, and exploit (the military term for reconnaissance or spying), plus the new aspect of social engineering. On a personal note, it is easy to read about social engineering and think "yeah, yeah, yeah," but I, among many others, friended Robin Sage, a fake personality created by a security researcher to see how much data could be collected, on Facebook.

Switching from the "what" to "how" in the later chapters, *Cyber Warfare* considers the "why," as the authors explore the ethics and legal issues of this new battlefield. Then the book defines and analyzes the challenges facing cyberspace. Finally, it looks at trends in this arena.

Cyber Warfare will provide readers with a strong foundational understanding of a threat they see every week in the news. Here is why that matters: In the beginning of this Foreword, I said my head was spinning. Why? Because there is so much new stuff that I can't keep track of? Actually, no. What amazes and scares me is that we are having the same conversations we had 13 years ago when I was chief for information warfare at the Ballistic Missile Defense Organization. Granted, today there are more acronyms, and more money is involved. But none of the fundamental issues have changed. Back then, the Russians were pursing international agreements to treat cyber attacks as strategic weapons. We did not listen, I think, because we thought our technology and techniques were superior. In addition, a lot of people were in denial—"Is this cyber attack stuff really an issue?" And far more people just did not have a clue. If it did not have to do with the Redskins or Cowboys, it could not possibly matter. But we forgot something. We had the most to lose. The United States has more information online than any other country, and that makes us the biggest target. We had an opportunity more than a decade ago to begin the dialog of government–private industry partnerships. We had an opportunity to begin to establish international agreements. We largely squandered those opportunities. Now they have returned. Compelling evidence suggests that there is a cyber threat. We need to educate ourselves, do our part, and encourage our legislators to engage. We need to hold the government accountable to spend our tax dollars wisely in the cyber warfare realm, not to just throw dollars in the air and hope they will land where they will do some good. *Cyber Warfare* will allow you to educate yourself, to form an opinion on where the nation should be moving and the risks we face if we take no action. More than a decade ago we missed our opportunity to take comprehensive action, and we have paid a terrible price. What are we going to do this time around?

Stephen Northcutt

References

[1] President Barack Obama. Remarks by the president on securing our nation's cyber infrastructure [home page on the Internet]. Washington, DC: The White House, http://www.whitehouse.gov/the_press_office/Remarks-by-the-President-on-Securing-Our-Nations-Cyber-Infrastructure/; 2010 [accessed 15.02.10].

[2] Allen V. Cyber warfare threats to U.S. are increasing: top spy [home page on the Internet]. New York: Thomson Reuters, http://www.reuters.com/article/2011/02/10/us-usa-intelligence-cyberspace-idUSTRE7194E320110210; 2010 [accessed 15.02.10].

Introduction

BOOK OVERVIEW AND KEY LEARNING POINTS

This book is designed to cover the strategic, operational, and tactical aspects of the conflicts in cyberspace today. The perspectives of the two authors balance the viewpoints of what many are calling cyber warfare today. One comes from a commercial background and the other brings the military viewpoint. The book is designed to help anyone understand the essentials of what is happening today, as well as provide a strong background on the issues we are facing.

This book is unique in that it provides the information in a manner that can be used to establish a strategic cybersecurity vision for an organization, but it is also designed to contribute to the national debate on where cyber is going.

BOOK AUDIENCE

This book will provide a valuable resource to those involved in cyber warfare activities regardless of whether their focus is policy maker, CEO, CISO, doctrinal development, penetration testers, security professionals, network and systems administrators, or college instructors. The information provided on cyber tactics and attacks can also be used to assist in engineering better and more efficient procedures and technical defenses.

Those in management positions will find this information useful, as well, from the standpoint of developing better overall risk management strategies for their organizations. The concepts covered in this book will help determine how to allocate resources and can be used to drive security projects and policies, in order to mitigate some of the larger issues discussed.

HOW THIS BOOK IS ORGANIZED

This book is designed to take the reader through a logical progression for a foundational understanding of today's cyber battlespace, but the content and organization of the topics in this book are built as standalone modules of information. It is not necessary to read the book from front to back or even in any particular order. In the areas where we refer to information located in other chapters in the book, we have endeavored to point out where the information can be found. The following descriptions will provide an overview of the contents of each chapter:

Chapter 1: What is Cyber Warfare?

In this chapter, we discuss how the concept of what a war means is changing and examine whether we are in a cyber war today. We discuss the differences between conventional and cyber wars and how conventional warfare is a poor standard against which to measure its cyber equivalent. We talk about how holding to the strict definition of warfare being one nation state declaring war on another sovereign nation may no longer be valid and how a cyber war, whether strictly cyber in nature or in combination with traditional war, could lead to an international disaster, changing economies, enabling an increased cyber crime wave, and facilitating unprecedented espionage, and why we need to act now to be prepared for these potential events.

Chapter 2: Cyber Threatscape

This chapter presents an overview of the cyber threatscape. It covers the methodology, tools, and techniques used by the different types of attackers, as well as a review of the key parts of the defensive infrastructure employed to protect our systems. In addition, it discusses the general categories of information that present prime targets for attackers.

Chapter 3: The Cyberspace Battlefield

In this chapter, we study the boundaries of cyber warfare and examine the many different perspectives that are used to define it. We cover the traditional war-fighting domains of land, sea, and air, and space both as they relate to cyber operations and what we can learn from them as cyber becomes more mature as the fifth war-fighting domain. We also review the different threats, the impacts they are having, and what their motivations might be. Finally we examine how acquisition is enabling and fettering cybersecurity.

Chapter 4: Cyber Doctrine

This chapter explores the state of current cyber warfare doctrine on both the nation state and military. We discuss how every country with a dependence on IT infrastructure is developing strategies and capabilities to protect and exercise national power and examine some of the traditional tactics and products that the military needs to adapt to the cyberspace environment. We also cover some of the directives used by federal agencies and governments to guide behavior in this virtual environment. Finally, we look at how organizations are training to both develop new doctrine and execute their current plans.

Chapter 5: Cyber Warriors

In this chapter, we examine who cyber warriors are. As cyber warfare is a rapidly developing field, we cover both the existing forces, and we talk about what might come in the future. We cover what those working in the cyber field presently look like from the standpoint of education, training, certifications, and experiences and what the differences between those that are selected for traditional warfare and cyber warfare might be. We also discuss the present cyber warfare forces in countries around the globe and what we might need to train the next generation of cyber warriors.

Chapter 6: Logical Weapons

In this chapter, we discuss the various tools that we might use in conducting Computer Network Operations (CNO) and the methods that we might use to defend against an attacker using them. We discuss the tools for reconnaissance, access and privilege escalation, exfiltration, sustaining our connection to a compromised system, assault tools, and obfuscation tools, many of which are free, or have free versions, and are available to the general public.

Chapter 7: Physical Weapons

In this chapter, we discuss the use of physical weapons in cyber warfare. We talk about the intersection of the physical and logical realms and how making changes to either realm can affect the other, sometimes to a disastrous extent. We also talk about infrastructure concerns, primarily those that have to do with the Supervisory Control and Data Acquisition (SCADA) systems that control the various industrial, infrastructure, and facility processes that are in constant use all over the world. In addition, we cover supply chain concerns and the potential consequences of corruption or disruption in the supply chain.

Chapter 8: Psychological Weapons

In this chapter, we cover social engineering and discuss how it can be a dangerous threat vector to all organizations and individuals. We look at this from a military mindset and pull lessons from how they conduct interrogations and conduct counterintelligence. We talk about how the security policies, culture, and training must be reinforced often to insure the work force stays vigilant and how a great technical security infrastructure can be subverted by just going after the people.

Chapter 9: Computer Network Exploitation

In this chapter, we discuss the basics of Computer Network Exploitation (CNE). We explain that exploitation in this context means reconnaissance or espionage, and then discuss how it is conducted. We cover identifying our targets, in the sense of both gleaning information from targets of attacks and identifying targets to be surveilled. We talk about reconnaissance and how it might be used to conduct planning operations for future attacks, including Computer Network Attack (CNA) and Computer Network Defense (CND). We cover the three major divisions of reconnaissance, Open Source Intelligence (OSINT), passive, and Advanced Persistent Threat (APT), and the differences between them. In addition, we go over surveillance tactics and techniques, and how they differ from reconnaissance.

Chapter 10: Computer Network Attack

In this chapter, we discuss Computer Network Attack (CNA). We talk about the different factors involved in cyber warfare, including the physical, logical, and electronic elements of warfare. We also discuss the different phases of the attack process: reconnaissance, scanning, accessing systems, escalating privileges, exfiltrating data, assaulting the system, sustaining our access, and obfuscating any traces that might be left behind. We compare how this parallels and differs from typical hacker attacks.

Chapter 11: Computer Network Defense

In this chapter, we discuss Computer Network Defense (CND). We talk about what exactly it is that we attempt to secure, in the sense of data and information, as well as security awareness and training efforts, in order to mitigate what sometimes is the weakest link in our defenses, this being authorized normal users. We also present some of the different strategies that we recommend be used to defend ourselves against attack.

Chapter 12: Non-State Actors in Computer Network Operations

In this chapter, we discuss the various non-state actors that might take part in cyber warfare, including the place of corporations in cyber warfare, how cyber terrorism comes into play in cyber warfare activities, and how cyber criminal groups are a major consideration in cyber warfare. We also cover the participation of autonomous actors in cyber activities.

Chapter 13: Legal System Impacts

In this chapter, we review the different legal systems across the world and some of the current laws that can impact how cyber warfare is conducted. The importance of these can be found in the overlap with Chapter 1 on the definition of cyber warfare, Chapter 2 on the warfighting domains, Chapter 3 on doctrine, and Chapter 13 on ethics. We look at the laws that impact cyber warfare due to the unique fact that it is the only warfighting domain that must use commercial infrastructure. We discuss the need to balance methods to fight the interconnected cyber crime, espionage, and warfare with the right to privacy. Finally, we dive into the need for digital forensics to support cyber warfare.

Chapter 14: Ethics

In this chapter, we discuss the ethical issues surrounding cyber warfare, such as the Law of Armed Conflict and Just War Theory. Such issues differ significantly from those in conventional warfare due to the potential for cyber attacks to be misattributed. We discuss attacking ethically in cyber war, including issues such as secrecy in attacks, noncombatant immunity, and what constitutes use of force in cyber warfare. We also cover issues that may arise as to the determination or improper determination regarding the specifics of an attack.

Chapter 15: Cyberspace Challenges

We define the thirty key issues that are impacting cybersecurity and map how they should be categorized. We then break them out into levels of difficulty and resources required to solve. We also discuss how they are interrelated. Finally, we look at both who and how they should be addressed, to include rough timelines on when they might be resolved.

Chapter 16: The Future of Cyber War

As we look to what lies ahead we examine the logical evolution based on current cyber-security trends. We then talk about the most likely and most dangerous course of action for conflicts in the cyber domain. Next, we examine potential impacts from some of the new technologies and problems on the horizon. Finally, we discuss what needs to be done through international interactions.

Appendix: Cyber Timeline

We have also included an appendix with a timeline of the major events that have impacted or driven the conflicts in cyberspace.

CONCLUSION

Writing this book was a true journey. A considerable amount of debate among all those involved in the book took place over what would build the best foundation to address the subject, but in the end a solid balance was struck between the broad perspective and specific practical techniques. The hope is that this book will contribute to the national discussion on both where cyberspace is headed and what role each one of us can play.

What is Cyber Warfare?

We are constantly bombarded with news about cyber events today. There are constant headlines: *cybercrime is up, watch out for the latest phishing attack trying to steal our identity, update our antivirus to avoid infection, patch the operating system to avoid a hacker taking control, new zero day attack against smartphones, Facebook privacy compromised, someone took down Twitter,* and now we cannot go for more than a week without hearing about cyber war.

When establishing the boundaries of the battlefield in the physical world it is usually straightforward. When two countries go to war there is a battlefront established between the two armies where active combat occurs. Wars have traditionally been fought over land, and typically on the very land the countries are fighting for but in the current war on terrorism, the reasons and boundaries are less defined, with no set battlefront where the forces clash, and distributed forces conducting guerrilla or asymmetric warfare with no formal rank structure or doctrine.

Still, even in unconventional warfare the two sides operate within the same geographical area; in cyberspace the traditional physical boundaries disappear.

WHAT IS CYBER WARFARE?

Background

We have been reading about cyber acts of aggression for years now. Cliff Stoll first published *The Cuckoo's Egg: Tracking a Spy Through the Maze of Computer Espionage* in 1989 about Soviet Bloc countries breaking into Department of Defense (DoD) sponsored networks. Seven years later we see a very similar storyline from both sides of the hack in

Take-Down: The Pursuit and Capture of Kevin Mitnick, America's Most Wanted Computer Outlaw-By the Man Who Did It by Tsutomu Shimomura and John Markoff with its opposing view in the book *The Fugitive Game: Online with Kevin Mitnick* by Jonathan Littman. Today we see a host of books on crime, hacking, defensive practices, and certification prep guides not to mention cyber plots in fiction books like *The Blue Nowhere* by Jeffrey Deaver, *Debt of Honor* by Tom Clancy, or *The Scorpion's Gate* by Richard A. Clarke.

NOTE

Here are some recent notable mentions around the topic of Cyber showing the national leadership of the U.S. is concerned about this domain:

- President Obama—Talked about cybersecurity in State of Union address and signed PPD-21: Critical Infrastructure Security and Resilience [1].
- Director of National Intelligence James Clapper told Congress that cyberattacks and cyberspying can damage critical infrastructure like power grids. But in prepared testimony, he says advanced cyber-actors like Russia and China are unlikely to launch such attacks unless they are threatened by conflict [2].
- Defense Secretary Leon Panetta has also been a strong advocate for increased governmental grip on the web and in October warned that the U.S. is facing a possible "cyber-Pearl Harbor" by foreign hackers [3].
- Homeland Security Secretary Janet Napolitano issued the warnings Jan 2013, claiming that inaction could result in a "cyber 9/11" attack that could knock out water, electricity and gas, causing destruction similar to that left behind by Hurricane Sandy [3].
- Representative Mike Rogers, a Michigan Republican who leads the House Intelligence Committee, has said foreign intruders "are stealing literally billions" of dollars from companies [2].
- Army General Keith Alexander, head of U.S. Cyber Command and the National Security Agency, called cybercrime "the greatest transfer of wealth in history" [2].
- Chief of Staff of the U.S. Air Force Gen. Mark Welsh III said he worried the investments made in cyber could be disappearing into a "black hole." Welsh will wait until he understands the cyber topic better, he said [4].
- Commander Army Cyber Command Lieutenant General Rhett Hernandez: Army Cyber Command/Second Army said he is tasked to operate and defend all Army networks and prepare for full-spectrum cyber-operations to support our forces worldwide [5].

We also see touches of cyber warfare in the movies starting with *War Games* in 1983 where a kid breaks into a military network and accidently almost starts World War III to *Sneakers* in 1992 where all data encryption is compromised to *Swordfish* 2001 where intelligence agencies use hacking to support their activities to the epic *Die Hard 4: Live Free* or *Die Hard* in 2007 when criminals pose as terrorists and take down the Internet and all the critical infrastructure it supports. There are a lot of great books and movies not mentioned but this sample list points to the evolution of Cyber Warfare into mainstream thinking and how it can be used as a tool to conduct espionage, crime, terror, and warfare.

America's information dominance tools, which helped win the Cold War, have become its Achilles heel of the cyber conflict we are in today. U.S. technology was far ahead of any competitor nation and we outspent them to keep the edge. Today we are more dependent on this technology than ever before, most of which is now available to our partners, competitors, and adversaries. At the same time the cost of entry into this arms race is incredibly low. Furthermore, the benefits of attacking someone far outweigh the dangers. This has led to what many are calling a Cyber War.

Definition for Cyber Warfare

A definition of Cyber Warfare is not easy. In fact definitions for Cyber or Warfare are both under debate. We will start with a simple definition of Cyber or Cyberspace. For the purpose of this chapter, we will frame the definition in the context of military environment.

DoD defines *cyberspace* as the "notional environment in which digitized information is communicated over computer networks" (Figure 1.1) [7]. There is no official definition for just "cyber." When you hear it by itself it could mean cybersecurity, computer network operations, electronic warfare or anything to do with the network. It is important to agree on what it means, for this book it will generally refer to cyberspace and be discussed in terms of computer network operations (attack, defend, and exploit).

The National Military Strategy for Cyberspace Operations defines *cyberspace* as the "domain characterized by the use of electronics and the electromagnetic spectrum to store, modify, and exchange data via networked systems and associated physical infrastructures" [6].

DoD (Joint Publication 3.0 Joint Operations 17 September 2006 Incorporating Change 2, 22 March 2010) defines *cyberspace* as a "global domain within the information environment. It consists of the interdependent network of information technology infrastructures, including

FIGURE 1.1 Cyber or computer network operations falls under this doctrinal manual JP 3-13 information operations [6]. Department of Defense (DoD) joint publication 3-13 information operations 13 February 2006.

the Internet, telecommunications networks, computer systems, and embedded processors and controllers."

Within cyberspace, electronics and the electromagnetic spectrum are used to store, modify, and exchange data via networked systems. Cyberspace operations employ cyberspace capabilities primarily to achieve objectives in or through cyberspace. Such operations include computer network operations and activities to operate and defend the Global Information Grid (GIG) [8].

United Nations (UN) defines cyber as "the global system of systems of Internetted computers, communications infrastructures, online conferencing entities, databases and information utilities generally known as the Net." This mostly means the Internet; but the term may also be used to refer to the specific, bounded electronic information environment of a corporation or of a military, government, or other organization [9].

For a definition of warfare we cannot turn to an authoritative source. The UN does not have a definition, so we will default to the two historical standards for military doctrine: *On War*, the exhaustive work documenting tactics during the Napoleonic War period in 1873 and *The Art of War* a more condensed version of how to conduct warfare composed in sixth century BC.

> ON WAR—We shall not enter into any of the abstruse definitions of war used by publicists. We shall keep to the element of the thing itself, to a duel. War is nothing but a duel on an extensive scale. If we would conceive as a unit the countless number of duels which make up a war, we shall do so best by supposing to ourselves two wrestlers. Each strives by physical force to compel the other to submit to his will: his first object is to throw his adversary, and thus to render him incapable of further resistance. War therefore is an act of violence to compel our opponent to fulfill our will [10].
>
> ART OF WAR—The art of war is of vital importance to the State. It is a matter of life and death, a road either to safety or to ruin. Hence it is a subject of inquiry which can on no account be neglected. The art of war, then, is governed by five constant factors, to be taken into account in one's deliberations, when seeking to determine the conditions obtaining in the field. These are: (1) The Moral Law; (2) Heaven; (3) Earth; (4) The Commander; (5) Method and discipline [11].

Are these definitions applicable to what is happening on the Internet today? Can these historical concepts be applied to the virtual world? Is the military perspective the right one to look at this problem through? The answer to all questions is a declarative: YES. That is where this book becomes applicable: to help solidify what cyber warfare means. First there is no governing body to determine what definition we should use, so the definition is normally based on the perspective of the person speaking. Governments, finance companies, Internet providers, international corporations, organizations with a specific cause, and lawyers all give us a different answer. As for historical concepts, there are many that are based on geography which no longer apply, but most principles and practices can be modified to be useful when it comes to the new World Wide Web's Wild West. Finally, we think if we are going to use the term warfare we should use the military perspective but throughout this book we will take the time to explore the other options because our systems are connected to the same battlefield on which the nation states are fighting!

Tactical and Operational Reasons for Cyber War

The motivations for war are as old as time. Whether individuals or nations, going to war generally is based on power/patriotism/greed versus protection of self/ideology/country.

Traditionally warfare was focused on controlling limited resources but today the power of a network is not determined by resources but the number of nodes on it which equates to the power of information/influence. Additionally in some cases resources may not be as important as ability to react quickly or cycle time. Be it access to proprietary information, classified networks, interconnections on a social network, applications, or data about customers or systems that run the critical infrastructure, the more connected, the more value.

> **NOTE**
>
> The tactical level of war is where individual battles are executed to achieve military objectives assigned to tactical units or task forces. In the Army this would normally be at the Brigade/Regimental level.
>
> The operational level of war is where multiple battles are combined into campaigns within a theater, or larger operational area. Activities at this level link strategy and tactics by establishing operational objectives needed to achieve the strategic objectives through a series of tactical battles. This would normally be at the Joint Task Force or Division level.
>
> The strategic level of war is where a nation, or coalition of nations, determines national political objectives that will be enforced by military forces and other instruments of national power. This is normally controlled at the Combatant Commander level and higher.

Today's critical infrastructure networks are key targets for cyber attack because they have grown to the point where they run the command and control systems, manage the logistics, enable the staff planning and operations, and are the backbone of the intelligence capabilities. More importantly today, most command and control systems, as well as the weapon systems themselves, are connected to the GIG or have embedded computer chips. Airplanes have become flying routers receiving and sending targeting information constantly. Air Defense and Artillery are guided by computer systems and they shoot smart munitions that adjust their flight based on Global Positioning System (GPS) updates to guide themselves to the target. The Intelligence Surveillance and Reconnaissance systems gather so much information the challenge is sifting through it to find the critical data. Today's infantry squad has communication gear, GPS, tracking devices, cameras, and night vision devices. The computer chip is ubiquitous and has become one of the U.S.' centers of gravity. It is both a nations' strength and could be turned into our weakness if taken away. The loss of GPS satellites would take away many of our advantages on the battlefield.

When we consider the military maxim "amateurs study tactics; professionals study logistics," [12][a] it quickly becomes clear how important the logistical systems are. When we deploy forces into a theater of operations our capability to fight is shaped by the forces, weapons, equipment, and supplies that can be moved to the right place at the right time. Today, that is calculated and controlled by computers. An enemy can understand our intentions and abilities by tracking what is happening in the logistics system. If they can modify actions and data, they can interdict, or at least impact, our capabilities.

---

[a]There is much dispute as to who uttered this military maxim. It has been attributed to General Omar Bradley and U.S. Marine Corps Commandant General Robert H. Barrow. In various other forms, it has also been attributed to Napoleon, Helmuth von Moltke, and Carl von Clausewitz. For the purposes of this book, its origin is far less important than its message.

We have discussed the tactical and operational considerations now let us look at the strategic reasons to fight on the cyber front.

Cyber Strategy and Power

There are some general principles we should look at when analyzing the virtual world. When deciding on military strategies we look to the Principles of War. When evaluating plans we evaluate ends, ways, and means. When we analyze sources of national power we weigh Diplomatic, Information, Military and Economic (DIME) factors. Finally when we think of the national level tools we break them into hard power, soft power, and smart power. We will look at how all these apply to cyber warfare.

The U.S. Principles of War are Objective, Offensive, Mass, Economy of Force, Maneuver, Unity of Command, Security, Surprise, and Simplicity [12]. As we look at cyber war we must decide if we are talking about the virtual battlefield of the Internet or the ubiquitous nature of cyber conflicts being enmeshed into the physical battlefield. Some of the principles do not easily transfer into the virtual battlefield but they all can be force multipliers in the physical battlefield. When deciding on a cyber strategy we must not throw out hundreds of years' worth of doctrine and tactics but rather understand how to modify them based on the new paradigm we are facing. This has been true of all the technical advancements on the battlefield that have caused a Revolution in Military Affairs. Looking at the traditional principles of war we see having a clear *objective* with a simple plan that utilizes surprise while protecting our infrastructure is still the key to success. The numerous news stories we see show that defending in cyber warfare is not easy, so *offensive* actions are still the best way to achieve victory (this is a military statement and ignores the legal/policy challenges that must be solved). *Mass* is still important to achieve impacts and is validated by botnets today. *Unity of Command* is key for command and control. *Security, Surprise* and *Simplicity* are important for any plan, real world or virtual. *Economy of force* and *maneuver* are more difficult to apply in a battlefield with attrition and terrain being relative terms.

> ## WARNING
>
> Botnets are large groups of computers networked together that use their combined computing power to accomplish missions like solving complex mathematical problems or, more nefariously, to cause denial of service attacks. These groups are built from vulnerable systems with no concern for to whom they belong. Our work system, our home computer, or the MRI system at the hospital all can become zombies on a botnet if they are not protected and monitored.

When developing a strategic framework to determine how to defeat the enemy center of gravity it is important to validate the plan by analyzing ends, ways and means. "Ends" is the objective, such as deny access to enemies command and control systems. "Ways" is the form through which a strategy is implemented, such as Computer Network Attack or full scope Information Operations. "Means" consists of the resources available, such as people, equipment, and technology to execute the plan. We will look more closely at the "means" when we analyze the sources of national power. Once we develop the plan that utilizes the principles of war we use Ends/Ways/Means to validate whether we can execute it.

FIGURE 1.2   Instruments of national power that could influence or be influenced by cyber actions [6].

When evaluating sources of national powers we analyze the *DIME* factors seen in Figure 1.2. *Diplomatic* is based on the actions between states based on official communications. It can go through organizations like the State Department, National level Computer Emergency Readiness Teams (CERT), treaty organizations like North American Treaty Organization (NATO), economic groups like the Group of Twenty Finance Ministers and Central Bank Governors (G20), or law enforcement agencies. Next is *information*. This power is based on controlling the key resource of the information age. It encompasses strategic communication, news and popular media, international opinion, social media sites, and Open Source Intelligence (OSINT) to include the collection, analysis, and dissemination of key national actors. *Military* is the final political or government controlled option, but today we must understand this is full spectrum, from unconventional warfare, peacekeeping, humanitarian assistance, nation-building, and finally large-scale combat operations. *Economic* power comes from the influence of trade, incentives like embargos and free trade zones and direct support like aid packages or sale of surplus DoD equipment. All these factors can be applied to effect behaviors in cyber warfare.

Note that the concept of what constitutes instruments of national power is under review but the key counter insurgency doctrinal manual (FM 3-24) still uses DIME. Other acronyms are: MIDLIFE (Military, Intelligence, Diplomatic, Law Enforcement, Information, Finance, Economic), ASCOPE (Areas, Structures, Capabilities, Organizations, People, and Events), and PMESII (Political, Military, Economic, Social, Informational, Infrastructure) [13].

With cyber warfare impacting the tactical, operational, and strategic levels of war both directly and indirectly, should we move to mitigate the possibility through international agreements?

NOTE

The U.S. military has six INTs that they use to manage intelligence collection. They are Open Source Intelligence (OSINT), Signals Intelligence (SIGINT), Geospatial Intelligence (GEOINT), Imagery Intelligence (IMINT), Human Intelligence (HUMINT), Technical Intelligence (TECHINT), and Measurement and Signature Intelligence (MASINT). The information from all these sources is fused into all-source analysis.

Cyber Arms Control

One idea that has become popular lately related to cyber warfare is the concept of arms control, or deterrence. The analogy is to the Cold War, where everyone understood the concept of Nuclear War being impractical because it would cause Mutually Assured Destruction (MAD). There were just a few countries that could develop nukes so they worked together to avoid a war. The thought is that if we can make cyber attacks expensive, or the consequences extremely painful, nobody would use it. This worked in the nuclear case because the cost of entry into the "Nuclear Capable" club was expensive and those in the club were all committed to not let anyone else in. Once both sides had the capability to kill the other side multiple times it led to a series of incidents that convinced both sides it was a no-win situation. Eventually a progression of international agreements reduced this threat. But MAD was an all-or-nothing scenario so is not a good fit for cyber warfare; let us look at another arms control agreement.

Another analogy are the international agreements on Biological Weapons from the 1970s. The issue is closer to cyber warfare in that it's easier to gain access to the weapons—if someone released a bio weapon it could impact the sender as much as the target, and once released it is impractical to control. The same problem exists with a computer virus released against a specific country; once someone reverse engineers it they could quickly send it back. The dangers were so intense that many countries agreed not to develop bio weapons. The challenge here was one of verification. It is impossible to track everyone who can develop these capabilities. Another challenge is there was not a dual use for bio weapons like there is for many of the malware weapons developed today. So with many groups having different goals or business plans (in the case of the criminal organizations) it is not a fair comparison.

Generally, when we talk about arms control it refers to Weapons of Mass Destruction (WMD), when we talk about cyber WMDs they are Weapons of Mass Disruption. There is no way to calculate the damage today. Rarely would a cyber attack result directly in deaths but could disrupt vital services that result in the damage to property, economic loss, or impacts to national security. This is not to say the potential is not there and we could see this become a method used by terrorists, but we are not seeing it today. The Cyber Policy Review of 2010 stated that industry estimates of losses from intellectual property to data theft in 2008 range as high as $1 trillion [14]. McAfee, Version and Symantec subsequently published reports ranging from trillion to 400 billion to 100 billion but there is no systematic analysis with empirical data to date. Most folks feel it is hard to justify raising cyber actions to the same level as systems that can cause mass causalities. The counter argument is there are so many critical infrastructure systems dependent on it that the unintended consequences of taking down major parts of the Internet could cause devastation at the national emergency level. As we approached year 2000 (Y2K) there was a lot of concern that systems all over the Internet would fail due to an error with how they handled calculating the date. This Y2K scare grew to the point that if we did not get everything patched we would find ourselves living at a tribal, apocalyptic level.

NOTE

There have been a lot of events like Y2K over the history of the World Wide Web (WWW) or as it is more commonly called today, the Internet. As you read this book there will be times when it would help to see them in a timeline, so we have provided a major event list by year in this book's appendix entitled, "Cyber Timeline."

Internationally, there was an effort as early as 2005 in the United Nations to establish a cyber treaty. There was a disagreement between the United States, which had concerns about human rights violations thinking it could be used to suppress dissents, and Russia, which was pushing for banning military actions in cyberspace. No verification process was laid out and it quickly died. Then in mid-2010 it came back with 15 nations supporting a modified version of the plan. The supporters were: America, Belarus, Brazil, Britain, China, Estonia, France, Germany, India, Israel, Italy, Qatar, Russia, South Africa, and South Korea. They compromised and focused on areas they could agree on like: establish accepted behaviors in cyberspace, exchange information on national laws and strategies, and strengthen computer protection in underdeveloped countries [15]. More recently, the EastWest Institute's Bilateral on Critical Infrastructure Protection committee published "Working Towards Rules for Governing Cyber Conflict—Rendering the Geneva and Hague Conventions in Cyberspace" which proposed joint recommendations for the private sector and governments. The European Commission has also made progress by publishing the Joint Communication to the European Parliament, the Council, The European Economic and Social Committee, and the Committee of the called "Cybersecurity Strategy of the European Union: An Open, Safe and Secure Cyberspace" laying out guidelines of behaviors. Finally, the Tallinn Manual on the International Law Applicable to Cyber Warfare was a positive collaboration how current laws map to cyberspace. Cyber is an international problem so a key part of the solution is these international agreements.

What is the United States Doing about the Threat of a Cyber War?

As the Internet started to become critical to running governments and economies, it soon became both an advantage and a valuable target. For the nations that operate in the information age it is a key enabler, for the emerging nations it offers them the ability to leapfrog many competitors, for those still fundamentally in the agricultural age it offers an ability to conduct asymmetrical operations. For the United States, it is a part of all our national strategies, with numerous presidential directives to include the George Bush Sr administration's heavily funded Comprehensive National Cybersecurity Initiative [16] designed to address the National Security level concerns as seen in Figure 1.3.

FIGURE 1.3 The 12 areas where the Bush administration invested in cybersecurity.

> **NOTE**
>
> Asymmetric warfare (sometimes called Irregular Warfare or Unconventional Warfare) is war between a dominant force and a smaller force where the smaller force uses indirect or guerrilla tactics rather than to engage in force-on-force battles.

The benefits of cyber espionage/attacks are high, with so much information being available. The costs are low, with remote access being easier than physical access in many cases. The risks are lower, with few laws governing cross-border Internet activity and attribution being so difficult. Though the costs of entry are low for basic capabilities, the more industrialized countries are developing advanced espionage and attack capabilities that can impact command and control systems, weapons, and classified networks at both the software and hardware levels.

During his first term, President Obama moved to define the cybersecurity problem by commissioning the Cyberspace Policy Review [17]. Seven months after the report was released, President Obama appointed a cybersecurity policy official, "cyber czar," responsible for coordinating the nation's cybersecurity policies and activities. Then finally he authorized the DoD stand up US Cyber Command in 2010. In 2011 he signed "International Strategy for Cyberspace – Prosperity, Security, and Openness in a Networked World." More recently, he has signed Presidential Directives on cybersecurity. There seems to be more emphasis on cyber in his second term but there is not much hope for any legislation around cybersecurity because of current congressional gridlock.

There are currently two major players in the protection of the nation's networks. First is the Secretary of Department of Homeland Security (DHS) which has established the U.S. CERT, published the National Incident Response Plan that included a Cyber Incident Annex and fielded the Einstein malicious cyber activity early warning system to all Federal departments and agencies (note the Einstein program is being phased out and replaced by system coming from National Security Agency (NSA) called Perfect Citizen). On the downside the DHS has suffered from a lack of a cyber budget, difficulty in hiring the right skill sets, and revolving door leadership challenges. The second major player is the dual-hatted Commander of U.S. Cyber Command (CYBERCOM) and NSA. Looking at budget, available personnel, and capabilities across the exploit, attack, and defense functions this individual will have the largest set of capabilities.

Although the United States has taken steps to address the cyber war concern, it is not ready to deal with a cyber war today. Many other nations have taken similar steps. The United Kingdom and Australia published *Cyber Strategies* in 2009 and have taken both organizational and legislative actions to secure their networks. Russia and China have taken public steps to address internal cybersecurity but have not done well with the international community as good cyber citizens. Organizations like NATO have very active cyber communities. Countries like India, France, Israel, Brazil, South Korea, and Estonia are emerging as cyber players moving to center stage.

HAVE WE SEEN A CYBER WAR?

The answer depends on the definition. To date no nation has declared a cyber war and, although many governments have spoken out about cyber activities, none have stated they suffered from an act of war. The two more talked about events are the 2007 cyber attacks against Estonia and the 2008 integrated cyber and kinetic attacks against Georgia. These both involve nation states and call on military action. There are many other incidents. Most have been called criminal acts. This trend is very reminiscent to the U.S. definition of terrorism. The

United States had a low level of terrorist acts because they were all listed as criminal acts, then after the Oklahoma bombing and 9/11 they updated the definition based on new priorities and the number of incidents shot up.

> **NOTE**
>
> Code Word—A word or a phrase designed to represent a program or activity while remaining inconspicuous to folks not cleared for the information. A code word should be assigned randomly and have no association with the program or activity it represents. Active code words are classified. If the name is compromised it is canceled and a new name is issued.

Historically, there have been a number of high visibility cyber incidents that could qualify as cyber attacks. Here is a short list of code word programs that have been exposed:

- Eligible Receiver—This was an exercise where NSA's Red Team conducted a no-notice Vulnerability Assessment/Penetration Test of critical government networks to include the DoD. The report showed the network was so poorly protected, the results were quickly classified.
- Moonlight Maze—A series of probes and attacks starting in 1998 against the Pentagon, National Aeronautics and Space Administration, as well as affiliated academic and laboratory facilities. These attacks were tracked back to Russia but as they will not cooperate in an investigation, it could not be proven whether it was state run, local hackers, or someone routing through their systems. This is still an open investigation.
- Solar Sunrise—A series of probes and attacks in 1998 that were initially believed to be Iraq intelligence breaking into DoD systems. This was a big wake up call for the military. However, it turned out to only be a couple of kids from California who were being taught how to break into systems by an Israeli hacker.
- Titan Rain—The name given to the systematic probes and attacks against both the DoD and the Defense Industrial Base that supports it. This was originally discovered around 2003 and made its way into public media when Shawn Carpenter for Sandia National Laboratories spoke out. These activities gave birth to the name "Advanced Persistent Threat" which is commonly used today to refer to the nation state level attacks.
- Buckshot Yankee (also known as Rampart Yankee)—An attack in 2008 designed to use thumb drives as the attack vector. A variant of an older worm called agent.btz got onto both classified and unclassified networks. This resulted in the banning of thumb drives on DoD networks which had an operational impact as workarounds were needed anywhere thumb drives had been used to store, collect, or transfer information.

> **TIP**
>
> Many of these compromises can only be detected by things like changes to a system's performance (machine hard drive being active when no one is logged on or the system is unusually slow) or monitoring traffic exiting the network (it is easy to see a connection from the Pentagon to a system in Russia causing a concern but the attackers are getting better at hiding this). It is a good idea to check what process you are running, review your logs, and occasionally monitor outbound traffic to make sure it is all authorized.

Case Studies

Now to look at some major events that were not code word events. First we will touch on Estonia. The Estonian government had leapfrogged from a paper-based government to a web-based infrastructure to conduct all business in the 1990s. In 2007 a statue of a Soviet soldier in the capital, Tallinn, was moved from the city center to a war cemetery. As part of the outcry from the Russian population (both in Russia and those of Russian heritage still living in Estonia) this resulted in a large-scale denial of service attack against most of the day-to-day government services, news sites, banking, and e-commerce. There is a lot of speculation on whether or not this was state directed/sponsored, or just spontaneous. If the Russia government was involved, was it a low level Russian official acting on their own or directed from official channels? Regardless, when a sovereign state is prevented from conducting its functions for two weeks it is clearly a national security issue.

Estonia called to NATO for support to fight off this attack. NATO sent military personnel with technical skills needed to defend against and recover from these attacks. Estonia has gone on to become one of the leaders in the area of Cyber Strategy and today hosts the NATO Cooperative Cyber Defense Center. Was this the first cyber war? By the simple definition of a "war" as an activity between two nations, then no; but if a nation calls upon its wartime treaty for protection many would say, yes, by definition it is a war.

Next we will look at the cyber attacks during the war in Georgia, over South Ossetia. South Ossetia became de facto independent from Georgia in 1991 but remained commonly recognized by the international community as part of Georgia. A peacekeeping force of Russian and Georgian forces controlled the region. In August 2008, hostilities flared and Georgia moved forces into South Ossetia to quell separatist activities. Russia counterattacked to protect South Ossetia citizens.

Before they attacked there was a cyber recon of Georgian networks and then a series of attacks. There were web page defacements, denial of services attacks against government systems, specific malware launched and spamming email flood attacks. There were also issues with traffic getting out of Georgia (turns out it is a bad idea to have the communication pipes running through the enemy's territory). It was a well-coordinated effort run by a group out of Russia. Again there was no clear evidence of state direction or sponsorship, but information given out via the Internet regarding methods for attacking Georgia, when and what to attack, and lessons learned correlated well with the Russian offensive. So this coordinated effort was not directly attributable to the Russian government/military but did result in a cyber blockade that helped make the Russian attack more successful.

Israel has had a number of cyber warfare-related events that cross from military using cyber to patriotic citizens entering the cyber battlefield on their own. In 2007 Operation "Orchard" used cyber to impact Syria's air defense systems. In 2009 Operation "Cast Lead" Israeli websites, mostly commercial, were defaced. A pro-Palestinian attack tool was used named after a Palestinian child allegedly killed by Israeli soldiers in 2000. On the pro-Israeli side a voluntary botnet called "Help Israel Win," was deployed. These cyber conflicts continue to flare up as recently early 2013 when "#OpIsrael" started attacking Israel to be countered by the "Israeli Elite Strike Force" which attacked sites in multiple countries warning they were willing to "fight fire with fire." An infamous group of hacker called Anonymous has also gotten involved by attacking websites, Facebook pages, Twitter accounts and bank accounts in what they call "Operation Israel." In retaliation the Anonymous site was hacked and set up to play "Hatikvah," Israel's national anthem.

Next we will look at an incident that fits into a gray area around the critical aspect of national power "Economic" that could become the type of incident that leads to hostilities. In 2010, Google announced they had been attacked by elements believed to be from China. Google was one of many high-level companies that had been attacked to gain access to information on dissidents and proprietary information. This event became known as Operation Aurora and there is some interesting analysis of how the attackers got access (some of the exploits were well-known exploits), but the more interesting question is how do we classify this—a crime or an act of war? First let us look at some of the events that unfolded after the attacks. Google threatened to pull out of China and stopped censoring search results. The end result was a compromise where Google agreed to operate out of Hong Kong without censorship. Google also started to openly share information with the U.S. National Security Agency (NSA) to work through this problem which reflected the importance and made it a national security matter. U.S. Secretary of State Hillary Clinton then spoke out on the incident, and called on China to conduct an investigation on the matter. China replied to these allegations by denying involvement. So we have a key U.S. company involved with a sovereign nation that pulls in the U.S. Intelligence Community (IC) and the State Department. By today's standards this was a crime, but it led to heightened tensions between the two countries and could have easily turned into a flash point.

These examples are far from complete. Studies like "Ghost Net," "Operation Shady RAT," "Unsecured Economies: Protecting Vital Information," "Night Dragon" and "Behavioral Risk Indicators of IP Theft" talk in more detail to the economic issues. Studies like "Project Grey Goose" and "Mandiant Intelligence Center Report" talk to the nature of military operations. Analysis of specific attack tools/software like Stuxnet, Flame, Gauss, Duqu and agent.btz give great insight into targeted attacks.

So have we had a cyber war? No, there has been no country that has declared a war or who has openly stated they have come under a hostile act of war. That said, the acts we have seen today could someday be deemed acts of war. Finally when there are nations making statements through the state department, calling on war treaties and developing military doctrine, we are at a level of tension that equals the Cold War.

The Debate (is it Real?)

Some will say that the current state of affairs is just the status quo. To have the kind of growth the Internet has experienced it had to be net neutral and wide open. This resulted in many vulnerabilities being imbedded into the system. Today so much is dependent on the Internet that we want it to be safe and have declared it a national security issue. Folks who do not like the term cyber war feel there is a lot of hype spreading fear about the dangers of a coming Cyber Pearl Harbor, or for the younger generation a Cyber 9/11, that is being used so the government can spend more on cyber protection and be used to erode our privacy rights.

In 2010 a debate was held called "The Cyber War Threat Has Been Grossly Exaggerated" sponsored by Intelligence Squared U.S. Four well-known cyber experts were selected to settle the matter. Marc Rotenberg and Bruce Schneier took the position that cyber war was exaggerated and VADM (Ret) John M. (Mike) McConnell and Harvard Law Professor Jonathan Zittrain stated that we are in a cyber war. The results showed: Pre-debate vote: For, 24%; Against, 54%; Undecided, 22%; Post-debate vote: For, 23%; Against, 71%; Undecided, 6%. The majority of the undecided shifted to a belief that the threat of a cyber war is real [18].

There are three recent point papers that offer a counter point to the warfare-based discussion around cyber today. "Cyber War Will Not Take Place" by Thomas Rid 2011, "The Fog of Cyberwar Why the Threat Doesn't Live Up to the Hype" by Brandon Valeriano and Ryan Maness 2012 and "Putting the 'war' in cyberwar: Metaphor, analogy, and cybersecurity discourse in the United States" by Sean Lawson 2012.

Rid argues that cyber war has never happened, that cyber war is not taking place today and that it is unlikely that cyber war will ever occur. He states that what we actually have is subversion, espionage, and sabotage (in order of increasing difficulty and impact). He also postulates that first world countries with advanced cyber forces would be better off if they openly shared their capabilities if they want to maintain their advantage on the defense [19].

Valeriano and Maness argue that the actual damage that has been caused by cyber attacks does not justify the amount of attention or resources that are being paid to it. They feel that over reaction could have negative impacts to the freedom and innovation the Internet fosters today as governments clamp down on it. They agree there are dangers but want to use proportionally and evaluate actual damage to judge cyber attacks and not succumb to hype [20].

Lawson highlights concerns with the use of major war metaphors and Cold War analogies. He covers the power of these collective story devices and how they can be misleading when used in the wrong context. He reviews current law, cold war deterrence, counterinsurgency and bioterrorism analogies. His conclusion focus on how most metaphors and analogies are not used appropriately when talking about cyber events [21].

With two distinct camps and multiple viewpoints, it may take a cyber-based event that impacts one of the DIME elements of national power to create a catalyst that will engage the "national will" and force everyone onto the same page (think Pearl Harbor or 9/11). Today, the fact is we are facing something more like the Cold War where espionage and military spending are the bullets that will determine the outcome of the war. Unlike the Cold War the cost of entry to cyber war is much lower, the ability to determine actions and attribute players much harder, and the pace of change exponentially faster so the lessons of the last war will not serve us in this one.

WHY CYBER WARFARE IS IMPORTANT

When we look at what is at stake we can see multiple critical infrastructures. The following areas are critical to national health and to a large extent are dependent on the Internet: Agriculture and Food; Banking and Finance; Chemical; Commercial Facilities; Communications; Critical Manufacturing; Department of Defense; Dams; Defense Industrial Base; Emergency Services; Energy; Government Facilities; Healthcare and Public Health; Information Technology; National Monuments and Icons; Nuclear Reactors; Materials and Waste; Postal and Shipping; and Transportation System and Water as laid out in Figure 1.4. These are national

FIGURE 1.4 Critical infrastructure dependant and vulnerable to cyber attacks [22].

capabilities or programs the U.S. Department of Homeland Security's (DHS) Critical Infrastructure and Key Resources (CIKR) protection plan tracks. They work to support assessing vulnerabilities, implementing protective programs, improving security protocols, implementing real-time information sharing, and assisting with contingency planning and recovery.

Although these critical infrastructure categories were identified by the U.S. government, they are applicable to every country. Some of these are more directly involved with cyber warfare. Communications, Transportation, Department of Defense, and the Defensive Industrial Base that supports them are the most important to war fighting. Most military communications tunnel through commercial circuits so any compromise of the commercial infrastructure would effectively cut off all communications for fixed military installations.

Much of the material support the military requires is delivered over commercial infrastructure, so to lose access to rail movement, or to have supplies misrouted, could cause significant delays in operations. Finally, the DoD depends on contractors for everything from staff support to equipment development and operation.

If another nation wanted to know how to defend against the latest weapon system or wanted to clone it they would try to steal the system design documentation. The traditional method would be to try to infiltrate a spy or compromise someone working on the program. Today it would be easier to break into the servers that had the information. In the U.S., there are two locations to go after that information, the DoD program office that controls the development and fielding and the contractor that designed and builds it. So, as you can see, the infrastructure that enables most of what we do today is both our strength and our weakness.

SUMMARY

Many U.S. citizens would say the last time the *country* was at war was World War II. Others would say Korea and Vietnam were wars but technically or legally they were police actions. If Korea was a war then we are still at war with North Korea (having stood on the Demilitarized Zone (DMZ) between the two countries, many soldiers would agree). Many presidents have openly talked about the Cold War but a "war" was never declared. The United States declared a "War on Drugs" and "War on Terrorism" but those were not wars against another country but rather on problems that had reached the level that they became a national security issue.

If this is the standard we measure by then we could have a pure cyber war. We have been in multiple wars in the Middle East (Iraq twice and Afghanistan) but these were not formally declared "wars"; some would say they are part of the "War on Terrorism." The last time the United States was in a congressionally declared war was World War II; however, the concept of what a war means is changing. These have been very traditional wars and if they are the standards we measure a "war" by, then there is no such thing as cyber war.

The term "war" has taken on many different meanings over time. If we had a Cold War and are in both a Drug War and a War on Terrorism then we are in a Cyber War. If we hold to the strict nation state declaring war on another sovereign nation then we are just facing a steady state complex problem that could become an international disaster, changing economies, enabling a massive crime wave, facilitating unprecedented espionage, and creating a new domain for warfare.

Today the Internet is more similar to how the Wild West is portrayed in movies than the Cold War. Over the course of a movie, settlers might have to deal with Indian attacks, Mexican banditos, bad weather, criminals from our own community, and Mexican Army invasions. To carry the analogy to the internet/cyber domain, Indian attacks are a form of guerilla warfare, banditos are non-state actors but may have informal support from their host nation, weather equates to the environmental impacts that create noise in systems, making things unpredictable, criminal acts if they get bad enough may become a threat to the community and may require the aid of the state or federal government, and military invasion is a full-scope war that could require the full weight of the country to address. Any of these can wipe the "settlers" out and may need to be addressed by the local "sheriff," the "rangers" or the "U.S. Army" depending on the scope of the problem, demands of the people and how the government reacts. So the question of if we are in a cyber war today is answered by the simple statement: "Stop debating on what to call the problem and get us some help!"

References

[1] Whitehouse website, http://www.whitehouse.gov/cybersecurity [accessed 17.03.13].
[2] The Hill (blog), http://thehill.com/ [accessed 17.03.13].
[3] RT website, http://rt.com/usa/napolitano-us-cyber-attack-761/ [accessed 17.03.13].
[4] FP National Security website, http://killerapps.foreignpolicy.com/posts/2012/09/18/air_force_chief_wary_of_cyber_black_hole [accessed 17.03.13].
[5] Secretary of Defense. DoD Publications, http://www.dod.mil/pubs/foi/joint_staff/jointStaff_jointOperations/07-F-2105doc1.pdf [accessed 17.03.13].
[6] Secretary of Defense. DoD Publications, http://www.dod.gov/pubs/foi/ojcs/07-F-2105doc1.pdf [accessed 17.03.13].
[7] Joint Electronic. Electronic Library Library, http://www.dtic.mil/doctrine/dod_dictionary/index.html; 2010 [accessed 17.03.13].
[8] United Nations. UN terms, http://unterm.un.org/dgaacs/unterm.nsf/375b4cb457d6e2cc85256b260070ed33/$searchForm?SearchView [accessed 17.03.13].
[9] Bassford C. The clausewitz homepage. On war [document on the Internet], http://www.clausewitz.com/readings/OnWar1873/; 2010 [accessed 17.03.13].
[10] Tzu S. On the art of war, http://www.chinapage.com/sunzi-e.html [accessed 17.03.13].
[11] Wright DP, Reese, CTR. ON POINT II: Transition to the New Campaign. The United States Army in Operation IRAQI FREEDOM May 2003-January 2005 Part IV Sustaining the Campaign Chapter 12 Logistics and Combat Service Support Operations, http://www.globalsecurity.org/military/library/report/2008/onpoint/chap12.htm [accessed 17.03.13].

[12] Joint Doctrine Division, J-7, Joint Staff. DOD dictionary of military and associated terms [document on the Internet], http://www.dtic.mil/doctrine/dod_dictionary/index.html; 2010 [accessed 17.03.13].

[13] Kem CJD (Retired). Understanding the operational environment: the expansion of DIME, http://www.thefreelibrary.com/Understanding+the+operational+environment%3A+the+expansion+of+DIME.-a0213693824 [accessed 17.03.13].

[14] Securing Our Digital Future. The white house blog, Washington, DC, http://www.whitehouse.gov/assets/documents/Cyberspace_Policy_Review_final.pdf; 2010 [accessed 17.03.13].

[15] Homeland Security Newswire. 15 nations agree to start working together on cyber arms control. Business of homeland security, http://www.homelandsecuritynewswire.com/first-15-nations-agree-start-working-together-cyber-arms-control [accessed 17.03.13].

[16] The National Security Council (NSC). National security council. The comprehensive national cybersecurity initiative [document on the Internet], Washington, DC, http://www.whitehouse.gov/cybersecurity/comprehensive-national-cybersecurity-initiative [accessed 17.03.13].

[17] Securing Our Digital Future. The white house blog [document on the Internet], Washington, DC, http://www.whitehouse.gov/assets/documents/Cyberspace_Policy_Review_final.pdf [accessed 17.03.13].

[18] IQ2US. Intelligence squared U.S. Debate—The cyber war threat has been grossly exaggerated, Washington DC, USA: s.n., http://intelligencesquaredus.org/index.php/past-debates/cyber-war-threat-has-been-grossly-exaggerated/ [accessed 17.03.13].

[19] Rid T. Cyber war will not take place. J Strat Stud 2012;35(1):5–32.

[20] Valeriano B, Maness R. The fog of cyberwar why the threat doesn't live up to the hype. J Strat Stud 2013;35 (1):5–32. National Defence University Department of Leadership and Military Pedagogy Publication Series 2 Article Collection no: 10 Helsinki. http://www.foreignaffairs.com/articles/138443/brandon-valeriano-and-ryan-maness/the-fog-of-cyberwar.

[21] Lawson S. Putting the "war" in cyberwar: metaphor, analogy, and cybersecurity discourse in the United States. First Monday 2012;17(7).

[22] Department of Homeland Security. Homeland security, www.dhs.gov [accessed 17.03.13].

2

Cyber Threatscape

HOW DID WE GET HERE?

In the early 1980s, when ARPANET was becoming the World Wide Web which grew into today's Internet, the focus was on interoperability and reliability as a means of communication and potential command and control in the event of an emergency. Everyone with access to the system knew each other and security was not a consideration. Then, in the late 1980s, trouble started; Robert Morris released the first worm (a self-replicating piece of malware) and Clifford Stoll discovered Soviet Bloc spies stealing U.S. secrets via a mainframe at the University of California, Berkeley. These were quickly followed by a number of incidents that highlighted the security risks associated with our new communication capability (see Appendix for list of major events through the years).

The key cyber events as they relate to and impacted the military occurred in the mid-to-late 1990s highlighted by Time magazine having a cover on "Cyber War." The 1998 Solar Sunrise incident hit the news as the Pentagon got hacked while America was at war with Iraq, but the instigators were actually just two kids from California. Then came Moonlight Maze, where the Department of Defense (DoD) found intrusions from systems in the Soviet Union (though the source of the attacks was never proven) and Russia denied any involvement (hackers will often route their attacks through countries that will not cooperate with an investigation so there was plausible deniability). By the early 2000s, a series of attacks, generally accepted as being from China, were identified and code named Titan Rain, the name was changed to Byzantine Hades after the Titan Rain code name was disclosed in the media and changed again when the Byzantine Hades code name was posted to WikiLeaks (current name is classified). The term "Advance Persistent Threat (APT)" has become the common reference term for this state-sponsored systematic electronic reconnaissance/digital espionage. By late 2000s, there was a physical aspect added to the entropic attacks which the DoD code named Operation Buckshot Yankee. Thumb drives used by U.S. Military were found to have malcode embedded which caused DoD to ban thumb drive usage on all military networks and systems.

In addition to attacks on the U.S. Military, some international incidents occurred in the 2000s. In 2007, hackers believed to be linked to the Russian government brought down the Web sites of Estonia's parliament, banks, ministries, newspapers, and broadcasters. Estonia called on the NATO treaty for protection and troops to help recover. A year later cyber attackers hijacked government and commercial Web sites in Georgia during a military conflict with Russia, creating a new form of digital signal jamming over the Web. In 2010, the Stuxnet worm attacked the systems that control Iran's nuclear material development causing damage to these systems. While the examples we have looked at, a nation calling on a mutual defense treaty—combined kinetic/non-kinetic war and physical destruction of a national security asset, could be considered to be cyber wars no nation state has formally acknowledged or accused another state of "cyber war."

There are some notable commercial cyber events that parallel the military's pains. In 2009, reports revealed that hackers downloaded data from the DoD's multibillion-dollar F-35 Joint Strike Fighter program, showing that the cyber attackers were going after defense contractors as well as the military itself. Then in 2009, Operation Aurora broke into the news when Google publicly revealed itself as being one of many commercial companies hacked by the APT, showing that the cyber attackers were also going after commercial intellectual property. There were two more troubling attacks in 2011: The first was a series of hacks exposed in the global energy report "Night Dragon" which showed how China was trying to gain a competitive edge in the energy market through espionage. The second was the RSA attack where stolen information would allow a hacker to replicate the number that showed up on the password token many organizations used to secure their networks, showing that the enemy was willing to attack the infrastructure used to protect the U.S. More recently, a very detailed report on China's cyber operations was published by the commercial consulting vendor Mandiant. These all point to an active campaign to steal intellectual property. Some of the information is taken to gain military advantage but the majority is to gain an economic advantage which as we look at countries' ability to fund their militaries has a direct impact.

For the past 30 years, there has been a continuous battle between defenders and attackers on networks around the globe. At first most of the hackers were motivated by curiosity, looking for entertainment or bragging rights. Then as more financial transactions were conducted on the internet, a criminal element followed. Soon we saw trends like botnets where it did not matter to the attacker if the target was military, government, or commercial, the attacker was just after as many computer systems as they could acquire. This was back in the days when it was popular to say "network security needs to be good enough so that you're not the low hanging fruit on the internet." That is no longer true as with many sophisticated threat organizations there are a lot of giraffes on the internet interested in only eating fruit from the top of the tree; security today needs to be good—not better than the next guy. Then as nation's governments, militaries and economies became more dependent on the internet we see nation states acting against each other in cyberspace. As each new threat grows new protective solutions are established and new attacks are developed to circumvent them, and the cycle continues.

The threatscape map in Figure 2.1 was designed to assist everyone in understanding this complex environment. As we look at it some will see the map of Mordor from J.R. Tolkien's fictional Middle-Earth while others see the old TV show's map of the Ponderosa. The map is designed to show how all the events we have covered in this chapter interrelate in cyberspace. It shows the methodology (upper left) and resources (lower left) that hackers use to break into systems. Then it provides the different categories of the attackers in the second column. These categories are divided by a solid line but it is important to realize that nation states can use criminal organization to accomplish their aims or for another example where they can cross is between insider threat and hacktivists. In the past an insider might post an organizations' critical information on the internet, either because they were disgruntled or a whistle-blower, but now hacktivists are behaving like an insider threat by not stealing information but rather by posting it openly on the internet. The center column shows the defensive mountain range to portray the "defense in depth" strategy used to protect networks today. Finally, the far right column shows the different types of data the attacker wants access to. It is broken out by the motivations of the threat actors from the second column.

ATTACK METHODOLOGY WITH THE TOOLS AND TECHNIQUES USED TO EXECUTE THEM

As we examine the manner in which networks are broken into, it is evident that the basic steps in the process are analogous to traditional military attack/defend doctrine. Similar to how South Korea and North Korea have built physical defensive fortifications between each other, we see the same principle and even term used by network administrators—Demilitarized Zone (DMZ). This is where one puts systems that must connect to the internet where they are in more danger. From the attacker point of view the same steps are necessary to attack a network as it is to break through the DMZ: conduct reconnaissance to determine vulnerability, marshal forces at the point of weakness, attack and penetrate the defense, then exploit the infiltration to gain control over the battlefield/network.

The major difference between kinetic (real world) and non-kinetic (virtual world) warfare methodology is the weapons versus software programs they use. We will walk through the steps and define a few of the tools used. The tools will be covered in more detail in later chapters so this will just be to gain an initial understanding.

WARNING

The only difference between a hacker tool and a cybersecurity professional tool is "written permission." Please do not load a tool you read about here like the password cracker on an operational computer at work to test your organization's security without authorization. People have been fired for using these tools despite their good intentions. Contact your manager and get approval, in writing, then test your security in a coordinated and safe manner.

FIGURE 2.1   This is a threatscape map designed to show the different components in the cyber environment and how they interact.

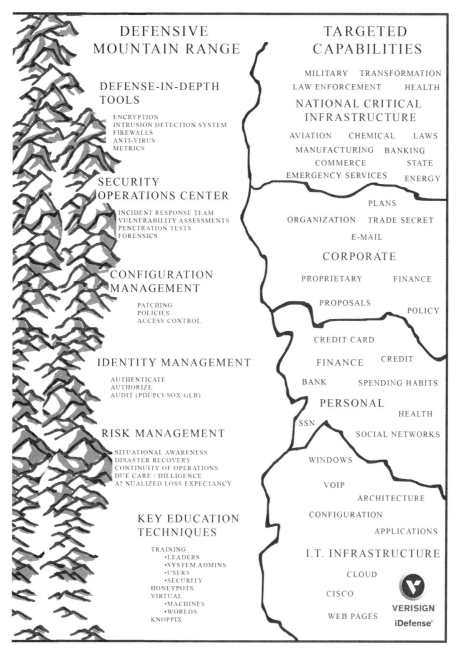

FIGURE 2.1—Cont'd

An attack methodology is the process or general steps used to conduct an attack of a target. The tools/techniques are what are used to execute the process. The major steps are recon, attack, and exploit. These steps can be a variety of activities, from launching machine to machine attacks to using social engineering. (Think of social engineering as scamming or conning a target out of information allowing the hacker to compromise a network.) Each of these steps or phases have a number of substeps to accomplish them and in many cases different hackers will both modify and automate them to suit their style.

Mapping Sample of Well-known Tools to the Process

- Reconnaissance
  - Scanners
    - Nmap
    - Nessus
  - Sniffers
    - Wiresharek
    - Ettercap
  - Packet Crafters
    - Netcat
    - Hping
- Attack
  - Exploit Vulnerabilities
    - Metasploit
    - Canvas
    - CoreImpact
    - Back Track
  - Compromise Applications
    - Web page—Cross-site Scripting
    - Database—SQL attack
  - Crack Passwords
    - Cain and Able
    - John the Ripper
- Exploit
  - Confidentiality
    - Steal data to use or expose
  - Integrity
    - Change data based on impact desired
  - Availability
    - DDOS based on critical timing
- SE
  - Via Technology
    - Social Engineering Toolkit
    - Maltego
  - Via Human or user
    - Phishing
    - Social Networking sites

To begin the recon phase a target is required. The target can be the specific systems that will be attacked or the personnel that use them. To attack the unique Internet Protocol (IP) address for a machine or Uniform Resource Locator for a Web page must be known. To conduct an attack via the users, a phone number could be all that is needed. IP addresses and phone numbers can be found with a quick Google search or with services like American Registry for Internet Numbers searches. Much of what is needed for a social engineering attack can be found on a business card.

Once the target is identified, the recon begins to find the weak point or vulnerability. The attack can be against the operating system or one of the applications on it (i.e., Adobe Flash, Microsoft Office, games, Web browsers, or an instant messenger). A scanner is run against the system to determine and list many of the vulnerabilities. Some of the more popular scanners are Nmap, Nessus, eEye Retina, and Saintscanner. Attack framework tools are available that both scan and then have the exploits to launch the attack matching vulnerabilities found built into the application. Some popular framework tools are Metasploit, Canvas, and Core Impact. Finally, there are tools that transform a machine into a Linux system by booting off of a Linux live CD. The most popular live CD attack tool is BackTrack.

Another tool that is useful during recon is a sniffer. This is a tool that has the attacker's system mimic every computer on the network so it gets a copy of all the traffic. It will allow the attacker to read all unencrypted emails and documents as well as see the Web pages being accessed by everyone on the network. Popular sniffers are Wireshark, Ettercap, and Tcpdump. On the wireless side tools include Aircrack-ng and Kismet.

While there are a lot of recon tools that are very powerful and easy to use, the one set of tools that shows how the threat environment has evolved is packet crafters. Someone with no programming skills can now craft unique attacks. Popular tools include NetCat and Hping. There are a host of other tools for recon but these represent the baseline tools used to discover the vulnerabilities that allow movement to the attack phase.

When attacking a system there are many types of malcode that can be used. At the code level there are worms or viruses that can use attack vectors like cross-site scripting or buffer overflows to install rootkits or a Trojan horse which acts as a backdoor into a system, and is used to spread the attack. A worm spreads without any help. It infects a system and then uses that system to find more systems to spread to. A virus needs some user interaction like opening any type of file (email, document, presentation) or starting a program (game, video, new app). Worms and viruses use techniques like cross-site scripting or buffer overflows which attack mistakes in the code in order to compromise it. Cross-site scripting is a Web-based attack that allows unauthorized code to be executed on the viewer's computer that could result in information being stolen or the system's identification certificates being stolen. An overly simplified example of a buffer overflow is when a program asks for a phone number rather than giving the 10 digits needed, the software sends 1000 digits followed by a command to install the malcode. Because the program does not have good error handling to deal with the large amount of unexpected extra data, it executes the malcode.

A rootkit is a program that takes over control of an operating system and tells lies about what is happening on the system. Once a rootkit is installed, it can hide the hacker's folders (i.e., hacker tools, illegal movies, stolen credit card numbers), misdirect applications (i.e., show the antivirus updating daily but do not allow it to update), or misrepresent the system status (i.e., leave port 666 open so the hacker can remotely access the system but show it as closed).

The first generation of rootkits was much like my daughter when she was 4 (called the fibbing 4s because that is when most kids learn to lie). Like a 4-year-old, the rootkits of the first generation did not lie very well. The generation we are on now is more like when she was 21 (she was MUCH better at telling a coherent story that was not easy to detect as a lie). The current generation of rootkits does a much better job of hiding themselves from detection. The next generation will be like someone with a masters in social engineering; almost undetectable. A Trojan horse backdoor is a program that masquerades as a legitimate file (often a system file: i.e., files ending in .sys on a Windows box or the system library on a Mac). These files are actually fakes and have replaced the actual system file. The new file both runs the system and opens a backdoor to the system allowing the hacker remote control of the system.

One use for worms and viruses is to build botnet armies. A bot (also called a zombie) is a computer that is a slave to a controller. Once someone builds an army of millions of bots they can cause a distributed denial of service (DDoS) by having all of the bots try to connect to the same site or system simultaneously. This can be done to blackmail a Website (pay or be blocked so no customers can get access), disrupt command and control systems, click fraud (if Acme.org gets paid one cent for every customer that clicks on link taking them to Selling.com a botnet could be used to do that millions of times a day) or compile complex problems (much like a distributed supercomputer).

> **NOTE**
>
> If the intent of an attack is to cause a Denial of Service (DoS) there are two ways to accomplish this. The first is to attack the system and take it down. The second (usually called Distributed DoS or DDoS) attacks the bandwidth. In cases where you are attacking the communication lines you can skip recon because you are not worried about finding a specific vulnerability, you just need a botnet army large enough to overwhelm a target's communication capabilities. If you are attacking an organization with distributed and redundant infrastructure then it would be necessary to develop malcode that attacks the organization's systems simultaneously to take it offline as it is impractical to take down all the communication capabilities.

There are a number of ways to launch attacks targeted at a specific system rather than the broad net a worm or virus would catch. The attack framework tools mentioned earlier are the most common. The key is to correlate the exploit to the vulnerability. Much like there has never been a bank built that cannot be robbed and there is not a computer or network that cannot be broken into given enough resources and persistence. If no vulnerability can be found then the attacker can go after the authentication via password attacks, credential compromises or attack the security infrastructure used to protect the network.

Cracking passwords can be done with brute force by having a program try every possible password iteration. This can be time consuming and is easy to detect but, depending on the strength of the password, is very effective. If the hacker can get access to the password file then tools like Cain & Able or Jack the Ripper can be utilized to crack them. Another technique that is available is called rainbow tables. These are databases where popular password encryption protocols have been run on every possible key combination on a standard keyboard. This precompiled list allows a simple lookup when the hacker gets access to the list of encrypted passwords. Many of these tables have done every combination for 8-20 characters and the length grows as hackers continue to use botnet to build the tables.

NOTE

Exploit has three meanings within the cyber community. When talking about code it refers to malcode that allows a system to be compromised. When talking about attack methodology it refers to what the payload of the attack is intended to accomplish. When talking about military doctrine it is used by the intelligence community to refer to cyber recon/espionage.

The exploit phase is where the attacker takes advantage of gaining control. There are generally three factors that the hacker can compromise: Confidentiality, Integrity, or Availability. When attacking confidentiality they are simply stealing secrets. Integrity attacks are when they change the data on the system or masquerade as a legitimate authorized or authenticated user. In a commercial setting this could be changing prices or customer data. On a military network it might be to change the equations used to calculate command and control guidance. Availability attacks are normally time based and can be accomplished by taking the system down or overwhelming the bandwidth. The type of exploit is based on the motivations of the attacker. They can use the system to attack more systems on the network, misrepresent the user (send fake emails), or load a rootkit with a backdoor to maintain long-term access. They will often try to avoid detection and might even use anti-forensic techniques like log wiping and time stomping. Some will patch the systems they have taken over so future hackers will not be able to break in and take them away. Finally, they may load digital tripwire alarms to tell them if they have been detected by security engineers using forensic tools.

If these technical attacks do not work another vector of attack is social engineering. In fact some threat organizations use social engineering as their primary means of attack. Social Engineering (SE) can be thought of as the act of influencing someone's behavior through manipulating their emotions, or gaining and betraying their trust to gain access to their system. The difference between social engineering and other attacks is the vectors are through the person, or as hackers say the "wetware." Think of any of the movies about stories or movies about con-artists, the difference being rather than money they want access to information on or about a target's computer systems. This can be done in person but is often done over the phone or remote communications like email. It starts with pre-texting, with includes researching an organization using sources like websites, social media, or even meeting people at places like a conference to exchange business cards. The most common attack today is via email. This kind of social engineering attack is called phishing (sending general email to multiple people), spear phishing (targeted at a specific person), or whaling (targeting a specific senior member of the organization). There are also technical tools like the "Social Engineer Toolkit" that are designed to assist attacking the workforce.

ATTACKERS (MAJOR CATEGORIES OF THREATS)

This section will focus on the different categories of attackers. As we look at the threatscape map (Figure 2.1) the attackers are not ranked or ordered in any particular way. Again it is important to note that while there are solid lines between them they can overlap or someone can belong to more than one category. The Advanced Persistent Threat (APT) can buy exploits from criminal elements, noobs can join hacktivist causes and, one particularly troubling paradigm shift that has happened recently, hacktivists can behave like insider threats as they steal information and then publish the stolen information on the websites like WikiLeaks.

Advanced Persistent Threat

APT is one of the key drivers of cyber warfare. The term APT is often used in different ways by the media, but, for purposes of this book, APT means state guided attacks. It is truly digital spying or espionage in the virtual world. Some of the most commonly referenced APT activities were discussed earlier (Titan Rain, Operation Buckshot Yankee, Aurora, Stuxnet, Night Dragon, APT1 Report). As we examine if the APT actions qualify as war we look to how war is defined.

Organized Crime

Organized crime on the Internet is widely covered in the news today. One of the most often joked about scams on the Internet is the "Nigerian royalty that just needs access to your bank account to get money out of the country" scam that sends phishing emails designed to steal identities and access the victims' bank accounts. The text of the emails from the Nigerian scams will talk about how they have money that they need to get out of the country and all they need is to transfer the money to a U.S. bank, but to do that they need access to the victim's account. The early versions used poor English but they have gotten much more sophisticated over time. These scams have been around long before the Internet but have become much easier to do in bulk and with little risk of incarceration, as the perpetrators are usually overseas. Another popular scam is selling fake medicine. While some of the sites are selling legitimate drugs most will send fake medicine if they send anything at all. Similar scams can be used to get members of the military or national security infrastructure to get involved in activities they would not do in the real world.

One of the more well-known criminal organizations is called the Russian Business Network (RBN) also known as the Russian Mob (note this is not one single organization). If someone graduates from a university in one of the old Soviet Union bloc countries with a degree in computer science one of the better paying jobs is with the RBN. There they will work full time on tasks like building custom exploits targeting specific financial institutions, building botnet armies, running identity theft networks, or any one of a dozen of "business ventures" for organizations like the RBN based on different revenue models. These organizations can be staffed in one country, use systems hosted in a different country (for a while RBN was using systems hosted in China) and commit crimes against citizens in a third country. This makes it very complex to prosecute when the crimes are discovered. A great reference that goes into detail is the book "Fatal System Error" by Joseph Menn. While we have talked about China and Russia they are not the only countries that have cyber-based criminal organizations; in fact the U.S. has similar groups.

Insider Threat

As we change to look at insider threat you will find a common rule of thumb is that insider threats represent 20% of the threat but could cause 80% of the damage (recent studies by CIS and Verizon show the real numbers of insiders are closer to 50%). The reason is the insiders understand what is valuable on the network and often have legitimate access to it. The three basic categories of insiders are: disgruntled employees, financially motivated (thieves), and users unintentionally causing damage. Disgruntled employees can cause problems by publishing information on the Web to competitors or to fellow employees (i.e., everyone's salary). They could also install a logic bomb that will cause damage if they stop working at the company (i.e., if Winterfeld does not show up on the employee payroll, reformat all servers in the data room). Financially motivated insiders will misuse the company assets or manipulate the system to steal. There are both intentional and unintentional insider threats. Examples of unwitting threats include users who unintentionally delete files causing loss of work or accidentally post classified documents on unclassified systems causing what is known as a spill. Spills could require destruction of the system and a lengthy investigation. Finally, users can open files or go to websites with malcode infecting the network.

Hacktivist

Hacktivists can be motivated by political views, cultural/religious beliefs, national pride, or terrorist ideology. The most notable example has been from a group called Anonymous. This group of loosely affiliated hackers from around the world banded together to attack organizations they felt were in the wrong. This cyber vigilante group attacked the Church of Scientology under project name Chanology in 2008 and started using their trademark saying "We are Anonymous. We are Legion. We do not forgive. We do not forget. Expect us" [1]. They have attacked MasterCard for stopping support of WikiLeaks, Law Enforcement Agencies for policy they do not support, political parties, HBGary Federal (in response to statement made by Aaron Barr), Sony (in response to a lawsuit they brought), the Bay Area Rapid Transit system (in response to their closing down cell phone tower coverage at the stations to prevent a protest), porn sites, and many government sites around the world. Their supporters can often be seen wearing Guy Fawkes masks from the movie "V for Vendetta." As of early 2013, the FBI has arrested many of the leaders of Anonymous, but the group is still active and expect more groups like this to sprout up. A good reference to read on the story is "We Are Anonymous: Inside the Hacker World of LulzSec, Anonymous, and the Global Cyber Insurgency" by Parmy Olson.

Script Kiddies/Noobs

The final group in this section is on Script kiddies or noobs (for new to hacker). These are pejorative terms for the less skilled hackers. These are the people who just use the tools that can be found on the Internet with little thought out methodology or technique. They have many different motivations to start hacking. Some are looking for a social experience and will try to join a hacker group (some groups will require proof of hacking ability before they grant membership), others enjoy the challenge or want to gain status across the hacker community, still others do it out of curiosity and think of it as entertainment. We can see many examples of these at hacker conferences like DEFCON, ShmooCon, or HOPE. The problem these script kiddies pose to the cyber warfare landscape is the amount of activity they produce. If there are millions of attacks launched by noobs every week, how can the APT or specific criminal activity be located? It is also important to understand that the tools script-kiddies use are very powerful and they will end up PWNing (slang for own) systems. The age old adage "the defender has to get it right every time while the attacker only has to get it right once" applies here. The Defense Information Systems Agency has consistently said the majority of systems compromised were from known exploits that could have been prevented if the systems were fully patched and configured to standard [2]. As script-kiddies gain more experience they will become hackers and usually end up being part of some group.

These groups are not represented in the threat list as they do not fit into an attacker category. When they join together they may prank each other, build tools (one classic example is the Cult of the Dead Cow's tool called "Back Orifice" in 1980), they may live near each other (i.e., 303 group in Denver), skill focused (Social-http://www.social-engineer.org/ group), startup conferences (B-Sides) or run a podcast (pauldotcom). This would be an example of the range of motivations—some are white hat and only use their skills when professionally contracted to test security, others are gray hat and do what they feel is the right thing for betterment of the Cybersecurity community and some are black hats who conduct illegal activities.

DEFENSE IN DEPTH—HOW ORGANIZATIONS DEFEND TODAY (DEFENSIVE MOUNTAIN RANGE)

On the threatscape map (center column of Figure 2.1) the Defensive Mountain Range shows many of the different methods used to protect networks today. It covers the infrastructure and processes used to secure the systems and detect any intrusions. Much like real-world defenses, they need to be constantly validated, monitored, and updated.

Defense-In-Depth or multiple layers of protection is how most networks are protected today. The issue is there are so many mobile systems (laptops, phones, tablets) and removable storage devices that it is becoming increasing difficult to keep all the systems inside the defensive perimeter. Some of the critical tools are firewalls to block the attacks, intrusion detection systems to alert on attacks, antivirus to kill the attacks that got through, and encryption of the data on the device so if the device is lost or stolen the information is still secure. The critical process needed is good security metrics. Metrics revolve around the need to quantify the impact of cyber events. They should support both the technical and senior leadership's ability to make decisions to protect the network and react to changes in risk assessment as well as support understanding of return on investment of security infrastructure. There has been a lot of work done, but there is no clear set of industry standard cyber metrics today. There are three basic types of metrics:

- *Technical:* Based on infrastructure and the incident response cycle.
- *Security return on investment:* Cost-based analysis on benefits from implementing new technology or policies. These goals must be set before they change and methods to track performance are established.
- *Risk posture:* Analysis on impact of cyber events/incidents to enterprise and operations.

Next comes the team that monitors the network, usually called the Security Operations Centers (SOC) or Computer Emergency Response Team. These cells typically contain the Incident Response Teams responsible for the response cycle—Protect, Detect, React, and Recover. This is very similar to the military OODA Loop (Observe, Orient, Decide, and Act). The SOC would also be responsible for conducting Vulnerability Assessments (VA) and Penetration Tests (PT). The VA is designed to look for vulnerabilities on the network then prioritize how to fix or mitigate them. The PT is designed to test the team's ability to respond to an intrusion. Penetration Tests can also be called Red Teaming depending on the scope and interaction of the two sides. The PT team will not only find the vulnerability but exploit it and once they break in will either grab a predetermined file (called the flag) or load a file on the system (called the golden nugget). Then the SOC team must determine how the PT broke in and what they did. This will validate the team's processes and tools. One key capability that is needed after an intrusion is the forensics expert. This is someone that understands the rules of evidence and can testify in court. This analysis is key to understand what happened to prevent it from reoccurring.

TIP

A forensics expert is a must-have team member, but, as they can be expensive, many organizations have someone they can call on demand as opposed to having a full time staff member. The forensics expert should be called if there is any possibility of a lawsuit, human resource action (firing), or prosecution of the hacker. There must be clear policies on when they are called because, much like a real crime scene, the more people that have accessed the data the more the crime scene is compromised. The military is slowly moving toward gathering evidence in a way that it can be presented in court as opposed to just getting the systems back on line quickly.

Configuration Management is a critical part of the defense. A well-configured and managed network is more secure. Think of walking up to a cruise liner to start your vacation only to find it is so covered in rust you cannot tell what color it used to be painted. Common sense would prevent you from getting on. Yet because we cannot see that our network devices are past their maintenance lifecycle we put our most valuable information on the equivalent servers. The basics require timely patching. Patches must be tested before they get installed on critical operational systems so the challenge is how much time is allowed for analysis (some suggest 72 h, but that can be expensive so there is a broad range). Well understood and enforced policies for both the users and network administrators are a must. They both can impact the security baseline with decisions on operations or processes but often do not examine the impact to security risks. Finally, access control must be managed so that only the people with a need are allowed to access the mission critical data. This can be done physically or through electronic policies. This is called the principle of least privilege and has been used for decades in the intelligence community.

Identity Management is one area that will help as users become more mobile. The three vital factors are authentication, authorization, and audit/compliance. Before someone logs into the system they should have to prove who they are with something they know (user name and password), something they have (electronic token), and/or something they are (biometrics, i.e., scan a fingerprint): this is authentication. Next they should be categorized by what kind of information they should have access to. The military uses Unclassified/ Secret/Top Secret but there are a number of organizations that have designed their own system. Finally, as was mentioned earlier, as every network will have a weakness over time it is prudent to assume that someone has penetrated the network and conduct audits to find them.

Compliance is based on the legal or regulatory requirements of the industry. Some examples are:

- Healthcare = Health Insurance Portability and Accountability Act (HIPAA)
- Finance = Gramm-Leach-Bliley Act
- Publicly traded companies = Sarbanes-Oxley Act
- Credit Cards = Payment Card Industry
- Energy Providers = North American Electric Reliability Corporation (NERC) Critical Infrastructure Protection (CIP) program
- Federal agencies = Federal Information Security Management Act (FISMA)
- U.S. Intelligence Community (IC) = Director of Central Intelligence Directive (DCID) 6/3
- DoD = DoD Information Assurance Certification and Accreditation Process (DIACAP)

Today most of these are based on annual reviews of the systems but they are moving to real-time monitoring.

Risk Management is what all these regulations have been driving to. The goal is to achieve Situational Awareness (SA). SA is the correlation and fusion of data from multiple sources that enable decision making. Ideally it will be presented visually through a Common Operational Picture that will facilitate true risk posture understanding and provide information in a format that enables decisions. If the network is lost then the Disaster Recovery (DR) and Continuity of Operations Plans (COOP) come into play. DR focuses on getting the network back up while the COOP is the plan to continue operations without any automation.

As we design systems and networks it is important to understand there are legal expectations of how the network will be protected. These principles are known as due care and due diligence. These should be based on the "Annualized Loss Expectancy" calculations (Vulnerability × Threat × Asset Value = Total Risk then Total Risk × Countermeasures = Residual Risk). This will help determine where the organization is in the security lifecycle: requirements definition, design and develop the protective measures, implement, and validate the defensive solution, operation maintain risk management controls. This will also allow security to be designed into the system rather that bolted on afterwards, something that is always more expensive and less effective.

One of the most effective protection techniques is education designed to alter the users' behaviors. The training must be targeted at the different types of users: leaders need to know how to manage cyber risk, system admins must understand the importance of configuration management and patching, general users need to understand how their behaviors can become vulnerabilities that hackers can exploit, and the cyber security team needs to understand the latest threats and protection tools/techniques. Some useful tools are honeypots, virtual machines, virtual worlds, and live CDs. Honeypots are systems that are deployed with no operational function so any interaction with them causes an investigation. If we install a server with data labeled "senior leaders evaluations and important financial data" it will attract insiders and hackers but as soon as they touch it the SOC will be alerted and quickly react. Virtual Machines (VM) are software-based computers that allow anyone to simulate multiple computers with various operating systems on their computer. This allows them to test hacking from one VM to another. Virtual worlds can be used to conduct training with no travel costs. A popular business-oriented virtual world is Second Life. Finally to boot your current computer as a Linux machine to use some of the tools we have discussed, use a live CD like BackTrack.

WHAT THE THREAT IS AFTER (WHAT WE SHOULD FOCUS ON DEFENDING)

Targeted Capabilities break out the variety of systems, types of information and industries that the enemy is trying to compromise. The major categories are National Critical Infrastructure, Corporate, Personal, and Information Technology (IT) Infrastructure. Critical infrastructure often has aspects of the other categories embedded within it. Corporate information will normally have personal and IT Infrastructure embedded.

National CIP includes: Banking, Law Enforcement, Laws/Legal System, Transportation, Health, Military, Chemical, Energy, State, Emergency Services, Plans, Manufacturing, Commerce, and Aviation. If any of these were not available for even short periods of time, there would be major impacts. The loss of faith in the security of aviation after the 9/11 attacks had secondary economic impacts. The loss of belief in the integrity of our financial systems could cause a run on the banks. If the power grid were to be taken down it would cause both economic and health impacts. The issue is that most of this critical infrastructure is managed by commercial companies that have to balance risk against profit and are generally driven by cost-effectiveness, functionality, and financial gain, rather than security.

Corporate assets such as email accounts, proprietary info/trade secrets, finance records, policy, proposals, and organizational decisions are all of value to the competition. Depending on the nature of the information nation states, criminal organizations, hacktivists, and insiders could all be after different parts of the company.

Personal data like health records and financial information (banking and credit card accounts) are high value targets for insurance companies, criminals, espionage targets, and your personal enemies. If someone wants to target a senior member of the U.S. Military today, finding out as much about the person on the Internet would be the first step. The same could be true of Law Enforcement Agencies that focus on the drug trade. Digital natives are putting more and more personal information on the Web. This information all ties back to two major issues: identity theft and social engineering.

IT infrastructure is a target for two reasons. Hackers may want to use the infrastructure for themselves (i.e., building a botnet) or they want to know what operating systems (i.e., Windows/OS X) and network devices (i.e., VoIP, applications, and specific Cisco devices) are available to allow them to find vulnerabilities. Understanding the architecture or mapping the Web pages could provide insight into how to gain unauthorized access.

SUMMARY

This has been an overview of the threatscape coving the methodology, tools, and techniques used by the different types of attackers and a review of the key parts of the defensive infrastructure employed to protect our systems as well as the general categories of information the attackers are after. These will all be covered in more detail in subsequent chapters but this foundation is intended to help tie it all together. Chapter 15 on Cyberspace Challenges is designed to give an overview of the cyber environment, focused on the challenges. It breaks out the problems in a way that they can be evaluated against each other and facilitates a discussion on prioritization and resource allocation.

The question most often asked after discussing this cyber threatscape is how someone should protect themselves at home. The answer is "safe behaviors!" The basics go a long way such as a firewall, up-to-date antivirus, patching all applications, keeping private and financial data on a removable hard drive that is only connected when in use, and BACK UP valuable data to a place that will not be destroyed if the system is stolen or destroyed. All are mandatory for basic security, but they can all be defeated by poor security practices such as weak passwords, surfing sites known to be hot spots for malcode, and opening emails or accepting invites on social networking sites from someone unknown. While there is no such thing as "security through obscurity" we should strive to not be the "low hanging fruit" that is easily PWNed.

References

[1] Anonymous. UNK [Online], http://www.webutation.net/go/review/anonymousarmy.webs.com.
[2] Brig, Gen. Patterson, LaWarren. Brief on operating, maintaining and defending the Army's global network enterprise. In: Cyberspace symposium, Colorado Springs; 2010.

3

The Cyberspace Battlefield

INFORMATION IN THIS CHAPTER

- Boundaries in Cyber Warfare
- Where Cyber Fits in the War-fighting Domains
- Review of the Threat Actors
- Fielding Systems at the Speed of Need

The boundaries of the battlefield in the physical world are usually straightforward. When two countries go to war there is a battlefront established between the two armies where active combat occurs. While there is not a clear forward area to the battlefront for counterinsurgency, irregular warfare, counterterrorism, and foreign internal defense battles even there are two sides with political goals fighting over geography.

The chief challenge in dealing with this new virtual cyberspace paradigm is the separation of activities from geography. Reconnaissance can now be done by folks distributed across the world. Planning can be done by cells of combatants who never meet. The Internet provides a means of communications via secure channels. The Internet can be both a resource and an attack vector. This new battlespace is an intricate problem. To understand it we will look at the boundaries of this new battlespace, how it fits into the historical war-fighting domains, the enemy forces we are facing, and the weapons needed to win on this virtual front.

BOUNDARIES IN CYBER WARFARE

Upon examining the boundaries of this virtual battlespace, we see three areas to analyze: physical, logical, and organizational. In the physical world boundaries can be legally recognized (*de jure*) like the borders between countries or practical (*de facto*) like the division of terrain between two units in the same army; these definitions are more difficult to apply in the virtual world. If we think of the World Wide Web as a connection of smaller networks with different configuration rules it is easy to see where to divide it. For the U.S. government this could be any system with .gov or .mil extensions which is the blend between the physical and logical. Generally each of these networks has a perimeter defended with a firewall, and anti-virus defending each machine. The more mature networks have a Security Operations Center (SOC) monitoring a Security Information and Event Management tool that includes feeds from Intrusion Detection Systems (IDS)/Intrusion Prevention Systems, correlation engines, web security proxies, centrally managed enterprise anti-virus/anti-spam servers, and forensics tools and compliance programs (ideally including training to help secure the users). These are the foundations for the defensive forces used in this battle. Finally there are organizations where a unit has multiple logical networks used by multiple groups (e.g., for a deployment to disaster relief) but also have multiple units that combine their networks to develop a single capability when they are part of a Joint or Multinational Command in an operational theater. This can present command and control challenges where physical presence does not line up with logical existence and the unit must coordinate action across many organizational boundaries to include government and commercial entities.

What do we mean by battlespace? The U.S. military definition is: "A term used to signify a unified military strategy to integrate and combine armed forces for the military theater of operations, including air, information, land, sea and space to achieve military goals. It includes the environment, factors and conditions that must be understood to successfully apply combat power, protect the force, or complete the mission. This includes enemy and friendly armed forces; infrastructure; weather; terrain; and the electromagnetic spectrum within the operational areas and areas of interest" [1]. In cyber operations, battlespace includes things like the networks, computers, hardware (this includes weapon systems with embedded computer chips), software (commercial and government developed), applications (like command and control systems), protocols, mobile devices, and the people that run them.

Defense in Depth

In cybersecurity, Defense in Depth is designed to build a wall of protection around the network or throughout the battle space. It must be enhanced to protect against insider threats and mobile devices that migrate in and out of the perimeter. It is the standard practice for logical construction of a network. At the lowest level we have an individual home network behind a local Internet Service Provider (ISP) router, and at the other end of the spectrum we have a national state network like China behind their Great Firewall. The U.S. government is behind several hundred access points monitored by the Department of Homeland Security. Sub-groups like Department of Defense, Department of Energy, Department of State, and Department of Treasury, etc., all sit behind their own security infrastructure. Organizations maintain their own networks but use a variety of techniques to administer and secure them. Some build and maintain everything, others outsource the infrastructure but keep security in house, some outsource everything but have the equipment in their building, and finally some prefer cloud solutions. Many of these organizations are geographically dispersed with users in multiple locations across the world. The amount of protection they deploy is based on their perception of risk and willingness to invest their profit back into security for the network. When we look at their defenses it is based on economic power rather than military power.

NOTE

Cloud computing uses Infrastructure as a Service (IaaS), Platform as a Service (PaaS), or Software as a Service (SaaS) to provide computing needs where the services are remote. Similar technology is Service Oriented Architecture (SOA) which is closely tied to web services. Both of these technologies often use Virtual Machines (VM) to host their systems on. These technologies provide benefits but come with new security issues to include data control, auditing, and configuration management. Like any system, they can be fraught with risk or very secure, based on how they are designed and maintained.

One concept that has been popular in the media is the concept of building a switch to isolate or "turn off the Internet" if we are under attack. These concepts show a fundamental lack of understanding of the Internet today. The Internet was a system originally built by Defense Advanced Research Projects Agency (DARPA) to provide communications capability after a nuclear war. As a result, it has resiliency and alternate path routing as part of the requirements. A good example of this can be seen in Iran's effort to suppress the protests following the 2009 presidential elections. Iran had government control over the communications systems and yet the Green Protest groups started a Twitter revolution using social media tools to get their message out (called the Twitter Revolution) [2]. We can quickly see that parts of the Internet can be turned dark, but only for a limited period of time and are actually a self-inflected denial of service.

Physical Infrastructure

Physical infrastructure includes power, backup generators, Heating Ventilating and Air Conditioning, surge control systems, connectivity (cabling), hardware, software, and people. The physical systems are vulnerable to surveillance, vandalism, sabotage, and attack. Much of this infrastructure is controlled by Industrial Control Systems (ICS), also commonly known as Supervisory Control and Data Acquisition (SCADA) programs which are vulnerable to hacking or denial of service attacks. Note that SCADA is a subset of ICS but has become synonymous in the media. This list does not address the potential environmental disaster factors. If the threat cannot conduct a kinetic attack or hack the system then there is always the wetware (human) vector. It is often easier to attack users than it is to attack the equipment. So when attacking the physical there are a number of options to create the desired impact.

NOTE

As with any subculture hackers have their own jargon. They use terms like: wetware for the human or user, noob or script kiddy meaning new or unskilled, PWN means to own, hacktivism is politically motivated hacking, and zombies/bots are systems that have been compromised and become part of a hackers network. There is also a unique way to write where letters and numbers are changed to make writing distinctive. Examples of this writing are elite becomes leet or 1337 or l33t and hacker becomes Haxor.

It is important to note that most of these infrastructure systems have systemic issues like: legacy systems, lack of lab environments to test patching, local management, and no SOC monitoring them. The programs are built on proprietary systems that originally ran on closed networks so were designed with high availability requirements but no confidentiality or integrity protections. SCADA owners believed that they would be protected by obscurity with nobody wanting to break into their systems. Also they felt that their programs were proprietary so would not be hackable, as the applications were unique. Most of these systems use the same protocols and are developed with the same programming languages as the rest of the applications on the market today so it has been relatively easy to find vulnerabilities in them. If we take a look at one critical infrastructure area like water, we have heard reports [3] about how terrorists could hack in and open dam gates to cause flooding or cause an infusion of the purification chemicals to the point where the water is toxic. The reality is cyber problems are competing with other issues with these systems. In many cases the cyber threats are not getting funding because fixing problems like repairing the dam gates to prevent maintenance failure, or cleaning the holding tanks that have toxic mold in them are a higher priority and consume all the funds that are available. Our infrastructure has many issues to be dealt with and cybersecurity is only a potential issue relative to the number of tangible issues they are facing today.

NOTE

U.S. Critical Infrastructure includes: Agriculture and Food, Banking and Finance, Chemical, Commercial Facilities, Communications, Critical Manufacturing, Dams, Defense Industrial Base, Emergency Services, Energy, Government Facilities, Healthcare and Public Health, Information Technology, National Monuments and Icons, Nuclear Reactors, Materials and Waste, Postal and Shipping, Transportation Systems, and Water. Note that most of these are in the private sector and government control varies widely depending on the sector.

Organizational View

Organizations can be divided into commercial (including critical infrastructure) and government (generally divided into federal agencies and the military but there are hybrids like the Tennessee Valley Authority which have elements of both). These organizations all approach cybersecurity differently based on their risk tolerance, regulations, and resources. Commercial companies are market-driven and must spend just enough on security to manage risk appropriately. These companies must make decisions based on Return on Investment (ROI) which leads to the eternal struggle between the Chief Financial Officer (CFO) and the Chief Information Officer (CIO). Today many CIOs calculate Return on Security Investment using formulas like Annualized Loss Expectancy (Vulnerability × Threat × Asset Value = Total Risk then Total Risk × Countermeasures = Residual Risk). This translates into the following sample scenario: the chance of getting a virus attack is 100% (in fact expect one a day), the cost of which is three hours of lost productivity and one hour of IT support times total number of employees (200) leads to the following equation—365 viruses × $450 labor × 200 people = $3,285,000, which indicates that a company is better off buying anti-virus at $40 per system for total of $8000 to reduce risk to an acceptable level. With the need for cost saving in the government, these types of calculations are becoming more common in the military today.

Companies also pull in the legal team to review what their due care/diligence responsibilities are in case they are sued. For example, if they were to lose customer privacy data, they might be sued. This evaluation is based on what a reasonable person would expect them to do to protect their information. The size and resources of the company play a big role in determining what "best practices" they should be following for their industry. Finally, depending on which market sector we are talking about, ROI could mean Risk of Incarceration based on laws like Health Insurance Portability and Accountability Act (HIPAA) of 1996, the Gramm-Leach-Bliley Act of 1999, or Sarbanes-Oxley (SOX) Act of 2002. One comparison many security professionals make is the amount spent on physical security and property insurance versus what is spent in Information Assurance versus their relative value to the success of the company. There is a balance between budget and level of risk. Some CIOs spread Fear, Uncertainty and Doubt to get their budget approved, rather than work the numbers, which has given the IT Security Industry a bad reputation. The simple fact is that today if a security team was given an unlimited budget they could not guarantee that there would not be any intrusions because there are constantly new vulnerabilities. Some CFOs feel it is a waste of money to do more than the minimum security protection measures. They point to examples such as when T. J. Maxx and Heartland were in the news for being hacked but they still made a profit the next quarter. There is a reasonable level of security that should be implemented based on which industry the company is in (i.e., financial institutions would spend more than manufacturing) and what risk the leadership is willing to take. The key is making sure the leadership understands the risk that they are accepting in this contested virtual economic battlefield.

Next we have the federal government, which has dispersed responsibility throughout the different agencies who all use different tools and processes. Most cybersecurity is based on compliance with regulations like National Institute of Standards & Technology (NIST) 800-XX series, the Federal Information Security Management Act (FISMA) of 2002, or Homeland Security/Presidential Directives. The White House has a cybersecurity coordinator but the major player is the Department of Homeland Security (DHS). The DHS controls the U.S. Computer Emergency Response Team, National Incident Response Plan, Critical Infrastructure Protection Plan, and the Einstein IDS program.

The Federal Bureau of Investigation (FBI) has a Cyber Division, the InfraGard outreach program, the Internet Crime Complaint Center, and the National Cyber Crimes Investigative Joint Task Force that add up to some impressive forensics capabilities. Their focus is domestic crime and counterterrorism not cyber war, but they have some useful tools and processes to help fight the cyber war. One major success the FBI had was the Darkmarket sting, when they took down a major identify theft ring [4]. They continue to get better at conducting computer investigations internationally [5] with 61 legal attaché offices around the world conducting joint investigations with countries like Romania, Estonia, Ukraine, and the Netherlands.

Another agency that is moving into the digital battlefield is the Federal Aviation Administration (FAA) with the Next Generation Air Transportation System (NextGen) project to move from analog to digital systems to provide safer, more convenient, and more dependable travel. As with any system, as it moves to the network it increases accessibility which also opens a new set of attack vectors.

The Department of Energy is becoming a major cyber player with Smart Grid and energy grid security. With the potential for everyone's appliances, heating/air-conditioning, entertainment systems, and home security systems being put online they are opening up a new field for the hackers to move into. DoE is working to build security into the smart grid but it is very complex. They have done some great work in their National Labs like Sandia National Laboratory and Idaho National Laboratory, to name two of the seven labs working on cyber solutions.

Finally, the Department of Justice (DoJ) must decide which cases to take to court and sets the tone for what is acceptable behavior by deciding where to put their prosecution resources. Today, the DoJ is focused on terrorism and drugs rather than hacking or cyber war incidents.

On the military side, the DoD has a very complex hierarchical authority structure. Despite standing up US CYBERCOMMAND, the individual services (Army, Air Force, Navy, and Marines) still have the authority and budget to decide how to implement cybersecurity. Each branch of the service has a name for their portion of the network. Defense Information Systems Agency (DISA) runs the Global Information Grid (GIG), the Air Force has C2 Constellation, the Army has LandWarNet, and Navy has FORCEnet. The emerging initiatives to transform network capabilities are Joint Information Environment (JIE), DoD Enterprise Portal Service, Enterprise Cloud Broker, and standardize mobility solutions. These are not formal programs of record but rather efforts to respond to new budget constraints and capability demands. There are also different levels of classification on information and networks. The DoD uses Unclassified, For Official Use Only (FOUO) or Controlled Unclassified Information (CUI) or Confidential, Secret, Top Secret, Sensitive Compartmented Information and Special-Access Program/Special Access Required (SAP/SAR). The associated networks are Non-Secure Internet Protocol Router (NIPR) for unclassified, Secure Internet Protocol Router (SIPR) for Secret and Joint Worldwide Intelligence Communications System (JWICS) for Top Secret. In addition, there are separate networks like the Defense Research and Engineering Network (DREN) for research. Finally, deployed forces build their own networks in theater that connect to many of these "reach back" networks as well as to fellow coalition nations via multinational forces networks. An example is if a unit from Fort Carson deployed to Afghanistan has to build a network in country or theater, they would want to connect back to resources at Fort Carson and to other international forces they are teamed with. It is not unusual to see a Tactical Operation Center (TOC) with 6-12 terminals representing the different networks. It is easy to see that there is not a clear chain of command for the network of networks supporting DoD.

As important as these networks are, they do not include the full scope of the modern virtual battlefield. Today command and control of forces is done digitally, weapon systems are connected to the network and depend heavily on computing power, intelligence dominance is key to our ability to wining on the modern battlefield, and it is completely dependent on computer applications/systems. For example in 2006 during a military simulation for an Air Operation Center (AOC), a young airman was asked what would happen if the network went down. He said they would have to stop flying missions. That is, of course, untrue as leaders of the pre-digital generation were flying similar missions long before computers were used for command and control and there are continuity of operation plans in place in the event that the network goes down; but the younger generation's perception and dependence on the network was astonishing. Note that the loss of the AOC's network would have a huge impact on the ability to process orders nearly as fast or accurately as the current "information dominance" systems allow but it would not stop them.

When we talk about CYBERCOM and the Services (Army, Navy, Air Force, and Marines) it is important to remember that the Services train and equip the forces and the Combatant Commanders call on the services to provide forces for their missions. Strategic Command (STRATCOM) has the mission to "ensure U.S. freedom of action in space and cyberspace" [6]. Cyber Command's (CYBERCOM) mission is to "plan, coordinate, integrate, synchronize, and conduct activities to: direct the operations and defense of specified Department of Defense information networks and; prepare to, and when directed, conduct full-spectrum military cyberspace operations in order to enable actions in all domains, ensure U.S./Allied freedom of action in cyberspace and deny the same to our adversaries" [6]. Each Service has a Cyber Unit that supports CYBERCOM, the Air Force has the 24th Number Air Force, the Army has Army Cyber Command (ARCYBER) or 2nd Army, the Navy has the 10th Fleet, and the Marines have Marine Forces Cyber. Closely aligned to these forces is the Intelligence Community, specifically the National Security Agency. This results in different priorities and authorities based on the different mission each organization has.

It is important to note that there are U.S. codes that set the rules for how these units operate. There are a number of titles that provide specific guidance. Title 10 is Armed Forces and is the law that regulates how war is fought [1]. Title 50 is War and National Defense and generally covers intelligence and counter intelligence [1]. It is interesting to note that some units had their authorized mission changed from being under Title 50 to Title 10 as part of the CYBERCOM stand up. Title 18 is Crimes and Criminal Procedure, which covers taking the attacking party to court [1]. Many people are now talking about the need to merge these three into one integrated process (sometimes called title 78). Other titles often used are Title 32, which is National Guard and Title 14 which is the Coast Guard [1]. These forces are not as restricted by laws like Posse Comitatus, which restricts the federal government use of the military for law enforcement. Today we see Joint Operation Centers with forces from multiple "title source" or "forces" to allow them to operate effectively based on the different rules they must comply with.

So we see the commercial sector is driven by the market, the federal agencies are all driven by their function and compliance requirements, and the military is driven by mission and the regulations they have to operate under, and everyone must deal with a limited budget! All of them are facing the similar threats and vulnerabilities. There are efforts to coordinate between them but there is no central authority to drive integration; again each organization is doing their best based on their mission and resources. So let us take a look at the domain we are talking about.

WHERE CYBER FITS IN THE WAR-FIGHTING DOMAINS

Cyber is ubiquitous throughout Land, Sea, Air and Space. Initially there were only two war-fighting domains: land and sea. Land is the area where combatants fought. Over time there were developments in weapons that would give one side or the other an advantage but they would face each other on the field of battle. Then the sea became both a separate war-fighting domain and a part of supporting the land domain fight. The Maritime domain [7] includes the oceans, seas, bays, estuaries, islands, coastal areas, and the airspace above these, including the littorals. Sea forces supporting a land force, usually with artillery fire, is known as littoral battle. Littoral support has two operational environments: Seaward, the area from the open ocean to the shore, which must be controlled to support operations ashore, and Landward, the area inland from the shore that can be supported and defended directly from the sea. Ships would fight battles to both control the sea and support land battles. As technology continued to influence the battlefield, airplanes were introduced. The air domain is the defined as "within the earth's atmosphere"; beginning at the Earth's surface and extending to the altitude where its effects upon operations become negligible [7]. The first airplanes were used for reconnaissance but were soon armed and fought both air-to-air and air-to-ground engagements. Then warfare reached space. Space is the environment corresponding to the space domain, where electromagnetic radiation, charged particles, and electric and magnetic fields are the dominant physical influences, and that encompasses the earth's ionosphere and magnetosphere, interplanetary space, and the solar atmosphere [8]. This was a unique domain as it was used by the other domains rather than a domain where combat was fought (though at some point it will become another battlefront). Finally Cyberspace became so vital to the war-fighters it was declared a domain. It is a global domain within the information environment consisting of the interdependent network of information technology infrastructures, including the Internet, telecommunications networks, computer systems, and embedded processors and controllers [8]. Modern commanders depend on it and are actively studying how to fight and win the next war on it. Next we will take a look at each of the first four domains (land, sea, air, space), and see how they relate to cyber.

Land Domain

As we look back at the progression of warfare on land we see there have been many Revolutions of Military Affairs (RMA). The rock gave way to the club, which was beat out by the spear and then the bow. Horse-mounted soldiers had an advantage over ground troops and then the stirrup gave them a tremendous advantage. Guns and artillery increased the rate at which armies could kill each other as well as the effective range at which they could kill. Next came the tank and machine guns. Each of these RMAs changed how armies organized and fought. New doctrine, tactics, and organizational structures had to be developed. Should we integrate the new weapons into every unit or build a unit of pure machine guns/tanks? The decision was tank units should consist of tanks by themselves but the machine gun should be integrated into every unit. The decision to make tank units of pure tanks has been reversed. Today, the tank is normally integrated with infantry to form "combined arms task forces" so the commander can leverage each unit's strengths. These historical lessons in transformation must be studied to find how to most efficiently develop methods of fighting in this latest RMA—cyberspace.

Sea Domain

In many ways the sea is an analogous battlefield to cyberspace. Similar to cyberspace it is a large area where ships can easily move without detection so the defender has the challenge of detecting where the threat is. No one side can control it. The criminal elements operating on the Internet are comparable to the pirates of old who would interdict and influence the lines of commerce. There were eventually international agreements developed to deal with these threats. Another example we can draw from the Navy is the development of the Flattop or Aircraft Carrier. For years the battleship was the measure of a nation's sea power but the introduction of the Flattop caused a paradigm shift and soon strategies, doctrine and tactics were built around it. Most senior officers had built their careers around the battleship and the defense industrial base was heavily investing in the battleship so they strongly resisted the transformation. They refused to see the need to change based on a new capability. This cultural blindness is impacting the transformation to computer network operations in many of today's organizations. At the tactical level many security professionals still base their strategies on outdated technologies, even though the industry and the battlespace have transformed and evolved. They are still focused on perimeter defenses and ignore the mobile devices being used by their workforce. At the senior leadership level the lack of understanding of the technology and its implications in some organizations impedes the development of doctrine to fight the next war.

Nowadays we have commanders who have grown up with the idea that weapon systems must be based on their ability to put "steel on target," and that the idea of a weapon system that does not destroy something via kinetic attack is ridiculous. They also do not feel that their "real" weapon systems (e.g., jets or tanks) should be considered part of the virtual battlefield because they are enabled with computer chips (despite the fact that they can be hacked into and modified). Some still believe that non-kinetic attacks are something that would only be an annoyance (like their email going down) or play a support role—not be part of a battlefield engagement strategy. These are the same professionals that study history and understand transformation but struggle to understand the technology running the systems they depend on. It is a challenge because they are steeped in tradition and have studied warfare based on the weapons that existed when they were junior officers and still in the field. It is a constant struggle to understand the changes that technology is bringing to the battlefield.

Air Domain

Airpower is similar to cyber power because it is a domain dominated by technological advancements. Early on there were major leaders developing strategies, doctrine, and tactics. General Giulio Douhet was an Italian officer who was one of the first real theorists supporting the use of Air Power [9]. He felt that there was no defense against bombers: it would terrorize populations into surrender. He advocated the use of explosive, incendiary and poison gas bombs against population centers as he felt the entire workforce contributes to the total war effort making everyone a legitimate target. General Douhet was court-martialed for his outspoken beliefs.

Billy Mitchell is considered the father of American Air Power. He came into World War I as a lieutenant colonel in the Army and ended up controlling all U.S. air forces [10]. He is a controversial figure because of the disagreements he had with the Army leadership over using air power against battleships and was court-martialed for insubordination. His passion for how air power could be used was key to the development of Air Force capabilities. Both these general officers understood the potential for air power and pushed for innovation at the expense of their careers, both eventually had their court-martials overturned and are considered heroes. We have not seen anyone with that level of forward thinking theories and dedication for cyber warfare in today's military.

Space Domain

Space is very comparable to cyberspace in that it is generally considered an enabler to the other domains. It provides communications paths for most long-haul communications systems, Command and Control (C2), Intelligence Surveillance and Reconnaissance, navigation based on Global Positioning System, phones, radios, television, financial transactions, and surveillance for wide area reconnaissance, weather, mapping and commercial imaging (i.e., Google maps). The George C. Marshall Institute produced a great series called "A Day without Space" which lays out all the impacts. Space provides some great examples on how to integrate a new technology into the armed forces. Space started as a military dominated domain that has transitioned to a commercial market just like cyber operations. It is a technology that integrated into the other domains to the point they are dependent on it. It is an area that requires unique skills so the management of the workforce presents a challenge. It takes time to build senior leaders for a new technology and as the commercial demand takes off the competition for the workforce gets fierce. It is very hard to retain skilled operators in cyber and space-related fields.

Cyber Domain

Cyber is ubiquitous in all the other modern domains. In 2010 Lt. Gen. William T. Lord, Air Force chief of war-fighting information said "I think that a day without cyber brings you back to about World War I days" [11]. When we talk about the cyber domain some will say it is limited to the hardware that runs the military networks (e.g., computers, routers, firewalls), others will say it is the military networks and the supporting infrastructure (e.g., defense contractors and long-haul communications providers), a few believe it is all government systems, still others feel it is all systems connected to the Internet (all private and government systems). As we look for precedents we can see maritime law could be used, or international space treaties could apply or maybe we could develop a cyber manifest destiny. Some of the answers are overly simple or fit within current legal rules but ignore the reality of how interconnected these systems are. The problem is complex and, much like defining the boundaries in an insurgency conflict, may require different answers for different audiences. This domain is in need of theorists, strategies, doctrine, and tactics that shape what the domain and cyber war itself is scoped to include and exclude.

Combined Arms

While we have talked about the domains as separate and distinct the military integrates them for maximum effect when conducting combat operations. Different branches of the military integrate to achieve force multipliers, for example an infantry brigade would have an armor platoon attached to each battalion, be supported by an artillery unit and close air support from the Air Force, have air defense to protect them from enemy aircraft and engineers to clear obstacles. In other scenarios the Navy, Space or Special Forces could be part of the force design. Now cyber must be both a domain to operation in and force to integrate.

REVIEW OF THE THREAT ACTORS

No analysis of war can be done without a thorough understanding of the enemy forces and their composition, disposition, strength, centers of gravity, and terrain. You will find this was true under Sun Tzu, Napoleon Bonaparte, Alexander the Great, and still today. We will look at the type of forces active in this battlespace, what impacts they are causing and what their motivations are. Understanding that these forces change quickly and they do not follow any set strategies, doctrine, or tactics we will categorize them by their actions.

> **NOTE**
>
> Center of gravity is the source of power that provides moral or physical strength, freedom of action, or will to act [12]. The center of gravity could be military forces or the will of the people to support the war. In cyber warfare, for a nation that bases its ability to win wars on information dominance, it could be their ability to collect, analyze, and act on data.

Most Active Threats

Let us get into the threat spectrum as seen in Figure 3.1. This is a different way to look at the information from Chapter 2 on Threatscape. There are a lot of folks out there trying to be "hackers." Most of them are what we call script kiddies. These are folks who just go out and grab tools off the Internet and try to break into systems. They are also known as noobs (as in newbies) because they are new to hacking and will generally only get the low-hanging fruit like unprotected home systems. Next come criminals. As soon as we started shopping and banking online the criminals saw the money and quickly followed to take advantage of the new opportunity. Many of these are professional organizations. If someone graduates with a degree in computer science in many poor countries the best paying jobs are with organized criminal gangs. The most famous is out of Russia and is known for the ISP they use called the Russian Business Network. Now they have well-educated people working 40-60 h a week trying to break into a specific target (i.e., Chase Bank or Ford for the latest designs). If they develop a zero day exploit it will only be used against that one company until the job is complete.

FIGURE 3.1   Ranking of different threats on the Internet.

Next we have hacker groups like the classic "Cult of the Dead Cow" who released a tool called "back orifice" at one of the more famous hacker conventions, DEFCON, starting back in 1998. These groups develop powerful tools but the Anti-Virus (AV) and IDS companies quickly analyze and post protections against them. Possibly the most dangerous group is the malicious insider. Typically, it is estimated that they represent 20% of the threat but cause 80% of the damage. Though studies like the annual Computer Security Institute (CSI) report show that number is growing [13]. Typically, we group insiders as disgruntled, or seeking financial gain. It is often hard to detect them as they are authorized users so we must look for unauthorized behaviors when most of the security today is on the perimeter looking for someone breaking in. Political/Religious groups practice recruitment, influence operations, and often attack the opposing viewpoint's websites or networks (commonly called Hacktivism).

Finally comes state-controlled or -sponsored groups, which have become known as the Advanced Persistent Threat (APT). These can be military units or loosely affiliated groups who may receive direct or indirect support from the government. The one we see in the news most today is China, which has been accused of systematically stealing information from both the military and the defense contractor base. However, there are many countries engaged in these activities. Some nations have devoted significant resources to these capabilities and we can only surmise their level of activities and capabilities.

Most Dangerous Threats

Now as we look at the impacts or damage the threat can cause, we see a very different order. It is important to measure out incidents based on the impact they have, rather than the amount of activity it caused. It would be easy to say that the slammer worm had a significant level of activity and compromised a large number of systems but when we consider that it had no payload to cause damage to our information it suddenly becomes only a nuisance. At the same time a spear phishing attack that successfully compromises the CEO of a Fortune 500 company would be an insignificant technical event but could cost the company millions. It is not the volume but the impact we need to measure, and to do that we must understand the criticality of the data on our systems.

If we sort the threats by the amount of damage caused, the order is APT/nation state, insider threat, terrorism, physical/environmental events, criminal attacks, hacker groups, unintentional, hacktivism, and Noob/Script Kiddy attacks (as seen in Figure 3.2).

Amount of damage they cause	
• APT/ Nation State	$$$$$$$$$
• Insider	$$$$$$$
• Terrorism	$$$$$$
• Physical / Environmental	$$$$$
• Criminal / Phishing	$$$$
• Hacker Groups	$$$
• Unintentional	$$
• Hacktivism	$$
• Noob / Script Kiddy	$

FIGURE 3.2   Ranking of level of impact different threats can have.

Today APT is stealing billions of dollars worth of intellectual property and sensitive military information. One of the most widely reported military incidents was the F-35, "Computer spies have broken into the Pentagon's $300 billion Joint Strike Fighter project—the Defense Department's costliest weapons program ever—according to current and former government officials familiar with the attacks" [14]. Looking at commercial incidents it would have to be the Aurora incident involving Google, mentioned in Chapter 1. These activities are conducted daily by many different countries. Though some say it is only espionage or spying, a better description would be a full-scale economic war.

Next on our list is the insider threat. It can be damaging in many ways. Some insiders embezzle funds or take valuable information with them, or even leave malicious code like a logic bomb behind to destroy information after they are gone. Or they could bring illegally stolen information into our company when they are hired and expose the new company to lawsuits.

As we look at terrorism, it is doubtful that a terrorist would conduct a purely cyber attack when they could use it to increase the impact of a physical attack by causing a denial of service attack against emergency phone services, police surveillance systems, and traffic control systems.

Physical and environmental attacks can be both natural and man-made. A simple backhoe could isolate large portions of a network, turning on the fire sprinkler system could flood the server room, and heat from a fire or from taking out the air-conditioning can wipe out a server room. There are a number of ways to use attacks against facilities to cause a cyber impact but these are generally very localized.

Criminal attacks are causing a steadily increasing level of pain. It is becoming a national security concern as the general population is losing trust in conducting commerce over the Internet. Identity theft is now a household word, every scam and con has been converted for use over the Internet, and both individuals and banks are losing millions every year [15]. Anyone can buy stolen credit cards, malicious viruses, and botnet armies on the Internet (though it is hard to find reputable vendors). These can all be used as resources for cyber war if that is the intent.

Hacker groups are still around but have become more mainstream. They now have podcasts and attend hacker conventions. They still release new hacker tools and vulnerabilities but they are often shared with the security community before they are shared with the public.

Unintentional actions are often as painful as the attacks, with user actions, patches, configuration changes, and loading new services that cause denial of service and loss of data. These can be mitigated through training, testing, and backups but few organizations have the resources to do these correctly.

Hacktivism sounds exciting and we have had events like the one in 2001 that caused the first major "hacker conflict" when a U.S. spy plane was forced to land in China. "As China and the United States attempt to peacefully end their diplomatic standoff sparked by the mid-air collision between a U.S. spy plane and a Chinese fighter jet, crackers from both countries continue to wage private wars on the Internet" [16]. There were a lot of attacks from both sides and no prosecution on either side but it made for great media coverage. We can see this kind of activity between citizens of different countries or between political parties in the same country. The concern from a cyber war point of view is we now have multiple factions joining the virtual battlefield. It is like watching a soccer game with the fans able to walk around on the field during play.

Finally we have the Noobs or Script Kiddies, who are the hackers that will grab well-known tools and just attack systems. They have little to no understanding of the hacker methodology (addressed in Chapter 6) or techniques to break into systems once the tool they are using does not work. Their biggest impact is they cause so much data or noise that it makes it very difficult to find the truly dangerous threats.

> **WARNING**
>
> It is odd that most companies today spend the same amount of money on protection of all their systems. Let us say someone spends $1M USD a year and they have 100K systems. That is $10 per system; now do all 100K systems have the same kind of info? No, some have no critical or mission-essential data and others hold the keys to all the corporate proprietary information. Yet we protect them all the same. This is one area where the economic war should force us to invest in Return on Security Investments by carefully categorizing our data based on its value and protecting it accordingly.

Motivations

Hacker's motives are varied but generally are ranked by amount of activity in this order: Money, Espionage, Skills for employment, Fame, Entertainment, Hacktivism, Terrorism and War (as seen in Figure 3.3). Most hackers are motivated by money; whether they are considered criminals or not depends on the country in which they live. Next comes the nation state or corporate espionage to gain some military or economic advantage. This is an area where it is often cheaper and more efficient to conduct cyber operations than use traditional spies. There is a high demand for these skills and many individuals are getting into the field because it is a hot job market but most do not have both a cyber and intelligence background. There is a lot of debate on whether it is smart to hire a "hacker" but just like some banks hire ex-cons to evaluate their security many network managers think we need to hire someone who thinks like the enemy to beat them.

Motivations

- Money
- Espionage
- Skills for employment
- Fame/Status
- Entertainment
- Hacktivism
- Terrorism
- War

FIGURE 3.3   Ranking of the motivations for the threats.

TIP

There is no governing body for computer security so we have no professional standards or definitions. Here are some quick and easy definitions we have come up with:

- Event—any recorded/logged activity (no logging = no events)
- Incident—any event we investigate (some turn out to be nothing = false positive)
- Intrusion—any compromise of a system (ranging from a virus to a person breaking into a system – most organizations break out 5-10 categories of intrusion, based on the severity of the compromise)
- Virus—malicious code that requires interaction to spread/execute (i.e., open a PowerPoint that has a script embedded that installs a program to compromise the system)
- Worm—malicious code that spreads/executes on its own (executes a vulnerability then compromises the system and uses the system to attack other systems)
- Trojan Horse—malicious code that masquerades as legitimate code (virus that is named a legitimate operating system file)
- Backdoor—code or configurations that allow access in the future (keep a port open and listening to allow the hacker to connect anytime they want)
- Rootkit—malware that compromises the brain of the operating system (called the kernel) so our system tells us what the malware wants us to see rather than what is really happening (lying about what files, processes, or programs are really running)
- Phishing—efforts to steal our identity or access credentials (usually via email)
- Pharming—efforts to steal mass groups worth of identity (usually compromise the database with all the financial information)
- Spear Phishing—effort to steal a specific VIP's identity (target a general officer or a chief level executive in a company)
- Zombies—systems on a network that are controlled by a hacker
- Botnets—group of networked systems controlled by hacker
- Honeynet/Honeypot—system whose sole purpose is to be compromised (allows security professionals chance to analyze the malware)

The days when system administrators saw a spike in the number of attacks during the summer and on spring break are long gone, but there are still individuals out there hacking for the challenge, entertainment value, or seeking fame. Others see it as a way to promote their beliefs through attacking the opposition, or simple vandalism of their web sites. The smallest groups are sometimes the most dangerous as they can concentrate skills and minimize exposure. There are organizations and countries that are developing the plans and capabilities to use the World Wide Web (WWW) to cause or increase the impact of terrorism and even full-scale wars.

FIELDING SYSTEMS AT THE SPEED OF NEED

One of the challenges facing most programs today is that there are no security requirements designed into the systems being built. A number of systems that are fielded today never have security designed in, so security has to be bolted on after they are fielded. This results in both weaker security and higher costs.

Another challenge is the time it takes to field a new system. In 2009 Deputy Secretary of Defense William J. Lynn, III said "A more nimble IT acquisition process is even more important with the transition away from supplemental appropriations bills which had allowed us to deliver crucial war-fighting technologies outside the usual budget acquisition processes. As we return to funding wartime programs through the base budget, we need to build greater responsiveness in our standing processes. We need to redirect IT systems from an 81-month march to obsolescence and put them on a path to meet war fighters' evolving needs" [17]. We need to change the acquisition system to move at "the speed of need." This does not mean fielding systems that have not been through testing but rather making sure we do the testing in a cost-efficient and rapid manner.

Moore's law demands that we keep our capabilities inside an 18-month window. For cyber attack weapons the shelf life could be weeks depending on who else discovers the vulnerability or if normal patching fixes it. The generation coming into junior leadership positions has grown up with technology and wants the same capabilities they have at home in the workplace and are not satisfied hearing that every device has to go through an evaluation process that could take a year before it can be used in a secure facility. In the commercial sector we are hearing that the employee is always right today and the IT department needs to give them the tools they want to get their job done. So there are a number of factors driving rapid deployment but they lead to a history of security issues. It was difficult to get security right when the process was methodical so how do we expect to build a secure network with a reduced acquisition cycle? The answer is focusing on risk management and understanding when and where to take risks. We need to spend less time analyzing the device and more time monitoring it. We also need to understand that this domain will always be in flux and our systems cannot always be secure but they can be well managed and monitored.

As we look at how government contracts involving cyber operations are done today we see some trends. Overworked contracting offices have little experience with cybersecurity so they are challenged to address it in the requirements sections of the contracts they are developing. Most contracts for IT services have cybersecurity embedded as part of the overall task list, but it is not a critical evaluation criteria. Many Program Managers think the first place you can cut cost is by dropping security capabilities because there is no perceived loss of functionality to the system. The pain of these cuts are not felt until there is a public cybersecurity incident and the users must demand a redesigned secure system. A few contracts are pure cyber contracts that require quantifiable criteria for selection but the criterion are not very mature as this is a relatively new field. These contracts are normally for monitoring or validating the security of the network. The advantage of these contracts is that we are just measuring the security capabilities so we will not end up with a strong overall program that has a weak security subsection. This also keeps the funding and management separate so security does not get subjected to other network concerns. In a cyber conflict it is vital to have the security team be independent.

Most contract requirements are driven by regulations not risk management. In the cyber field these come from compliance rules and regulations. There is the NIST 800-XX series, North American Electric Reliability Council (NERC) has issued eight reliability standards on cybersecurity, DoD Information Assurance Certification and Accreditation Process

(DIACAP), and the Intelligence Community uses Director of Central Intelligence Directive (DCID) 6/3. There are laws and international agreements. There are commercial standards like International Organization for Standardization (ISO) and Information Technology Infrastructure Library (ITIL). All of these provide a starting point to develop standards for performance on contracts.

SUMMARY

We have studied the boundaries of cyber warfare and examined the many different perspectives that are used to define it (logical, physical, and organizational). These all have complexities that end up causing multiple strategies and solutions to be used.

We studied the traditional war-fighting domains of land, sea, air, and space both as they relate to cyber operations and what we can learn from them as we develop cyber as a war-fighting domain.

We reviewed the different threats (most active to least active: Script Kiddies, Criminals, Hacker Groups, Insiders, Political/Religious, APT/Nation State), the impact they have (high level of impact to low level of impact: APT/Nation State, Insider Threat, Terrorism, Physical/Environmental Events, Criminal Attacks, Hacker Groups, Unintentional, Hacktivism, Noob), and their motivations are (most common to least common: Money, Espionage, Skills for Employment, Fame, Entertainment, Hacktivism, Terrorism and War).

Finally, we examined how acquisition is enabling and fettering cybersecurity. All of these areas are immature and in need of policy, law, doctrine, tactics and education to ensure that if the next war is in or employs cyberspace we are ready.

References

[1] Congress. US house, http://uscode.house.gov/; 2010 [accessed 17.03.13].
[2] Leyne J. BBC news. How Iran's political battle is fought in cyberspace, http://news.bbc.co.uk/2/hi/8505645.stm; 2010 [accessed 17.03.13].
[3] FBI, Testimony of Ronald L. Dick, director, National infrastructure protection center, congressional testimony, http://www.fbi.gov/news/testimony/testimony; 2010 [accessed 17.03.13].
[4] FBI. Headline archives, http://www.fbi.gov/page2/may09/cyber050509.html; 2010 [accessed 17.03.13].
[5] FBI. Headline news, http://www.fbi.gov/page2/oct08/darkmarket_102008.html; 2010 [accessed 17.03.13].
[6] DoD. STRATCOM. Strategic command, http://www.stratcom.mil/; 2010 [accessed 17.03.13].
[7] DoD. Joint electronic library, http://www.dtic.mil/doctrine; 2010 [accessed 17.03.13].
[8] DoD. Dictionary of military and associated terms, http://www.dtic.mil/doctrine/dod_dictionary/index.html; 2010 [accessed 17.03.13].
[9] Air force historical studies page. Out of print, http://www.au.af.mil/au/awc/awcgate/readings/command_of_the_air.pdf; 2010 [accessed 17.03.13].
[10] Museum, Maxwell Air Museum. Air chronicles, http://www.airpower.maxwell.af.mil/airchronicles/cc/mitch.html; 2010 [accessed 17.03.13].
[11] Grant R. Battling the phantom menace. Airforce-magazine.com, http://www.airforce-magazine.com/MagazineArchive/Pages/2010/April%202010/0410menace.aspx [accessed 17.03.13].
[12] DoD. Dictionary of military and associated terms, http://www.dtic.mil/doctrine/; 2010 [accessed 17.03.13].
[13] Computer Security Institute. CSI computer crime and security survey 2009, http://gocsi.com/; 2010 [accessed 17.03.13].

[14] Gorman S, Cole A, Dreazen, Y. Wall Street J Tech 2009, http://online.wsj.com/article/SB124027491029837401.html; 2010 [accessed 17.03.13].

[15] IC32009 annual report on internet crime released, http://www.ic3.gov/media/2010/100312.aspx; 2010 [accessed 17.03.13].

[16] Delio M. Crackers expand private war. Wired, http://www.wired.com/politics/law/news/2001/04/43134; 2001 [accessed 17.03.13].

[17] Defense, Department of Defense. Office of the assistant secretary of defense (Public Affairs). Speech, http://www.defense.gov/speeches/speech.aspx?speechid=1399; 2010 [accessed 17.03.13].

Cyber Doctrine

Doctrine is the fundamental principle by which the military forces or elements thereof guide their actions in support of national objectives. It is authoritative but requires judgment in application [1]. Doctrine is what militaries base their plans on and it is influenced by tradition, guides, and tactics, techniques, and procedures (TTPs). We will cover what doctrine exists today, what doctrine needs to be translated to cyberspace, what adjacent guidance exists in non-military agencies, and, finally, what exercises are being conducted to develop doctrine.

CURRENT U.S. DOCTRINE

The U.S. military does not have a definition for cyber warfare today. Over time this capability has been called computer security, Information Security (InfoSec), Net Centric Warfare, Information Assurance (IA), Information Warfare, Cybersecurity, and now Cyber Warfare. These terms generally focused on the defense; today when military planners use the term cyber they include offensive capabilities as well. Cyber is generally understood to be Computer Network Operations (CNO). There are three functions under CNO: Computer Network Exploitation (CNE), Computer Network Attack (CNA), and Computer Network Defense (CND). These functions map to traditional doctrinal terms: CNE is not what most security professionals think of as exploiting a system by compromising it but is focused on

```
┌──────────────────────────────────────────────┐
│            Information Operations (IO)          │
│  Core capabilities                              │
│  • Psychological operation                      │
│  • Military deception                           │
│  • Operations security                          │
│        o Computer network operations            │
│               ▪ Computer network attack         │
│               ▪ Computer network defense        │
│               ▪ Computer network exploitation   │
│  • Electronic warfare                           │
│  • Electronic attack                            │
│  • Electronic protection                        │
│  • Electronic support                           │
│  Supporting capabilities                        │
│  • Information assurance                        │
│  • Physical security                            │
│  • Combat camera                                │
│  • Counterintelligence                          │
│  • Physical attack                              │
│  Related capabilities                           │
│  • Public affairs                               │
│  • Civil-military operations                    │
│  • Defense support to public diplomacy          │
└──────────────────────────────────────────────┘
```

FIGURE 4.1   Information operations framework.

reconnaissance or espionage and will be covered in Chapter 9, CNA is offense and is covered in Chapter 10, and CND is defensive operations, which are examined in Chapter 11.

CNO falls under Information Operations (IO) which has a set of core, supporting, and related capabilities (see Figure 4.1 for details). There are two areas that overlap: CNO and Information Assurance (IA). CNO is defined by the three functions listed above while IA is defined as measures that protect and defend information and information systems by ensuring their availability, integrity, authentication, confidentiality, and non-repudiation. This includes providing for restoration of information systems by incorporating protection, detection, and reaction capabilities [1]. So we can think of IA as building and maintaining the networks while CNO is planning and conducting battle on them, much like the difference between maintaining the Tanks in an Armor Battalion and using them to fight a battle.

There are some concerns with how cyber doctrine is being developed today. The key Joint doctrine for cyber (JP 3-13) was published in 2006. Doctrine is not normally updated quickly, so when we have the environment operating under Moore's Law (capabilities doubling every 18 months) there is concern that the doctrine will quickly become out of date. Another potential issue is that the services do not follow the same terminology; for example the Army and the Air Force have different definitions of Information Operations. Then there is the challenge of having much of the doctrine classified. This leads to different groups having access to different information and basing decisions on only the information they have access to. Finally there is the problem with basic attitude on the importance of cyber as part of combat operations with some leaders' belief that cyberspace is only a supporting function for administrative activities, while others feel cyberspace is embedded in everything from to-day's command and control systems to the weapons systems and it is the critical center of gravity for the nation (often this division runs along the lines of techies and luddites).

U.S. Forces

The White House released its International Strategy for Cyberspace in May 2011 with focus on prosperity, security, and openness in a networked world. "The United States will pursue an international cyberspace policy that empowers the innovation that drives our economy and improves lives here and abroad. In all this work, we are grounded in principles essential not just to American foreign policy, but to the future of the Internet itself. Focus on freedom of information and privacy" [1]. It has an overall goal with key diplomatic and defensive objectives:

- *Goal*: the United States will work internationally to promote an open, interoperable, secure, and reliable information and communications infrastructure that supports international trade and commerce, strengthens international security, and fosters free expression and innovation. To achieve that goal, we will build and sustain an environment in which norms of responsible behavior guide states' actions, sustain partnerships, and support the rule of law in cyberspace.
- *Diplomatic Objective*: the United States will work to create incentives for, and build consensus around an international environment in which states—recognizing the intrinsic value of an open, interoperable, secure, and reliable cyberspace—work together and act as responsible stakeholders.
- *Defense Objective*: the United States will, along with other nations, encourage responsible behavior and oppose those who would seek to disrupt networks and systems, dissuading and deterring malicious actors, and reserving the right to defend these vital national assets as necessary and appropriate.

The Department of Defense (DoD) Strategy for Operating in Cyberspace was released in July 2011 and has five initiatives:

- Strategic Initiative 1: Treat cyberspace as an operational domain to organize, train, and equip so that DoD can take full advantage of cyberspace's potential.
- Strategic Initiative 2: Employ new defense operating concepts to protect DoD networks and systems.
- Strategic Initiative 3: Partner with other U.S. government departments and agencies and the private sector to enable a whole-of-government cybersecurity strategy.
- Strategic Initiative 4: Build robust relationships with U.S. allies and international partners to strengthen collective cybersecurity.
- Strategic Initiative 5: Leverage the nation's ingenuity through an exceptional cyber workforce and rapid technological innovation.

U.S. Cyber Command (CYBERCOM) has been given responsibility for cyberspace operations and must execute the strategies listed above. In a memo signed 23 June 2009, the U.S. Secretary of Defense established the new command [2]. General Keith Alexander (who is also the current director of the NSA) is its first Commander and in 2010 statement to Congress said, "The Department of Defense networks that we defend are probed roughly

250,000 times an hour" [2]. As early as 2006 the Department determined that 10-20 TB of data had been remotely exfiltrated from NIPRNet [2]. General Alexander then quoted Deputy Secretary William Lynn's 2010 comment that the key function for CYBERCOM is its "linking of intelligence, offense, and defense under one roof" [2]. The National Security Agency (NSA) contributes essential expertise to accomplish this. General Alexander further explained to Congress in his 2010 statement, "U.S. Cyber Command has three main lines of operation. We direct the operations and defense of the Global Information Grid so the Department of Defense can perform its missions, we stand ready to execute full-spectrum cyber operations on command, and we stay prepared to defend our U.S. nation's freedom of action in cyberspace" [2]. Cyber Command will use five principles for the Department's strategy in cyberspace: remember that cyberspace is a defensible domain; make our U.S. defenses active; extend protection to our critical infrastructure; foster collective defenses; and leverage U.S. technological advantages [3]. This focus on bringing cyber doctrine and policy to the highest level of command in the military shows how much emphasis the leadership is placing on this new warfighting domain. There is not a lot of money to make this happen until the new Command catches up with the DoD Program Objective Memorandum (POM) budgeting cycle, so DoD has had to reallocate funds, but they are making this happen now because they feel it is vital to the future success of the military. With sequestration and continuous resolutions in the U.S. it is not clear when they will be part of the annual budget cycle.

While this command has been stood up the Honorable W. "Mac" Thornberry Chairman of Subcommittee on Emerging Threats and Capabilities Committee on Armed Services House of Representatives has called out the fact "DOD does not yet have an overarching budget estimate for full-spectrum cyberspace operations including computer network attack, computer network exploitation, and classified funding. During February and March 2011, DOD provided Congress with three different views of its cybersecurity budget estimates for fiscal year 2012 ($2.3 billion, $2.8 billion, and $3.2 billion, respectively) that included different elements of DOD's cybersecurity efforts [4]. The three budget views are largely related to the Defense-wide Information Assurance Program and do not include all full-spectrum cyber operation costs, such as computer network exploitation and computer network attack, which are funded through classified programs from the national intelligence and military intelligence program budgets" [5].

NOTE

The key to understanding where the authority controlling cybersecurity is the same as any other function of the government: follow the money. A new command or presidential directive without funding is more posturing than executing a plan of action. Naming someone into a new position or declaring a new committee that does not have budget authority is more public relations than fixing a problem. When we look at a lot of the activity it is vital to see who controls the resources.

Joint Doctrine

The 2013 compendium of Key Joint Doctrine Publications noted that the pace at which Joint doctrine changes has accelerated in recent years. "One third of approved joint publications have been revised or new ones created in just the last two years ... Approximately 41% of the joint publications are under revision or in development." [6] Doctrine is still focused on joint and multinational integration of forces but now must deal with irregular warfare/counterinsurgency, U.S. Federal interagency coordination, counterterrorism, various humanitarian assistance and civil support operations, support to homeland security, national communications strategy and cyberspace operations.

Recent updates to Joint Pub 1 Doctrine for the Armed Forces of the United States published in 2013 have incorporated cyber into the two basic forms of warfare (traditional and irregular). A useful dichotomy for thinking about warfare is the distinction between traditional and irregular warfare (IW). Traditional warfare is characterized as a violent struggle for domination between nation-states or coalitions and alliances of nation-states. With the increasingly rare case of formally declared war, traditional warfare typically involves force-on-force military operations in which adversaries employ a variety of conventional forces and special operations forces against each other in all physical domains as well as the information environment (which includes cyberspace). IW is characterized as a violent struggle among state and non-state actors for legitimacy and influence over the relevant population(s). In IW, a less powerful adversary seeks to disrupt or negate the military capabilities and advantages of a more powerful military force, which usually serves that nation's established government [7]. This formal recognition of cyber shows commanders are looking at cyberspace and cyber operations as part of both their operational environment and as a capability that can be employed.

Joint Publication 3-13 Information Operations published 27 November 2012 focuses on IO being a force multipliers to create a desired effect. There are many military capabilities that contribute to IO and should be taken into consideration during the planning process. These include: strategic communication, joint interagency coordination group, public affairs, civil-military operations, cyberspace operations (CO), information assurance, space operations, military information support operations (MISO), intelligence, military deception, operations security, special technical operations, joint electromagnetic spectrum operations, and key leader engagement. The two key aspects of cyber warfare, cyberspace operations and information assurance, are defined below [7]. It is important to note there is a move away from the current definition of Information Operations which includes Computer Network Operations (composed of Attack/Defend/Exploit) to cyberspace operations and information assurance.

- Cyberspace Operations (CO)
  a. Cyberspace is a global domain within the information environment consisting of the interdependent network of information technology infrastructures and resident data, including the Internet, telecommunications networks, computer systems, and embedded processors and controllers. CO is the employment of cyberspace capabilities where the primary purpose is to achieve objectives in or through cyberspace. Cyberspace capabilities, when in support of IO, deny or manipulate adversary or potential adversary decision making, through targeting an information medium (such as a wireless access point in the physical dimension), the message itself (for example, an encrypted message in the information dimension), or a cyber-persona (an online identity that facilitates communication, decision making, and the influencing of audiences in the cognitive dimension). When employed in support of IO, CO generally focuses on the integration of offensive and defensive capabilities exercised in and through cyberspace, in concert with other IRCs, and coordination across multiple lines of operation and lines of effort.

b. a process that integrates the employment of IRCs across multiple lines of effort and lines of operation to affect an adversary or potential adversary decision maker, IO can target either the medium (a component within the physical dimension such as a microwave tower) or the message itself (e.g., an encrypted message in the informational dimension). CO is one of several IRCs available to the commander.

- Information Assurance. IA is necessary to gain and maintain information superiority. The Joint Forces Commander relies on IA to protect infrastructure to ensure its availability, to position information for influence, and for delivery of information to the adversary. Furthermore, IA and CO are interrelated and rely on each other to support IO.

The inclusion of the cyberspace domain, cyber operations and evolution of doctrine at the strategic, operational and tactical level shows that the DoD is endeavoring to keep pace with military/doctrinal intricacies of the information age.

Finally a new addition to the doctrinal library is being published. "JP 3-12, Joint Cyberspace Operations, was initiated based on the National Military Strategy for Cyberspace Operations Implementation Plan, which directed USSTRATCOM to assess joint doctrine in support of operations in cyberspace and the five National Military Strategy Cyberspace Operations Ends. Initially a joint test publication (JTP), there was unanimous support by the joint doctrine development community to end development of the JTP and instead develop a Joint Publication (JP). This JP will address the uniqueness of military operations in cyberspace, clarify cyberspace operations-related command and operational interrelationships, and incorporate operational lessons learned" [7]. This will be a classified document.

The Joint Operational Access Concept (JOAC) of Jan 2012 envisions a greater degree and more flexible integration of space and cyberspace operations into the traditional air-sea-land battlespace than ever before. Three emerging trends in the operating environment promise to complicate the challenge of opposed access for U.S. joint forces: (1) The dramatic improvement and proliferation of weapons and other technologies capable of denying access to or freedom of action within an operational area, (2) the changing U.S. overseas defense posture, and (3) the emergence of space and cyberspace as increasingly important and contested domains [7]. As the U.S. military is predominantly a force projection capability they must ensure they address these new trends to ensure operational freedom.

NOTE

In February 2013 Defense Secretary Leon Panetta announced the creation of the Distinguished Warfare Medal, to recognize "extraordinary achievements that directly impact on combat operations, but do not involve acts of valor or physical risks that combat entails." The medal will rank immediately below the Distinguished Flying Cross—higher than the Bronze Star—in order of precedence, according to a Defense Department chart. It can be awarded for any actions after September 11, 2001 [8]. This addition of a medal can be applicable to cyber warriors, and is a significant recognition of the importance of the domain.

One challenge the military faces is highlighted by Colonel U.S. Army Bryant David Glando in "Cyber Warfare —A New DoD Core Mission Area." The new primary and current core mission areas do not adequately address cyberspace warfare as a way to shape the National

Security Strategy (NSS) of the United States. However, they subsume cyberspace capabilities as a service enabler across all the mission areas. This approach does not address the art of the possible, but limits the U.S. in its ability to develop a strategic approach using cyberspace capabilities as a means to achieve strategic objectives. Cyberspace warfare that uses cyberspace capabilities to conduct cyberspace operations could ensure the U.S. achieves its national security objectives. These issues are being addressed but highlights that most of the capabilities are service-specific.

U.S. Air Force

The first U.S. Air Force commander of 24th NAF Major General Richard E. Webber in 2010 told Congress his number one priority for 24th AF is developing and improving cyberspace situational awareness. The 24th has also established a Cyber Operations Liaison Element (COLE) to act as liaison officers (LNO) to facilitate the requisite exchange of expertise between mission planners and cyber planners [9]. The Air Force has made the earliest efforts to establish cyber operations integration into their forces. They were the first to move to stand up a cyber command unit, and have aggressively tried to take the lessons learned from developing doctrine and organizational structure for space and apply it to cyberspace.

United States Air Force published their Cyberspace Science and Technology Vision 2012-2025 in Dec 2012. It states, "Cyberspace is essential to all Air Force (AF) missions. It is the only service to not stand its subordinate command up at Fort Meade but collated with its key cyber units in San Antonio. It is a domain in which, from which, and through which AF operations are performed. Actions in cyberspace can have digital, kinetic, and human effects. Increasingly, the cyberspace domain is contested and/or denied. Yet our ability to address opportunities and threats is constrained by time, treasure, and talent." and has the following recommendations:

- Assuring, empowering and enhancing mission system security standards, making more effective use of authorities (e.g., Title 10/50/32), synchronizing multi-domain effects, and increasing the cost of adversary cyberspace operations.
- Improving cyber accessions and education and developing Air Force Cyberspace Elite (ACE) forces.
- Requiring and designing-in security and securing weapon systems throughout their full life cycle.
- Rapid, open, and iterative acquisition that engages user and test communities early.
- Integrating cyber across all core functions, advancing partnerships, aligning funding, and orchestrating effort and effects across domains.
- Complexity reduction to ease verification and reduce life cycle cost, the development of trusted and self-healing networks and information, the creation of agile, resilient, disaggregated mission architectures, and the advancement of real-time cyber situational awareness/prediction and cyber S&T intelligence across all Air Force domains of operation.
- Using science and technology to improve foundations of trust, enhance human machine interactions, enhance agility and resilience, and assure and empower missions, in collaboration with the Air Force's partners.

The Air Force also published Air Force Instruction 51-402 *Legal Reviews of Weapons and Cyber Capabilities* in 2011 which states the Judge Advocate General will "Ensure all weapons being developed, bought, built, modified, or otherwise being acquired by the Air Force that are not within a Special Access Program are reviewed for legality under Law of Armed Conflict (LOAC), domestic law and international law prior to their possible acquisition for use in a conflict or other military operation." This public statement shows the challenge faced by commanders in deploying their cyber weapons. This statement applies to the U.S. military which operates under U.S. title 10 codes for legal authority, the intelligence agencies operate under U.S. title 50 codes.

U.S. Navy

The U.S. Navy is moving out to develop their cyber capabilities as well. Retired Vice Admiral David J. "Jack" Dorsett, the first Deputy Chief of Naval Operations for Information Dominance (N2/N6) and Director of Naval Intelligence (DNI), in his Information Dominance and the U.S. Navy's Cyber Warfare Vision stated that the Navy is prominent and dominant in the fields of ISR, Cyber Warfare, C2, and Information & Knowledge Management, and as information becomes a Main Battery of U.S. Navy warfighting capability, warfighting wholeness will replace today sub-optimal stovepipes. The Navy will move from platform-centric to information-centric processes, into unmanned, machine autonomous technologies, and create a fully-integrated intel, C2, and Cyber & Networks Capability. Finally they will focus on the following principles: every platform is a sensor; every sensor is networked; build a little, test a lot; spiral development/acquisition; plug-n-play sensor payloads; reduce afloat/airborne manning; transition to remoted; automated; one operator controls multiple platforms; and emphasize UAS and autonomous platforms [10]. The Navy looked to its history and wanted to take lessons learned from standing up the 10th fleet during World War II to deal with the new submarine threat and apply that same methodology of innovation and focus on how new technology is impacting the battlespace. They have made some hard choices like reorganizing the staff functions to increase efficiencies and integration by joining the N2 (Intelligence) and N6 (Communications/Networks) functions into the Information Dominance directorate. These changes show the level of importance and time sensitivity the Navy is placing on the potential for cyber warfare. They do not want to be caught preparing to fight the last war.

The current Deputy Chief of Naval Operations for Information Dominance Director of Naval Intelligence Vice Admiral Kendall L. Card recently stated, "Whether characterized as cyber, intelligence, surveillance, reconnaissance, networks, communications, space, meteorology, oceanography, or electronic warfare, the Navy is inextricably and irreversibly dependent on information. In fact, I would argue that information lies at the core of the Navy's missions of sea control, power projection, deterrence and forward presence. The degree to which we master and control information will yield either a decisive operational advantage or an incapacitating weakness. Therefore, mastering the information domain is critical to the Navy's success. We refer to that mastery as information dominance—the advantage gained from fully integrating the Navy's information functions, capabilities and resources to optimize decision making and maximize war fighting effects" [11].

The Navy has also recently published their view of cyber in "Navy Cyber Power 2020 – Sustaining the US global leadership: priorities for 21st century defense" in Nov 2012. The Navy vision is that cyberspace operations provide Navy and Joint commanders with an operational advantage by [12]:

- Assuring access to cyberspace and confident C2. The Navy operates, defends, exploits, and engages in cyberspace effectively to ensure Navy forces retain access to cyberspace for all mission critical functions and to provide Navy and Joint commanders with resilient C2 capabilities.
- Preventing strategic surprise in cyberspace. The Navy effectively evaluates adversary actions in cyberspace through dedicated cyber intelligence collections and analysis and by fully integrating timely and relevant cyber information and threat warnings into the commander's operational picture.
- Delivering decisive cyber effects. The Navy delivers cyber effects at a time and place of its choosing across the full range of military operations in support of commanders' objectives.

U.S. Army

The U.S. Army's is formally addressing cyber doctrine development today. The primary Field Manual is FM 3-13 which was called Information Operations but was renamed Inform and Influence Activities in January 2013. This is based on the view that IO was looked at as a shaping operations. Army Doctrine Reference Publication (ADRP) 3-0 (which superseded FM 3-0) refined the elements of combat power so the mission command warfighting function includes two staff tasks—conduct inform and influence activities (IIA) and conduct cyber electromagnetic activities—as well as additional tasks of conducting military deception and information protection. The Army's concept of IIA is the integration of information-related capabilities that informs and influences audiences simultaneously. They view Cyber electromagnetic activities as the combination of electronic warfare, cyberspace operations and electromagnetic spectrum management operations [7].

The U.S. Army's key units are 1st Information Operations Command (Land), the 780th Military Intelligence Brigade at Fort Meade, the theater information operations groups, and supporting elements. The key officer skill is the Army functional area, 30 officers who are trained for the role of a joint information operations planner.

The U.S. Army Training and Doctrine Command (TRADOC) has coordinated concept development for cyber with stakeholders across the Army, and in January 2013 published a Cyberspace Operations Concept Capabilities Plan (CCP) which outlines the framework under which the Army expects to conduct cyber operations in the timeframe 2016-2028. They are focusing on three dimensions of cyber in the current operational environment: psychological contest of wills, strategic engagement, and the cyber-electromagnetic contest. Commanders seek to retain freedom of action in cyberspace and in the electromagnetic spectrum, while denying the same to adversaries at the time and place of their choosing; thereby enabling operational activities in and through cyberspace and consequently the other four domains. CyberOps encompass those actions to gain the advantage, protect that advantage, and place adversaries at a disadvantage in the cyber-electromagnetic contest. CyberOps

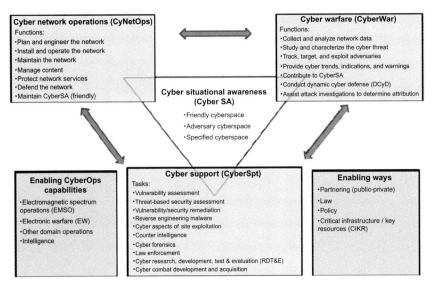

FIGURE 4.2   Cyber Net Ops.

are not an end to themselves, but rather an integral part of full spectrum operations and include activities prevalent in peacetime military engagement, which focus on winning the cyber-electromagnetic contest. CyberOps are continuous; engagements occur daily, most often without the commitment of additional forces. Consequently, the framework developed for Army Operations establishes four components for CyberOps: cyber warfare (CyberWar), cyber network operations (CyNetOps), cyber support (CyberSpt), and cyber situational awareness (CyberSA). See Figure 4.2 for how they interrelate [13]. The Army is the service that focuses the most on publishing doctrine. They integrate it in their school house curriculum (at every level) as a way to push new doctrine into the field. This is a different approach from the other services that are focused on reorganization; the Army wants to reeducate their force to understand the new environment.

DoD INFOCONs

The last thing we will cover in current U.S. military doctrine is Information Operations Condition (INFOCON) system procedures [14]. This is the guidance for all DoD systems to direct the state of the defensive posture the military networks must take when under attack. The INFOCON increases from 5 to 1 when under more severe attacks.

- INFOCON 5 (normal activity). This is the normal state of readiness of information systems and networks (i.e., "Routine" Network Operations (NetOps)) that can be sustained indefinitely. System and network administrators will create and maintain a snapshot of each server and workstation in a normal operational condition. This snapshot then becomes the normal operational baseline that can be compared against future changes to identify unauthorized activities.
- INFOCON 4 (increased vigilance procedures). System and network administrators will establish an operational rhythm to validate the known good image of an information

network against the current state and identify unauthorized changes. Additionally, user profiles and accounts are reviewed and checks are conducted for dormant accounts. Impact to end-users should be negligible.

- INFOCON 3 (enhanced readiness procedures). System and network administrators will further NetOps readiness by increasing the frequency of validation of the information network and its corresponding configuration. Impact to end-users should be minor.
- INFOCON 2 (greater readiness procedures). System and network administrators will increase the frequency of validation of NetOps readiness for the information network. Impact to end-users could be significant for short periods, which can be mitigated through training and scheduling.
- INFOCON 1 (maximum readiness procedures). This is the highest condition of NetOps readiness. This condition addresses intrusion techniques that cannot be identified or defeated at lower readiness levels. During INFOCON 1, System and Network Administrators may reload the operating system software on key infrastructure servers from an accurate baseline. Once baseline comparisons no longer indicate anomalous activities, INFOCON 1 would be terminated. Impact to end-users could be significant for short periods, which can be mitigated through training and scheduling.
- Tailored Readiness Options (TROs). TROs are supplemental measures to respond to specific intrusion characteristics. They are narrowly focused and meant to supplement the current INFOCON readiness level. TROs will document, in standard language, all supplemental INFOCON measures to ensure a common understanding of the level of readiness and mission impact of each measure.

There are some issues: these INFOCONs are not regularly exercised and there is some doubt as to the viability of the current IT staffs to be able to execute this intensive schedule. The good news is these are much better reaction guidelines than the old set which led to organizations disconnecting themselves during an attack causing a self denial of service. Any local commander can increase the level of INFOCON but may not lower the level of protection below the next higher command. Finally, a TRO is a unique reaction to a specific threat; the most recent example is the reaction to malware on thumb drives. DoD disallowed the use of thumb drives deciding that the operational impact of losing the capability was less than the threat of compromising their network.

WARNING

When dealing with an attack or intrusion, the normal response is to recover systems as soon as possible. This will often destroy evidence necessary to determine how the systems were compromised in the first place. If we do not do the forensic work before the reload, it will be impossible to figure out what we need to fix to prevent the threat from coming right back. The key is to ensure we have a process to preserve the evidence offline while the systems are recovered.

SAMPLE DOCTRINE/STRATEGY FROM AROUND THE WORLD

We will now review some of the cyber doctrine and strategies being developed by other nations. We will start with China and some of the other major Asian countries, and then cover

European countries. While Russia is a major player, most of their impact is in crime versus warfare so we will not call them out uniquely. Iran is active and trying to be a major player in cyber but there is not much open source information on what their national cyber strategy is. Finally, we will look at possibility of private or mercenary organizations. These countries are meant to be a sampling of cyber stratagems rather than a holistic representation of the cyber strategy landscape.

Background

There have been some studies that shed light on broad trends. The RAND Corporation's study "Cyber-security threat characterization: A rapid comparative analysis" prepared for the Center for Asymmetric Threat Studies (CATS), Swedish National Defence College, Stockholm does a great job breaking out the nations by focus [15]. Below are two of the many countries analyzed as an example of what the report covers:

Comparator	Level of Prioritization	Characterization of Threat	Lead Responding Authority
Russian Federation	Most prominent	Internal (crime and corruption)	Security Council of the Federation/Ministry of Defence
		External (state, terrorists, foreign competition)	National system of information protection and intelligence community
USA	Priority (one of four)	Criminal hackers	Distributed across a number of organizations with inter-agency policy committee
		Organized criminal groups	
		Terrorist networks	
		Advanced nation	

The *"Cybersecurity and Cyberwarfare Preliminary Assessment of National Doctrine and Organization"* report by the Center for Strategic and International Studies (CSIS) is a useful reference. Using open-source literature, CSIS reviewed policies and organizations in 133 states to determine how they are organized to deal with cybersecurity, whether they have a military command or doctrine for cyber activities, and whether they have or plan to acquire offensive cyber capabilities. There are clear limitations to open-source data. CSIS identified 33 states that include cyberwarfare in their military planning and organization. These range from states with very advanced statements of doctrine and military organizations employing hundreds or thousands of individuals to more basic arrangements that incorporate cyberattack and cyberwarfare into existing capabilities for electronic warfare. They also discuss another 36 states where there is no public discussion of a military role in cyberspace and where civilian agencies charged with internal security missions, computer security or law enforcement are responsible for cybersecurity [15]. This is a great reference for finding a half page summary of country doctrinal positions.

These and other studies show a continued trend toward public declarations of national cyber strategies, formal policy and doctrine, standing up of military and civilian agencies charged with cyber missions and ensuring all elements of national power are secure. Following are examples on some key countries and their doctrinal/strategic activities.

Chinese Doctrine

The first nation we will look at is China. As early as 1999, China was developing doctrine on how to compensate for military technological inferiority against the United States. Some of their senior strategists published a document called "Unrestricted Warfare." It was insightful that they were thinking about the value of network warfare already, but statements like, "Technology is like 'magic shoes' on the feet of mankind, and after the spring has been wound tightly by commercial interests, people can only dance along with the shoes, whirling rapidly in time to the beat that they set" [16], shows how differently a culture can shape how doctrine is developed.

Taiwan watches Chinese strategies very closely, and published a good analytical review of new doctrine being considered by the People's Liberation Army (PLA) [17]. The following is a list of the more pertinent concepts:

- Highly controlled war is a new form of warfare in which "the direct purpose is to control a political regime, and in which political, economic, diplomatic, and other resources are integrated effectively to control the scale, form, means, and results of the war, with the backing of absolute military superiority."
- Acupuncture war establishes the examination of critical points in a network. Much like the pressure points in martial arts, when taken out, this type of war can shut down an entire system. Here, using Electronic Warfare (EW) can enable "the first battle being the final battle."
- Strategic information war is the integration of political, economic, military, diplomatic, and other areas to produce an overall or comprehensive information victory. The targets of strategic Information Warfare (IW) include national political, monetary, communications, and other crucial sectors down to single weapon systems such as aircraft carriers.
- Work Web sites establish distant learning capabilities and databases for quick access to information not readily available in the past.
- Intangible war focuses on strategies, market competition, legal systems, and intellectual property rights.
- Net Force is a brand new type of "Grand War" scheme that combines high-tech knowledge with politics, economy, psychology, and information networks and that is "all people being soldiers, the integration of peace and warfare, and dual usage for the military and civilians."
- Surgical warfare aims to attack the vulnerability of high-tech weapons systems to achieve final victory, namely, attacking one point to cripple the whole system.
- Space warfare capability puts the crowning touch on China's asymmetric warfare capability: the ability to sabotage or destroy an enemy's space systems.

The US-China Economic and Security Review Commission Report on the *Capability of the People's Republic of China to Conduct Cyber Warfare and Computer Network Exploitation* states "The government of the People's Republic of China (PRC) is a decade into a sweeping military modernization program that has fundamentally transformed its ability to fight high-tech wars. The Chinese military, using increasingly networked forces capable of communicating across service arms and among all echelons of command, is pushing beyond its traditional missions focused on Taiwan and toward a more regional defense posture. This modernization effort, known as informationization, is guided by the doctrine of fighting 'Local War Under Informationized Conditions,' which refers to the PLA's ongoing effort to develop a fully networked architecture capable of coordinating military operations on land, in air, at sea, in space and across the electromagnetic spectrum" [18]. This open source study reveals how seriously China is modernizing their Cyber Forces for today's ongoing cyber war and the next integrated kinetic/non-kinetic war.

The Annual Report to Congress Military and Security Developments Involving the People's Republic of China 2011 states that China's development of capabilities for cyber warfare is consistent with authoritative PLA military writings. Two military doctrinal writings, Science of Strategy and Science of Campaigns identify information warfare (IW) as integral to achieving information superiority and an effective means for countering a stronger foe. Although neither document identifies the specific criteria for employing computer network attack against an adversary, both advocate developing capabilities to compete in this medium.

In a separate report it was pointed out that as few as 12 different Chinese groups, largely backed or directed by the government there, do the bulk of the China-based cyberattacks stealing critical data from U.S. companies and government agencies, according to U.S. cybersecurity analysts and experts. The aggressive, but stealthy attacks, which steal billions of dollars in intellectual property and data, often carry distinct signatures allowing U.S. officials to link them to certain hacker teams. And, analysts say the U.S. often gives the attackers unique names or numbers, and at times can tell where the hackers are and even who they may be [19]. This targeting can result in accusations and political posturing but to date no military action has been authorized. Much like the Cold War it is more about gathering information, but unlike the Cold War where military capabilities were displayed as part of a show of force but not used, today many of the cyber weapons are being actively used.

From WikiLeaks documents, and several other sources, the identity and location of the main Chinese Cyber War operation is now known. The Chinese Chengdu Province First Technical Reconnaissance Bureau (1st TRB) is a Chinese Army electronic warfare unit located in central China (Chengdu), and is the most frequent source of hacking attacks traced back to their source. The servers used by the 1st TRB came online over five years ago, and are still used. The Chinese government flatly refuses to even discuss the growing pile of evidence regarding operations like the 1st TRB [20]. So we can see China is using both civilian hackers and military Computer Network Attack units to engage in cyber operations.

TIP

The information being posted to WikiLeaks has changed the paradigm of insider threats. Both commercial and government organizations are now relooking at internal trust. With hackers breaking in and posting information to Wikileaks and insiders handing over large amounts of data that reporters can pour through, it is time for senior leaders to reevaluate their insider protections and risk acceptance.

What does all this focus on modernization and cyber doctrine mean? The level of effort and types of activities mentioned above show that China is preparing to fight the next war utilizing the electromagnetic spectrum and plans to deny access to its enemy. China understands how dependent the West has become on the IT infrastructure, and will attack that center of gravity. It is conducting reconnaissance today that will give it the advantage. China has the infrastructure to conduct denial of service attacks, and has talked about attacking the integrity of systems so an enemy cannot trust its command and control systems to give accurate reports. China is not alone in this level of cyber warfare doctrinal development but they are in the front of the pack.

The recent "APT1 Exposing One of China's Cyber Espionage Units" by Mandiant specifies that APT1 is believed to be the 2nd Bureau of the People's Liberation Army (PLA) General Staff Department's (GSD) 3rd Department, which is most commonly known by its Military Unit Cover Designator (MUCD) as Unit 61398. The report estimates that Unit 61398 is staffed by hundreds, and perhaps thousands of people based on the size of Unit 61398's physical infrastructure [21].

Similarly, Bloomberg BusinessWeek magazine February 2013 also had a cover story on how Joe Stewart of Dell SecureWorks tracked down the specific individual responsible for the APT malware he was investigating. "There is a tremendous amount of manpower being thrown at this from their side," Joe says. Investigators at dozens of commercial security companies suspect many if not most of those hackers either are military or take their orders from some of China's many intelligence or surveillance organizations. In general, they say the attacks are too organized and the scope too vast to be the work of freelancers. Secret diplomatic cables published by WikiLeaks connected the well-publicized hack of Google to Politburo officials, and the U.S. government has long had classified intelligence tracing some of the attacks to hackers linked to the People's Liberation Army (PLA), according to former intelligence officials. None of that evidence is public, however, and China's authorities have for years denied any involvement [22]. These two examples of commercial companies that are uncovering espionage while protecting commercial companies show the level of activity that is going on today.

Other Asian Countries

Japan has placed their strategy under the Japanese Ministry of Defense (MoD) Self-Defense Forces National Information Security Center (NISC). In 2005, NISC was established following a surge in cyberattacks. The government-wide agency was set up to co-ordinate efforts to protect computer networks. In February 2009, the Japanese government adopted the Second National Strategy on Information Security (NSIS) for the years 2009-2011. The 3-year plan included four subjects: central and local governments, critical infrastructure, business entities, and individuals. As part of the NSIS process, the Japanese government adopted "Secure Japan 2009." One-fourth of its 212 policy items are aimed at the improvement of central and local governments. In the areas devoted to critical infrastructure and business entities, private enterprises serve as the subjects of its actions while the government provides support [23]. Japan is developing cyber doctrine with a broader government focus; they want to ensure the country is secure from attacks, and are willing to leverage their military capabilities to achieve it.

South Korea and North Korea: South Korea's Defense Security Command (DSC) and the Ministry of National Defense (MND) stated in December 2009 that hackers had accessed classified military plans drawn up by South Korea and the U.S. Details of "Operation Plan 5027," which outlines how South Korea would be defended in the event of war, were said to have been transferred to an internet protocol (IP) address in China but thought to be compromised. The reaction was to stand up a cyber warfare command to protect its military computer systems, the plans are part of the ministry's strategy known as "Defense Reform 2020" [24]. The Korea Internet & Security Agency (KISA) was also formed in 1996 to promote internet cooperation and security.

North Korea has built capabilities under Unit 121, which was stood up in 1998. The mission is to increase their military standing by advancing their asymmetric and cyber warfare capabilities through both offensive and espionage methods. This unit is trained by the Mirim Academy in Pyongyang. Their annual budget is estimated to be ~$56M [25]. With the struggle on the Korean peninsula still going on, it is easy to see why North Korea would carry the battle to cyberspace. This could give North Korea an advantage as it is not as dependent on IT infrastructure as most countries, but at the same time it will have to come a long way to overcome the lack of a computer workforce to draw from.

Terrorists have no formal published doctrine but they are very interested in understanding the doctrine of the countries that they want to attack. It would be important to know what a country's response to specific attacks would be in order to plan attacks that accomplish their objectives. They also have many locally developed doctrinal practices for reconnaissance, communication, and recruiting on the internet so they are leveraging the capabilities it offers. Finally, it should be assumed that they understand how many of the countries in the west depend on cyber so have actively sought out capabilities to exploit this vulnerability but to date no plans have been seen on how they would accomplish it.

European Countries

The Cooperative Cyber Defense Center of Excellence (CCD COE) located in Tallinn, Estonia, was formally established on the 14th of May, 2008, in order to enhance North Atlantic Treaty Organization's (NATO) cyber defense capabilities. The Center received full accreditation by NATO and attained the status of International Military Organization on the 28th of October, 2008. Its mission is to enhance the capability, cooperation, and information sharing among NATO, NATO nations, and Partners in cyber defense by virtue of education, research and development, lessons learned, and consultation [26]. This center is designed to allow NATO to integrate cyber doctrine. There are political, legal, doctrinal, and technical issues that must be worked out when operating in a multi-national task force. It has taken years to develop the processes to do this in the real world and NATO is moving to establish the same functionality in the virtual world.

The United Kingdom is developing strategies and doctrine for cyber as well. The "Cybersecurity Strategy of the United Kingdom safety—security and resilience in cyber space" was published in June 2009 by UK Office of Cybersecurity and UK Cybersecurity Operations

Center. This document states there is an ongoing and broad debate regarding what "cyber warfare" might entail, but it is a point of consensus that with a growing dependence upon cyberspace, the defense and exploitation of information systems are increasingly important issues for national security. It recognizes the need to develop military and civil capabilities, both nationally and with allies, to ensure we can defend against attack, and take steps against adversaries where necessary. Furthermore, these include criminals, terrorists, and states, whether for reasons of espionage, influence or even warfare [27]. This acknowledgement that cyber war is a distinct possibility and they are preparing for it is a clear statement that the UK is treating this as a matter of national security. They expanded the scope of cyber battle space to include criminals and espionage but treat them as separate from warfare; this inclusion in the statement shows the overlap that is one of the challenges in cyber doctrine.

France's government published a white paper on defense and national security which says cyber war is a major concern. The white paper develops a two-pronged strategy: (1) a new concept of cyber defense, organized in depth and coordinated by a new Security of Information Systems Agency under the purview of the General Secretariat for Defense and National Security; (2) the establishment of an offensive cyber war capability, part of which will come under the Joint Staff and the other part will be developed within specialized services [28]. Though not a national strategy, this white paper does call out France's belief that cyber is a military problem with the need for offensive capabilities under their special services units. They have followed the model that most countries are going to—stand up a new and separate organization to handle cyber war. Very few are trying to integrate a cyber capability into their traditional forces. This follows in the same pattern that Space support went through before it was integrated into tactical operations on the battlefield.

From The Fog of Cyber Defence by Eds. Jari Rantapelkonen and Mirva Salminen, we get a view of the Nordic countries. Finland aims to be a globally strong player in the field of cyber and cyber defense. Originally known as information security, cyber defense has become an issue on the strategic and individual levels. Norway released a revised "National Strategy for Information Security" in late 2012. The Norwegian national CERT has been provided increased funding for 2013, and the Norwegian Armed Forces Cyber Defence (NOR CYDEF) changed its name in the second half of 2012 in order to underscore the increased importance of cyber defense in the military sector. Swedish cyber defense aims at protecting Sweden and the Swedish interests against cyber-attacks from resourceful and advanced players. This includes strategic control and planning, cooperation and coordination as well as operational protection measures. Coordination, exercises and exchange of information with skilled and well-informed parties internationally is a top priority for the Swedish Armed Forces, as well as for other authorities that are in charge of national cyber security [29]. There is a high degree of cooperation between these three countries.

The Czech Republic has published their cybersecurity strategy for 2011-2015. This states, "Essential objectives of the cybersecurity policy include protection against threats which information and communication systems and technologies (hereinafter 'ICTs') are exposed to, and mitigation of potential consequences in the event of an attack against ICTs. The implementation, operation, and security of credible information and communication systems is a duty of the Czech Republic and a responsibility of all levels of government and administration, the private sector and the general public, the objective being to maintain a safe, secure, resistant, and credible environment that makes use of available opportunities offered by the digital age. The strategy focuses mainly on unimpeded access to services, data integrity, and confidentiality of the Czech Republic's cyberspace and is coordinated with other related strategies and concepts." It is worth noting they call on their general public as part of the solution [30].

Private or Mercenary Armies

"In an age where cyber warfare is more common than the physical battlefield, it may be necessary for the private sector to stop playing defense and go on offense," Gen. Michael Hayden said on August 1, 2011. Hayden, who led the National Security Agency and Central Intelligence Agency under president George W. Bush, said during a panel discussion at the 2011 Aspen Security Forum that the federal government may not be the sole defender of private sector companies—and that there is precedent for such action. "We may come to a point where defense is more actively and aggressively defined even for the private sector and what is permitted there is something that we would never let the private sector do in physical space," he said. "Let me really throw out a bumper sticker for you: how about a digital Blackwater?" he asked. "I mean, we have privatized certain defense activities, even in physical space, and now you have got a new domain in which we do not have any paths trampled down in the forest in terms of what it is we expect the government—or will allow the government—to do" [31]. Blackwater is a private military contractor that has changed its name to Academic after incidents in Iraq gave them a negative image. If companies decide to hire forces (hackers) to strike back or conduct recovery operations it could change the cyberspace battlefield dramatically.

KEY MILITARY PRINCIPLES THAT MUST BE ADAPTED TO CYBER WARFARE

There are a number of Tactics, Techniques, and Procedures (TTPs) that are used to implement doctrine. Some of the fundamental TTPs are Intelligence Preparation of the Operational Environment (IPOE), Force Analysis using Joint Munitions Effectiveness Manual (JMEM) factors, Measures of Effectiveness (MOEs), Battle Damage Assessment (BDA) to determine if MOEs were achieved, Close Air Support (CAS) to integrate air and land forces, and Counterinsurgency (COIN) to adapt classic force on force doctrine to asymmetric battlefield.

Intelligence Preparation of the Operational Environment

Intelligence Preparation of the Battlefield (IPB) has evolved to become Intelligence Preparation of the Operational Environment (IPOE) in today's complex wars. It is, "the analytical process used by joint intelligence organizations to produce intelligence estimates and other intelligence products in support of the joint force commander's decision-making process. It is a continuous process that includes defining the operational environment; describing the impact of the operational environment; evaluating the adversary; and determining adversary courses of action" [32]. This requires evaluating both traditional enemy capabilities and terrain but also now includes many new demographics (i.e., economic, race, religious, gender, ethnic, and cultural). When looking at lines of communication, influence operation, and terrain it is now necessary to include cyberspace in that analysis. Cyber IPOE is vital to keeping inside the enemies OODA loop (Observe/Orient/Decide/Act). "IPB must be: timely, accurate, usable, complete, and relevant to be useful. In most cases, the basic groundwork needs to be 80% complete before operations and logistics can start planning" [33]. So with terrain that can change by the minute, forces that can be spread across the world and motives as diverse as the groups involved IPOE must relook at how it produces products like "enemies most likely course of action" but these products are still vital to the commander and must not be ignored in cyberspace.

Joint Munitions Effectiveness Manual

Joint Munitions Effectiveness Manual (JMEM) is formal capabilities analysis that determines effectiveness of different weapon systems (e.g., can an AT4 bazooka destroy a T64 Tank). These estimates may be generated using probabilistic mathematical models that take into account the target's critical vulnerabilities, performance data on the assets contemplated for application against the target, and means of delivery or they can be done via field testing. These predictions are based on historical data using strike performance and analyses of likely success given the specific planned weapon/target pairings (e.g., Air-to-Surface, Special Operations Target Vulnerability, or Surface-to-Surface) [33]. This is fairly straightforward when measuring kinetic effects but there are a multitude of factors that can impact the effectiveness of a cyber-weapon. We need to establish a standard to measure effectiveness that is used for a baseline so a commander can understand which cyber munitions are best for their needs. The standard will be based on some type of effect like "time not available" or "ability to influence decision."

There has been some work on this under the title JOINT NON-KINETIC EFFECTS INTEGRATION (JNKEI) which was completed in September 2010. The purpose was to develop joint TTPs to assist joint planners in integrating the non-kinetic effects of electronic attack, computer network attack, and offensive space control capabilities into operational planning. The following was accomplished:

- Improved integration of non-kinetic capabilities during operational planning that expand the range of possible courses of action for joint force commanders.
- Information exchange requirements based on the JNKEI TTPs and incorporated into the Integrated Strategic Planning and Analysis Network (ISPAN) and Virtual Integrated Support for the Information Operations Environment (VisION) collaborative tools.
- Input provided to Joint Publication (JP) 5-0, Joint Operational Planning; Joint Test Publication 3-12, Cyberspace Operations; JP 3-13, Information Operations; and JP 3-60, Joint Targeting.
- JNKEI TTPs provided to Joint Information Operations Planning Course (Joint Forces Staff College), Joint Targeting School (USJFCOM), and Advanced Integrated Warfighter Weapons Instructor Course (US Air Force Weapon School).
- JNKEI TTPs provided to USEUCOM; USPACOM; US Force, Korea; and USSTRATCOM to enhance existing standard operating procedures.

Measures of Effectiveness

Measures of Effectiveness (MOEs) assess changes in system behavior, capability, or operational environment that is tied to measuring the attainment of an end state, achievement of an objective, or creation of an effect. They do not measure task performance. When evaluating a course of action or combat assessment we need to evaluate it based on the impact or MOE it will have. These MOEs should use assessment metrics that are relevant, measurable, responsive, and resourced so there is no false impression of task or objective accomplishment [33]. This can be very complex if we are talking about influence operations or information operations. We need to establish a standard by which every branch of the military and federal agencies measure both impact and effectiveness. It will need to be a matrix that can deal with compromise to confidentiality, denial of access, and loss of integrity that reflects the consequences to the aspect of national power that was affected (military, economic, information, or diplomatic). It should be done in an unclassified format so that everyone trains and uses it to the point that it is universally understood.

Battle Damage Assessment

Battle Damage Assessment (BDA) is another key TTP. It is the estimate of damage resulting from the application of lethal or non-lethal military force. Battle damage assessment is composed of physical damage assessment, functional damage assessment, and target system assessment. The purpose of BDA is to compare post-execution results with the projected/expected results generated during target development. Comprehensive BDA requires a coordinated and integrated effort between joint force intelligence and operations functions. Traditionally, BDA is composed of physical damage assessment, functional damage assessment, and functional assessment of the next higher target system [33]. BDA is vital to determining if the attack method has a successful MOE. For example, the Air Force would not launch aircraft until they were sure the enemy's anti-aircraft batteries were destroyed. Similarly, Cyber forces would not launch their exploit until they knew they could bypass the defensive firewalls. Generally, it is best to use "all source" information (indicators from all the Intel Functions) to provide accurate analysis.

Close Air Support

Close Air Support (CAS) is air action by fixed- and rotary-wing aircraft against hostile targets that are in close proximity to friendly forces and that require detailed integration of each air mission with the fire and movement of those forces [33]. This TTP reminds us that combined forces are more powerful when they are integrated. The United States does not fight wars alone, but rather as part of multinational coalitions. The Army rarely fights alone, but rather as part of a Joint Task Force. A cyber war will most likely be part of the integrated effort using multiple aspects of national power.

Counterinsurgency

Counterinsurgency (COIN) is comprehensive civilian and military efforts taken to simultaneously defeat and contain insurgency, and address its core grievances. COIN is primarily political, and incorporates a wide range of activities, of which security is only one. Unified action is required to successfully conduct COIN operations and should include all host nations (HN), the United States, and multinational agencies or actors [33]. Combating insurgency is the most prevalent type of conflict the United States has been engaged in recent history. In this kind of environment Information Operations and Influence Operations are key force multipliers. Cyber is a critical weapon for both sides in this kind of fight. As commanders analyze how to fight and win on today's battlefield they must understand how to dominate cyberspace. The same tools they use to fight on the local terrain can be modified to be used in cyberspace if we force the staff functions to focus on the right requirements.

GUIDANCE AND DIRECTIVES

Not all national strategy comes from military doctrine; much of it is in the rest of the federal government as guidance and directives which can act as both constraints and permission. For cyber strategy we have the Comprehensive National Cybersecurity Initiative (CNCI), National Cyber Incident Response Plan (NCIRP), Homeland Security/Presidential Directives (HSPDs), and National Institute of Science and Technology (NIST). On the civilian side we have supporting organizations like academic institutions, commercial associations, and government/civilian partnerships. All of these contribute to a tapestry of efforts to secure the Internet.

Comprehensive National Cybersecurity Initiative

Comprehensive National Cybersecurity Initiative (CNCI) consists of a number of mutually reinforcing initiatives with the following major goals designed to help secure the United States in cyberspace that were covered in Chapter 1. The key tasks were creating, or enhancing, shared situational awareness of network vulnerabilities, threats, and events within the federal government—and ultimately with state, local, and tribal governments and private sector partners. Tasks also include to: defend against the full spectrum of threats by enhancing U.S. counterintelligence capabilities and increasing the security of the supply chain for key information technologies; strengthen education, research, and development; and to define and develop strategies to deter hostile or malicious activity in cyberspace [34]. This effort was funded by the government in acknowledgement of the critical threat cyber vulnerabilities are to national security. We covered CNCI in Chapter 1 as it is the major investment the United States has made to secure cyberspace.

Department of Homeland Security

The Department of Homeland Security (DHS) has published the National Cyber Incident Response Plan (NCIRP). The NCIRP is designed in full alignment with these initiatives to ensure that federal cyber incident response policies facilitate the rapid national coordination needed to defend against the full spectrum of threats. The NCIRP focuses on improving the human and organizational responses to cyber incidents, while parallel efforts focus on

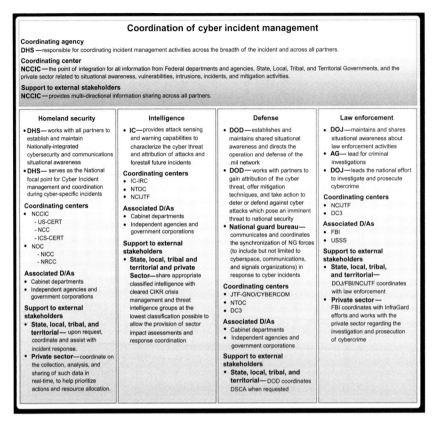

FIGURE 4.3   Federal cyber incident lanes.

enhancing the community's technological capabilities. NCIRP was developed according to the principles outlined in the National Response Framework (NRF) and describes how the nation responds to Significant Cyber Incidents [35]. This plan is designed to bridge the DoD capabilities to federal agencies and ultimately to the national critical infrastructure. The plan lays out the roles and responsibilities across the federal government, military, intelligence community, and law enforcement. This integration is as vital to the nation as joint operations are to the military. See Figure 4.3 to understand the roles and responsibilities that have been laid out to facilitate cooperation.

DHS has made progress creating a baseline to measure the impacts we mentioned in the military TTP section. They have classified Significant Cyber Incidents as a set of conditions in the cyber domain that requires increased national coordination. This increase in national coordination is triggered when the National Cyber Risk Alert Level (NCRAL) system reaches Level 2 (see Figure 4.4 to understand the different levels).

A key new development is the "Strategy for Homeland Defense and Defense of Support of Civil Authorities" signed by Defense Secretary Leon Panetta in Feb 2013. The executive summary states, "We are now moving beyond traditional distinctions between homeland and national security. National security draws on the strength and resilience of our citizens,

Level	Label	Description of risk	Level of response
1	Severe	Highly disruptive levels of consequences are occurring or imminent	Response functions are overwhelmed, and top-level national executive authorities and engagements are essential. Exercise of mutual aid agreements and Federal/non-Federal assistance is essential.
2	Substantial	Observed or imminent degradation of critical functions with a moderate to significant level of consequences, possibly coupled with indicators of higher levels of consequences impending	Surged posture becomes indefinitely necessary, rather than only temporarily. The Department of Homeland Security (DHS) Secretary is engaged, and appropriate designation of authorities and activation of Federal capabilities such as the Cyber UCG take place. Other similar non-Federal incident response mechanisms are engaged.
3	Elevated	Early indications of, or the potential for but no indicators of, moderate to severe levels of consequences	Upward shift in precautionary measures occurs. Responding entities are capable of managing incidents/events within the parameters of normal, or slightly enhanced, operational posture
4	Guarded	Baseline of risk acceptance	Baseline operations, regular information sharing, exercise of processes and procedures, reporting, and mitigation strategy continue without undue disruption or resource allocation

FIGURE 4.4   National cyber risk alert levels.

communities, and economy. This includes a determination to prevent terrorist attacks against the American people by fully coordinating the actions that we take abroad with the actions and precautions that we take at home. It must also include a commitment to building a more secure and resilient nation, while maintaining open flows of goods and people. We will continue to develop the capacity to address the threats and hazards that confront us, while redeveloping our infrastructure to secure our people and work cooperatively with other nations." This increases the level of the U.S. military in the active defense of critical infrastructure, pushes for more information sharing, and acknowledges cyberspace as an aspect they must protect.

Homeland Security/Presidential Directives

Homeland Security/Presidential Directives (HSPDs) are issued by the president on matters pertaining to Homeland Security. While they are not part of the military doctrine they provide a similar function for the other elements of national power—specifically diplomatic and economic. They are intended to provide guidance, set standards, and increase coordination across all federal agencies [36]. Following are the HSPDs that impact cyberspace.

- HSPD—1: Organization and Operation of the Homeland Security Council. Ensures coordination of all homeland security-related activities among executive departments and agencies and promotes the effective development and implementation of all homeland security policies.
- HSPD—5: Management of Domestic Incidents. Enhances the ability of the United States to manage domestic incidents by establishing a single, comprehensive national incident management system.
- HSPD—7: Critical Infrastructure Identification, Prioritization, and Protection. Establishes a national policy for federal departments and agencies to identify and prioritize United States critical infrastructure and key resources and to protect them from terrorist attacks.

- HSPD—8: National Preparedness. Identifies steps for improved coordination in response to incidents. This directive describes the way federal departments and agencies will prepare for such a response, including prevention activities during the early stages of a terrorism incident. This directive is a companion to HSPD-5.
- HSPD—12: Policy for a Common Identification Standard for Federal Employees and Contractors. Establishes a mandatory, government-wide standard for secure and reliable forms of identification issued by the federal government to its employees and contractors (including contractor employees).
- HSPD—23: National Cyber Security Initiative. Details are classified but are generally focused on a series of efforts covered in Chapter 1.
- HSPD—24: Biometrics for Identification and Screening to Enhance National Security. Establishes a framework to ensure that federal executive departments use mutually compatible methods and procedures regarding biometric information of individuals, while respecting their information privacy and other legal rights.
- Presidential Policy Directive (PPD)—20 is a classified directive relating to cyber operations which establishes principles and processes for the use of cyber operations so that cyber tools are integrated with the full array of national security tools we have at our disposal.
- PDD 21—Critical Infrastructure Security and Resilience advances a national unity of effort to strengthen and maintain secure, functioning, and resilient critical infrastructure.

NOTE

The key to understanding where the authority is for cyber is the same as any function: follow the money. A new command or presidential directive without funding is more posturing than executing a plan of action. Naming someone into a new position or declaring a new committee that does not have budget authority is more public relations than fixing a problem. When we look cyber-related activity it is vital to see who controls the resources.

National Institute of Standards and Technology

The one agency that is at the center of establishing standards for the nation is the National Institute of Standards and Technology (NIST). The government has stated that for cyber and network security NIST is focused on ensuring three security objectives of information technology systems: confidentiality, integrity, and availability. NIST does not publish rules like Defense Information Systems Agency (DISA), NSA, and DoD but instead provides the groundwork for those organizations to create regulations. The Cyber and Network Security Program addresses NIST's statutory responsibilities in the domain and the near- and long-term scientific issues in some of the building blocks of IT and network security, including cryptography, security testing and evaluation, access control, Internet-working services and protocols (Domain Name System, Border Gateway Protocol, IPv6, Wi-Max, etc.), security metrics, vulnerability analysis, security automation, and security properties. These efforts will provide a more scientific foundation for cybersecurity, while maintaining a focus on near-term security issues in emerging technologies [37]. NIST is responsible for determining how the government will protect systems today, setting guidelines and shaping Institute of Electrical and Electronics Engineers (IEEE) standards for the future. They have traditionally

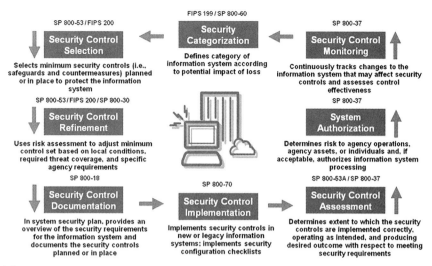

FIGURE 4.5 NIST risk management framework.

been focused on configuration management, compliance validation, and vulnerability detection but are shifting to a real-time situational awareness model.

Currently, there are over 300 NIST information security documents. This number includes Federal Information Processing Standards (FIPS), the Special Publication (SP) 800 series, Information Technology Laboratory (ITL) Bulletins, and NIST Interagency Reports (NIST IR). The Federal Information Processing Standards (FIPS) Publication Series is the official series of publications relating to standards and guidelines adopted and promulgated under the provisions of the Federal Information Security Management Act (FISMA) of 2002. The Special Publication 800-series reports on ITL's research, guidelines, and outreach efforts in information system security, and its collaborative activities with industry, government, and academic organizations. Each bulletin presents an in-depth discussion of a single topic of significant interest to the information systems community. Bulletins are issued on an as-needed basis [37]. See Figure 4.5 to understand the flow of the documentation. These are the foundation for all government cybersecurity guidance and compliance specifications. These standards are the baseline for multiple regulations but are implemented differently by each.

Academia and Industry Associations

Two key supporting functions to doctrinal development come from the commercial sector. First is academia for both skills and innovation and the second are industry organizations like National Defense Industrial Association (NDIA) or Armed Forces Communications and Electronics Association (AFCEA). First we will talk about some of the key academic institutions (though there are far too many to mention all the great work being done). To find a list of what universities are nationally ranked we refer to National Centers of Academic Excellence. NSA and the Department of Homeland Security (DHS) jointly sponsor the National Centers of Academic Excellence in IA Education and research programs. The goal of these programs is to reduce vulnerability in our national information infrastructure by promoting higher education and research in IA, and producing a growing number of professionals with IA expertise in various disciplines [38]. Next, we will look at a couple of universities that have been consistently doing great work in the field: Purdue's Center for Education and Research in Information Assurance and Security (CERIAS) and Carnegie Mellon University with both the Computer Emergency Readiness Team (CERT) and CyLab. These are just two of a number of outstanding programs but are good examples of what is being done. All these institutions are training the future cyber warriors and helping develop the future tools need to conduct CNO.

There are two basic types of associations: industry based and government partnerships. Industry associations focus on certifications, awareness training, and ethical standards. A sample list of these include: International Information Systems Security Certification Consortium (ISC)2®, Information Systems Security Association (ISSA), and Information Systems Audit and Control Association (ISACA). Partnerships are sponsored by many different government agencies, including: Executive Office with Advisory Councils on Infrastructure, Telecommunications and Science & Technology; DHS with National Security Information Exchange (NSIE); Industrial Control System Joint Working Group; National Cyber Coordination and Integration Center; Information Sharing and Analysis Centers and Defense Industrial Base (DIB) Program; DoD with Domestic Security Alliance Council; Counterintelligence Strategic Partnership-Business Alliance and Science Boards; FBI with InfraGard; Dept of Treasury with Advisory Committees on Information Policies and Telecommunications; and Department of State with Information Security and Privacy Advisory Board, to name a few. These partnerships are designed to help share policy within the government and encourage industry self-governance. The partnerships face challenges like companies who are unwilling to share because of the fear of exposure. These companies do not want to lose credibility by letting the public know they were hacked into. The government in many cases will not protect information the companies would share from Freedom of Information Act (FOIA) so anyone could ask for the details on who was compromised and publish it. Another concern companies have is in regards to how much of their shared information can be used by any agency of the government, in particular prosecution by the Department of Justice.

OPERATIONS AND EXERCISES

Finally, we have to train and practice to be successful when it comes time to execute. There are many efforts in the federal government, military, academia, and jointly (both commercial and international) to exercise the different cyber plans. There are two basic types of exercises, Table Top and Simulations. Table Top exercises are scripted and designed to take the organization through the thought process, while simulations are designed to recreate the environment and take the team through the actual actions they would take in the real world. Exercises can be purely cybersecurity focused, or cyber can be an active part built into an operational exercise. There are federal exercises, military exercises, and academic exercises.

Federal Exercises

For the U.S. government, the major exercises are Cyber Storm and National Level Exercises (formally known as Top Off). Cyber Storm is focused on the National Cyber Incident response plan. Cyber Storm IV: 2011-2012 was the latest installment of the series, Cyber Storm IV

(CS IV), it was designed as a set of building block exercises, which began in fall 2011 and concluded in 2012. It promoted more focused exercise activities, allowing participants to delve deeper into particular cyber issues. Members of the cyber incident response community are actively collaborating with DHS in the design and execution of these building block exercises [39]. Cyber Storm was the primary vehicle to exercise the newly developed National Cyber Incident Response Plan (NCIRP)—a blueprint for cybersecurity incident response—to examine the roles, responsibilities, authorities, and other key elements of the nation's cyber incident response and management capabilities and use those findings to refine the plan. The goals were increased federal, state, international, and private sector participation (multiagency, over 20 states and nations). The National Level Exercise 2009 was designated as a Tier I National Level Exercise. Tier I exercises are conducted annually in accordance with the National Exercise Program (NEP), which serves as the nation's overarching exercise program for planning, organizing, conducting, and evaluating national level exercises. The NEP was established to provide the U.S. government, at all levels, exercise opportunities to prepare for catastrophic crises ranging from terrorism to natural disasters [40]. These exercises are vital to building relationships and procedures for the different agencies to work together. The downside to them is there are many problems that are identified and not addressed. We need formal After Action Reviews (AARs) with a plan of action to remedy the issues identified. This goes back to the problem that there is no one person responsible for solving the problems identified so as the participants get back to their normal jobs they focus on the near term problems they are directly responsible for.

TIP

Most organizations do not have disaster recovery/continuity of operations plans. Those who do often do not exercise them. Find out if your company has a plan and organize a Table Top walk through the plan. Get the IT department to transfer one application to your alternate site for a week every year. These little steps could prevent your company from going under given a major catastrophe.

DoD Exercises

The U.S. military has built cyber warfare into some of their key exercises. Below is a list of exercises (broken out by major commands and services) that have significant cyber Mission Event Synchronization List (MESL) events:

- EUCOM—Austere Challenge, Agile Response, Flexible Leader
- PACOM—Terminal Fury, Ulchi Focus Lens, RSOI
- CENTCOM—Unified Endeavor
- NORTHCOM—Ardent Sentry, Northern Edge, Vigilant Shield
- SOUTHCOM—Fuertas Defensas, Blue Advance
- STRATCOM—Global Lightning, Global Shield, Bulwark Defender
- TRANSCOM—Turbo Challenge, Turbo Distribution
- USA—Warfighter Program (simulation)
- USN—JTFeX
- USAF—Black Daemon
- U.S. Marines—MEFEx, FEDOS

Although these exercises have a cyber component, they cost millions of dollars to run, and the cyber events are not allowed to have a severe impact on the exercise. There is no exercise that is designed to see how the military would operate without cyber. How well the military could perform without cyber-enabled command and control systems may never be known until they are forced to.

Educational Exercises

There are also some very strong educational sponsored exercises. At the high school level there is CyberPatriot, at the college level is the National Collegiate Cyber Defense Competition (NCCDC) and for the U.S. Military Academies is the Cyber Defense Exercise (CDX). UK has officially launched its Cyber Security Challenge to find and attract new talent to the IT security industry. In the "hacker" community there is a competition called Capture the Flag contest (CTF) at DEFCON (since 2010 there have been both a network and social engineering contests). Finally, SANS (a major commercial training company) hosts NetWars. The educational sponsored exercises are very defense-oriented. DEFCON and SANS have both attack and defending aspects. These are designed to encourage development of the skills needed to be successful in this new domain. These competitions are monitored by federal agencies, DoD, and commercial companies in search of cyber talent.

Sample MESLs

We include some sample MESL events for organizations considering conducting an exercise:

1. Disaster Recovery Plan/Continuity of Operations Plan execution
   a. Analyze team response (focus on legal, HR, public relations actions)
2. Major IT support vendor failure to perform (i.e., going out of business)
3. Vulnerability Assessment/Penetration Test
   a. Both external and internal threat test with full staff response to incident
   b. Conduct Forensic analysis of simulated incident and determine response
4. Detection of a Massive Data Exfiltration or Theft of IP
5. Sample Vignettes to talk through at staff meetings

   • Zero Day Attack takes down over 20% of the companies systems
   • Critical System failure (key application or email server)
   • Degraded Connectivity/Denial of Service impacts access
   • Insider accidental data deletion
   • Insider proprietary information theft
   • Insider malicious activity
   • Insider inappropriate activity
   • Partner network compromise
   • Compromised web page
   • Discovery of software license abuse
   • Compromise of privacy information
   • Unauthorized Device on the enterprise network

SUMMARY

This chapter has explored the state of current cyber warfare doctrine on both the nation state and military. Every country with a dependence on IT infrastructure is developing strategies and capabilities to protect and exercise national power. We then examined some of the traditional tactics and products that the military needs to adapt to the cyberspace environment. We covered some of the directives used by federal agencies and governments to guide behavior in this virtual environment. Finally, we took a look at how organizations are training to both develop new doctrine and execute their current plans.

Today we are at the beginning of a new era of culture, individual and nation state influence, and possibly warfare (both economic and force on force conflicts). Governments and militaries all over the world are aggressively working on developing doctrine to defend, fight, and win in this new domain.

References

[1] DoD. Joint electronic library, http://www.dtic.mil/doctrine/; 2010 [accessed 17.02.13].

[2] DoD. Secretary of Defense Robert Gates. Wall Street J Resource Documents, http://online.wsj.com/public/re sources/documents/OSD05914.pdf; 2009 [accessed 17.02.13].

[3] Alexander, General Keith B. Statement of commander United States Cyber Command before the house committee on armed services; 2010.

[4] Gates, Secretary of Defense Robert. Wall Street J Resource Documents [online] DoD, http://online.wsj.com/pub lic/resources/documents/OSD05914.pdf; 2009.

[5] Congressman W. Mac. Thornberry (R) definitions, focal point, and methodology needed for DOD to develop full-spectrum cyberspace budget estimates, http://www.gao.gov/products/GAO-11-695R; 2011 [online].

[6] Compendium of Key Joint Doctrine Publications Compiled by Deputy Directorate, Joint Staff, J-7 Joint and Coalition Warfighting Joint Doctrine Support Division as of 7 January 2013.

[7] DoD. Joint electronic library, http://www.dtic.mil/doctrine/; 2010 [accessed 17.02.13].

[8] Baldor LC. Pentagon creates new medal for cyber, drone wars. Washington: Associated Press; 2013 [accessed 17.03.13].

[9] Major General Webber RE. USAF. U.S. House of Representatives House Armed Services Committee. Presentation to the subcommittee on terrorism and unconventional threats. US Navy. http://www.airforce-magazine. com/SiteCollectionDocuments/Testimony/2010%20docs/092310Webber.pdf; 2010 [accessed 17.02.13].

[10] VADM Jack Dorsett DCNO for Information Dominance. Information dominance and the U.S. Navy's cyber warfare vision. The Defense Technical Information Center. US Navy, http://www.dtic.mil/ndia/2010SET/Dorsett. pdf; 2010 [accessed 17.02.13].

[11] Vice Admiral Kendall L. Card interview on cyber http://defensesystems.com/articles/2011/06/17/chief-of-na val-intelligence-card-navy-technology.aspx [accessed 17.03.13].

[12] Navy Cyber Power 2020 – Sustaining the US global leadership: priorities for 21st century defense, www.public. navy.mil/fcc-c10f/Strategies/Navy_Cyber_Power_2020.pdf.

[13] U.S. Army. TRADOC pam 525-7-8, Cyberspace operations concept capability plan 2016–2028; 2010.

[14] Department of Defense. TRICARE. Military health system information assurance guidance, http://www.health. mil/Libraries/ia-files/14-INFOCON-10102008.pdf; 2008 [accessed 17.02.13].

[15] Robinson N, Gribbon L, Horvath V, Robertson K. Cyber-security threat characterization: a rapid comparative analysis. Stockholm: Prepared for the Center for Asymmetric Threat Studies (CATS), Swedish National Defence College; 2013.

[16] Liang Q, Xiangsui W. Unrestricted warfare. Beijing: PLA Literature and Arts Publishing House; 1999.

[17] Thomas T. Air Force Space Command High Frontier. Taiwan examines Chinese information warfare. Air Force, http://www.afspc.af.mil/shared/media/document/AFD-090519-102.pdf; 2009.

[18] Krekel B. Capability of the people's republic of China to conduct cyber warfare and computer network exploitation. The US-China Economic and Security Review Commission, http://cdm266901.cdmhost.com/cdm/singleitem/collection/p266901coll4/id/3130/rec/12; 2009 [accessed 17.02.13].

[19] Associated Press 12 Chinese Hacker Teams Responsible for most US Cybertheft. http://www.foxnews.com/scitech/2011/12/12/12-chinese-hacker-teams-responsible-for-most-us-cybertheft/; 2011 [online].

[20] Strategy Page The Mighty 1st Technical Reconnaissance Bureau. http://www.strategypage.com/htmw/htiw/articles/20110417.aspx; 2011 [online].

[21] Mandiant APT1 report, www.mandiant.com [accessed 17.03.13].

[22] Bloomberg Businessweek February 18-24 cover story [accessed 17.03.13].

[23] Yasuhide Y, Atsuhiro Y, Katsumi BT. Comparative study of the information security policies of Japan and the United States, J Natl Security Law 2010; http://infosecmgmt.pro/sites/default/files/us-japan_information_security_comparison_4_yamada.pdf [accessed 17.03.13].

[24] Yong-sup H. Analyzing South Korea's Defense Reform 2020. Korean J Def Anal 2006;XVIII(1) [accessed 17.03.13].

[25] Bermudez Jr. JS. SIGINT, EW, and EIW in the Korean People's Army, Honolulu: Asia-Pacific Center for Security Studies; 2005. http://www.apcss.org/Publications/Edited%20Volumes/BytesAndBullets/CH13.pdf [accessed 17.03.13].

[26] Cooperative Cyber Defence Centre of Excellence. NATO and attained the status of International Military Organisation, http://www.ccdcoe.org/12.html [accessed 17.02.13].

[27] Centre, Office of Cyber Security and Cyber Security Operations. Cyber Security Strategy of the United Kingdom. Cabinet Office, http://www.cabinetoffice.gov.uk/media/216620/css0906.pdf; 2009 [online].

[28] République, Présidence De La. The French White Paper on defence and national security. Le Livre blanc sur la défense et la sécurité nationale, http://www.livreblancdefenseetsecurite.gouv.fr/IMG/pdf/white_paper_press_kit.pdf; 2007 [online].

[29] Rantapelkonen J, Salminen M, editors. The fog of cyber defence. Helsinki: National Defence University Department of Leadership and Military Pedagogy; 2013, Publication Series 2 Article Collection no: 10.

[30] Czech Republic Czech Cyber Security Strategy for 2011–2015 published [online] August 2011, http://www.enisa.europa.eu/media/news-items/czech-cyber-security-strategy-published.

[31] Andrew Nusca Hayden Digital Blackwater may be necessary for private sector to fight cyber threats, http://www.zdnet.com/blog/btl/hayden-digital-blackwater-may-be-necessary-for-private-sector-to-fight-cyber-threats/53639; 2011 [online].

[32] Steve W. GSEC gold credentials. Cyber IPB, http://www.giac.org/paper/gsec/1752/cyber-ipb/103147; 2001.

[33] Department of Defense. Joint electronic library, http://www.dtic.mil/doctrine/; 2010 [accessed 17.02.13].

[34] National Security Council. White house comprehensive national cybersecurity initiative, http://www.whitehouse.gov/cybersecurity/comprehensive-national-cybersecurity-initiative; 2008.

[35] Department of Homeland Security. Federal news radio. National cyber incident response plan. DHS, http://www.federalnewsradio.com/pdfs/NCIRP_Interim_Version_September_2010.pdf; 2010.

[36] Department of Homeland Security. White house homeland security presidential directives, http://www.dhs.gov/xabout/laws/editorial_0607.shtm; 2010 [accessed 17.02.13].

[37] National Institute of Standards and Technology. Cyber and network security. Information technology laboratory, http://www.nist.gov/itl/cns/index.cfm; 2010 [accessed 17.02.13].

[38] National Security Agency. National centers of academic excellence. Information assurance, http://www.nsa.gov/ia/academic_outreach/nat_cae/index.shtml; 2010 [accessed 17.02.13].

[39] Department of Homeland Security. Cyber storm: securing cyber space, http://www.dhs.gov/files/training/gc_1204738275985.shtm; 2010 [accessed 17.02.13].

[40] National Exercise Program. http://www.dhs.gov/files/training/gc_1179350946764.shtm; 2010 [accessed 17.02.13].

Cyber Warriors

In looking at the people that are and will be conducting cyber warfare, there are two somewhat distinct areas to examine. At present, many of those that are carrying out such operations are likely to not have been trained from the beginning to do so, due to the relatively recent arrival of the field, and their skills are carried over from other fields. Although this is not a bad thing, and may indeed serve to give them a better and generally more broad technical view, some needed areas will tend to lack focus as the vast majority of the information security field is presently defensively focused.

In the future, as cyber conflicts become more prevalent, and more specifically trained personnel are required, we will need to recruit appropriate people and teach a more focused set of skills to them. In doing so, we will need to look at what these training requirements might be, and the potential consequences of passing on such information.

WHAT DOES A CYBER WARRIOR LOOK LIKE?

The general description of a person engaged in cyber operations may be a difficult order to fill. As the field has only recently begun to become formalized, and most of the personnel are originally from other fields in security and general computing, they have quite a broad range of skills, experiences, and other attributes. We can likely expect this to change in the future as cyber warfare forces become more specifically structured to the task, but at present things are a bit of a hodgepodge.

Certifications

Although the world of information security lacks some of the formal credentials of other fields, such as engineering, there is a glut of security credentials, primarily in the form of certifications, to be found, covering nearly any aspect of information security that we should examine. Of primary, but certainly not exclusive, interest, we might commonly find certifications in general information security, penetration testing, and forensics among the groups of people currently conducting cyber warfare tasks. There are, of course, also people conducting these tasks that have no certifications at all.

There are three main types of certifications to be found across the technical computing industry: those that are vendor neutral and sponsored by a collective of organizations, those that are vendor neutral and put forth by a single organization, and those that are vendor specific and launched by the vendor itself.

In the general information security field, the single certification that holds the most weight at present is the Certified Information Systems Security Professional (CISSP®) from the International Information Systems Security Certification Consortium (ISC)$^{2®}$. The CISSP®, although considered to be a management certification, has become the "gold standard" against which security professionals are weighed, and without which a job above entry level might be very difficult to find in the security industry. Also of note in general information security certifications are a variety of offerings from the SysAdmin, Audit, Network, Security (SANS) Institute, with certifications provided by Global Information Assurance Certification (GIAC), the certification body associated with them, as well as the offerings from the Information Systems Audit and Control Association (ISACA).

In the penetration testing field, certifications are somewhat fewer and farther between. Again from SANS/GIAC, the GIAC Certified Penetration Tester (GPEN) certification has become well known in the last few years. Although a solid certification, the GPEN test does not include a hands-on assessment, which raises criticism from some regarding what exactly is being tested for this very results-oriented specialty of the security field. A relative newcomer to the penetration testing certification cadre, and one that had gained a considerable amount of attention, is the Offensive Security Certified Professional (OSCP), a certification created by the same group that develops the BackTrack pen testing Linux distribution. The OSCP test is offered online and consists largely of being able to successfully attack and exploit a number of systems in order to retrieve specified information, a scenario much more closely matched to what we might find in a cyber warfare operation.

In the forensics field, we can again find several offerings from SANS/GIAC, in a few different subspecialties of forensics.

We can also find several offerings that are vendor specific, often from forensics software vendors, such the EnCase Certified Examiner (ENCE) certification from Guidance Software, the makers of the commonly used EnCase forensic toolset.

While this by no means represents a complete list of all of the certifications, nor of specializations, that we might find in information security professionals, and in those capable of conducting cyber warfare, it is a relatively representative sample.

TIP

Many security classes and certifications come with a very high price tag, including those from SANS. For those willing to put in a little bit of work in exchange, SANS offers a workstudy program that allows training classes to be attended for a considerably reduced cost. This renders the road to certification considerably more accessible, at least from a monetary perspective. Further information can be found at http://www.sans.org/security-training/volunteer.php.

Education and Training

In general, those that work closely with information security in general, or in the cyber warfare arena specifically, tend to be rather well educated and trained. Outside of lower-level jobs, entry into positions in these fields is not always easy and tends to be rather competitive. We will generally find that such people are, in general, relatively well educated to begin with, and undergo continual rounds of training, attend conferences and seminars, and generally try to keep their skills as current and sharp as possible.

Education

Education, in the sense of formal university degrees, in the information security field can vary widely, although it does tend toward the higher end of the scale. In general, studies that have been done on information security professionals show that around half of them have at least a bachelor's degree, with some relatively large fraction of that group having a master's degree as well. Additionally, we will find a very small percentage with terminal degrees [1]. Such degrees, although largely technical in nature, also expand to include the arts, history, and many other non-technical areas. Technical degrees such as those in computer science, computer engineering, information technology, information assurance, and others in the same vein have some direct applicability to cyber warfare, although such academic knowledge not tempered with practical experience is of considerably less utility.

At present, a large portion of those conducting cyber warfare operations in the United States are current or former military, and of those that are or were commissioned officers, a certain number will have come through one of the military academies. Defense contractors, who are often providing the actual personnel for such efforts, tend to favor former military due to skill set and clearance issues. In addition to the benefit of the college degree earned at the academy for their particular branch of military service, such people will also have gained knowledge of strategy and tactics as a part of their educational process, knowledge that could be quite useful in conducting cyber warfare operations. In particular, those that have been through such schooling in the last few years may very well have had educational experiences that spoke specifically to cyber warfare. This dimension of warfare has recently come considerably closer to the forefront in military circles, and this focus is reflected in the content at many military academies [2].

Also worthy of mention is the National Security Agency (NSA) Center of Academic Excellence (CAE) institutions. The NSA reviews the information security curriculum and the credentials of the school in question, and makes a determination on the quality of the security-related programs that are offered by school. The CAE is awarded when a school meets or exceeds the criteria for information security training that have been set by the NSA.

Training

A very large portion of those in the information security and cyber warfare fields go through quite a bit of effort to keep their training and skills current. In this particular profession, being linked so closely to technology, and, in particular, to keeping technology secure, means that keeping up on training and staying abreast of events is vital to staying current. This is generally done by attending formal training sessions, going to conferences, watching the news outlets that are specific to security, reading new books and papers that come out, and other similar activities.

In the world of formal security training, there are a large variety of options to choose from, but most of them cover the same relatively limited pool of information. The focus of such offerings changes with the focus of the industry, so there are sure to be a glut of classes for whatever the hot topic is at any given time. At present cyber warfare is the hot new thing in the security industry, so many training vendors are pushing penetration testing, the nearest thing to directly address the topic. Outside of a few vendors that produce unusual training, most such classes will fit into penetration testing, incident handling, digital forensics, law, auditing, or development relatively neatly. In such classes, we will find often our cyber specialists in attendance.

One of the other main avenues of keeping up to date with the security and cyber fields is to attend the various conferences, seminars, and other similar events that are available in a near continuous stream. These events can arrive as everything from very large general security conferences to very specialized and more exclusive events on particular sub-topics. In the last several years, we have seen quite a few more events that are specific to cyber warfare; however, these are often sponsored and attended almost entirely by military and government organizations and often do not enjoy the attention of the general public.

Experience and Skills

The experience and skills held by those in cyber operations can be quite wide and varying, but often maps well to several of the general information security and computing fields. If we make a fairly broad generalization, we can break such skill sets down into reconnaissance, offensive, and defensive skills.

Reconnaissance skills such as network traffic sniffing, packet analysis, network and system mapping, forensics, reverse engineering, binary analysis, and other such capabilities allow us to examine the infrastructure, systems, traffic, and often data of those that oppose us on the cyber battlefield. Such skills are commonly used in the troubleshooting of systems, applications, and networks, although usually with a slightly different focus. We may find people with such experience working in system administration, development, network engineering, and security roles.

Offensive skills are somewhat more specific and focused in the direction of attack and, as such, do not overlap with quite as many non-security fields, although they still do to some extent. The set of skills found in hackers (ethical or otherwise) and penetration testers maps almost directly across, although with a slightly different focus and rules of engagement. The skills of fields such as network engineering, development, and others can also be of use here by changing the goals from keeping infrastructure, systems, and applications running to taking them down.

Defensive skills are already rather prevalent in the computing industry in general, although generally not with the sole focus of withstanding a concentrated cyber attack from a determined enemy with the resources of a nation state to back them. These standard skills are found in system administration, penetration testing, network engineering, and many other common areas. Although they are skills found in most IT departments, we are less likely to find individuals that have the particular focus of defending against a large scale attack, outside of a few major providers or hosting services that have been through such trials already. For example, Akamai, a company that provides, among other things, hosting services for many large companies, and is attacked quite regularly.

As we have noted, the skills used to conduct cyber warfare are not uncommon ones, but they have a different focus than their industry counterparts. When looking for those that are experienced in the cyber warfare area, we are unlikely to find the very specific skills that we are looking for, unless the person in question is already working in the cyber area, conducting research, or a related field. The better candidates for such positions will have a broad variety of technical skills and a good general understanding of hacking, networking, development, system administration, and other similar areas, and an ability to be creative and thing outside of the box. Although specialists do have their place, they can be blind to particular areas and may be better focused on single tasks.

DIFFERENCES FROM TRADITIONAL FORCES

In selecting candidates for cyber warfare operations, we may find, and the U.S. military has found, that those suited to this particular task may differ in some rather significant areas from those that are traditional in fighting forces the world over. Although we may desire a certain set of qualities from someone for taking a hill or shooting someone a long distance away, these same qualities may not be significant for conducting cyber warfare.

Age

Age can be significant in several ways for traditional fighting forces. We may want our troops to be young enough to be in or near their physical prime, so that they can withstand the rigors of combat, but not too young or too physically underdeveloped. We are also less likely to value those that are of a more advanced age, due to the physical concerns and lessening of strength and stamina past a certain point.

In the world of combat on a largely logical level, many such concerns vanish entirely. When conducting operations from behind a computer screen, measures of age-related physical strength and fitness become exponentially less important, if they are a consideration at all.

On the other side of the coin, mental factors such as maturity, intelligence, and problem-solving skills become dramatically more important in this type of engagement.

The reduced reliance on attributes related to age gives us a considerably larger potential pool of candidates from which to select. We can potentially recruit, where other factors permit, from a range much younger or older than would normally be considered for operations of a militaristic nature. We still need to consider health factors, maturity level, and other such items, when making such selections.

Although this could be considered a positive thing from a personnel perspective, we would also need to consider the psychological effects that having "kids" or "seniors" presents in such conflicts. Even away from physical frontlines and out of danger of immediate physical harm to their persons, we might see a variety of effects on other segments of our fighting forces, and a certain amount of backlash that might be associated with using such candidates, just as we have seen with discussions in the introduction of other groups potentially not conforming to the military image, namely homosexuals. Nonetheless, we must maintain an awareness of possible candidates, regardless of the ageism present in many modern societies.

Attitude

When considering the ideal type of mind that we may seek out to conduct cyber warfare operations, a few attributes present themselves: creative, intelligent, good problem solving skills, independent, and other similar terms. Unfortunately, or perhaps fortunately, depending on perspective, these types of attributes do not generally produce people that tend to follow rules well, or possess any willingness to follow strong authority figures. People, of course, vary greatly and in unexpected ways, so this will by no means be a universal issue, but it will be prevalent enough to pose some difficulty when attempting to attract large numbers of people with such qualities, and will need to be accounted for when attempting to do so.

Additionally, as we discussed above when we covered the broadened age range that we have to select from when assembling a non-physically oriented force, attitude issues may accompany those at either end of the age spectrum. For those that are at the younger end of the spectrum, we may encounter issues such as maturity and impulse control. At the older end of the spectrum, we may have societal issues involving a perceived lack of respect of deference from those that are considerably younger. Again, these types of problems can be highly situational and vary greatly from one individual to the next, but definitely need to be accounted for and prepared for.

Physical Condition

The physical condition of dedicated cyber warfare forces, security professionals, and those that work with computers for a living, in general, tends to be very different than that of the membership of the militaries and other fighting forces in most countries. While generally good physical fitness, granting the ability to move quickly over long distances, engage in physical combat with enemy forces, and other such strenuous activities, may be very valuable in traditional combat, this is not necessarily the case when seeking to conduct cyber warfare.

In the case when the truly valued assets of our cyber warrior revolve largely around mental abilities, creativity, technical skills, and the ability to sit in a chair for long periods of time, all the while tracking multiple activities on a series of displays, physical fitness may tend to take a back seat. Although it is obviously desirable for our best and brightest to be fit enough to allow them to function relatively normally, some are of the opinion that such traditional military measures of physical performance, such as timed runs around a track are not necessarily applicable. On the other side of the discussion is the potential for cyber forces to be deployed in an area where a traditional ground/air war is being carried out. In this case, it may be vital for such forces to be physically fit.

It is the nature of modern conflicts involving new and complex technologies that will force a paradigm change in the way that a soldier is viewed. Even in traditional warfare, we can see a surge of new technologies, such as the use of unmanned and remotely piloted drone aircraft, that usher in a wave of chair-bound and technically savvy operators, having many of the same skills, background, and characteristics as our cyber warriors.

Although this attitude regarding the physical fitness of tech workers is commonly accepted in the civilian world, it is one that is sure to be a very difficult change to internalize in many organizations of a military and governmental nature. Although such changes may not be commonplace at this time, they are sure to become considerably more so in the future.

Credentials

An interesting anomaly in the security world, and in the world of technology in general, is the importance of credentials, or lack thereof, depending on the given situation. In many other disciplines that depend heavily on complex domain expertise, such as civil engineering or medicine, the ability to legally practice such skills is tightly regulated, and justifiably so. We do not want to see a bridge erected or an appendix removed by someone who has a set of knowledge bounded by a weekend with a "<skillhere> for utter morons" book. In the commercial security field, we can often see examples of exactly this, and the world is awash with self-proclaimed experts in this area.

In some cases, primarily in military and government, we can see some steps that have been taken to avoid such situations. An excellent example in the U.S. military can be found in Department of Defense (DoD) Directive 8570.1, commonly referred to as DoD 8570, or just 8570. DoD 8570, in a nutshell, requires that those in the direct employ of the DoD who are performing information assurance-related functions be trained and certified to be capable of carrying out their particular role, and that certification for these functions are carried out by a vendor on a relatively short approved list. The vendors that are on the approved list also enjoy a certain amount of fame in the civilian world, as they presumably measure up to a higher level of quality for having been so included. The present, as of this writing, table of approved certifications for various DoD career fields and levels can be seen in Table 5.1 [3].

The interesting dichotomy in this situation is that certification does necessarily equate to skill or knowledge, and lack of certification is not always a good indicator of lack of knowledge or skill. When selecting candidates for cyber warfare, unlike picking a doctor to remove our appendix, we cannot presently afford to immediately discard those that do not possess a given certification in the security field. In the future, we may see a more closely regulated security industry, but at present, we may be as likely to find our best prospects waiting tables or arranging flowers as anywhere else.

TABLE 5.1   DoD Approved Baseline Certifications

IAT Level I	IAT Level II	IAT Level III
A + CE	GSEC	CISA
Network + CE	Security + CE	CISSP (or Associate)
SSCP	SSCP	CASP
		GCIH

IAM Level I	IAM Level II	IAM Level III
CAP	CAP	GSLC
GSLC	GSLC	CISM
Security + CE	CISM	CISSP (or Associate)
	CISSP (or Associate)	
	CASP	

IASAE I	IASAE II	IASAE III
CISSP (or Associate)	CISSP (or Associate)	CISSP—ISSEP
CASP	CASP	CISSP—ISSAP

CND Analyst	CND Infrastructure Support	CND Incident Reporter	CND Auditor	CND-SP Manager
GCIA	SSCP	GCIH	CISA	CISSP—ISSMP
CEH	CEH	CSIH	GSNA	CISM
GCIH		CEH	CEH	

PRESENT CYBER WARFARE FORCES

Although the idea of formal cyber warfare forces is a relatively new one, only going back a few years, many countries and organizations have at least taken steps in that direction.

In a few cases, large organizations have sprung into existence virtually overnight, even if they are not entirely operational and ready to take on a large conflict. Even the question of what exactly constitutes operational is somewhat up in the air, as many of these units and organizations have not been tested under live circumstances.

Looking at Figure 5.1, we can see that even when only accounting for the major players in the cyber warfare arena, we still have a large percentage of the globe that could potentially be involved in such a conflict.

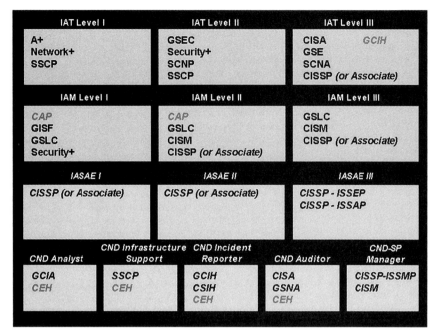

IAT Level I	IAT Level II	IAT Level III
A+ Network+ SSCP	GSEC Security+ SCNP SSCP	CISA GCIH GSE SCNA CISSP (or Associate)

IAM Level I	IAM Level II	IAM Level III
CAP GISF GSLC Security+	CAP GSLC CISM CISSP (or Associate)	GSLC CISM CISSP (or Associate)

IASAE I	IASAE II	IASAE III
CISSP (or Associate)	CISSP (or Associate)	CISSP - ISSEP CISSP - ISSAP

CND Analyst	CND Infrastructure Support	CND Incident Reporter	CND Auditor	CND-SP Manager
GCIA CEH	SSCP CEH	GCIH CSIH CEH	CISA GSNA CEH	CISSP-ISSMP CISM

FIGURE 5.1   The major forces in the cyber warfare arena.

U.S.

The U.S. government has one of the more complex groupings of cyber warfare forces, at least on paper. In reality, though these organizations and agencies exist, they are not all staffed, operational, and completely ready to carry out such operations on any large scale.

U.S. Cyber Command

The U.S. Cyber Command (CYBERCOM) is a unified command under U.S Strategic Command (STRATCOM), composed of units from the Army Cyber Command, the Fleet Cyber Command (10th Fleet), the 24th Air Force, and the Marine Corps Forces Cyberspace Command [4]. The seal of CYBERCOM can be seen in Figure 5.2 [5].

CYBERCOM is headed by the Director of the National Security Agency (DIRNSA), who serves both roles, and is assisted in technical matters by the Defense Information Systems Agency (DISA). The Cyber Command is specifically responsible for the protection of DoD networks only, leaving the protection of civilian networks up to the Department of Homeland Security (DHS) [6].

China

The public face of cyber warfare in China rests with the People's Liberation Army (PLA), although the specifics are a bit sketchy on exactly the composition and duties of cyber warfare units within the PLA are. It is believed that the majority of such capabilities lie within

FIGURE 5.2   The seal of the United States Cyber Command.

the General Staff Department (GSD), 4th Department, GSD 3rd Department, several of the Technical Reconnaissance Bureaus (TRB), and the Information Warfare Militia Units [7].

> **NOTE**
>
> As we discuss the cyber capabilities of the various countries in this section, please note that they are in no particular order and their positioning in the chapter does not indicate strength, ability, or any other factor.

Also to be considered are the informal, or at least not publically recognized, groups of hackers, hacktivists, malware authors, cyber criminals, and other such similar elements that are frequently discussed in the media. Although we might suppose that all of the attacks attributed to China are not actually sponsored by the state, if they originate from the country at all, there may be at least some element of truth present here. The large population of China also equates to a large number of potentially unsecure systems that could be used as attack platforms. We will discuss the attribution issue in Chapter 9 and criminals and criminal organizations at greater length in Chapter 11.

Russia

It is clear from the events in Estonia and Georgia that we discussed in Chapter 1, that Russia has a strong capability to conduct cyber warfare. Presently these capabilities are housed in the Federal Security Service of the Russian Federation (FSB), the Federal Guard Service, and the General Staff [8]. Until it was abolished in 2003, the Federal Agency for Government Communications and Information (FAPSI) solely handled such matters in Russia [9].

France

The cyber warfare capability of the French springs from the French Network and Information Security Agency (ANSSI), which is an organization under the Secretary General for

National Defense (SGDN) and exists to "detect and early react to cyber attacks" [10]. This organization is, as are those of many countries at this point, relatively new, having been in existence for only slightly over a year at the time of this writing.

Israel

As with many other aspects of warfare, Israel is and has been for some time very proactive in the area of cyber warfare. Israel reportedly has had at least some cyber warfare capability since the early 1990s, and these capabilities have matured and evolved over time. In 2002, a special unit of the Israel Security Agency (ISA) was charged with matters of defense against cyber attacks. At present the task of cyber warfare operations appears to be somewhat of a contested split between the C4I (command, control, communications, computers, and intelligence) Directorate of the Israel Defense Force (IDF) and Unit 8200 (signals intelligence) of the Directorate of Military Intelligence which is commonly known as Aman [11].

Brazil

In Brazil, a country that is no stranger to cyber crime issues, the responsibility for issues related to information security lies with the Institutional Security Cabinet (GSI), which ultimately acts through other related organizations such as the Ministry of Science and Technology, Ministry of Communications, and the Brazilian Network Information Center [8]. The technology industry in Brazil is evolving quickly, so we will likely see a more formalized organization or set of organizations here in the very near future.

Singapore

In Singapore, the Singapore Infocomm Technology Security Authority (SITSA), a division of the Internal Security Department of the Ministry of Home Affairs (MHA) is responsible for securing Singapore against cyber attacks [8]. SITSA, as with many other such agencies, is relatively new and has only existed for slightly over a year as of this writing.

South Korea

Although the stance on cyber warfare in South Korea was previously very disjointed and was divided among a variety of government agencies numbering into the dozens, in 2009, they began an effort to consolidate and standardize the agencies that would be responsible for handling such matters. At present the Korea Internet & Security Agency, composed of the former Korea Information Security Agency (KISA), National Internet Development Agency of Korea (NIDAK), and the Korea IT International Cooperation Agency (KIICA) appears to now be officially responsible for cyber operations [12].

North Korea

The capability of the Democratic People's Republic of Korea (DPRK), otherwise known as North Korea, to conduct cyber warfare is questionable, but may actually exist, at least according to the South Korean intelligence services. Two North Korean educational institutions, Mirim College and Moranbong University, appear to exist for the nearly sole purpose of producing experts in espionage and warfare, of which cyber war is reported to be at least a portion. Additionally, a unit of the Korean People's Army (KPA), dedicated to cyber warfare, is rumored to exist [13]. Outside of a few attacks on South Korea which were tenuously attributed to North Korea, examples of such capabilities are thin indeed.

Australia

In Australia, the Cyber Security Operations Centre (CSOC), under the Defense Signals Directorate (DSD), was launched in 2009, and populated with personnel from the DSD, the Defense Force, the Defense Intelligence Organization, the Federal Police, and the Australian Security Intelligence Organization. The CSOC is responsible for cyber matters pertaining to government computer systems. For civilian systems, the responsibility falls to CERT Australia [14].

Malaysia

In Malaysia, the responsibilities for cyber warfare are spread over several government agencies. The Malaysian Communications and Multimedia Commission (MCMC) acts as a coordinator and has responsibility for ensuring the overall well-being of the network as a whole. The Police Cyber Crime Unit is responsible for preventing and investigating cyber crime. The Ministry of Science, Technology, and Innovation (MOSTI) is responsible for cyber defense and security, and the Malaysian Administrative Modernisation and Management Planning Unit (MAMPU) is responsible for both government and civilian CERTs and monitoring cyber threats [8].

Japan

In Japan, the Information Security Policy Council (ISPC) and the National Information Security Center (NISC), both under the Cabinet Secretariat, are largely responsible for cyber issues. The ISPC focuses on developing and reviewing security policies and strategies, while the NISC handles implementations. Also under the Cabinet Secretariat, the National Police Agency (NPA), is responsible for maintaining computer and network security and investigating cyber incidents. The interface between the public and government cyber concerns lies with the Capabilities for Engineering of Protection, Technical Operation, Analysis, and Response, or CEPTOAR [7].

Canada

In Canada, the Canadian Cyber Incident Response Center (CCIRC) is responsible for monitoring cyber threats to the Canadian network infrastructure. The CIRC falls under Public Safety Canada, the Canadian equivalent to the Department of Homeland Security in the United States. Several agencies are involved in responding to cyber threats and incidents including the Canadian Security Intelligence Service (CSISS), Communications Security Establishment Canada (CSEC), and the Canadian Department of National Defense (DND) [7].

United Kingdom

In the United Kingdom, two main agencies are responsible for cyber issues, the Office of Cyber Security (OCS) and the Cyber Security Operations Centre (CSOC). OCS provides strategic leadership across the whole of the government, while CSOC provides monitoring and coordinates incident response. Additionally, the Centre for the Protection of National Infrastructure (CPNI) runs a CERT for responding to attacks [8].

Other Countries with Cyber Forces

Many other countries currently field, or are in the process of standing up, cyber forces. Some countries may not, at this point, have any significant resources devoted, and others may not be advertising their capabilities. At the time of this writing, considerable confusion and wild speculation in the media and in the industry do not help to make the cyber landscape any more clear. In addition to the countries mentioned above, the following are known to have some presence, but this is by no means an exhaustive list and exact capabilities are not clear [8]:

- Austria
- Belgium
- Estonia
- Finland
- Germany
- Hungary
- India
- Iran
- Italy
- The Netherlands
- New Zealand
- Norway
- Poland
- Spain
- Sweden
- Switzerland

Corporate

Given the increased focus on cyber warfare in the last few years, and the current focus on the topic in both government and industry, a large number of companies have, predictably, become involved in cyber warfare in one fashion or another. In the world of companies that primarily focus on defense contracts we can find the following non-exhaustive list of companies [7]:

- BAE Systems
- Boeing Integrated Defense Systems
- Booz Allen Hamilton
- General Dynamics Corporation

- GreyLogic
- Lockheed Martin Corporation
- ManTech International Corporation
- NetWitness Corporation
- Northrop Grumman Corporation
- QinetiQ Group Plc
- Raytheon Company
- Science Applications International Corporation (SAIC)
- TASC, Inc.
- Thales Group

The list of companies below, also not exhaustive, does not primarily focus on the defense market, although we can almost certainly find most of them in the market to a certain extent [7]:

- F-Secure Corporation
- iDefense
- Kaspersky Lab
- McAfee Inc.
- Microsoft Corporation
- PGP Corporation
- Spirent Communications
- Symantec Corporation

In addition to these companies, we can find thousands of others that have similar foci, products, services, and customers. The market for cyber-oriented offerings is very rich at present, and promises to be so for several years to come, so we are sure to see more entries as time passes.

Criminal

In addition to the various countries and organizations that we discussed above, we must also consider the criminal elements in our list of cyber warfare forces. These can range from the lowest spammer annoying us with promises to enlarge various portions of a man's anatomy, to identity thieves that have managed to parlay stolen information into tens of millions of dollars in funds, to botnet operators that are capable of disrupting the network operations of large corporations or small countries.

Such criminal elements are not as easy to define and point out as the formal cyber warfare forces of a country, but they can be every bit as powerful, and are not bound by the same sets of rules that other forces might be, which can make them very dangerous. We will discuss such elements in greater depth in Chapter 11.

STAFFING FOR CYBER WAR

Given the current situation in which most countries in the world are arming themselves for cyber warfare, there is a large demand around the globe for people with the skills to carry out such operations. In the United States, many of the defense contractors that actually provide the staff for such roles are constantly recruiting, and doing so in such a fashion as to catch the attention of a younger and more technically savvy group of people. Likewise, many military organizations, such as those in the United States and China, are actively recruiting for such positions, once again, with a large target on the backs of younger and potentially more technically able recruits. As we discussed in the "Differences from Traditional Forces" section earlier in the chapter, though age may not be a factor in determining the capacity of a person to carry out cyber operations, technical skill certainly is. The general perception appears to be that such skills can be found to a greater degree in younger people or digital natives.

Particularly given the high level of demand, there is a shortage of people with the technical skills needed to step directly into roles such as these [15]. Defense contractors tend to favor, if not require, potential candidates that have prior military experience. Military recruits have the hurdle of going through rigorous and time-consuming training processes before they can even begin to learn the technical specialties that would make them valuable to such operations. Conversely, if such skills are not used and maintained, they will quickly become outdated.

In short, many countries are in a crunch for qualified people to man these positions, and they may have to alter their current standards to get them. Although this may change in the future, especially if the demand for cyber capable candidates keeps up or increases, for now the situation in the staffing world is rather tight.

Sources of Talent

Sources of sufficiently talented people for recruiting into cyber warfare efforts could potentially come from a wide variety of areas, but a couple present themselves as the most likely sources, namely hacking competitions and schools. Although groups from the two of these may overlap, they ultimately tend to produce a slightly different variety of skills and experiences.

Hacking competitions often referred to as Capture the Flag, or CTF, events value practical skills almost entirely. The general goal of a CTF competition is to exploit one or more machines in order to gain information to either reach the end goal itself, the flag, or to gain information to exploit additional machines with the end goal in mind.

NOTE

There are a large number of such competitions, both inside and outside of the United States, including the National Collegiate Cyber Defense Competition,[a] the Cyber Defense Exercise[b] (CDF), the Defcon CTF[c] competition, Netwars,[d] and Cyber Patriot High School Cyber Defense Competition.[e]

[a] http://www.nationalccdc.org/

[b] http://www.nsa.gov/public_info/press_room/2010/cyber_defense.shtml

[c] http://www.defcon.org/

[d] https://netwars.info/

[e] http://www.highschoolcdc.com/

In academic settings, attention is often more focused on learning the basics and theory behind information security thoroughly, with considerably less emphasis on the practical implementations. Where such situations are discussed, they are often limited to purely defensive topics. Of course there are some schools that are exceptions to this rule, but they are not common.

Ideal candidates are those that have both a deep understanding of the principles of information security, as well as practical knowledge and experience in the specific areas in which they will be working. Such people are not only somewhat more difficult to come by, but chances are that they will either be employed in the field already, or will be actively recruited for their somewhat unique attributes.

Training the Next Generation

Training the next generation of those who will carry out cyber warfare is an interesting prospect. Not only are we training those that are new to the field, but also retraining existing personnel to cope with newer paradigms. Although we can presently muddle through, to a certain extent, by depending on the small core of capable forces that do exist, we are largely depending on being able to retune the skills of those security professionals that already exist in a few small fields in the information security industry.

Currently when such security personnel fail at their jobs, we see something along the lines of a large breach of Personally Identifiable Information (PII), such as contacts information, financial information, medical data, and the like, often closely followed by a rash of identity thefts.

Although such occurrences are unfortunate and can certainly lead to no small amount of financial and emotional trauma for the victims, they pale in comparison to the damage that could be caused by a well backed attacker intent on causing physical harm by attacking critical infrastructure and systems. These attacks have the potential to be orders of magnitude worse if targeted at power infrastructure systems, safety systems, distribution networks for food, and the like.

To train specifically to carry out and defend against an actual cyber conflict, our training focus will need to shift in order to be able to cope with the change.

The Training Paradigm

One of the realities of being closely linked to a constantly changing slate of computing technologies is that change comes at a lightning pace. Although we have yet to see cyber warfare on a large scale, we see a relatively constant stream of small conflicts between various countries, criminal organizations, corporations, and individual players. The lack of a large altercation has less to do with the technology to carry it out not being present, and more to do with a determined attacker having yet to step up to carry out such an attack. In other words, we could find ourselves embroiled in a true cyber war at any point. The prospect of this begs the need of an immediate influx of new blood to be trained for just such an occasion.

Although the need for such training in the immediate future is clear, the practicality of being able to functionally provide such knowledge may be more difficult than it might immediately seem. The U.S. does have a number of commercial training institutions that presently teach on more sedate, but similar, topics, and they presently provide the majority of such training for personnel, civilian, government, or otherwise. These training venues would need to not only retool their training in a much less commercially and perhaps publically, palatable direction, but might also need to keep such training out of the hands of the general public. The necessity might arise to move the delivery of such training inside of the organizations where it would be used, which would require a rather large paradigm shift in the training industry as well.

Teaching the Needed Skills

As we discussed earlier in the chapter in the "Experience and Skills" section, the chief skills required to conduct cyber warfare are reconnaissance, attack, and defense. In the information security world at present, the gross skills that comprise what we need for reconnaissance and attack already exist to a large extent.

Defense, unfortunately, is an area in which most organizations are severely lacking. True defense against concerted attacks, such as large scale Distributed Denial of Service (DDoS) attacks, at this point usually revolves around ignoring the attack in some fashion until it goes away, either by bringing redundant systems online, or some similar strategy. In order to successfully withstand attacks on the scale that we might see in a cyber conflict, we will need to develop new methods of defense and be allowed the freedom to use existing ones. An excellent example of the issue of defense at present is that of the rampant and unchallenged use of botnets. The major issue behind the botnet problem lies in the fact that the simple steps that need to be taken to dismantle a botnet are illegal in many countries. This is largely due to the unauthorized intrusion onto the systems that comprise the botnet that would be required to take it down. Because the skills required to employ such methods of defense are not generally allowed to be used outside of research labs, these skills are not well developed. When examining the skills required to conduct cyber warfare, many such examples present themselves.

Issues in Training for Cyber Warfare

When looking to train large groups of people to conduct cyber warfare, we also need to look to the potential consequences of doing so. At present, the majority of formal training that is oriented in the direction of hacking, our current closest analog to cyber warfare, is firmly directed at what is called "ethical hacking." Ethical hacking, red teaming, and penetration testing are often interchangeable terms, and tend to point at the same set of carefully carried out, with advanced permission being granted, attacks that are intended to root out (pun intended) vulnerabilities so that they can be mitigated before a malicious attacker can find them. This type of training is fairly universal and is provided to those in the corporate world and those in the government world alike. Such training is often expensive enough to be out of the reach of those that do not have the backing of a corporation or government entity.

When we shift our training slightly to focus on cyber warfare instead of ethical hacking, we move somewhat away from the carefully regulated world of ethical hacking, and we almost certainly would not be granted the permission of the party being attacked. In such an environment, the definition of the party conducting the attack becomes almost entirely a matter of perspective. The attacking party may see such an operation as contributing to the defense of their country in both a physical and logical sense, but the opposing party may see such actions as those of a malicious attacker. In this way, one potential viewpoint of training personnel for cyber warfare is also training them for cyber crime.

With traditional forces, when the conflict is over, or when they have been released from their duties, the harm that can come from their training is relatively minimal. They will likely have not been allowed to depart their service with any form of advanced weaponry, although they will still be in possession of the strategic and tactical knowledge in which they were trained. They will also have the benefit of the ingrained lessons of discipline that have been drilled into them over a period of time. These factors will generally allow them to be a normally functioning member of society.

In the current theoretical world where large numbers of individuals have been trained in the conduct of cyber warfare, the peaceful reintroduction of combatants into society may not necessarily be the case. In such circumstances, the mitigating factors that we looked at for traditional forces may not be present at all, or may be lessened.

In cyber warfare, stripping our troops of weaponry when they leave our service may be a difficult prospect. We can certainly attempt to remove their direct access to the systems that would facilitate such attacks, but we will have likely also trained them specifically to subvert such attempts at access control. Even in the case of being able to successfully remove access to such resources, the tools with which cyber warfare is carried out are not (presently anyway) unusual by any means. More often than not, such tools are free, open source, and easily available to the public. Additionally, if we have done a proper job in our training, we should be producing people sufficiently skilled as to be little inconvenienced by the removal of a few specific tools.

Speaking to the issue of discipline ingrained over time by exposure to strict training, we have discussed some of the differences in those that would be suited to cyber warfare from those that are ideally suited to be soldiers in a traditional conflict. As one part of the issue, we may find ourselves surrounded by people that are naturally questioning authority, are independent thinkers, and are particularly bright. On the other hand, the need for such capabilities is now, and lengthy training may not be an option. The combination of the two of these sets of factors does indeed have the potential to be troublesome moving into the future.

SUMMARY

In this chapter, we discussed cyber warriors. As cyber warfare is a rapidly developing field, we covered both the existing forces, and talked about what might come in the future.

We talked about what those working in the cyber field presently look like from the standpoint of education, training, certifications, and experiences. Because this is a relatively new field, we looked at how such skills overlap several other related fields. We also discussed the sources that such skills might come from, and how they are maintained.

We covered what the differences between those that are selected for traditional warfare and cyber warfare might be. Here we talked about how factors such as age, attitude, physical condition, and credentials might apply differently to people fighting from a chair rather than a traditional ground war.

We discussed the present cyber warfare forces in countries around the globe. The list of countries that have formal cyber warfare forces is a relatively short one, but many other countries are developing such capabilities. We also covered how corporate and criminal organizations fit into the picture.

Lastly, we discussed training the next generation of cyber warriors. We covered the training paradigm and how a change might be required to support a true cyber war. We discussed the skills required for cyber warfare and how they differ from the related skills that now exist. We also covered the implications of training people for cyber war and later releasing them into society.

References

[1] Frost & Sullivan. THE 2013 (ISC)2 Global information security workforce study. s.l: (ISC)2®, https://www.isc2.org/uploadedFiles/(ISC)2_Public_Content/2013%20Global%20Information%20Security%20Workforce%20Study%20Feb%202013.pdf; 2013 [accessed 04.04.13].

[2] Witte B. Military academies teach more cyberwarfare. Navy Times, http://www.navytimes.com/news/2010/03/ap_cyberwarfare_030810/; 2010 [accessed 04.04.13].

[3] Assistant secretary of Defense for networks and information, integration/Department of Defense chief information Officer. DoD 8570.01-M Information assurance workforce improvement program incorporating change 3, January 24, 2012. s.l.: United States Department of Defense, http://www.dtic.mil/whs/directives/corres/pdf/857001m.pdf; 2012 [accessed 04.04.2013].

[4] U.S. Strategic Command – Fact Sheets. United States strategic command, http://www.stratcom.mil/factsheets/cc/; 2010 [accessed 04.04.13].

[5] United States Cyber Command. cybercom_seal_large1. United States cyber command, s.l.; 2010.

[6] Deputy Secretary of Defense William J. Lynn, III. Remarks at the defense information technology acquisition summit; 2009.

[7] Visiongain. Cyberwarfare market 2012–2022; 2011.

[8] Buckland BS, Schreier F, Winkler TH. Democratic governance challenges of cyber security; 2010.

[9] Pike J. Federal Agency for Government Communications & Information (FAPSI). FAS intelligence resource program, http://www.fas.org/irp/world/russia/fapsi/index.html; 2003 [accessed 04.04.13].

[10] About ANSSI. Agence Nationale de la sécurité des systèmes d'information, http://www.ssi.gouv.fr/site_rubrique97.html; 2013 [accessed 04.04.13].

[11] Ben-David A. Israel Is serious about cyberwarfare. Aviation week, http://www.aviationweek.com/Article.aspx?id=/article-xml/AW_03_29_2010_p56-212531.xml; 2010 [accessed 04.04.13].

[12] Korean Internet & Security Agency. Korean Internet & Security Agency, https://www.kisa.or.kr/eng/main.jsp; 2013 [accessed 04.04.13].

[13] Mecca for North Korean Hackers. Daily NK, http://www.dailynk.com/english/read.php?cataId=nk01500&num=5161; 2009 [accessed 04.04.13].

[14] Defense Signals Directorate. The cyber security operations centre. Defense signals directorate, http://www.dsd.gov.au/infosec/csoc.htm; 2013 [accessed 04.04.13].

[15] Evans K, Reeder F. A Human Capital Crisis in Cybersecurity. Center for strategic & international studies, http://csis.org/publication/prepublication-a-human-capital-crisis-in-cybersecurity; 2010 [accessed 04.04.13].

6

Logical Weapons

INFORMATION IN THIS CHAPTER

- Reconnaissance Tools
- Scanning Tools
- Access and Escalation Tools
- Exfiltration Tools
- Sustainment Tools
- Assault Tools
- Obfuscation Tools

Logical tools are the weapons that we likely envision when discussing cyber warfare. These are the set of tools that is used to conduct reconnaissance, scout out the networks and systems of our opponents, and attack the various targets we might find. When we look at the use of such tools in a cyber warfare context, we might ask how they are different than the tools used in everyday penetration testing of applications, systems, and networks. The answer is that, in many cases, they are not conceptually different to any great degree, but the scope of their use is greatly increased in a cyber warfare scenario. In April of 2013, the U.S. Air Force officially designated six cyber capabilities as weapons systems: Air Force Cyberspace Defense, Cyberspace Defense Analysis, Cyberspace Vulnerability Assessment/ Hunter, Cyber Command and Control Mission System, Air Force Intranet Control, and Cyber Security and Control System [1]. This reflects the changing nature of attitudes regarding cyber warfare as "real" war.

Where penetration testers may be bound, contractually in some cases, to shy away from the tools or settings in tools that are labeled "dangerous" due to their possible deleterious effects on the target at the other end, such effects may be acceptable, or even desirable in a cyber conflict. This may not always be the case, and we certainly may still want to be stealthy and cautious in some scenarios, but this opens up the use of the common tools in such a way that we do not normally see in penetration testing outside of a lab environment.

Another common question that arises in discussions of tools that might be used during cyber warfare is that of "secret" military or government tools. There are always rumors of gigantic military botnets that are a billion nodes strong, or tools that can cut through encryption like butter. As we have yet to see a no-holds-barred cyber war publicly erupt, the good answer to this question is that although such tools may exist, we will not know the specifics regarding them until they are brought out of hiding and publicly deployed.

Given past examples of military weapons that were held in extreme secrecy, such as the Manhattan Project and the Stealth Fighter, we would certainly be rash to assume that similar projects do not exist for cyber weaponry, or that super-skilled hackers are not being trained in the bowels of the National Security Agency (NSA). However, from the examples that we can see publicly, government and military cyber warriors are going through the same training, in many areas, and using many of the same tools as their counterparts in the civilian world.

In the case of individuals, corporations, hacktivists, criminal organizations, and other nonstate actors, we are more likely to see the use of common rather than custom developed tools. Such groups are often presumed to be the origin of many of the more pervasive items of malware, attack websites, and the source of any number of small-scale cyber attacks. As such, they are on a good footing to participate in cyber warfare on a larger scale and certainly can be considered a serious threat.

When we discuss the broad categories of tools: reconnaissance, scanning, infrastructure, application, and operating system, we might also consider the sources of such tools. A very large portion of the tools in the arsenal used by cyber warriors, penetration testers, hacktivists, and terrorists are free and/or open source, and are regularly maintained and enhanced by their base of users. There are also quite a few commercial tools, or tools that are free with commercial components, some of which are very good indeed, but can be quite expensive.

> **NOTE**
>
> The selection of tools available for use in cyber warfare, penetration testing, and security in general is truly staggering. Although a complete discussion of the various popular security tools would have been great to be able to include, we would have had to devote an entire book to it to have been able to do so. In this chapter, we discuss a few of the highlights, but for those still wanting more, Insecure.org is a great resource. They maintain lists of password crackers, sniffers, vulnerability scanners, web scanners, wireless tools, and numerous other tools of the trade.

We may very well find commercial tools in the hands of cyber warfare forces that are backed by, or in the employ of, nation-states, but we are less likely to find them in the hands of individuals or small groups. Nonetheless, in skilled hands, the free tools can be highly effective, if less automated, and are used regularly by a variety of attackers.

RECONNAISSANCE TOOLS

Reconnaissance tools, as should be clear from the name, are those that we use to gather information, usually in a passive state, about the networks and systems that we might plan to take action against in a logical sense. Such efforts may include gathering information from public websites, looking up Domain Name System (DNS) records, collecting metadata from accessible documents, retrieving very specific information through the use of search engine, or any of a number of other similar activities. Many such tools match closely with Open Source Intelligence (OSINT) techniques.

General Information Gathering

When looking for general information that can be used to provide intelligence on a target, there are a variety of sources that we can turn to. We can mine websites for data on companies and individuals, we can search job postings for a variety of information, we can look for personal and technical information in resumes, we can use search engines both in a general and very specific sense, and we can also use specialized searching tools such as Maltego. In all likelihood, we will utilize a combination of such techniques to assemble a more complete picture of our target.

Websites and Web Servers

All manner of interesting information can be found on the websites of individuals and organizations. Some such information may be intentionally displayed, such as corporate organizational information, and some of it may be shared in an unintentional or unauthorized manner.

In 2007, the U.S. Internal Revenue Service (IRS) conducted an internal audit to inventory servers with the aim of ensuring that security maintenance and patching activities were taking place properly. In the course of the audit, 1811 unauthorized web servers were discovered, constituting 87% of the total web servers discovered. Of these servers, 661 were being used for legitimate business purposes, but were still operating outside of the processes that would have ensured that they were operating in secure configurations [2]. When compliance failures are found in environments that are theoretically highly secure, the implications regarding the security of servers in less strictly regulated environments are frightening indeed.

Search Engines

Search engines, such as Google, can be of great use when conducting research for an attack. They can be used to collect information regarding a particular target, look up application or hardware details, or even collect very specific information to locate vulnerabilities in the target environment.

Even more specifically, search engines can be used to collect data that does not appear during casual searching. Such methods often involve very specifically targeted queries to the standard search engines, or the use of specially tuned search engines, such as Pipl.com, that return information within a particular area of focus.

Google Hacking

Google hacking is the use of advanced operators in search engine queries, in order to enable more directly targeted searches. Although the name would tend to indicate that such searching would be specific to the Google search engine, in actuality, similar search parameters can be used with almost any search engine. Lists of such operators can generally be found on the page for the search engine in question. For Google, the advanced operators can be found at https://sites.google.com/site/gwebsearcheducation/advanced-operators and for Bing at http://msdn.microsoft.com/en-us/library/ff795620.aspx. For most search engines, we can find an advanced operator listing by searching for the engine name and "advanced operators." Although we will likely find some variation in advanced query construction from one search engine to the next, the construction is often fairly similar. For example, if we wanted to search Google for pages on the Syngress.com website that contained the string "advanced operators" in the page text, we could put together a search string like:

```
http://www.google.com/search?hl=en&lr=&ie=UTF-8&oe=UTF-8&
q=intext: "advanced operators" site:syngress.com
```

More specific to security-related issues, we can also construct searches like:

```
http://www.google.com/search?hl=en&lr=&ie=UTF-8&oe=UTF-8&
q=intext: "enable secret 5$"
```

Such searches will often locate configuration files for Cisco devices that contain the encrypted (and easily decrypted) administrative passwords for the device in question [3]. Such configuration files can also contain IP addresses for the networks on which they rest, effectively giving the keys to the kingdom to the entirety of the Internet.

Quite a bit of very specific information pertaining to these types of searches is available for public consumption. The book *Google Hacking for Penetration Testers, Volume 2* (ISBN: 978-1-59749-176-1, Syngress) by Johnny Long is an entire volume dedicated to this specific subject. Also available from and maintained by the same author is the Google Hacking Database (GHDB) at http://www.hackersforcharity.org/ghdb/. The GHDB contains a wide variety of security specific searches and makes them available to the public through a few simple clicks.

The Deep Web

When search engines crawl the Internet to construct the indexes on which their search results are based, they touch only the very surface of the information that is available. Great unexplored depths of information exist unplumbed due to the nature of such indexing. When we are conducting research on a target, we may very well like to see some of this information.

In recent years, several specialized search engines, such as Shodan,[a] have come into being to provide access to some portion of this hidden information. These search engines are generally rather specialized in the information that they provide.

Whois

Whois is a tool used to query the globally distributed set of databases that contain the information regarding domain names around the world. The databases contain information

---

[a]http://www.shodanhq.com

FIGURE 6.1 A Whois query from the command line.

regarding when the domain was registered or last updated, which registrar it was registered with, contact information for the owners of the domain, and the name servers that are used to resolve requests sent to the domain name. We can see part of the reply from a basic whois query in Figure 6.1. One of the more interesting items of information displayed here is the nameserver to which the domain name is directed, which will lead us to additional information in the next section.

The information displayed in Figure 6.1 is the result of a command line whois query, a tool often found in Linux and Unix operating systems, but not so common in others, such as those distributed by Microsoft. We can also run such queries through a variety of web pages dedicated to such purposes, one of the more common being whois.net.

In some cases, the contact information found in the data returned from whois queries will contain a great deal of useful information, such as a physical address, phone number, and contact name from someone directly associated with the domain. Such information can be used as the basis for conducting searches for additional information when researching a target. In recent years, however, it has become more common for domains to be registered through a service that acts as a proxy for domain contact information, thus hiding the actual contact information for those associated with the domain.

In addition to conducting whois queries on domain names, we can also run queries on IP addresses. The information from these queries is returned from the databases maintained by the Regional Internet Registries (RIR), who keep track of IP address assignments for their particular regions. The RIRs are distributed as follows:

• North America and some of the surrounding regions—American Registry for Internet Numbers (ARIN).

```
                            root@kali: ~                              _ □ ×

  File  Edit  View  Search  Terminal  Help
 root@kali:~# whois 66.33.206.206
 #
 # The following results may also be obtained via:
 # http://whois.arin.net/rest/nets;q=66.33.206.206?showDetails=true&showARIN=fals
 e&ext=netref2
 #

 NetRange:      66.33.192.0 - 66.33.223.255
 CIDR:          66.33.192.0/19
 OriginAS:
 NetName:       DREAMHOST-BLK1
 NetHandle:     NET-66-33-192-0-1
 Parent:        NET-66-0-0-0-0
 NetType:       Direct Allocation
 Comment:       ADDRESSES WITHIN THIS BLOCK ARE NON-PORTABLE
 Comment:       ** For abuse issues, please contact abuse@dreamhost.com **
 RegDate:       2002-04-26
 Updated:       2012-03-02
 Ref:           http://whois.arin.net/rest/net/NET-66-33-192-0-1

 OrgName:       New Dream Network, LLC
 OrgId:         NDN
 Address:       417 Associated Rd.
 Address:       PMB #257
```

FIGURE 6.2   A Whois query on an IP address.

- Europe, the Middle East, and some of Asia—Réseaux IP Européens Network Coordination Centre (RIPE NCC).
- Asia Pacific—Asia Pacific Network Information Centre (APNIC).
- Latin America and the Caribbean—Latin American and Caribbean Internet Address Registry (LACNIC).
- Africa—AfriNIC.

Shown in Figure 6.2 are some of the results of an IP address query against an IP controlled by ARIN.

We can also conduct such queries based on information other than an IP address, such as a point of contact or an organization name.

DNS

Given the nameservers of our target from the whois queries that we have conducted, we can query them for still more information. The DNSs are responsible for fulfilling name resolution requests for clients that are attempting to resolve the domain name to an IP address.

Numerous tools are available to aid us in our quest for DNS information. We can conduct command line queries in most operating systems by using the nslookup command, shown in Figure 6.3. Nslookup will generally return the IP address of the DNS server, which we can then interrogate for additional information.

Ideally, we would like to conduct a zone transfer against the DNS server, causing it to send us a complete copy of the record that it has, and allowing us to get a fairly complete view of

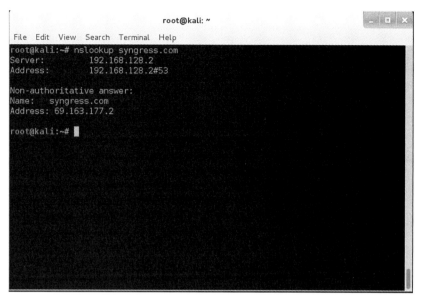

FIGURE 6.3 Nslookup information for Syngress.com.

the machines that it knows. In some cases, we can still use nslookup for this purpose. In Windows, we can do this with an interactive mode command like:

```
nslookup
> server [DNS server name or IP]
> set type=any
> ls -d [domain name]
```

In most cases, this will fail to return the information we are looking for, as DNS servers will not generally perform a zone transfer to an arbitrary requestor on the Internet. Additionally, nslookup may have the zone transfer functionality disabled in some operating systems. A similar tool to nslookup, called dig, can be found on most Linux systems and is capable of conducting zone transfers where the DNS server in question is willing to cooperate.

Even in the case of not being able to get a full zone transfer from a DNS server, we can still query other useful information. In Figure 6.4, we can see the results of a dig query asking for the MX records for the domain syngress.com. In this case, we now have a starting point for further investigation on this domain, as we have located its mail server.

As with the whois records, DNS information can also be requested from a variety of public servers on the Internet. One of many sites that provide such functionality is dnsquery.org. Additionally, a variety of other tools exist to query DNS servers, even to the point of brute forcing through possible subdomain and hostnames, using tools such as dnsenum.

Metadata

Metadata is data about data. For instance, if we have a file containing the text of this chapter, and the file has a file size, last accessed timestamp, and bits set for file permissions, none of

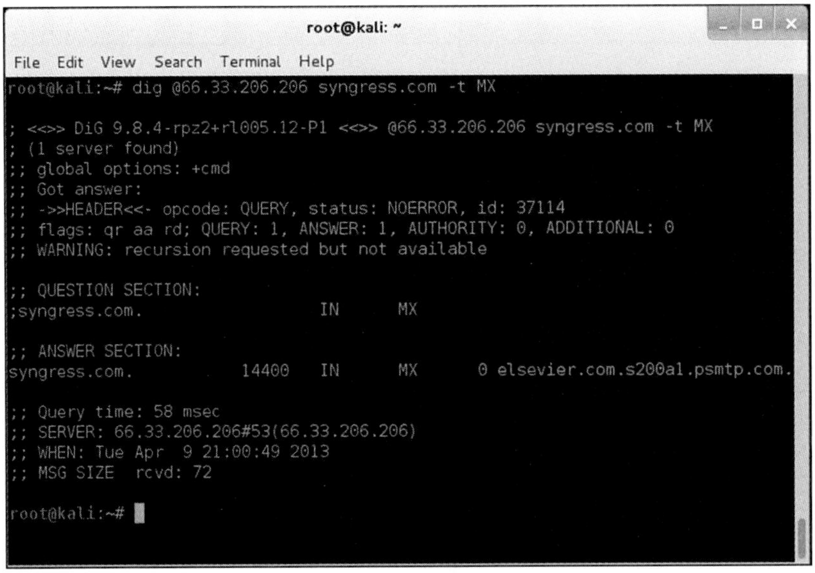

FIGURE 6.4 Dig information for Syngress.com.

this data has anything directly to do with the contents of the file itself, but is data about the file storing the text. Although such information may seem to be rather mundane outside of digital forensics circles, some of the information contained in document or image metadata may be very interesting indeed. We may find items such as the usernames that have edited the file, paths where the file has been stored, previous revisions of the text, coordinates that indicate where a picture was taken, image thumbnails, or any of hundreds of other items of information, all stored in the file with the actual intended content.

Metagoofil

Metagoofil is an excellent tool for hunting down metadata. Metagoofil is a script that conducts very directed Google searches, using some of the advance operators that we discussed earlier in the Google hacking section of this chapter, to locate documents that are stored on the web servers of a given domain name. In Figure 6.5, we can see the launch of a Metagoofil search on the domain syngress.com.

Once these documents have been located, they are downloaded and parsed for interesting information in the document metadata, which is then displayed in html format for easy perusal of the user.

Exiftool

Exiftool is another wonderful tool for extracting metadata from documents and images. Exiftool is named for a type of metadata, called EXIF data that is normally attached to image files. This data can include information regarding the equipment that the image was created on, including serial numbers, thumbnails of the original image, coordinates where the image was created, for GPS-enabled devices, and a host of other information.

FIGURE 6.5   Metagoofil information for Syngress.com.

WARNING

When taking pictures on most GPS-enabled devices, including almost all modern cell phones, and quite a few cameras, the location information is often embedded in the EXIF data of the image file. On some devices, this functionality cannot be disabled without disabling the GPS entirely. When posting images for public consumption, it is always a good idea to review the EXIF data beforehand to see what exactly we will be sharing.

Strings

Strings is a utility that will parse a given file for strings of text, generally consisting of several printable characters in a row. Strings can be very helpful in finding data hidden in files, even data, such as deleted content, which may not be accessible through normal applications that are used to access and manipulate the file. Strings is a common tool on Linux and Unix distributions and is available as a download for Microsoft operating systems.

We can use strings to locate metadata not only in documents and images, but also in a variety of other files as well. Although some of the other metadata-centric tools may be more efficient at finding known metadata, strings will find all of the strings in a given file. We may get back quite a bit of irrelevant or useless data, but we will likely get back all of the data that is in the file in plaintext.

Maltego

Throughout this section, we have discussed a number of types of data that can be helpful when conducting reconnaissance on a target. We have also talked about a number of tools that can be used to collect various items of such information. Several tools exist that can collect multiple items of information, but one particular tool shines in this particular area: Maltego from Paterva. Maltego allows us to start with a particular item of information, such as an email address, phone number, or IP address and use this information as the basis to collect other information. In Maltego, such links between information are referred to as transforms and can be very powerful for collecting large amounts of information in a very short period of time. A screenshot of the results of such a search can be seen in Figure 6.6, using a domain name as the basis for a search.

Maltego is available in both free and commercial editions, varying largely in the information available and what can be done with the information once it is discovered. Maltego often returns information that would have required a considerable amount of manual searching to discover.

Defense

Defense against the various tools that can be used for reconnaissance against a target generally revolves around one simple concept: limit the sources of data and the data that is available from each source to the greatest extent that is reasonable. Although it may not always be feasible to completely sever the flow of outgoing data, and in some cases may be outright harmful to do so, we can certainly attempt to keep a handle on the information that we do allow out.

In the case of information gained from general data found on websites, we can limit the information to a certain extent, but, in the case of a business, we cannot afford to be without such methods of communication. We can, however, be careful not to release overly detailed information, particularly in cases where we can very easily leak information, such as the job postings that we discussed earlier in this section. We can also implement policy in organizations to guide those who might post sensitive information to internal or external websites or social networking sites.

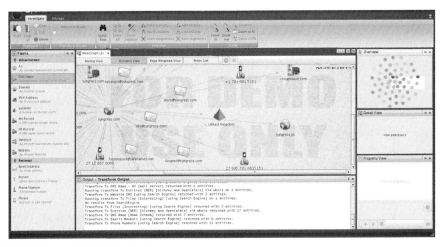

FIGURE 6.6   Maltego information for Syngress.com.

For information that might be gained from DNS servers, we are somewhat limited in the steps that we can take to not over share our data. We can deny zone transfers to unknown machines, so as to not give our information away wholesale. We can also use domain registration and hosting services that are willing to proxy our actual information so that we do not share network or company data that might be of use to an attacker. Such actions might not always be appropriate for a business environment, as we may not wish to hide this information from our customers, depending on our line of business.

Data leakage via metadata is one area in which, at least from a technical perspective, we can easily limit what we are sharing to the outside world. Recent versions of many tools that are used to produce documents these days, such as Microsoft Word or Adobe Acrobat, have functionality built into the application to scrub the metadata from them before they are released externally. These tools often do a very good job, but it often pays to check with a secondary source, such as the strings utility, just in case something was missed. As images often do not undergo the same processing as a document before they are used, we will also want to use something along the lines of Exiftool to ensure that we have not inadvertently included any information that we did not intend to.

SCANNING TOOLS

Scanning tools are the category of tools that we use to find more information about our target environment, the systems within it, and the details of those systems. With such tools, we can be very general, in the case of running ping sweeps; somewhat more specific, in the case of running port scans; or very specific, in the case of grabbing banners or enumerating users on particular systems.

Given the limits of our discussion on tools in this chapter, we have grouped network mapping, port scanning, and enumeration tools together in one section. Each of these areas could deservedly be the focus of its own chapter, but we will go over some of the highlights here.

Nmap

Nmap is a wonderful tool. It is principally a port scanner, but can do quite a bit more as well. It can be used to ping IPs, detect vulnerabilities, fingerprint operating systems, run traceroutes, and much more. Almost all of the uses to which nmap can be put can also be tweaked in various ways to avoid detection, alter the speed at which it carries out its processes, change methods of communication, and more. Nmap is truly a versatile tool. Additionally, nmap is a free tool and ships with many Linux and Unix operating systems. Nmap is also available for Windows. In addition to the command line version that we will be looking at in this section, there are also a variety of GUIs that can be used as a frontend to nmap, including Zenmap which was created by the author of nmap.

Depending on what our actual goal is when running nmap, we might construct a command in a variety of ways. To do a basic ping sweep of a subnet, we might do something like this:

```
nmap -nsP -n 10.0.0.1-254
```

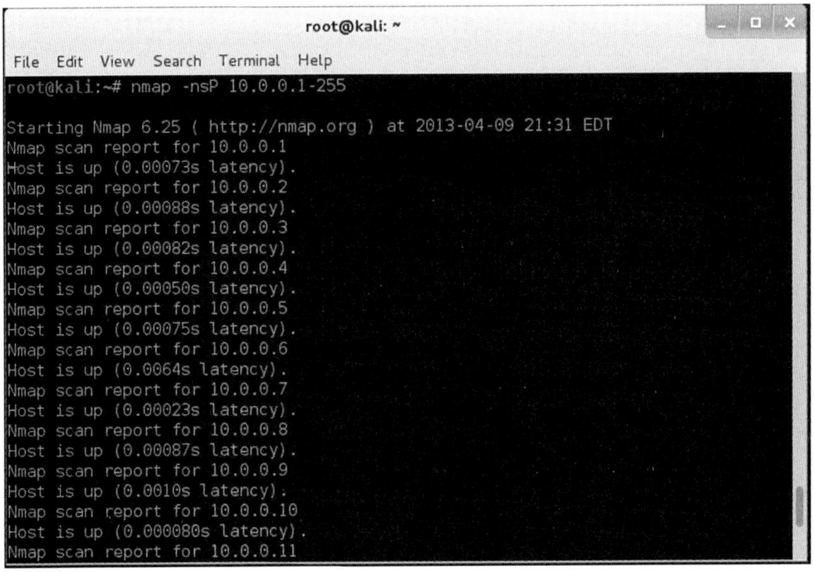

FIGURE 6.7   Nmap scan results.

This example performs a basic probe of each IP in the specified range to see if anything responds (-sP), and does not attempt to resolve names (-n), which will speed us up a bit. We can see the results in Figure 6.7. If we wanted to get a little more information back, we could alter our command to conduct a ping sweep, like so:

```
nmap -nsT 10.0.0.247
```

This will both probe each IP to see if anything responds and conduct a port scan using the default settings when a device is found (-sT). By default, nmap will scan the 1000 most commonly used ports. As we can see from Figure 6.8, this returns us quite a bit of useful information.

When running both the ping sweep and the port scan, we can see quite a bit of difference in the amount of time that each takes. Given the small range of IPs that we are scanning, the ping sweep will likely return in a minute or so, whereas the port scan could take hours.

TIP

Although an nmap scan is running, we can press enter (or one of several other keys) in the terminal window to get an estimated time of completion. We can watch the flow of packets that nmap is sending by pressing p in the terminal window to enable packet tracing. To switch back to the normal nmap mode, press shift + p.

We can continue to add complexity to our nmap searches by adding additional features and can indeed spend quite a bit of time constructing complex nmap commands. One compound switch that incorporates several of the others is the -A switch:

```
nmap -A 10.0.0.1-254
```

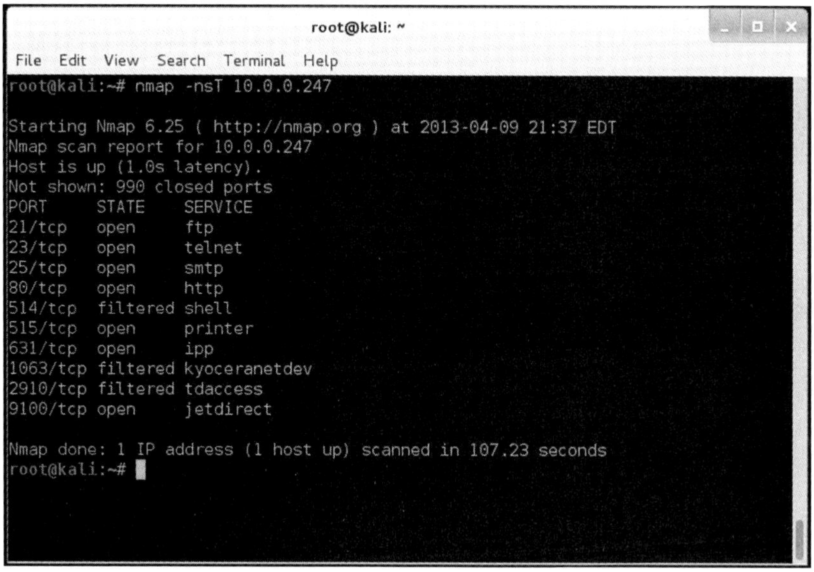

```
                        root@kali: ~                    _  □  X

 File  Edit  View  Search  Terminal  Help
root@kali:~# nmap -nsT 10.0.0.247

Starting Nmap 6.25 ( http://nmap.org ) at 2013-04-09 21:37 EDT
Nmap scan report for 10.0.0.247
Host is up (1.0s latency).
Not shown: 990 closed ports
PORT       STATE     SERVICE
21/tcp     open      ftp
23/tcp     open      telnet
25/tcp     open      smtp
80/tcp     open      http
514/tcp    filtered  shell
515/tcp    open      printer
631/tcp    open      ipp
1063/tcp   filtered  kyoceranetdev
2910/tcp   filtered  tdaccess
9100/tcp   open      jetdirect

Nmap done: 1 IP address (1 host up) scanned in 107.23 seconds
root@kali:~# █
```

FIGURE 6.8   Nmap scan results.

This will execute a scan of our IP range while conducting OS fingerprinting and version detection against the 1000 most common ports.

The examples above only just scratch the surface of nmap's capabilities. There are many more switches that enable various features and functionality, without even getting beyond the standard portions of the tool. In addition to this, we can use the Nmap Scripting Engine (NSE) to extend the functionality of nmap to do other interesting things. The author of nmap, Fyodor, has written an excellent book on the wide variety of things that we can make this tool do called Nmap Network Scanning: The Official Nmap Project Guide to Network Discovery and Security Scanning—ISBN-13: 978-0979958717. This is a highly recommended reference for those that use nmap frequently.

Nessus

Nessus is primarily a vulnerability scanning tool, but, as we discussed with nmap, a variety of other features have crept in over the years in order to add to its utility. Nesssus was, once upon a time, an entirely free and open source tool. In 2005, Nessus was changed to a closed source license, and certain features were restricted to the commercial version. A free version is still available, but is limited in the circumstances under which it may be used and the vulnerability listing that it is allowed to access. An alternative open source solution has been created, which we will discuss later in this section.

Nessus classifies vulnerabilities into sets of plugins, with each family of plugins focusing on a particular type of vulnerability. These families include a variety of different operating systems, databases, protocols, and services. The professional plugin feed includes swift

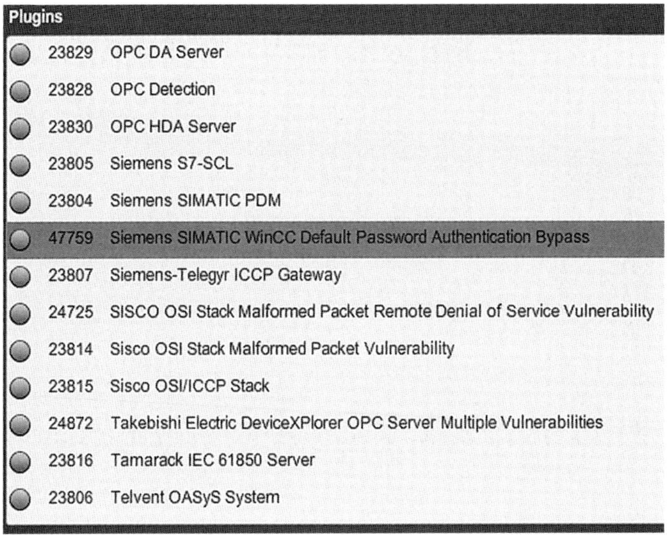

FIGURE 6.9   Nessus SCADA plugins.

access to the newest plugins, and some reserved categories of plugins as well, such as those for detecting vulnerabilities in Supervisory Control and Data Acquisition (SCADA) systems, as shown in Figure 6.9.

> **NOTE**
>
> As of the time of writing, the full impact and activities of the Stuxnet worm are still being discovered. For the latest information on Stuxnet, check into the most recent documentation from any of the major antivirus vendors.

The easiest way to use Nessus, due to the complexity of the product, is through the GUI. Although earlier versions of the Nessus client featured a self-contained client, the current version, as of this writing, is accessible through a web browser. In Figure 6.10, we can see a partially completed Nessus scan, showing the machines located; the current state of completion for the scan of each device; the number of vulnerabilities in the high, medium, and low categories; and the number of open ports on each device.

Drilling down into a specific device, as shown in Figure 6.11, we can then see the information for the specific ports found, the services in use on these ports, the count of vulnerabilities related to the particular service, again segmented into high, medium, and low categories of risk. At this level, we can start to get a better idea of how a given machine might be vulnerable to attack, and start to formulate a more specific strategy for attacking it.

From here we can step down to the listing of all of the vulnerabilities on a given service for the device in question. This will give us yet another level of specificity for where the gaps in security might be, but the truly interesting bits are one level further down still, in the specific vulnerability detail, as shown in Figure 6.12. This detailed listing will give us a specific

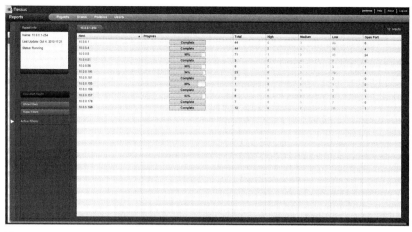

FIGURE 6.10 Nessus scan in progress.

Port ▲	Protocol	SVC Name	Total	High
0	udp	general	1	0
0	tcp	general	7	0
0	icmp	general	1	0
137	udp	netbios-ns	1	0
139	tcp	smb	2	0
445	tcp	cifs	14	2
1900	udp	upnp-client	1	0
3689	tcp	www	3	0
5353	udp	mdns	1	0

FIGURE 6.11 Nessus port scan results.

FIGURE 6.12 Nessus vulnerability listing.

description of how the vulnerability might be used to attack the device, as well as references to other possible sources of information.

If we wish to extend or automate the functionality of Nessus, the Nessus Attack Scripting Language (NASL) enables us to do so. This also allows us good access to run Nessus through the command line. For those interested in NASL and more in-depth coverage on Nessus in general, an excellent book on the topic is *Nessus Network Auditing, Second Edition* (ISBN: 978-1-59749-208-9, Syngress) by Russ Rogers.

For those looking for an open source alternative to Nessus, there is a Nessus variant called the Open Vulnerability Assessment System (OpenVAS). OpenVAS is a fork of Nessus from when the product was open source, thus sharing many of its characteristics. OpenVAS is largely compatible with the standard Nessus plugins, as well as being able to use custom plugins written in NASL. OpenVAS also offers its own plugin feed to the public, containing many of the same or similar plugins that are available from the Nessus plugin feed. Comparison tests have been done between Nessus and OpenVAS which, although declaring Nessus to be the superior product, noted that OpenVAS still performed well and was a reasonable alternative [4].

Defense

Protecting information from scanners can be a difficult prospect. If a scanner is positioned in such a way as to have network access, or be able to eavesdrop on network traffic, particularly if the target is exposed to the Internet, then we are likely vulnerable to scanning attacks. A common maxim in martial arts is that "the best defense is to not be there" [5]. This concept directly applies to preventing information leakage to scanners. In our case, not being there means not sending traffic out in ways that it is easily visible to unauthorized listeners, not running services on standard ports, not sending unencrypted traffic, and any of a number of similar hardening measures.

Many scanning tools depend on services existing on common ports and open access to information to generate their reports. In many cases, until a version scan has been attempted, scanning tools will report a service to be running based on the associated port being open. For example, if the scanner finds a port open on 21, it will generally assume that the service behind it is FTP. Changing these basic parameters in an environment can very quickly invalidate the information being returned by a scanning tool and can force the attacker to put quite a bit more time and effort into discovering what exactly is running on a given device.

ACCESS AND ESCALATION TOOLS

A great number of the hacking and penetration testing tools available, both open source and commercial, are focused on gaining access to systems and escalating our level of privilege once we are able to access the system. There are far too many tools for us to discuss any number of them individually, so we will cover some of the more common and more popular tools in this section.

Password Tools

As poorly constructed passwords are all too common, password attack tools are a good place to start when attempting to access a machine or get into an account with a higher level of privilege. Two of the most common tools used when conducting such attacks are Hydra and John the Ripper.

Hydra[b] is a tool for conducting password guessing over a variety of services and protocols. Hydra can run on a variety of operating systems and from the command line or GUI, as shown in Figure 6.13.

Hydra can be used with single usernames and passwords, or can work from lists of either or both. Given a weak password policy on the target system, and a reasonable password list to work from, we stand a reasonable chance of guessing the password for an account, given enough time to do so. With a bit of searching, we can find password lists containing default

FIGURE 6.13   Hydra GUI.

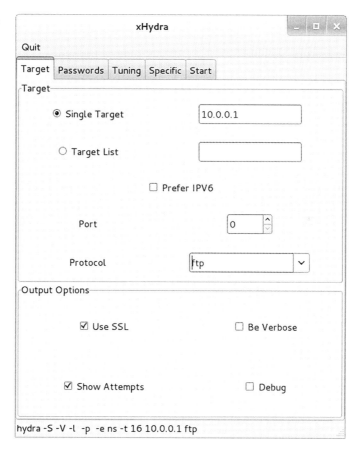

[b]http://freeworld.thc.org/

passwords for a variety of hardware devices,[c] or common passwords in a number of languages.[d]

John the Ripper[e] takes a slightly different approach to attacking passwords. Instead of guessing passwords from a list, as Hydra does, it takes the encrypted form of the password, commonly referred to as a password hash, and attempts to recover the password from this. Password hashes are mathematical functions that are, when properly implemented, generally considered impossible to reverse. We can work around this, when we know what hashing algorithm has been used, by using the known algorithm to hash a variety of guesses as to what the password might be, until we find a matching hash. At this point we now know what the password represented by the hash is. John the Ripper, commonly known as John, can perform this exercise with password hashes from many operating systems and can run on a variety of operating systems as well.

The Metasploit Project

The Metasploit Project[f] is a well-known collection of open source security tools, launched by HD Moore in 2003. In 2009, Metasploit was acquired by Rapid7, and now enjoys greatly increased funding for development. This has led to Metasploit branching out into more fully featured commercial versions, in addition to continued development on the original free tools. Metasploit is, at the time of this writing, available in three main versions: the free Metasploit Framework and the commercial Metasploit versions, Express and Pro.

The Metasploit Framework

The Metasploit Framework is the free offering of Metasploit and, prior to the Rapid7 acquisition, was the only version available. Framework is primarily intended to be used as a command line tool. Although there is a rudimentary GUI available, it does not offer access to the full might of the toolset that is available from the command line, as shown in Figure 6.14.

The process of using Framework to attack a system is, in broad strokes:

- Collect information about the target system using scanning and vulnerability assessment tools, such as nmap and Nessus
- Select an exploit that matches the system based on the collected information
- Select a payload to accompany the exploit, often a remote shell
- Execute the exploit and payload

Framework offers, at the time of this writing over 600 exploits with over 200 payloads that can be used in conjunction with them. Framework also supports more advance attacks, such as proxy pivoting, communication with other tools, such as Nessus, via Extensible Markup

[c]http://www.phenoelit-us.org/dpl/dpl.html

[d]http://www.cyberwarzone.com/cyberwarfare/password-cracking-mega-collection-password-cracking-word-lists

[e]http://www.openwall.com/john/

[f]http://www.metasploit.com/

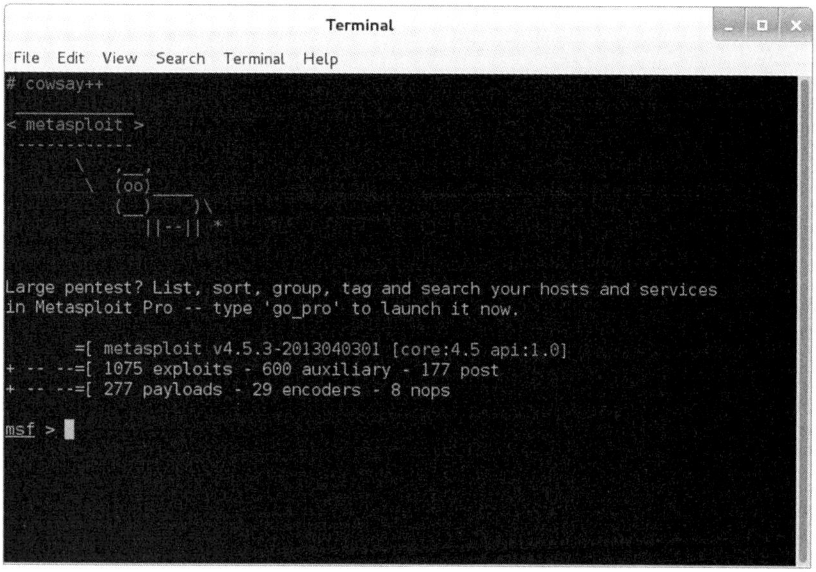

FIGURE 6.14   Metasploit framework.

Language Remote Procedure Call (XML-RPC), and extensibility through the Ruby language, which the current version of Metasploit is developed in. Framework has a truly massive set of functionality, much of it contributed by the security community, and is an extremely versatile tool.

Metasploit Express and Metasploit Pro

In 2010, we saw the arrival of commercial Metasploit offerings, which are, of course, not free. Metasploit Express, the first released commercial Metasploit version, contains all of the functionality of Framework, but adds a number of new features. One of the most immediately apparent features in Metasploit Express and Pro is the implementation of a fully featured GUI, as shown in Figure 6.15.

In addition to the functionality that is provided by Framework, Express adds a number of features designed to automate and ease the use of Metasploit in larger attack or penetration testing environments. Express includes automation for network discovery, attacks against accounts, and the use of exploits. Additionally, for use in team environments, Express adds workflow features, evidence collection and audit, and improved reporting tools. Being a commercial tool, support arrangements are also available for users of the tool.

Metasploit Pro is the latest addition, to the Metasploit family. Pro has all of the features and functionality of Framework and Express, with the addition of the ability to do Virtual Private Network (VPN) pivoting and web server scanning and exploitation, as well as additional features that allow better team collaboration and reporting.

The leap in functionality between Express and Pro is really oriented at those that would use the tool in larger environment where multiple people or teams of people are attacking closely

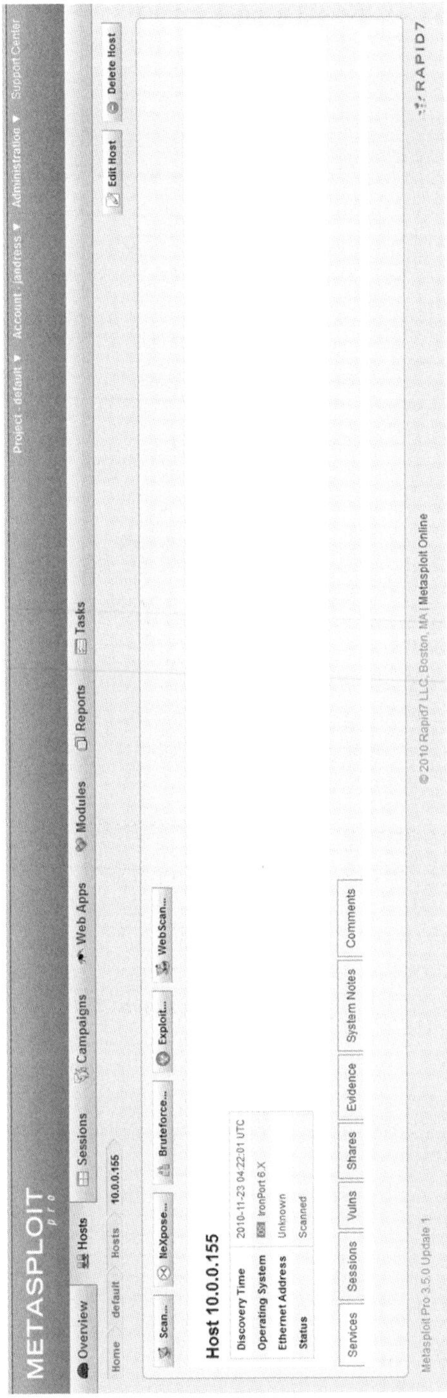

FIGURE 6.15 Metasploit Pro.

related targets. One of the gaps in the Metasploit tools has always been what to do with the information and access once it is gained, and Pro addresses this issue directly.

Immunity CANVAS

CANVAS Professional[g] from Immunity is a tool that enables access and exploitation of systems in a semi-automated or automated fashion. CANVAS contains a good selection of exploits and payloads (around 300 exploits at the time of this writing), as well as a number of exploit packages from third parties that allow access to truly bleeding edge exploits. Although some might point out that CANVAS does not have as large of a library of exploits as some of the other tools, it does tend to be updated very quickly to include some of the newer and more interesting exploits soon after, or in some cases before, they are publicly released.

CANVAS is developed in Python, and includes both GUI, as shown in Figure 6.16, and command line interfaces. In addition to some of the other functionality that we expect from this class of tools, such as pivoting (Immunity calls it bouncing), network scanning, client side attack tools, and other functionality, CANVAS also includes some more unique features.

One such feature that some might find convenient is the geolocation and mapping feature, allowing target systems to be displayed on a world map within the interface. Additionally, CANVAS has several areas in which the GUI can be used to display graphical

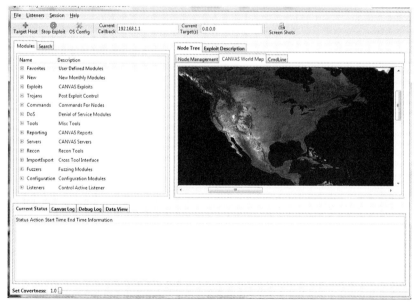

FIGURE 6.16   Immunity CANVAS.

[g]http://www.immunitysec.com/products-canvas.shtml

tools, such as VisualSploit for graphically building exploits, or GUI tools that can be used to explore remote file systems. Being written in Python, CANVAS is also a highly configurable tool and can be tweaked by the savvy user. Immunity prides themselves on producing a tool that is intended for use by experienced security professionals. It is extremely versatile, but like any good tool, has some sharp edges that the inexperienced wielder should be wary of.

Defense

Defenses against access and escalation tools largely revolve around well-written and implemented password policy, patching, and system hardening. All are common and well-known security techniques, and are, in theory, some of the most basic security measures that we can put in place when securing our environment, but they are not as ubiquitously implemented as we might think.

Protection against password guessing and cracking tools largely revolves around ensuring that we have strong passwords in place. The common standard for strong passwords is: minimum length of eight characters, at least one uppercase character, at least one lowercase character, at least one number, and at least one symbol. Although this may seem excessive to some, we can see the difference in using such a password versus a more simple password quite easily.

An eight-character password using only lowercase and uppercase characters has 200 billion possible combinations. Given a reasonably powerful workstation (100,000,000 guesses per second), we could brute force our way through all of the possible combinations in around 30 min. Using the stronger password scheme that we specified above (uppercase, lowercase, numbers, symbols), our eight-character password has 7.2 quadrillion combinations and would take a little over 2 years to brute force [6]. Increasing the password length and adding additional character sets continues this trend, and can quickly make password guessing or cracking infeasible entirely, even for very powerful or distributed cracking tools.

Another key step to take, particularly in the case of defending against tools such as Metasploit or CANVAS, is to ensure that our systems are quickly patched. Many such tools can penetrate a system in a few seconds given unpatched vulnerabilities with which to work, and this is an easily avoidable situation. We can argue that installing application and operating system patches immediately after they are released is foolhardy and that we may cause more problems than we will fix, and this is likely true. We should absolutely take the time to test patches before we apply them, with exceptions to this being very few and far between. It is likely true that the exploits with which attackers gain entry to our systems will be older and more common, rather than cutting edge, but we should be patching for everything that we reasonably can, as soon as we can.

Lastly, we should harden our systems as much as we reasonably can and still allow them to execute their functions. The more ports, services, accounts, and so on that we leave enabled on a system, the larger attack surface that we present to those that would seek to compromise it. In many cases individual systems have very few tasks that require leaving outside access open, either incoming or outgoing, and closing down such potential methods of access greatly limits the set of tools that we leave for an attacker to utilize.

EXFILTRATION TOOLS

Exfiltrating data from an environment can be an interesting and challenging problem, particularly if the environment in question is secured against exactly the activities that we are attempting to carry out. In broad strokes, some of the main methods that we can use to exfiltrate data are to physically carry it out, to use steganography or encryption to disguise the data, to make use of common protocols that are normally allowed to leave the environment, or to use out of band methods.

Physical Exfiltration

Physical removal of data is one of the methods most proof against detection, even in the most carefully guarded environments. The shrinking size of storage media makes such methods even more easily hidden on a person or in equipment, with the latest, at the time of this writing, standard for microSDXC memory cards topping out at a theoretical limit of 2 TB of storage and with dimensions of 11×15 mm at 1 mm thick, roughly the size of a fingernail [7]. Given the ability to store such amounts of data in a package so small, items to be exfiltrated could be secreted nearly anywhere and are beyond the reasonable realm of detection, even in the case of an extensive physical search.

Encryption and Steganography

Various tools exist for hiding data in formats that are not immediately visible to casual search, or in some cases, even to exhaustive search. Encryption tools in general can be useful for hiding data in such a fashion, rendering the data with which we are concerned potentially invisible, or at least unreadable. Certain encryption tools, TrueCrypt[h] for instance, can create encrypted volumes on storage media which appear to be random noise on the media and are neither detectable nor recoverable without the proper keys or passwords. Such a volume could easily be created on portable storage media, such as a flash drive or MP3 player and would appear to be empty space.

Steganography is the science of creating messages that are hidden from those that do not already know that they exist. Such methods have existed from time immemorial, using special inks, works of art, and numerous other methods, but the age of computers has provided us with a far more suitable and information dense media in the mass of information that flow around the globe on a daily basis. Files which contain a certain amount of noise, such as graphic, video, or audio files can be used to encode information within them without altering the presentation of the file contents to the point of being detectable to the naked eye.

Steganography tools such as OpenPuff[i] or OutGuess[j] can make secreting such data in digital files a relatively simple task. Once hidden in such a file, our data can be exfiltrated by placing an image on an externally facing web server, in a background graphic or logo attached to an email, or even in an audio message transmitted over a Voice over IP (VoIP) connection.

[h]http://www.truecrypt.org/

[i]http://embeddedsw.net/OpenPuff_Steganography_Home.html

[j]http://www.outguess.org/info.php

Using Common Protocols

Even in highly secure environments, there are likely to be a few protocols, perhaps closely monitored, that are allowed to leave the environment. We can generally find Hypertext Transfer Protocol (HTTP) and the various email protocols to be allowed some degree of freedom, as well as protocols that are more infrastructure related such as Domain Name System (DNS) and Dynamic Host Configuration Protocol (DHCP). We can simply, in the case of mail protocols, ship our information out in encoded and in small pieces, or if need be, we can tunnel over various protocols, using tools such as OzymanDNS.[k]

In some cases where the use of our favored protocols is prohibited, we can even create a tunnel to move Secure Shell (SSH) over HTTP using utilities such as Corkscrew,[l] and utilize the provided proxy server to exfiltrate our data. Given an unmolested SSH connection to the outside world, we can accomplish a great number of tasks, including exfiltrating our data.

Out of Band Methods

We can use a number of methods that step outside of the purview of the security and detection mechanisms that are put in place in order to prevent the leakage or deliberate exfiltration of data. In the case of application or host level security that would use any number of technical controls in order to prevent data from leaving the system in an unauthorized fashion, we need merely to move to methods that such systems are not capable of detecting or controlling. For such systems, we can hand copy data onto paper, take pictures of the information on the display, memorize the data for later retrieval, or any number of similar methods. Such methods can be very simple or very complex, depending on the density of the information that needs to be communicated, and could be as simple as leaving a light turned on during the day or closing the blinds in a window. Such methods are highly effective and can be extremely difficult to detect when properly executed.

Defense

Defending against exfiltration of information can be a very difficult task, depending largely on the inherent security posture of the environment. Preventing data exfiltration other than in the most egregious cases can be all but impossible, especially in a standard corporate setting, where personnel are able to move freely in and out of the environment, in both a physical and a logical sense, at will and are not prohibited from bringing personal electronics devices into the environment and not searched when entering or leaving the premises. In such environments, there are so many avenues, both physical and logical, that could be used to move data out that we will never be able to protect them all without making major changes.

The answer to this issue is to move to a more secure footing, such as what we would find in the environments used by many militaries and governments. In such environments, the

[k]http://dankaminsky.com/2004/07/29/51/

[l]http://www.agroman.net/corkscrew/

activities of personnel, both physical and logical, are very restricted and closely monitored. Additionally, personnel are often much more tightly screened before being allowed access to the environment at all, often in the form of extensive background check and security clearances. In any case, if a determined attacker is able to penetrate the environment in a physical or logical fashion and is sufficiently patient and persistent, they will likely find a way eventually to exfiltrate the data that they are interested in removing.

SUSTAINMENT TOOLS

Once we have gained access to a system and reached the desired level of access, we will likely want to ensure that we can continue to access the system in the future. Although we may have been able to successfully use a particular vulnerability or similar means to access the system in the first place, we cannot necessarily depend on the same hole to still exist in the future.

Adding "Authorized" Access

One of the simplest and, at times, most effective means of securing our access to a system is to add ourselves to the list of users that is legitimately allowed access. This is typically accomplished with built-in operating system commands such as `useradd` on Unix-like systems and the `netuser` command on Windows systems. In addition to adding simple users, we can also create additional access to applications, networks, and any number of other systems in the environment. Although such access may eventually be audited and removed in many environments that do not operate on an enhanced security posture this may not happen for several years, if ever.

We can see an example of such a tactic in the TJX breach that occurred in 2006. Once the TJX systems were penetrated, the attackers were able to install accounts on Internet accessible applications in order to access the information that they wished to obtain [8]. At this point, the vulnerabilities that originally allowed the attack to be successful were no longer a weak point in maintaining access to the environment, as they were then able to enter through the virtual front door of the system.

Backdoors

Adding backdoors to a system or application is another method that we can use in order to sustain our access. A great variety of such backdoors exist for any number of applications, and an attacker with a good knowledge of programming can easily create custom varieties. One useful set of web-based backdoors can be found in the Web Malware Compilation,[m] which is also included in recent versions of the Backtrack/Kali Linux distributions[no].

[m]https://code.google.com/p/web-malware-collection/

[n]http://www.backtrack-linux.org/downloads/

[o]http://www.kali.org/downloads/

There are many subtle ways that we can use to create backdoors on systems, but the old standby tool netcat can perform this task for us very nicely. Versions of netcat can be found for many operating systems, and it can often be found to already exist on many Unix-like operating systems. Creating a listening port that will allow us access to a shell on the system with netcat is very simple and can be accomplished with a command on Linux such as:

```
nc -l -p 1234 -e /bin/bash
```

And we can accomplish the same on Windows with a slight tweak, like so:

```
Nc -l -p 1234 -e cmd.exe
```

In each case, we are telling netcat to listen for connections on port 1234 and to execute a program that will give the connecting client a shell. Although the listening process will be obvious to any administrator who takes the time to look for odd processes or ports being listened on, clever naming of the tool and selection of the port number can help to minimize this. Additionally, the command can be run as a scheduled job, set to run when the system boots, or a variety of other methods to ensure that the backdoor stays in place. More on backdoors using netcat can be found in *Netcat Power Tools* (ISBN: 978-1-59749-257-7, Syngress).

Defense

Defending against backdoors being inserted requires a twofold approach. We first want to make sure that successfully inserting such backdoors is difficult to begin with. We can help to mitigate such attacks by ensuring that our systems and applications are as hardened as we can reasonably make them, and that both our outgoing and incoming traffic is as restricted as we can make it and still function properly. We can also lock down administrative access to our systems through the use of utilities such as powerbroker and Cisco Security Agent (CSA). These will help to prevent the insertion of backdoors and make a considerably more difficult task for those that are attempting to attach to them.

The second portion of defending against backdoor attacks is auditing. If we carefully audit accounts, system access, open ports, and other items that could be used to create a backdoor, we at least stand a chance of quickly catching anything that has been put in place. Unfortunately, this type of auditing is a time-consuming and thankless task, and so is not commonly implemented. In many environments, a subtly implemented backdoor many never be found, largely due to lack of anyone looking.

ASSAULT TOOLS

The tools that can be used to assault a compromised machine are many and varied. They can take the form of simple changes to configurations or environment variables on a system, to purpose-built botnets that can conduct a concentrated Denial of Service (DoS) attack on a given system or environment. Such tools of destruction can generally be categorized into those related to software or oriented on hardware.

Meddling with Software

Most software is not built to withstand deliberate tampering by authorized users, as such users are generally more interested in it functioning properly than in causing it to fail. Additionally, by the point that we have decided to use such tools, we have likely compromised the target machine already and have administrative rights, which allow such tampering to take place regardless of the software vendors wishes. Even in the cases where we might not have such rights, there are often still steps that we can take.

System Resources

System resources can often be affected, even by unprivileged users. Although such measures will be immediately obvious to anyone investigating the subsequent issues, such users can start a sufficient number of long-running processes as to use large amounts of system resources such as memory, CPU, and hard disk, thus preventing other processes from being able to access them. Any number of simple commands can be used to create such resource drains. In order to quickly fill a file system on a Unix-like operating system to the point of nonfunctionality we can use a command such as:

```
cat /dev/zero>file
```

This command will attempt to place the contents of /dev/zero, a never ending stream of zeros, into the file called file. Based on experimentation by the authors on an average system, this command will produce 4 GB of zeros in a little over a minute. Depending on where it is run in the file system and how much free space exists, this can bring a system to its virtual knees in a few minutes. Similar commands can be used to highly utilize the CPU and memory, and such tactics can also be used on Microsoft operating systems.

System Environment

Altering the system environment can also be used to throw a wrench in the works of many environments. Many applications, particularly in more complex cases, depend on a delicate balance of environment and operating system settings. Interfering with these settings can have a variety of deleterious effects on said software.

One such setting that can wreak havoc with systems in a variety of ways is to alter the way in which the system calculates time. Various tools depend on the system time being both correct and consistent over a period of time. When the system time is altered in either direction, sped up or slowed down, the system date is changed, or the time zone is incorrect for the location of the system, a multitude of effects that are generally undesirable to the system owners can ensue. For example, we could use the following:

```
tzutil/s "Ulaanbaatar Standard Time"
```

This command will change the time zone on a Windows system to that of the capital of Mongolia. This, for many countries, would change the system time considerably, and perhaps even the date. Changing such settings repeatedly would skew timestamps in logs, send times on email, entries in calendars, and any number of other places in which timestamps are utilized. This is a small change, but can have far-reaching effects.

There are a multitude of similar small changes that we can make. Another example is to change the `umask` setting on a database server. This command can change the permissions on newly created files. If the permissions are not exactly right on files that the database creates and uses, it will fail. It can be a rather difficult proposition to figure out what exactly has happened.

Across many operating systems, environment variables are used to hold a variety of information critical to keep the systems in working order. Environment variables hold information pointing to locations in the file system where various utilities are stored, where library files can be found, aliases to commands, and a multitude of other bits and pieces. Altering environment variables, depending on the variable in question, can very specifically effect an individual application, or can bring the entire operating system to a screeching halt. In addition, we have many other similar settings, such as those that alter the functionality of the operating system kernel, which behave similarly. If, on a Linux operating system we were to run:

```
# echo "fs.file-max=1" >> /etc/sysctl.conf
```

We would change the kernel parameter that specifies number of files that can be opened at once, across the entire operating system, to one file. Most busy systems will need to open something on the order of thousands of files at a time, so, of course, this will very quickly bring the system down once it takes effect.

Attacking Hardware

There are a variety of ways that we can attack computing and related hardware with the intent of disabling it in some fashion or other. In many items of hardware, we can find Read Only Memory (ROM) modules, consisting of electronically reprogrammable memory. Such ROMs often contain firmware that regulates how the specific piece of hardware functions or communicates with other hardware. Using somewhat universal ROM flashing tools, such as flashrom,[P] we can rewrite the contents of such modules in order to reprogram them to alter the functionality of the hardware, or, easier yet, to disable the hardware entirely. Using flashrom in particular, we can flash ROMs from remote on a variety of operating systems, presuming that we have administrative access.

Another easy way to disrupt hardware, although generally on a temporary basis, is to alter the software that controls communications with it. In the sense of drivers, we can fairly easily disrupt the files of which they are composed. Usually, this will be sufficient to prevent the device from being used until the driver is reinstalled, potentially requiring physical access to the machine to do so. On a somewhat more simple level, we can alter the way that the software talks to the hardware, often through the use of configuration files. We can change the settings of videos cards in order to temporarily render displays nonfunctional, disrupt a hard disk array by changing its composition, or any number of other small changes. As we said, such changes are unlikely to have any long-term effects on the hardware itself, but may have profound effects on the systems that depend on the availability of that hardware.

[P]http://www.flashrom.org/Flashrom

One of the most impactful ways that we can presently hold up as an example for potential outright hardware damage is in interfering with SCADA systems. Much supposition has been done about the potential for damage to such systems, and there are a few examples. An excellent example, discovered in July of 2010, occurrence was shown to exist in the Stuxnet worm. In addition to the other effects of Stuxnet, which we will discuss at greater length in Chapter 8, Stuxnet appears to interfere with the frequency of the motors that are used in the gas centrifuges used to enrich uranium. Not only can this impede the uranium enrichment process, but it can also potentially cause the centrifuge to catastrophically fly apart [9]. Clearly, this would be less than optimal, considering the environment in question.

Defense

Defending against software and hardware manipulation is a difficult prospect. Once an attacker has administrative rights on a machine, there is little that we can do to prevent them from taking such steps. Conversely, if an attacker does not have administrative rights on a machine, they are generally prevented from taking such measures. In short, the defense against such actions largely revolves around preventing attackers from gaining administrative rights on the system, a task often involving system hardening and including many of the methods that we have covered in the various defense sections in this chapter.

OBFUSCATION TOOLS

To obfuscate means to "confuse, bewilder, or stupefy"; "to make obscure or unclear"; or "to darken" [10]. This definition perfectly suits the set of tools that we might use to cover our tracks when operating on a system or in an environment. In general, there are three main types of tasks that we are concerned with in such cases: obscuring our location, manipulating logs, and manipulating files.

Location Obscuration

One of the chief concerns when conducting Computer Network Operations (CNO), which we will discuss at length in Chapters 10–13, is hiding or obscuring the location, in either a logical or a physical sense, from which we are operating. Generally, this is accomplished through the use of some sort of proxy, whether this is a purposely built network specifically for doing so, or merely a compromised system through which we are operating.

The Onion Router (Tor) is a system, developed with the support of the U.S. Naval Research Laboratory [11], with the specific purpose of insuring the anonymity of communications over the Internet. Tor is used by the Navy for open source intelligence gathering, by law enforcement agencies for surveillance and intelligence gathering [12], and by a large number of organizations and individuals for various purposes where privacy and secrecy of communications are desired. Tor provides this anonymity by routing communications through several intermediary proxies, other nodes operating in the network, before the traffic reaches an endpoint and is delivered to its final destination. In practice, this makes the traffic very difficult to trace back to its origin, but, depending on the configuration of the client and the type of traffic, not impossible.

WARNING

Tor and similar proxy networks, sometimes referred to as mixed networks, are great tools for obscuring the origination of traffic and adding a layer of security and/or privacy to our activities, but they are not a magic bullet. Depending on the exact configuration of the systems involved, the traffic being sent, the source and ultimate destination, and a number of other factors, it may be possible to trace the origin of the traffic. For those interested in reading further on such issues, see the paper Low-Resource Routing Attacks against Anonymous Systems.[q]

Similar proxy networks to Tor, such as Bitblinder, Perfect Dark, and I2P exist as well, and all have similar issues to one degree or another. Other measures can be taken to ensure some measure of anonymity, such as the use of VPNs, or even using one or more compromised machines as a sort of manual proxy. Such simpler measures obviously do not provide the same level of anonymization of communications, but they also do not have some of the same issues. Measures of such a simple nature can also be useful in the case where we do not necessarily desire to entirely hide the end point of an attack, but instead wish to implicate another party. This is commonly considered one of the reasons for the large number of attacks that appear to originate from China.

Log Manipulation

With nearly any activity that we might care to conduct on or against a system, we are sure to generate some sort of an entry in logs of systems and network devices. Depending on what exactly our purpose is when conducting such operations, we may wish to remove such traces in order to hide our presence from future investigators, system administrators, and the like.

On Unix-like systems, presuming that we have the proper permissions to do so, logs can often be altered through the use of a text editor. In some cases, we may find that a particularly savvy system administrator has set attributes for the logs that we are interested in in order to make them append only. Additionally, it is possible to disable the capability that would allow us, even as root, to remove such a flag from a log file. In such cases, by the time that we have discovered that these measures are in place, we have likely left a great deal of evidence behind in various logs, and may need to adopt somewhat of a scorched earth approach, as we discussed in the Assault Tools section of this chapter.

On Windows systems, the logs are stored in a somewhat more protected format, and are difficult to manipulate directly, by design. Not only is the file format resistant to tampering, but the logs are generally held in a constantly locked state by the logging processes. Any account with administrator access can clear the event logs entirely, but this is a heavy-handed tactic, and generally very obvious. Fortunately, some tools do exist that will allow us to selectively manipulate these logs, usually the Security log being our specific concern. One such tool is WinZapper,[r] which enables us to easily, given administrator access, remove specific

[q]http://citeseerx.ist.psu.edu/viewdoc/summary?doi=10.1.1.133.4562

[r]http://www.ntsecurity.nu/toolbox/winzapper/

events from the log on Microsoft operating systems from Windows NT 4.0 to Windows Server 2003. For more recent operating systems, such as Windows 7/8 and Server 2008/2012, the holes that allow these types of tools to function have been patched; fortunately, other vulnerabilities, such as MS10-041, do exist and can be used to carry out log manipulation in a similar fashion on unpatched systems.

In many operating systems, writing to logs files is not restricted to the same extent as is manipulating them, and in some cases, is not restricted at all. In such cases, when we have failed to remove data from the log files in a cleaner fashion, we can simply fill the logs with our own events in order to push the log past its retention period in order to obscure our own activities. Depending on how the logging mechanisms in question are configured, we may simply find that the log entries are overwritten past a certain time or size specified, as is common in many Windows implementations, or we may find that the logger rolls to a new file and that the older log is renamed and stored. In such cases, writing authentic looking events to the log, such as the repeated events that we might find from a hardware or software failure of some sort, or a replay of older events, may more easily escape notice than just writing garbage to the logs.

File Manipulation

When attempting to hide files on systems in which we are operating, there are a variety of approaches that we might take. We can simply use the built in commands of the file systems in order to hide files, which may work to a certain extent, for casual users. We can also rename our files to something obscure which matches the system files of the operating system on which we are operating and hide them in the midst of similar files, which will likely enjoy some measure of success. On Microsoft OSs using the NTFS file system, we can place data in Alternate Data Streams (ADS). ADS are storage areas in a file that are typically intended to store metadata, such as thumbnails for image files. Using tools such as streams,[s] we can easily access ADS and insert information that will be invisible to those that are not specifically looking for it.

> **WARNING**
>
> Using rootkits, and malware in general, is a form of attack that should be used very carefully. Even in the case of custom malware, such tools may behave in unexpected ways outside of our testing environment.

As somewhat of a final measure, we can also use rootkits to hide our files, which will be a nearly impenetrable method, as long as we still have control of the operating system itself. Given a kernel mode rootkit, we can prevent nearly any tool or utility from finding our files through the simple expedient of telling such tools that our files do not exist.

---

[s]http://technet.microsoft.com/en-us/sysinternals/bb897440.aspx

In the course of manipulating various files on the systems in which we are operating, we will have likely modified the timestamps of said files in the process of doing so. Particularly with files on which the timestamps are set to a commonly known value and not frequently changed, such as the files that comprise portions of an operating system, our efforts may cause these altered timestamps to clearly stand out to someone looking for the signs of compromise. Fortunately, such timestamps, again given appropriate administrative permissions, are relatively easily reset. On Unix-like systems, timestamps can be reset with the touch command. On Windows systems, timestamps can be reset with utilities such as Timestomp[t] or through the use of PowerShell commands like the following [13]:

```
$(Get-Item ).creationtime=$(Get-Date "mm/dd/yyyy hh:mmam/pm")
$(Get-Item ).lastaccesstime=$(Get-Date "mm/dd/yyyy hh:mmam/pm")
$(Get-Item ).lastwritetime=$(Get-Date "mm/dd/yyyy hh:mmam/pm")
```

Given sufficient attention by a skilled forensic investigator, it may be possible to eventually discover some traces of such file manipulation; however, our primary concern here is to keep from attracting such attention in the first place. If we are sufficiently diligent in our obfuscatory efforts, traces of our activities should be very difficult to find and should be all but invisible to casual users of the environments concerned and to the administrators as well.

Defense

Defending against obfuscation measures can be very difficult or very easy, depending on where exactly the manipulation is taking place. When dealing with the tactics that an attacker can use to obscure their location, the countermeasures that can be taken to reverse such efforts can fall solidly into the very difficult category. Although we can take steps to attempt to work our way backwards through the proxies and perhaps other steps that an attacker has taken, this is very much a manual process and would require the cooperation of the owners of each intervening layer, and would be rather unlikely to bear fruit. This being said, with the resources of a nation-state to back up such an investigation, and placing sufficient importance on recovering the information, it is not impossible that we could do so successfully. In any case, such tactics are almost entirely reactive in nature and would be carried out in the aftermath of the incident that prompted them.

In the case of file and log manipulation, there are many defensive measure that can be put in place to ensure that the efforts of our attacker are unsuccessful. We can use tools such as Tripwire[u] to monitor for file manipulation in real time and issue alerts when something untoward takes place. We can also send copies of our log entries to remote servers that are hardened against attack. These two measures will go a great deal of the way to ensuring that if such attacks do occur, they will not go unnoticed.

[t]http://www.offensive-security.com/metasploit-unleashed/Timestomp

[u]http://www.tripwire.com

SUMMARY

In this chapter we discussed the various tools that we might use in conducting cyber warfare, and the methods that we might use to defend against an attacker using them.

We discussed the tools that we might use for reconnaissance, for activities including: general information gathering, searching whois and DNS records, and metadata from media and documents. We covered scanning tools, such as Nmap and Nessus, that we might use to find systems and detect potential areas where vulnerabilities might exist. We went over access and privilege escalation tools, such as Metasploit and CANVAS, that we might use to gain entry to a system and work our way into accounts with greater levels of access to the system. We talked about exfiltration methods, using tools to encrypt, hide, or smuggle data over common protocols in order to remove it from a compromised system. We looked at means that we might use to sustain our connection to a compromised system, such as adding backdoors or additional access, so that we can still operate on the system if our original method of access is removed. We went over assault tools, which we might use to damage or disrupt systems that we have compromised, often using common operating system utilities. Lastly, we discussed obfuscation tools that we might use to hide our location, in both the logical and physical sense, while we are attacking.

The majority of the tools that we discussed in this chapter are free, or have free versions, and are available to the general public. It is important to realize that the tools that are required to conduct pure cyber warfare are freely available, unlike many of the tools that are required to conduct conventional warfare on any large scale. This easy access to such tools means that nation-states may find themselves facing enemies that are fully capable of causing severe damage to computers and the systems to which they are attached.

References

[1] Shalal-Esa A. Six U.S. Air Force cyber capabilities designated "weapons". Reuters, http://www.reuters.com/article/2013/04/09/net-us-cyber-airforce-weapons-idUSBRE93801B20130409; 2012 [accessed 05.22.13].

[2] Aitoro J. IRS finds unauthorized web servers connected to its networks. Nextgov.com, http://www.nextgov.com/nextgov/ng_20080904_3324.php; 2008 [accessed 04.09.13].

[3] Offensive Security. Google Hacking Database. Exploit Database, http://www.exploit-db.com/google-dorks/?function=detail&id=795; 2013 [accessed 04.09.13].

[4] Laboratory for Systems and Signals. Nessus/OpenVAS comparison test. s.l.: faculty of electrical engineering and computing, University of Zagreb, http://security.lss.hr/images/stories/documents/Nessus_vs_OpenVAS_en.pdf; 2009 [accessed 03.24.13].

[5] Morris D. Ninja Billy Fun Page. Ninjabilly.com, http://www.ninjabilly.com/fun.html; 2009 [accessed 03.24.13].

[6] Lucas I. Password recovery speeds. Lockdown.co.uk, http://www.lockdown.co.uk/?pg=combi; 2009 [accessed 03.24.13].

[7] SD Association. SDXC. SD Association, https://www.sdcard.org/developers/overview/capacity/; 2010 [accessed 03.24.13].

[8] Vijayan J. TJX violated nine of 12 PCI controls at time of breach, court filings say. Computerworld, http://www.computerworld.com/s/article/9044321/TJX_violated_nine_of_12_PCI_controls_at_time_of_breach_court_filings_say; 2007 [accessed 03.24.13].

[9] Keizer G. New Stuxnet clues suggest sabotage of Iran's uranium enrichment program, http://www.computerworld.com/s/article/9196458/New_Stuxnet_clues_suggest_sabotage_of_Iran_s_uranium_enrichment_program?taxonomyId=17&pageNumber=1; 2010 [accessed 03.24.13].

[10] Dictionary.com. Obfuscate. Dictionary.com, http://dictionary.reference.com/browse/obfuscate; 2013 [accessed 03.24.13].

[11] U.S. Naval Research lab. onion routing, http://www.onion-router.net/; 2010 [accessed 03.24.13].

[12] The Tor Project, inc. Tor: overview. Tor project, http://www.torproject.org/about/overview.html.en; 2010 [accessed 03.24.13].

[13] Hull D. Touch on Windows via PowerShell. trustedsignal. blogspot.com, http://trustedsignal.blogspot.com/2008/08/touch-on-windows-via-powershell.html; 2008 [accessed 03.24.13].

[14] Mills E. Stuxnet: fact vs. theory. CNET news, http://news.cnet.com/8301-27080_3-20018530-245.html; 2010 [accessed 03.24.13].

Physical Weapons

INFORMATION IN THIS CHAPTER

- How the Logical and Physical Realms are Connected
- Infrastructure Concerns
- Supply Chain Concerns
- Tools for Physical Attack and Defense

When we think of cyber warfare, we most likely envision legions of über-nerds, staring intently at banks of monitors while madly typing away at their keyboards. Although there may be some measure of truth to this particular mental picture, we also need to consider the place of conventional warfare in such conflicts.

When we look at how the physical and logical realms intersect, we find that they are very closely linked. The logical systems, such as software and applications, are entirely dependent on the physical systems and infrastructure on which they run. Changes made to either the physical or logical components can have profound effects on each other, with one sometimes rending the other completely useless.

Just as in any large conflict of a physical nature, we are concerned with the infrastructure and supply chains that make our operations possible. If either of these components is removed or subverted by opposing forces, conducting warfare becomes considerably more difficult, at best. At worst, we may find ourselves unable to act entirely, nullified by supply chain issues such as food poisoning from a batch of contaminated egg salad in a mess hall or cafeteria.

When looking at the tools we can use for physical attack and defense, we have a wide variety of options available to us. We can use conventional explosives, cut cables, jam transmissions, pick locks, and nearly anything else that come to mind. For defense, we can harden our facilities and equipment against the attacks that we consider to be the most likely, and we can take steps to ensure that those attackers that do make it through our perimeter are frustrated in their attempts and quickly detected.

HOW THE LOGICAL AND PHYSICAL REALMS ARE CONNECTED

The logical realm depends on physical hardware and network. Though the idea of the virtual world riding on the physical world is indeed a simple one, some of the second order effects of intersections between these two worlds may not be as clear or immediately obvious.

When looking at the physical network infrastructure on which such systems are maintained, we have two primary issues to consider in cyber operations: keeping our own systems and infrastructure intact and functional while rendering the opposing systems and infrastructure unable to do so.

Logical systems can also be used to make changes in the physical world. In complex items of physical hardware, software often regulates the way that the hardware functions. Changes made to the software can affect whatever the hardware interfaces with, including networks, other systems, or even people.

Logical Systems Run on Physical Hardware

The logical world runs on a variety of network infrastructure, computer systems, home automation devices, refrigerators, cars, and so on. When such a complex device loses connection to the various utilities that are critical to its functionality, mainly power and communications media, it becomes considerably less useful, often times to the point of being rendered a very expensive paperweight.

When conducting operations in a cyber conflict, whether offensive or defensive, keeping the physical hardware running that enables such activity can be challenging. Even in conventional warfare, an element of advanced technology has begun to enter the fray in the form of numerous computer systems and network-connected devices, and the intelligence provided by such technology can provide critical information on which to base cyber, as well as conventional, operations.

Many recent military actions in which the United States has participated, such as those in Iraq and Afghanistan, have taken place in desert locations that tend to be very hot and sandy, with little existing infrastructure to speak of. Operating in such bleak environments tends to be less than optimal for the continued functionality of computing equipment. The cost to environmentally harden equipment is often more than replacing off the shelf computers. In addition, such equipment may pose a tempting target for opposing forces to attack, both on a physical and a logical level. In such cases, ruggedized equipment is often required in order to have any expectation for the devices to function over a period of time.

Additionally, at a higher level, the infrastructure needs to be kept working for such systems to utilize. This type of infrastructure technology is commonly found in data centers and other areas that house critical computing equipment, although it is not commonly hardened to withstand the levels of attack that we might find in a cyber conflict. By using redundant systems, infrastructure, utilities, and other such necessities, we can make it very difficult to take systems down due to the high level of resiliency. On the other hand, because the technologies that enable resilient systems and infrastructures are generally available, we will likely find them implemented by our opponents as well.

On the reverse side of this issue is the problem of attempting to render the equipment and infrastructure of the opposing forces inoperable from a physical perspective. Particularly when physical operations are being conducted on foreign soil, those under attack may have a distinct "home court" advantage. In some situations, such as the conflict in Afghanistan, we may be dealing with an opponent that does not rely on a sophisticated technological infrastructure at all. In other cases, we may be facing well-constructed data centers that are hardened and have sufficient backup resources to provide power and communications in emergencies. These can prove to be very difficult to take offline. Often it is a mix of legacy equipment with some cutting edge technology (i.e., encrypted phones) combined with using nontraditional methods like internet-based drop boxes.

During Operation Iraqi Freedom in 2003, several rounds of cruise missiles were required to disrupt the Internet access in Baghdad. Although the civilian Internet Service Providers (ISPs) were taken down with relative ease, with much of the traffic originating from behind a single Cisco network switch, the traffic coming from the Iraqi government was not so easily silenced as it was part of a more resilient network. After direct hits on two telecommunications switching centers, several satellite dishes, and a server housed in the Iraqi Ministry of Information building, the official Iraqi government website and the associated email server were taken offline. It later appeared that communications were being carried through a satellite gateway that had been shipped to Dubai by the manufacturer and later brought into Iraq [1].

Given the ease of constructing backup systems on a variety of infrastructures, it is entirely possible that multiple systems would need to be taken down to remove the cyber capability of an opponent. Internet access can be provided over microwave, cell, ham radio, phone lines, and a variety of other solutions and can be shared through mesh networking to enable a great degree of redundancy. Given today's technologies a system could even be made to function at a minimal level from a laptop and a data connection from a cell phone. In such cases, a combination of physical and logical attacks may be required to completely take a system offline.

Logical Attacks can have Physical Effects

Just as physical attacks can affect logical systems, logical attacks can affect physical systems. To a great extent, physical computing systems are controlled by the operating systems and applications that are running on them. As a very simple example, for almost all systems that are physically connected to a network cable, changes to the network configuration can be made in such a way as to remove a device from the network.

> **TIP**
>
> Web administration interfaces are typically wonderful for knocking devices off of the network. They often have poor security, if the security features have been enabled on them at all. Although they have relatively limited functionality in most cases, many of them do have the capability to change basic network settings. Typically setting the IP address on such a device to 0.0.0.0 will disable its network functionality handily.

In the case of a device being removed from the network, a backup communications method could potentially be used to restore communications to the device, or a person will be required to physically travel to the device to reconfigure it. Such an attack may be very simple and ultimately very easy to fix, but using it to disrupt network infrastructure across an enterprise could bring an entire organization to a halt in very short order, and be very time consuming to fix.

Attacks on physical systems can also have effects of a much more serious nature that can go far beyond merely annoying network and system administrators. Attacks on implanted medical devices, such as pacemakers and pumps for dispensing medication, have become all too common in recent years, to the point of research being done to create firewalls for such devices [2].

Although such attacks are nontrivial to carry out, requiring considerable amounts of research and specialized hardware, but the concept is well proven. To make matters even worse for future attacks along these lines, in 2009 the first wireless and Internet connected pacemaker was installed in a patient [3]. Remotely connecting to and disabling all such devices under the control of a particular doctor, a cardiologist at the White House, for instance, might have quite a profound effect in the political world.

In addition to such concerns around generic computing devices, these attacks can also be used to affect the critical systems that control the components running industrial processes around the world. Such systems control the distribution of power and water, communications systems, manufacturing, and any number of other important processes.

INFRASTRUCTURE CONCERNS

When we mention the word infrastructure in the company of those that work in the computing and technology worlds, the common tendency is to assume that we are referring specifically to network infrastructure. Although this infrastructure is indeed important and many processes would be completely nonfunctional without it, it is only a portion of the infrastructure on which the industrial world runs.

Of chief concern when we discuss infrastructure and the associated systems are the systems that actually control these items. These control systems regulate power, water, communications, manufacturing processes, and any number of other tasks. Properly referred to, such systems are industrial control systems (ICS). ICS are made up of Supervisory Control and Data Acquisition (SCADA) systems, Distributed Control System (DCS), Human–Machine Interfaces (HMIs), Master Terminal Units (MTUs), Programmable Logic Controllers (PLCs), Remote Terminal Units (RTUs), Intelligent Electronic Devices (IEDs), and other such items [4]. A typical SCADA layout can be seen in Figure 7.1 [5].

These categories are often grouped together under the umbrella of SCADA, rather than calling them by the less familiar term ICS. In essence, the distinction between SCADA and ICS revolves around the specifics of where and what is actually being controlled or coordinated. In many cases, such distinctions are not standard between industries, and the term SCADA is often used where ICS may be more accurate in a technical sense.

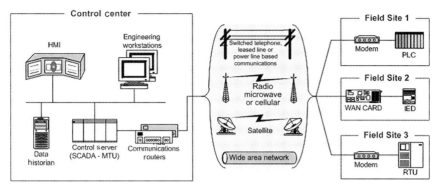

FIGURE 7.1   SCADA system general layout.

What is SCADA?

SCADA systems are used to control and monitor a variety of processes. Such processes can be industrial, infrastructure, or facility based [6]. Industrial processes can involve manufacturing facilities, generation of power, petroleum refineries, mining, or any number of similar activities that take place in factory-like environments. Infrastructure processes revolve around water and wastewater systems, pipelines used to distribute petroleum and natural gas, the transmission of electrical power, communications systems such as landline or cellular phone systems, and other systems that provide goods and services that are commonly considered utilities. Facility processes are those that regulate processes in individual facilities such as heating and air conditioning, or energy usage.

SCADA systems are integrated into nearly everything that we come into contact with. While we are putting gas in our cars, surfing the web, cooking dinner, or flushing the toilet, we are only steps away from such systems, if not directly interacting with them. Figure 7.2

FIGURE 7.2   A remote monitoring sensor for utility usage.

shows the sensor for a remote monitoring system that allows water usage to be read by a utility company. Remote sensors such as these have become increasingly common in many residential areas, as it enables utility companies to gain greater accuracy in meter reading, and does not require a person to manually visit each reader in order to collect information.

Without such systems to maintain and monitor the modern world, we would quickly be without heat, food, communications, and many other necessities. Needless to say, although such systems are designed for industrial usage and, in some critical systems, are multiply redundant, they are based on computer technology and therefore vulnerable.

What Security Issues are Present in the World of SCADA?

Many of the systems that fall under the category of SCADA depend on security through obscurity [7]. These systems use interfaces, software, operating systems, and protocols that are either proprietary or not generally well known outside of the industries in which they are implemented. In theory, in order for attackers to penetrate a SCADA system, they would either need inside knowledge of the design for the particular, and potentially unique, system, or they would need to spend the time gaining access to and learning how things worked in order to carry out attack.

Unfortunately, we are well into the information age, and a vast store of information awaits those willing to venture into the wasteland that we call the Internet. Manufacturers conveniently put manuals online for their customers to download, internal materials leak out to the public, and odd industrial systems can be bought for pennies on eBay. Although such systems do tend to be considerably more customized than the average server, we are well beyond the point of being able to depend on the obscure nature of a system conveying any large measure of protection against attackers. Indeed, systems and software that have not had the trial by fire of exposure to the Internet and outside attackers may very well be weaker for lack of having had their security flaws pointed out to the manufacturer.

As a case in point, in July of 2010 a multipart malware named Stuxnet was discovered and its main target is SCADA systems. Stuxnet is composed of a worm which spreads over USB drives via a Windows exploit, and a Trojan that specifically looks for a particular model of Siemens SCADA systems. Also included is a rootkit to prevent its discovery. If Stuxnet finds that it is on the Siemens systems, it uses a hard-coded password to access the database that the SCADA system uses as a back end. It then looks for industrial automation layout files and control files and uploads them to a remote system, as well as attempting various acts of sabotage. Stuxnet then waits for additional commands from the remote system [8].

Stuxnet has been found in SCADA systems in a number of countries, including China, India, Iran, and Indonesia, with a possible point of origination in Israel. At first it appeared that the goal of the malware was industrial espionage. It was later discovered that Stuxnet attempted to actively sabotage such systems under certain circumstances and may have been responsible for the loss of an Indian communications satellite [9]. In addition to such threats, as SCADA systems become more commonly connected to public and private networks, we are then exposed to the standard types of attacks with which many common systems are concerned. Distributed denial of service attacks (DDoS), side effects from malware attacks, patches that introduce security vulnerabilities, and a host of others now become issues for SCADA systems.

What are the Consequences of SCADA Failures?

In the case of serious SCADA failures, the potential consequences are quite far reaching. Considering that we are referring to the control systems for electrical power, communications, the flow of petroleum, and other such critical processes, a major disaster resulting from a SCADA failure seems likely indeed. We saw an example of the potential for such a failure during a large-scale power blackout in 2003.

In parts of the United States and Canada, in August of 2003, we saw the outcome from a SCADA failure that would, at first, seem to be relatively minor in nature, involving electrical distribution. Ultimately, a failure in a software monitoring system at a utility company in Ohio led to an outage at a local power plant. The failure of the power plant caused power to be drawn from other power plants in the area. Heavily loaded power lines, as seen in such outages, tend to physically sag, which several did. Sagging lines at multiple locations came into contact with improperly trimmed trees, causing these lines to also fail. While these failures were taking place, operators at the utility companies in Ohio neglected to inform controllers at utility systems in the surrounding states.

At that point, the utility systems in Ohio begin to draw power from the systems in Michigan, causing numerous issues as the system attempted to balance its load. Additional lines failed in Ohio and Michigan, causing power generating stations to go offline due to the absence of a load on them. Additional power was routed from plants on the east coast as the system continued to attempt to balance itself, causing plants on the east coast to overload and shut down. Due to the massive power grid issues, grids in Michigan and Ohio began to disconnect from each other. Connections to Canada also began to fail, and instabilities in the grid caused grids in Canada to begin disconnecting as well. Ultimately, grids in Ontario, New York, New England, Windsor, New Jersey, and Philadelphia were affected [10].

At the end of the blackout, 256 power plants were offline and 55 million customers were without power [11]. If we look all the way back at the beginning of the problem, the failure of a single monitoring system led to this enormous issue. Such situations have the potential for enormous loss of life and destruction, depending on the industry in which we see the failure. The blackout of 2003 was ultimately the result of a software bug, but was entirely accidental. Given the attention of a determined opponent, such attacks have the potential for great disruption and destruction.

SUPPLY CHAIN CONCERNS

In addition to the infrastructure concerns that we discussed earlier, awareness of our supply chain is also critical. We are now many years into a process of globalization that extends across nearly every large industry we might care to examine. Many countries import hardware and components to build infrastructure; a wide variety of foodstuffs, both processed and fresh; fuel; raw materials; clothing; and a number of other items, large and small, that are far too extensive to enumerate.

Although this has a number of benefits, it also poses severe problems, particularly when we look at the possibilities of warfare in either the conventional or cyber sense. When we look at the infrastructure that we might rely on to conduct such attacks, or in the reverse situation, the infrastructure that might be under attack, the majority of the components, from individual items of equipment, all the way to the components from which they are constructed come from a few major manufacturing areas around the globe.

Compromised Hardware

Of major concern is the specter of hardware that has been compromised for strategic or intelligence purposes. Critical items, such as routers or switches, firewall appliances, industrial control units, or any of a number of other components may be deliberately engineered to clandestinely report information, fail given a particular signal or set of conditions, include a backdoor, or any number of other similar activities. This can place the party suffering such attacks at a distinct disadvantage, if not cripple their capacity to operate entirely.

In the late 1970s and early 1980s, the U.S. Central Intelligence Agency (CIA) learned of plans by the Russian Committee for State Security (KGB) to steal plans for a SCADA control system and its associated software from a Canadian company. Allegedly, the CIA was able to insert malware into the software for the system, which was later used in a trans-Siberian gas pipeline. In 1982 a massive explosion is reported to have taken place as a direct result of the flawed control system install [12]. There is some debate as to the validity of this report, but it does nicely illustrate the point.

To illustrate the concept of introducing such modified hardware into the market, we can look at the case of Operation Cisco Raider, a 2-year investigation run by the U.S. Federal Bureau of Investigation (FBI). In this operation, the FBI broke up a counterfeiting ring that had sold equipment to, among others, the U.S. Navy, U.S. Marine Corps, U.S. Air Force, the U.S. Federal Aviation Administration (FAA), and the FBI itself [13].

In this particular case, the aim of the counterfeiting ring was profit rather than sabotage or espionage, and the amount of equipment concerned was very large. Under more stealth-focused circumstances, it is exceedingly unlikely that a few pieces of equipment that carried modified chips would be found, even given the government programs in place to do exactly this. We will discuss this issue in further depth, as well as some of the potential solutions, in Chapter 16.

Deliberately Corrupted Components

In addition to the specifically targeted and timed attacks that we discussed earlier, a much more simple supply chain issue can be brought about with the introduction of deliberately inferior or corrupted components. Particularly when looking at equipment with electronic components, this is a relatively simple type of attack to carry out. Considering the wide variety of components found in a typical item of electronic equipment and the large number of vendors that such components come from, such failures would be very wide reaching.

A specific case of an enormous number of issues related to a single bad component is that of the "capacitor plague" [14] that started in the late 1990s. A large portion of the issue relates to industrial espionage between capacitor manufacturers. Reportedly, the formula for the electrolyte used in capacitor manufacturing was stolen from a Japanese company and resold to several Taiwanese capacitor manufacturers. Unknown to any of the thieves, the formula was incomplete and lacked several key additives that would normally keep the capacitor from bursting. Although this allowed the capacitors to function for a short period of time, it caused them to fail at generally less than half of their expected lifetime. According to some, this problem is still being seen in the market, with devices that have been produced nearly a decade after the original issue [15].

In this particular case, the issue was caused by an effort on the part of the legitimate manufacturer of the capacitors as a defense mechanism against the theft of their intellectual property, and only got out of hand because the information was spread so widely. If this were a deliberate attempt at disrupting the supply chain of electronics components, it would be possible to produce components that were designed to fail in a very specific way, or at a particular time, as we covered in the previous section "Compromised Hardware." Such components could potentially find their way into missiles, tracking systems, aircraft avionics, or any number of other critical systems.

Nontechnical Issues

Of course when discussing supply chain issues, there are measures that could be used as attacks that do not directly relate to items of technology. Numerous issues relating to the supplies needed to conduct cyber warfare could present themselves to a sufficiently determined opponent and could prove profoundly effective at preventing such operations from being carried out. Additionally, given the potential for conducting such operations from centralized locations, such disruptions might be trivially easy to plan and implement.

In the words of Napoleon Bonaparte, "An army marches on its stomach [16]." The consumable supplies that are necessary for our forces to conduct operations whether they are toothpaste, cold medicine, drinking water, food, or other such items, are all susceptible to contamination, whether deliberate or otherwise. We have seen many examples of the outcome of such events in countries around the globe.

In October of 2012, a restaurant named Flicks in Belfast, Ireland was the source of an outbreak of food poisoning from *E. coli* contamination. Over the course of roughly 2 weeks, 293 cases of poisoning related to this incident were reported [17]. This particular case was accidental in nature, but still had very wide-reaching consequences. If such contamination were to be deliberately carried out, particularly in a centralized location such as a cafeteria, a targeted group of people could be incapacitated or worse.

Similar issues can appear with nearly any item that is required to support our forces, both conventional and cyber, particularly in locations that are not considered on the frontlines of a particular engagement. Security in a protected remote location is likely to be much more lax than that found on any battlefield. Intentionally created supply issues are more likely, when carried out carefully and subtly, to be attributed to chance, rather than an outright attack.

TOOLS FOR PHYSICAL ATTACK AND DEFENSE

As we look at some of the conventional tools or weapon systems used for offense we turn to direct fire weapons like machine guns and tanks, and indirect weapons like artillery and jets.

For defense we think of defensive minefields and dug-in troops. If we switch to reconnaissance we consider tools like satellite imaging, espionage or spies, and sending out scouts. The same concepts that apply to the physical aspects of the battlefield also apply to the cyber battlefield.

First we will explore some of the precision attack tools available during a conventional attack. Cutting cables with tools such as a wire snip or backhoe is very effective. Next is attacking the power system supporting the building housing the key network nodes. Attacks against the personnel supporting the network can be effective in preventing recovery and extend the impacts of other attacks. The goal of these attacks is to cause a denial of service. Physical attacks do not normally impact confidentiality or integrity, but rather just availability. Raids designed to capture hardware can be effective attacks against confidentiality.

Next we will examine defensive tools. At the physical plant level these include guards, gates, and guns. We need personnel monitoring and reacting to attacks and they need sufficient force to repel the attacks. This means patrolling the lines of communications (network cables and the power grid). We will need fences that have deterrent features like razor wire, force protection features to prevent vehicle attacks, and fences that are electrified. We need buildings that are built to Telecommunications Electronics Material Protected from Emanating Spurious Transmissions (TEMPEST) standards, Electromagnetic Pulse (EMP) hardened, and blast reinforced. We need redundant power capabilities (uninterrupted power supply and backup generators). We need alternate communications paths to ensure connectivity.

Finally we must protect ourselves from prying eyes. This is traditionally called Operations Security (OPSEC) in military terms. Our policies and procedures are what protect us here. We need to train the workforce to not talk about work in public places or with casual acquaintances (in real life or online). We need to train them how to guard their documents, laptops, and mobile devices when outside the office. We must get them to conduct risk assessments as part of their everyday life.

Electromagnetic Attacks

Electromagnetic attacks can be very useful in an environment where cyber conflicts are taking place. As such operations often depend on relatively delicate electronics, we can use this to our advantage. Such equipment can be affected by EMP weapons, transmissions can be jammed, and emanations from such equipment can be eavesdropped upon.

Electromagnetic Pulse Weapons

EMP weapons are a somewhat common player in movies, such as *Oceans 11* and *The Matrix*, and books, but not quite as common in the real world. EMP weapons work by creating a very intense energy field which is very disruptive to nonhardened electronics. Such devices do exist in military arsenals, generally in the form of High Altitude Electromagnetic Pulse (HEMP) or High Power Microwave (HPM) weapons.

HEMP devices produce an EMP over a wide area, commonly produced by detonating a nuclear device high in the atmosphere. Obviously, if we are to the point of countries lobbing nuclear devices into the sky, things have gotten rather out of hand in the world of warfare, and we will likely have other concerns than cyber attacks in fairly short order. The more

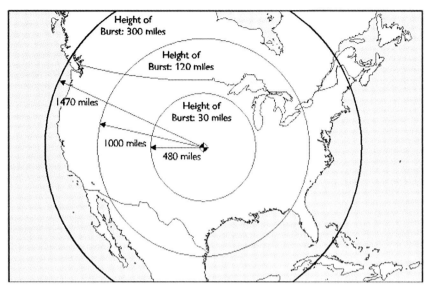

FIGURE 7.3   Estimated area affected by high altitude EMP.

realistic scenario, at present, for such a device being used is as an act of terrorism. As shown in Figure 7.3, a HEMP device triggered at 300 miles altitude over central North America would affect an area covering most of the continent [18].

HPM devices can produce a similar effect, although on a smaller scale and with smaller equipment. Instead of needing a nuclear device, a HPM can use chemical explosives or very powerful batteries, in conjunction with a type of coil called a flux compression generator, to produce a powerful pulse. HPM devices can also limit the effect of the pulse produced to a smaller area over a shorter distance. Additionally, the pulse produced by the HPM is much more effective against electronics and is more difficult to harden devices against [18].

Jamming

Particularly in many forces of a military nature, jamming technologies can be quite advanced. This set of technologies generally falls under the heading of Electronic Warfare (EW). EW systems can be used to jam nearly anything that utilizes the electromagnetic spectrum including radio, radar, sonar, infrared, laser, and a host of other technologies. Such technologies are very complex and expensive, but are common to many militaries.

On the other end of the spectrum, jamming can also be done very simply. Radio equipment can often be repurposed to interfere with transmission and receiving on other equipment, and plans for purpose-built home-brewed jamming equipment can be found on the Internet. Additionally, appliances such as portable phones, microwaves, and items that operate in the general area of the frequency to be interfered with can often be used to some effect.

Defense Against Conventional Attacks

When we are looking to defend against attacks in the physical and electromagnetic realms, there are two main areas in which we can deploy our defenses: we can harden the facilities and equipment against expected attacks, and we can develop redundant infrastructures in place. In this way we can attempt to prevent the attack from impacting us in the first place, and we can hopefully mitigate the effects of any portion of the attack that does get through.

Redundant Infrastructure

In the case of not being able to protect our facility against attack or disaster, it is important that we have a backup site from which we can resume operations. There are three main types of backup sites: cold sites, warm sites, and hot sites [19].

Cold backup sites are the most basic and the least expensive of the three types. In a cold backup site, we basically have a facility from which we can resume operations, but not much more than that. To bring a cold site online, we might need to have utilities turned on; order, configure, and build systems; and send copies of any backups that we might need to the site. Bringing a cold site online may take weeks or more.

Warm backup sites may have some portion of the hardware and software that is needed and connectivity at a certain level, although not necessarily what is needed to operate at the full scale of the primary site. Systems may need to be configured and have software or applications installed. We may have some backups on site, but they will likely be a few days or weeks behind and will need to be restored. Warm backup sites can generally be brought online in a few days.

Hot backup sites have a completely redundant set of hardware and software, communications, and everything else needed to fully replicate the primary site. Data is usually synchronized with the primary site, so that we have very little if any data loss when switching to the backup site. The primary delay with such a site in time of disaster will usually be related to rounding up the people needed to actually work from the backup site. Hot sites themselves can generally be brought online in a matter of hours.

In the light of disasters such as those that happened at the World Trade Center and during Hurricane Katrina, the view of the technical industry on backup sites changed dramatically. Not only have organizations been made much more aware of the need for solid disaster recovery plans, but government agencies such as the Federal Communications Commission (FCC) in the United States have mandated improvements to infrastructure in order to better cope with disasters on this scale [20].

Facility and Equipment Hardening

Facilities and equipment can be hardened in a variety of ways against a broad spectrum of attacks. In many cases, such hardening involves a multilayered approach. The factors in such hardening are many and varied, depending on the physical location, potential threats, and so on. We may protect a facility against electromagnetic attacks, kinetic attacks, radiation, cold, heat, flooding, or a variety of other attacks, depending on the threats that are thought to be likely for the facility in question.

We can harden both facilities and equipment against electromagnetic attacks. In general, we are concerned with the propagation of electromagnetic energy in undesirable ways. For purposes of HEMP, HPM, and other similar events, we want to ensure that the pulses from such events do not penetrate our facilities, and in particular our equipment.

> **NOTE**
>
> There is an entire field of security, known as Emissions Security (EMSEC), devoted to the prevention of intelligence-bearing emissions in the electromagnetic spectrum. Such concerns are often referred to by the name TEMPEST, which was the name of a project concerned with securing such emissions. For those interested in further reading on the subject, James Atkinson's Tempest 101 [21] gives a good overview and pointers to additional materials.

In principle, the approaches for ensuring protection for each are similar. Using a combination of shielding, faraday cages, waveguides, power and signal filters, and other similar measures, we can largely electromagnetically shield the facility or equipment in question.

Location of the facility is one of the primary layers of security. Buildings designed with security in mind are generally placed in areas that are easy to control access to, outside of flood zones and areas with frequent environmental issues, and so on. Physically hardening the facility itself might involve steps to prevent unauthorized entry to the immediate area, such as the use of fences, gates, or bollards. Inside the perimeter we may find an additional layer in the form of patrolling guards or dogs. At the facility itself, we may find structural reinforcements, locks, turnstiles or man traps, laminated glass windows, and additional physical segmentation of the facility inside.

Covert Activity

Covert activity provides the counterpoint to conventional warfare. Although in conventional warfare, our solutions generally involve overt actions with explosions and other obvious physical results, this is not necessarily the case in cyber warfare. In some situations, such activities are more damaging or more obvious than we care to be when conducting cyber warfare.

Many other alternatives are open to us when we want to carry out operations of a more subtle nature. We can use a variety of eavesdropping methods. We can jam radio-based devices, we can cut communications cables, we can pick locks, or any number of other similar methods. For a more complete discussion on some of the sneakier methods that we might want to use in such a cyber scenario, see *Ninja Hacking: Unconventional Penetration Testing Tactics and Techniques* (ISBN: 978-1-59749-588-2, Syngress).

Eavesdropping on Electromagnetic Emissions

In addition to jamming the signals of our opponents, we can also listen to the signals and eavesdrop on their emissions in the electromagnetic spectrum. Some such emissions, such as those from 802.11 wireless networks, are very trivial to eavesdrop on as they are broadcast to the world. Some emissions, such as those from keyboards or monitors, are somewhat more subtle, but are not particularly difficult to pick up either. We can even get rather esoteric and discover intelligence from the pattern of flickers on LEDs indicating network activity on servers or other such equipment.

Although it is possible that we might find our potential eavesdropping targets to be shielded against such eavesdropping, the vast majority of such devices, save a few in highly security military facilities, have absolutely no protection in this area. In the United States, the National Security Agency (NSA) is responsible for certifying facilities and equipment as being properly shielded against electromagnetic eavesdropping under the Certified TEMPEST Test Services Program (CTTSP). Such certifications indicate compliance with both the CTTSP Technical and Security Requirements Document (TSRD) and the National TEMPEST Standard, NSTISSAM TEMPEST/1-92, Compromising Emanations Laboratory Test Standard, Electromagnetics, collectively the cookbook for implementing such shielding [22].

Vandalism/Denial of Service

In the realm of technologies that depend heavily on the presence of power and communications lines, such as those used in cyber attacks, simple vandalism can be very effective. In many places, communications and power lines are buried in the ground, at best. Often access to such cables can be found by simply lifting a manhole cover. Even well-protected facilities of a military nature are often connected to public utilities, with some delay before they can revert to backup systems.

In April of 2009, exactly such an attack occurred, affecting the Santa Clara, Santa Cruz, and San Benito counties in California. Ten fiber optic cables were cut at four locations, all within easy access of manholes. In several cases, backup cables ran right next the primary cables and both were cut. Tens of thousands of phone customers using both land and cell lines were without services, as well as hospitals, police, fire departments, 911 services, and a broad variety of others [23].

Attacking Physical Access Controls

When we are looking to attack a physical access control, such as a locked door, taking a page from Occam's [24] book, going with the simplest approach will often lead to the best path. If we can avoid directly attacking a physical access control by finding an alternate way around it or by bypassing it somehow, we can often save ourselves quite a bit of pain.

Tailgating

Tailgating can be one of the easiest methods to bypass a physical access control. In a nutshell, tailgating is when we follow directly behind someone through a physical access control, generally without the person's consent, and without being authorized to pass through ourselves. In busy buildings, this is often very easy to accomplish, and, in fact, rather difficult to prevent without specific physical controls. Tailgating will beat tackling a lock every time, presuming that security at the facility in question is relatively lax.

Locks

Tackling locks directly can be very easy or very hard, depending on the environment and the lock in question. There are a number of methods that can be used to open a lock, including bypassing it or picking it.

Bypassing a lock involves working around the actual locking mechanism itself to cause the lock to open. This can commonly be done with a lower end padlock or combination lock by using a shim, a very thin piece of metal, to release the mechanism that holds the shackle closed. Similarly, a credit card can sometimes be used to slip the bolt on a door or a coat hanger can be used to unlock a car door. Such methods depend on low levels of security in the lock and the surrounding mechanism, and are generally not reliable in highly secure environments.

WARNING

Picking or bypassing locks that we don't own, or have permission to attack, is, of course, entirely illegal. In some states in the United States, merely having the tools with us can land us in a lot of trouble. That being said, learning to pick locks is a great deal of fun and can be useful for those employed in the security profession. For a great book on the topic, check out Deviant Ollam's book *Practical Lock Picking: A Physical Penetration Tester's Training Guide* (ISBN: 978-1-59749-611-7, Syngress). Additionally, a large number of demonstration videos can be found by searching for "lock picking" on YouTube.

Picking locks is a bit of a combination of art and science. The theory of lock picking is simple enough. A tool such as those shown in Figure 7.4, or even an improvised tool, in a pinch, and we use it to manipulate the mechanism of the lock, allowing the lock to open without the use of the key.

Figure 7.5 shows a view of what a lock might look like with the proper key inserted into it. In this case, because the key is in place, we see that the two parts of each pin stack, the key pins and the driver pins, are lined up so that the space where the two pins meet, called the shear line, is lined up with the edge of the plug, allowing the plug to rotate, opening the lock. This is the science piece.

Where the art comes into play is in being able to use the tool at hand to manipulate the pins in the lock in such a way as to manually line up the shear lines in the pin stacks so that the lock

FIGURE 7.4 A set of common lock picks.

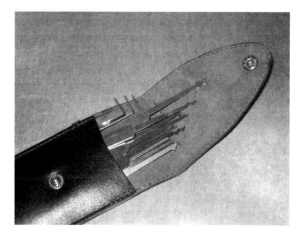

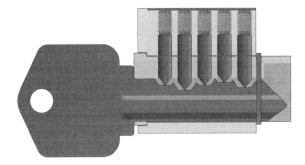

FIGURE 7.5 A key fully inserted into its lock *Courtesy of Deviant Ollam.* From *Practical Lock Picking: A Physical Penetration Tester's Training Guide* (ISBN: 978-1-59749-611-7, Syngress).

will open without the key. This is done by touch and, in some cases, by ear as well. As the pins are being manipulated with the pick, we put a small amount of pressure on the plug using a tension wrench, causing the plug to turn ever so slightly. Then, one pin at a time, we manipulate the pins until we reach the shear line. Done in the proper order, we should see the plug move a very small amount as each pin stack lines up properly. This is repeated until we are through all of the pins and the plug is able to rotate completely, hopefully opening the lock.

Picking simple pin-tumbler locks using the process that we just walked through can be relatively easy. There are several other varieties of locks, and many more in the world of high security locks, that can be much more difficult.

Defending Against Covert Attacks

Defending against covert attacks is a relatively simple, if expensive and inconvenient proposition. We can put measures into place that will keep people from tailgating, prevent locks from being bypassed, or picked, or most any other measure to subvert physical security that can be dreamed up. The problem with doing so is in the inconvenience to the people that legitimately need to pass through such controls; the trouble and expense to purchase, install, and maintain them; and the relationship to the value of what we are securing. If what we are protecting is valuable enough, then perhaps this is justified, but we can still never be 100% sure that it is completely secure.

Antitailgating measures can be relatively easy to implement, depending on the environment. On any door that we wish to absolutely prevent tailgating, we only need to install a floor to ceiling turnstile that is only big enough for one person. We can also put a guard in place, monitor the area with cameras, install a mantrap, or any of a variety of similar measures. In most cases, these types of controls are only found at government facilities with a very high level of security and are only a single layer of the physical security that is present. Additionally, we can help to mitigate tailgating through proper security awareness and training.

High security locks can contain a wide variety of measures to prevent the lock from being improperly opened or bypassed. They may contain multiple sets of pins, pins that are shaped to specifically prevent picking, specially cut keys, oddly shaped keyways, or any number of other such features. Such locks are by no means completely proof against picking or bypassing, but they will likely take a much longer period of time to do so. In the areas where such locks are used, we will often find them backed up by several layers of additional security.

Multilayered physical security may involve antitailgating measures, biometric systems, such as retina or iris scanners, guards and/or dogs, high security physical locks, proximity badge locks, and any number of other similar controls. Such environments are generally not conducive to an intruder spending several minutes picking a high security lock open, as they are considerably less likely to enter the facility in the first place and much more likely to be caught if they do. As with almost any security system, physical, logical, or otherwise, defense in depth is the key. For those not familiar with the concept, defense in depth is the use of multiple and differing layers of security. The concept being that we will never be able to universally keep everything secure, but we can try to delay the attacker for long enough that they are detected by one of our other security measures or give up.

SUMMARY

In this chapter we discussed the use of physical weapons in cyber warfare. We talked about the intersection of the physical and logical realms and how making changes to either realm can affect the other, sometimes to a disastrous extent.

We talked about infrastructure concerns, primarily those that have to do with the SCADA systems that control the various industrial, infrastructure, and facility processes that are in constant use all over the world. We covered some of the security issues present in SCADA and the potential consequences of failures in such systems.

We covered supply chain concerns and the potential consequences of corruption or disruption in the supply chain. We discussed the potential for espionage or sabotage by either deliberately corrupting components or by adding additional functionality beyond the original design of the component. We also talked about issues in supply chains on the nontechnical side.

In the last section of the chapter, we went over tools of a physical nature that can be used for attack and defense. We talked about the use of conventional explosives, vandalism or denial of service attacks, and attacks revolving around the electromagnetic spectrum. We also discussed hardening methods to help prevent such attacks and backup strategies that might aid us if such attacks do get through.

References

[1] McWilliams B. Iraq goes offline, Salon.com, http://dir.salon.com/story/tech/feature/2003/03/31/iraq_offline/index.html; 2012 [accessed 22.03.13].
[2] Venere E. New firewall to safeguard against medical-device hacking. Purdue University News Service, http://www.purdue.edu/newsroom/research/2012/120412RaghunathanHacking.html; 2012 [accessed 22.03.13].
[3] Reuters. New York woman receives wireless pacemaker, PCMag.com, http://www.pcmag.com/article2/0,2817,2351371,00.asp; 2009 [accessed 22.03.13].
[4] Motorola, Inc. Whitepaper: SCADA systems, http://www.motorola.com/web/Business/Products/SCADA%20Products/_Documents/Static%20Files/SCADA_Sys_Wht_Ppr-2a_New.pdf; 2007 [accessed 22.03.13].
[5] Stouffer K, Falco J, Karen K. Guide to supervisory control and data acquisition (SCADA) and industrial control systems security; 2006.
[6] Juniper Networks, Inc. Architecture for secure SCADA and distributed control system networks, http://www.juniper.net/us/en/local/pdf/whitepapers/2000276-en.pdf; 2009 [accessed 22.03.13].
[7] Strategic Security. Cyber security focus in the oil and gas sector to increase significantly. Strategic Security, http://www.resilienceoutcomes.com/organisations/unpatched-control-systems-in-the-oil-and-gas-industry-predicted-to-drive-significant-increase-cybersecurity-requirements/; 2013 [accessed 22.03.13].

[8] Mills E. Details of the first-ever control system malware. Cnet News, http://news.cnet.com/8301-27080_3-20011159-245.html; 2010 [accessed 22.03.13].

[9] Woodward P. Israel: smart enough to create Stuxnet and stupidenough to use it. War in context, http://warincontext.org/2010/10/01/israel-smart-enough-to-create-stuxnet-and-stupid-enough-to-use-it/; 2010 [accessed 22.03.13].

[10] U.S.-Canada Power System Outage Task Force. Final report on the August 14, 2003 Blackout in the United States and Canada: causes and recommendations, https://reports.energy.gov/BlackoutFinal-Web.pdf; 2004 [accessed 22.03.13].

[11] Highleyman WH. The Great 2003 northeast blackout and the $6 billion software bug. s.l.: the availability digest, http://www.availabilitydigest.com/private/0203/northeast_blackout.pdf; 2007 [accessed 22.03.13].

[12] Weiss G. The farewell dossier. Central Intelligence Agency, https://www.cia.gov/library/center-for-the-study-of-intelligence/csi-publications/csi-studies/studies/96unclass/farewell.htm; 2008 [accessed 22.03.13].

[13] Lawson S, McMillian R. FBI worried as DoD sold counterfeit Cisco gear. InfoWorld Security Central, http://www.infoworld.com/d/security-central/fbi-worried-dod-sold-counterfeit-cisco-gear-266; 2008 [accessed 22.03.13].

[14] Passalacqua C. How to identify, Badcaps.net, http://www.badcaps.net/pages.php?vid=5; 2010 [accessed 22.03.13].

[15] Moore S. Leaking capacitors muck up motherboards. IEEE spectrum. http://spectrum.ieee.org/computing/hardware/leaking-capacitors-muck-up-motherboards/0; 2003 [accessed 22.03.13].

[16] Moore R. Maxims of Napoleon bonaparte: on war. Napoleonic guide. http://www.napoleonguide.com/maxim_war.htm; 1999 [accessed 22.03.13].

[17] Marler, B. *E. coli* Poisons 293 in Belfast—someone needs to read poisoned. Centers for Marler Blog, http://www.marlerblog.com/case-news/e-coli-poisons-293-in-belfast-someone-needs-to-read-poisoned/; 2012 [accessed 23.03.13].

[18] Wilson C. High altitude electromagnetic pulse (HEMP) and high power microwave (HPM) devices: threat assessments s.l.: congressional research service, http://www.dtic.mil/cgi-bin/GetTRDoc?Location=U2&doc=GetTRDoc.pdf&AD=ADA529982; 2008 [accessed 22.03.13].

[19] Chapple M. Which disaster recovery site strategy is right for you? Biztech. http://www.biztechmagazine.com/article/2012/06/which-disaster-recovery-site-strategy-right-you; 2012 [accessed 23.03.13].

[20] Emmerson Network Power. Emerson network power's dusty becker addresses impact of post-katrina FCC mandate on backup power for telecom sites. Emmerson Network Power, http://www.emersonnetworkpower.com/en-US/About/NewsRoom/NewsReleases/Pages/EmersonNetworkPower%27sDustyBeckerAddressesImpactofPost-KatrinaFCCMandateonBackupPowerforTelecomSites.aspx; 2008 [accessed 22.03.13].

[21] Atkinson J. Tempest 101. Granite Island Group, http://www.tscm.com/TSCM101tempest.html; 2010 [accessed 22.03.13].

[22] National Security Agency. TEMPEST company POCs. National Security Agency/Central Security Service, http://www.nsa.gov/applications/ia/tempest/tempestPOCs.cfm; 2010 [accessed .22.03.13].

[23] Sabotage attacks knock out phone service. San Francisco Chronicle. http://www.sfgate.com/cgi-bin/article.cgi?f=/c/a/2009/04/10/MNP816VTE6.DTL&tsp=1; 2010 [accessed 22.03.13].

[24] Hiroshi S. What is Occam's razor? Phys.ncku.edu.tw, http://www.phys.ncku.edu.tw/mirrors/physicsfaq/General/occam.html; 1997 [accessed 22.03.13].

8

Psychological Weapons

INFORMATION IN THIS CHAPTER

- Social Engineering Explained
- How the Military Approaches Social Engineering

- How the Military Defends Against Social Engineering

We have talked about technical attacks in Chapters 6 and 7. Now it is time to talk about using the target's behaviors to gain access to their information. Psychological Operations (PSY OPS) are planned operations to convey selected information and indicators to foreign audiences to influence their emotions, motives, objective reasoning, and ultimately the behavior of foreign governments, organizations, groups, and individuals [1]. Militaries have been conducting PSY OPS, or Influence Operations, for centuries. The United States stood up Army Special Forces (Green Berets) to win the hearts and minds of the local population rather than just force to achieve victory. There has been a lot of change to doctrine based on lessons learned during operations in the Middle East, in fact the new Army FM for what was PSY OPS is now called Inform and Influence Activities and encompasses public affairs operations, military information support operations, combat camera, Soldier and leader engagement, civil affairs operations, civil and cultural considerations, operations security (OPSEC), and military deception. OPSEC and Force Protection are the defensive aspects for what we are talking about. Comparable techniques are used by Human Intelligence (HUMINT) collectors and the Intelligence Community to get enemy personnel to betray their countries by becoming spies. Similar techniques have been used in civilian society by con artists who make a living using their ability to gain someone's trust so they can take advantage of them. Many of the methods are used by salespeople to influence buyers to purchase the most expensive car. Now these techniques are being modified by hackers to get users to violate policies and common sense, thus allowing them access to critical data and are commonly referred to as Social Engineering.

SOCIAL ENGINEERING EXPLAINED

Social Engineering (SE) is the act of influencing someone's behavior through manipulating their emotions, or gaining and betraying their trust to gain access to their system. This can be done in person, over the phone, via an email, through social media, or a variety of other methods. The difference between SE and other attacks is the vectors are through the person, or as hackers say the "wetware."

The goal of an SE attack is to create a relationship, gain the target's trust, and get them to take an action or provide some information that is a violation of their organization's policies or personal basic security practices. Some folks have the gift of gab and can do it with a cold call but most attackers will take time to prepare a story based on information known about the target. This attack vector has grown rapidly in the past few years and for some target sets is the dominant technique.

Is SE Science?

How is this science? There have been many recent publications on kinesics (the study of body and facial expressions) like Paul Ekman's books on micro-facial expressions and *What Every Body Is Saying: An Ex-FBI Agent's Guide to Speed-Reading People* by Marvin Karlins and Joe Navarro. These, combined with books on subjects like *Emotional Intelligence: Why It Can Matter More Than IQ* by Daniel Goleman, *Blink: The Power of Thinking Without Thinking* by Malcolm Gladwell, *Thinking Fast and Slow* by Kahneman, or any of the books by Dan Ariely that talk about how intuition is based on insights the person may not be consciously aware of, start to develop a body of knowledge that can be applied as a science rather than an art. These studies are developing the baseline to take this discipline from an art to a science.

This leads to the question: can SE be taught, or is it a natural ability? There is some debate on whether SE skills can be taught, but this is basically the same debate that exists for leadership, salesmanship, or any other ability. Though the arguments are often very passionate, most will agree in the end that some people have natural tendencies that make them great when they study and train in the discipline they want to master whereas others can go through the same process and only become average. So whereas some individuals will naturally become very proficient at technical hacking they may struggle to use SE techniques like the "cold call" but everyone can learn the basics and find where their talents lay. Many of the tactics, techniques, and procedures (TTPs) we will discuss are a blend of technical and SE attacks.

> **NOTE**
>
> The difference between SE and interrogating the person that you're trying to gain information from is interrogating is under the control of the questioner so direct questioning is the most common technique. According to Joint Pub 2-01.2, intelligence-based interrogation is the systematic process of using approved interrogation approaches to question a captured or detained person to obtain reliable information to satisfy intelligence requirements, consistent with applicable law. The key being all techniques and methodologies undergo legal approval and review.

SE TTPs

A typical SE exploit depends on the target. There are two general scenarios: general access attacks and specific targeted access attacks. To set the stage, let's use the basic metaphor of stealing a car, keeping in mind that most metaphors when applied to cyberspace are dangerous as they don't reflect the complexity of the environment. In a general access attack, we could be looking for any car to steal. This could be relatively easy to accomplish. We could sit outside a convenience store waiting for someone to leave his/her car running and then jump in and drive away (remember to check for a baby seat) or we could use a gun and carjack someone at a light; we could go old school and learn to hotwire a car or any number of other techniques. Stealing a specific car—the mayor's car, for example—would be a different story. In the first scenario we didn't need to do any reconnaissance; now we need to put a lot of effort into recon. We have to learn what the mayor drives and figure out the best attack. We would need to understand which attack has the least chance of getting caught, as the mayor controls the police force. Depending on our motivations we may want the theft to go unnoticed for a period of time, or we may want it to be dramatic so it gets on the evening news. The same rules are true with cyber attacks but as there is an element of personal interaction in SE it is even more relevant to understand the target.

General Access Attacks

First let's look at general access attacks. These are attacks where the goal is to gain entry to any system or network. The attacker is indifferent to the owner of the system. A general phishing attack would be a good example (see note for definitions of types). The cost of sending out the emails is low; in 2010 there were about 183 billion spam emails sent a day and 2.3% were phishing attacks [2]. Compromised systems can then be used to attack other systems (making them "zombies"). Harvesting a large number of systems is useful to build systems in between the attacker and the targets. There is NO need for reconnaissance as the attacker doesn't care where the system is or what it does; they can move directly to the attack phase and, due to the low costs, accept a lower number of compromised systems.

The next example of a general attack is to release a virus. A virus is a malcode program that the user needs to run to have it work. Attackers can load a virus into a Word document, PDF, PowerPoint, picture, or even a game. These infected files will open and run (i.e., someone can open the PowerPoint document and go through the slides) at the same time the virus infects the system. The downside to an attack like this is that it can go viral (hence the name virus) and end up infecting systems it was not intended to attack. This kind of an attack can also be done with a worm which is a malcode program that doesn't need user interaction; it will infect a system and use it to infect others but this would not be a SE attack. It would be categorized as a technical attack. The proliferation of translation sites on the web and access to interesting news from the target's homeland have made this type of attack much easier to develop believable scenarios with proper grammar and cultural context that will get potential victims to take the bait.

Specific Targeted Access Attacks

Now we will analyze Specific Targeted Access Attacks. The attacker will approach the target after learning as much about them as they can via what the military calls Open Source Intelligence. Civilians would just call this "googling" someone. The attacker wants to understand the victim's interests, fears, motivations, attitudes, and desires. This will allow the attacker to tailor the attack and increase the chances of success. Key information includes knowledge of significant dates (birth, marriage, etc.), addresses, phone numbers, family members, interests, relationships, photographs, and work and education histories. If the target is active on social networking sites this is a great place to start; the greater their electronic footprint the better. There are many places to learn about the target:

- Personal info can be found on social media sites like Facebook or MySpace (this includes relationships, activities like sports, volunteering, religious practices, political beliefs, and so on)
- Professional information is on networking sites like LinkedIn or job sites like Monster (this also tells you what they are working on)
- Geolocation info on sites like Google Earth or location-based services like Foursquare
- Financial information like tax records and home ownership records
- What they are thinking can be read on via their Twitter pages or blogs
- Involvement in virtual worlds like Second Life or gaming site (where people can meet as any avatar they create)
- Membership info from organizations like academic alumni, clubs, professional organizations, or hobbies

diaries as part of their public web pages. Their expectations of privacy are different than most of the folks running the militaries and intelligence communities today. These digital natives can become vectors for attack if they have relationships with someone that has been targeted. It is important that everyone understand what is being posted and what is acceptable.

Types of SE Approaches

Once the attacker has gathered the background information necessary to understand some options to approach the target they must decide how aggressive they want to be. From least to most aggressive the approaches are: observation, conversation, interview, interrogation, and torture. They can start by digital or physical observation. Next comes a conversation (electronic, telephonic, or in person). This is often the phase where the attacker will determine who they want to recruit or attack. Typically this is known as elicitation which is generally the extraction of information through what seems to be a casual conversation. To phrase this another way it is "where the con is based on the social engineer's" ability to spin a lie. This ability comes from pretexting which is developing a scenario where the SE gains the trust of the person who owns or has access to the information in order to get them to break their policies or violate common sense and give the information to the attacker. One method that is used in every type of attack but is especially useful here is mirroring. For example by adopting the target's speech mannerism (or email style) it will be much easier to get them to engage in a conversation.

WARNING

The Financial Modernization Act of 1999 more commonly known as the Gramm-Leach-Bliley Act makes pretexting a crime. Under federal law it's illegal for anyone to [3]:

- Use false, fictitious, or fraudulent statements or documents to get customer information from a financial institution or directly from a customer of a financial institution.
- Use forged, counterfeit, lost, or stolen documents to get customer information from a financial institution or directly from a customer of a financial institution.
- Ask another person to get someone else's customer information using false, fictitious, or fraudulent statements or using false, fictitious, or fraudulent documents or forged, counterfeit, lost, or stolen documents.
- The Federal Trade Commission Act also generally prohibits pretexting for sensitive consumer information.

The next technique is to conduct an interview or outright interrogation. Both of these require the victim to submit to the attacker's authority. This can be done by posing as a customer who needs the information to make a decision, pretending to be someone from the government who has the right to the information, or through intimidation. These attacks can be done cold or after a relationship has been developed. The attacker can perform them in person using props like badges or over the phone/email using spoofing to make it appear like the

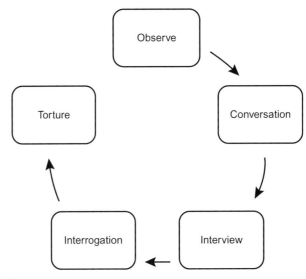

FIGURE 8.1 Approach techniques from least to most aggressive.

contact is from a legitimate source. An example would be to call someone as the Tech Department or Help Desk and tell them they have to reset their account because of a mistake made during a recent update. Most people want to be helpful and automatically trust their computer. That desire to help or trust in their system is the key to compromising them. Both of these techniques are not by their nature antagonistic. Often the most effective techniques are based on establishing common bonds. All of these techniques require building a relationship based on trust. Finally, after interrogation comes torture, but that is beyond SE practices. Figure 8.1 shows the flow of these Techniques.

Types of SE Methodologies

Some typical methodologies for general collection are divided into physical and electronic. Physical techniques include things like: dumpster diving (digging through target's trash), shoulder surfing (looking at a target's screen or keyboard while she/he works), observation (tracking a target's activities—think stakeout), spy gear (like directional microphones/ hidden cameras), and impersonation (posing as utility worker). Electronic techniques include: open web search (using all the features of a search engine—i.e., Google will just search blogs), Pay for Service sites like Intelius or U.S. Search, Credit Information Requests, social networking site searches, and professional networking site searches and geolocation sites (e.g., Google Street View).

Though this information is generally openly available the social engineer may need some tools to make the research more effective. These include web sites and tools like:

- SE Toolkit (technical hacks against the user)
- American Registry for Internet Numbers (IPs and phone numbers for North America)
- Freedom of Information Act requests

- Social media—OpenBook (Facebook searches), LinkedIn, Friendster, Monster, Yelp, Craigslist, Jigsaw, FriendFinder, PiPl, Plaxo, wordpress, Shodan
- Maltego and Maltego Mesh (link mapping)
- BeEF (webpage redirection)
- TwitScoop and Tweepz (Twitter searches)
- Creepy [http://ilektrojohn.github.io/creepy/] and TwitterMap (geolocation)
- Edgar [www.sec.gov/edgar] (corporate info)
- Sites like Spokeo (people search) and Telespoof.com (caller ID spoofing)

Additional tactics include:

- Camouflage
  - Fake business cards, disguises (facial or uniforms), and fake or cloned badges
  - Props (everything from clipboards to toolkits to deliveries)
- Lock Picking/Tailgating
- Cameras/hacking into video system
- GPS tracker

This is just a quick list of some of the different types of tools that can be employed as part of SE.

One recent event that has captured the media's attention was the SE Capture the Flag (CTF) event at the 2012 DEFCON 20 called "The Battle of the Sexes." There has always been a network-based CTF event but in 2010 DEFCON started SE CTF. The latest competition is an evolution to compare results based on gender (women captured more flags). There have also been competitions for youth to train the next generation. Here is an excerpt from the report on the event:

> Contestants were assigned a target company, with each having two weeks to use passive information gathering techniques to build a profile. No direct contact between the contestant and the target was allowed during this time. The information was compiled into a dossier that was turned in and graded as part of the contestant's score. During DefCon, contestants were then allowed 25 min to call their target and collect as many flags as possible, which made up the remainder of their score. Flags were picked to be non-sensitive information, and each was assigned a point value based on the degree of difficulty in obtaining the information associated with the flag. A few examples of the 25 flags are: In House IT Support, New Hire Process, Anti-Virus Used, Is there a Cafeteria, Wireless On-Site, Badges for Bldg Access and What OS Used.
>
> Complex searches lead the contestants to gather quite a few PDFs or web pages that answered each of their inquires in full detail. One interesting surprise was the use of Google Street View as an information gathering tool. A primary factor in the success or failure of the contestant was the planning of the overall attack. The most interesting aspect of this has to do with how quickly and easily information could be obtained from all companies in a relatively short period of time, even with the caller under pressure. Final results were 15 companies called and 14 of them had flags captured [4].

HOW THE MILITARY APPROACHES SE

The military has been in the spy-counterspy business from the beginning; they are also experts at interrogation. Spying is the long con, whereas interrogation is generally the method used to get access to information in an immediate situation. This section will focus on the near term gathering of data (or the short con). We will look at the techniques used to extract information and discuss how they apply to SE.

First, we must understand that these techniques have been developed to work in both peacetime operations and combat situations. They are normally done in a controlled environment and are very similar to the techniques used by law enforcement agencies. The basic principles are similar to SE and the foundational principles and many of the techniques apply well to SE attacks. The military trains interrogators that stay in that discipline their entire careers. They become proficient in the languages and culture of their assigned region. HUMINT operators or interrogators are trained to deal with screening refugees, debriefing U.S. and allied forces, interrogating prisoners of war, interviewing collaborators, exploiting captured material, liaising with host nation, acting as interpreters if needed, and interacting with the local population.

Army Doctrine

We will discuss how the army deals with interrogation as they are the ones who are on the ground dealing with these issues. The basic techniques we will cover are from "FM 2–22.3 HUMAN INTELLIGENCE COLLECTOR OPERATIONS" September 2006 [5].

Goal: collector's objective during this phase is to establish a relationship with the source that results in the source providing accurate and reliable information in response to the HUMINT collector's questions.

Key principles: From a psychological standpoint, the HUMINT collector must be cognizant of the following behaviors:

- Want to talk when they are under stress and respond to kindness and understanding during trying circumstances.
- Show deference when confronted by superior authority.
- Operate within a framework of personal and culturally derived values.
- Respond to physical and, more importantly, emotional self-interest.
- Fail to apply or remember lessons they may have been taught regarding security if confronted with a disorganized or strange situation.
- Be more willing to discuss a topic about which the HUMINT collector demonstrates identical or related experience or knowledge.
- Appreciate flattery and exoneration from guilt.
- Attach less importance to a topic if it is treated routinely by the HUMINT collector.
- Resent having someone or something they respect belittled, especially by someone they dislike.

These principles are used to develop an approach, build rapport, and establish a relationship in which the HUMINT collector presents a realistic persona designed to evoke cooperation from the source. In the military things are usually done in accordance with established procedures and if it is a mission (like an interrogation) should have a documented plan. This is not to say soldiers are not flexible and resist innovation but rather to say they want to increase the chances of mission accomplishment and have found these lead to greater success. The HUMINT collector must ensure their body language and personal representation match their approach.

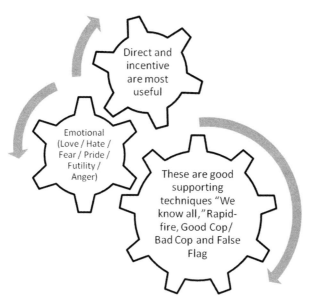

FIGURE 8.2 The various approaches must be integrated.

Some standard operating approach techniques are: direct, incentive, emotional (Love/Hate/Fear/Pride/Futility/Anger), "we know all" or "file/dossier," rapid-fire (don't let them talk), Mutt and Jeff or good cop/bad cop, and false flag (misrepresentation of oneself). See Figure 8.2 for how these relate to each other. The direct approach is simple and straightforward. It is simply telling the person what they want and using interview/interrogation skills to convince them to cooperate and share the information. This technique is useful in a conventional war but not very useful in counterinsurgencies or for SE. Statistics from interrogation operations in World War II show that the direct approach was effective 90% of the time. In Vietnam and in Operations URGENT FURY (Grenada, 1983), JUST CAUSE (Panama, 1989), and DESERT STORM (Kuwait and Iraq, 1991), the direct approach was 95% effective. The effectiveness of the direct approach in Operations ENDURING FREEDOM (Afghanistan, 2001-2002) and IRAQI FREEDOM (Iraq, 2003) is still being studied; however, unofficial studies indicate that in these operations, the direct approach has been dramatically less successful [5]. The military is still analyzing the reasons but one common assumption is that the motivations of religious fanaticism are harder to compromise than traditional nationalism. There are some general types of direct questions that are useful: Initial (get the discussion going), Topical (focused on establishing how much they will communicate and what their level of knowledge is), Follow-up (making sure we have gained all the primary and peripheral information), Nonpertinent (establishing rapport and keeping discussion going), Repeat (seeing if they are consistent), Control (establish baseline), Prepared (for areas interviewer is unfamiliar with or highly technical topics). One of the key questions here is the control or baseline question. It establishes how someone behaves when they are telling the truth. Much like a polygraph test that starts with baseline questions like name and address then gradually that builds to questions related to guilty actions to compare stress reactions against, a social engineer must understand how the target behaves when not under stress.

The indirect approach, or using elicitation, can often be useful as we combine information gathering from normal conversations with targets of interest without them knowing they are being interrogated. Elicitation is a sophisticated technique used when conventional collection techniques cannot be used effectively. Of all the collection methods, this one is the least obvious. However, it is important to note that elicitation is a planned, systematic process that requires careful preparation [5]. This is where the more the interviewer knows about the target the better, so they can have a natural flowing conversation. For example, they may start by sharing information they have so the target assumes they know all about it and will openly discuss the details.

Next comes incentive. This is basically offering the target something they want or need. The first thing that comes to mind is bribing them, but it can be as simple as an email offering to increase their speed or access to the Internet. This approach can be very effective when tied to the right emotions. The emotional approach is where the target's emotions are brought into the interaction to get them to take an action that they would not normally do. A recent example of this is what is known as scareware. A good example is when a pop-up box announces there is a problem on the user's system that can be fixed by installing a free update. In reality this scareware update is a Trojan horse whose only function is to compromise the user's system. This approach is based on Fear, other emotions that can be used are: Love (in its many forms), Hate or Anger (us against them), Pride (in themselves or their organization), and Futility (there is no other option). Picking the right emotion is easier in person because we can read the body language or on the phone where we can judge the tone of voice and modify the approach based on the situation. The goal of this method is to manipulate the target's emotions so they override their natural cognitive reactions.

Other well-known techniques are: "we know all" or "file/dossier"; this is where the interrogator comes in and lays a folder labeled "witness statements" or a DVD labeled "surveillance footage" on the desk. This fake evidence contains no actual information but allows the interrogator to start by saying something like, "we have the evidence we need but want to get your side of the story before we submit our final report." For a social engineer/interrogator the presentation of material that supports the belief that the interrogator knows the basics but just needs the target to provide the details. If target is still not talking freely it may be time to try the rapid-fire method where the interrogator keeps interrupting the target so they get frustrated and jump in with key facts so we will listen. The rapid-fire method is also used when the target is going to tell a lie that the interrogator doesn't want them to say like "I have never been to that site" because once they tell a lie they are committed to it. To get to the truth we first must make the target to admit they lied.

The last two methods we will discuss are Mutt and Jeff, or good cop/bad cop, and false flag. We have all seen the aggressive and compassionate interview team in movies. The target will identify with the compassionate person and tell their story so the good cop will shield them from the aggressive cop. This method can also be modified so a really abusive interrogator is followed by one who apologizes for the unprofessional behavior of their colleague. Typically the good cop would help the target rationalize their actions so they can talk openly. One way this method can be used by social engineers is on social networking sites; we could present a Fakebook (fake FaceBook) personality created for the attack as a cyber bully and a second as someone defending the target.

Finally using the false flag, for the military this might be having a new interrogator come in and pretend to be from a friendly country or a nongovernment origination like the Red Cross. This is very useful as it is simply misrepresentation and is a bedrock of SE.

We can see that most of the techniques used by the military are directly applicable to the civilian sector and can be applied to both physical and cyber environments. The most important aspects the military brings are proven TTPs and careful mission preparation and planning. These when applied to SE will give the attacker a strong capability to be successful on their mission.

HOW THE MILITARY DEFENDS AGAINST SE

As discussed earlier, the military has been in the spy-counterspy business from the beginning. The counterspy techniques are the same skills needed to defend against SE. Today's solider needs to understand counterintelligence (CI), counterterrorism, force protection, and Operational Security (OPSEC) techniques. This section will focus on the tactical level actions that can be done for CI. First let's review the doctrinal definitions for the key concepts:

- CI: Information gathered and activities conducted to protect against espionage, other intelligence activities, sabotage, or assassinations conducted by or on behalf of foreign governments or elements thereof, foreign organizations, or foreign persons, or international terrorist activities [6].
- Cyber CI: Measures to identify, penetrate, or neutralize foreign operations that use cyber means as the primary tradecraft methodology, as well as foreign intelligence service collection efforts that use traditional methods to gauge cyber capabilities and intentions [6].
- Counterespionage: That aspect of CI designed to detect, destroy, neutralize, exploit, or prevent espionage activities through identification, penetration, manipulation, deception, and repression of individuals, groups, or organizations conducting or suspected of conducting espionage activities [6].
- Counterterrorism: Actions taken directly against terrorist networks and indirectly to influence and render global and regional environments inhospitable to terrorist networks [6].
- Force Protection: Preventive measures taken to mitigate hostile actions against Department of Defense personnel (to include family members), resources, facilities, and critical information. Force protection does not include actions to defeat the enemy or protect against accidents, weather, or disease [6].
- OPSEC: A process of identifying critical information and subsequently analyzing friendly actions attendant to military operations and other activities to: (a) identify those actions that can be observed by adversary intelligence systems; (b) determine indicators that adversary intelligence systems might obtain that could be interpreted or pieced together to derive critical information in time to be useful to adversaries; and (c) select and execute measures that eliminate or reduce to an acceptable level the vulnerabilities of friendly actions to adversary exploitation [6].

The military depends on confidentiality and secrecy. They deploy encryption, data classification, clearances for their personnel, and a thorough set of processes and regulations. Soldiers, airmen, seamen, and marines understand the trust they have been given and the level of national security compromise that could occur (not necessarily through a single loss of data but the aggregate knowledge impact as well). Cybersecurity has become a critical component of the National Counterintelligence Strategy (see Figure 8.3). The mission to secure the nation against foreign espionage and electronic penetration of the IC, DoD, and to protect U.S. economic advantage, trade secrets, and know-how is becoming a core responsibility for the military.

CI has an offensive aspect as well. There is a need to set up internal traps or as they are called in cyberspace "honey pots" to attract insiders accessing information they are not authorized for. These honey pots will also capture outside threats that have gained access. Another technique organizations should consider is to have enticing files with embedded beacons that report back on where they end up when stolen to provide situational awareness on what has leaked out and who did it. Organizations need to fund programs to gain access to

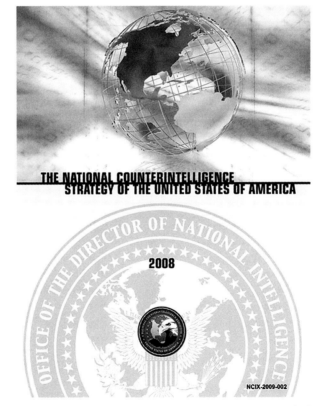

FIGURE 8.3   Counterintelligence is a national concern; this is the U.S. strategy to deal with it [7].

the types of organizations that have the motives and means to attack the United States and see what they have stolen. Organizations need to conduct exercises and tests on our personnel to assess our readiness level. Finally, we need to enforce consequences on individuals caught violating policies.

How the Army Does CI

Army regulation (AR 381-12 Threat Awareness and Reporting Program 4 October 2010 (for the old soldiers this was called Subversion and Espionage Directed against the U.S. Army or SAEDA)) establishes the training requirements and reporting procedures. It also lays out indicators or suspicious activities, such as foreign influence or connections, disregard for security practices, unusual work behavior, financial matters, foreign travel, undue interest, soliciting others, and extremist activity. This is basically a process that encourages every member of the staff to become a security officer and help police both themselves and their coworkers. The program is built around two key principles: situational awareness and behavior monitoring, both for themselves and their coworkers. If done well, it will counter the whole spectrum of crime, internal threats (disgruntled or unstable workers), external threats (foreign operatives and terrorist), and today's social engineers. If done poorly, it allows incidents like the recent unauthorized release of a large number of classified documents relating to the U.S. war in Iraq to WikiLeaks to occur.

An Air Force Approach

The Air Force Public Affairs Agency has published a "Social Media Guide." Top 16 tips include items like: differentiate between opinion and official information and no classified information [8]. This is a very good example as it does a couple of things well. First the guide is more about what we should use rather than why we should not use the many different communication applications on the web. Second it is a formal policy that includes punitive consequences for misbehavior.

An important aspect of this defensive capability is to analyze the information that is leaking and conduct the appropriate investigation to determine what actions need to be taken. Historically there are examples of traditional espionage like Aldrich Ames, Robert Hanssen, Colonel Vladimir Vetrov, a KGB defector known as the Farewell Dossier, Gregg Bergersen, and the 11 Russian spies recently deported from the United States, but these operations are time consuming, expensive, and risky where we can get much of the same material through cyber spying. The risk of getting caught is lower, the time to gain access is faster, and the cost is cheaper. We have talked extensively about computer network exploitation; when we combine that with SE we have a paradigm shift in spying capabilities. This requires us to look at the techniques that got these traditional spies caught, including careful analysis, auditing financial records, tips from co-workers, offensive operations to gain access to enemy files to see who they had turned into spies, and encouraging defectors to switch sides.

For the sake of brevity, we're not going to delve into the processes of the Navy and Marine Corps, although they're both quite capable in their own right at these processes and procedures.

SUMMARY

SE is a very dangerous threat vector to all organizations and individuals. It requires training and vigilance to defend against. For example, a simple questionnaire sent to a target on a social networking site asking the target to answer question about themselves so they can become closer friends could include the same questions asked by the company to reset the target's password and now the target's organization is compromised. We need to make sure people are vigilant and cautious (remember you're not paranoid if they are out to get you). We can leverage lessons learned in the military to understand how these SE attacks work and how we defend ourselves. Defenses against SE must be focused on behaviors.

The policies, culture, and training must be reinforced often to insure the workforce stays vigilant. Training the staff to have situational awareness is key to a good counter-SE program. This training must be continuous with messages from multiple sources—emails, meetings, and formal training. There need to be exercises to test the staff like emails asking employees to go to a site and enter their password only to find a message from the company that they would have allowed hackers to gain access to the network if it was a real attack. Security audits should include SE attacks to validate that the training is effective. There is a saying in the hacker community: "You can't patch stupid," which often refers to the fact that if an organization has a great technical security infrastructure and the attacker could not penetrate them, just go after the people. People are not stupid; they just don't understand the risks they are taking with their actions. Training is a critical step to fixing this threat vector.

The bottom line is: this is the growth area for threat vectors via social media and the only way to defend against it is executive awareness, user training, and validation exercises.

References

[1] Department of Defense. Joint electronic library, http://www.dtic.mil/doctrine/ [accessed 17.01.13].
[2] Commtouch Software Ltd Q1 2010 internet threats trend report, http://www.commtouch.com/press-releases/well-known-web-names-misused-to-give-spam-deceptive-legitimacy-according-to-new-report-by-commtouch/ [accessed 17.01.13].
[3] Financial Modernization Act of 1999. Federal Trade Commission. Facts for consumers, http://www.ftc.gov/bcp/edu/pubs/consumer/credit/cre10.shtm [accessed 17.01.13].
[4] Hadnagy CJ, Aharoni M, O'Gorman J. Defcon 20 social engineering CTF, http://www.social-engineer.org/social-engineering-ctf-battle-of-the-sexes [accessed 17.01.13].
[5] Army, U.S. FM 2–22.3 (FM 34–52) Human intelligence collector operations. Public affairs, https://www.fas.org/irp/doddir/army/fm2-22-3.pdf; 2006 [accessed 17.01.13].
[6] JP 1–02 from Department of defense. Joint electronic library, http://www.dtic.mil/doctrine/ [accessed 17.01.13].
[7] Office of the director of national intelligence's office of the national counterintelligence executive, http://www.ncix.gov/publications/strategy/docs/2008_Strategy.pdf [accessed 17.01.13].
[8] Air force social media guide 2012, http://www.af.mil/shared/media/document/AFD-120327-048.pdf [accessed 17.01.13].

Computer Network Exploitation

The term Computer Network Exploitation (CNE) is a cyber warfare term of military origin, and one that may be slightly confusing to those that are not on the inside of the environment. Although we might be tempted to think that the "exploit" in CNE refers to exploits used against systems in order to gain privileges or remote shells on them, this is not the case. In actuality, exploit in this case refers to the ability to exploit the data or information gathered on our target for our own purposes. Officially defined, CNE is "Enabling operations and intelligence collection capabilities conducted through the use of computer networks to gather data from target or adversary automated information systems or networks" [1] Such operations are the cyber equivalent of good old-fashioned spying or espionage. CNE is the phase of cyber warfare that we are experiencing globally at this point. We commonly see cyber intelligence, reconnaissance, and surveillance (ISR) activities taking place, but we do not yet commonly see outright cyber attacks between nation-states.

Although such intelligence gathering activities are a standard part of warfare and of the normal conduct of government, in the cyber world, the mechanisms that allow such activities to be conducted can be a bit easier to carry out than they are in the physical world. When we store our darkest secrets on computer systems that are connected, however indirectly, to the global Internet, we leave a pathway open for skilled attackers to access this information.

Even when such sensitive information is not directly available, we can imply a great deal of information by examining systems and networks, even from the outside, in preparation for future attacks. Such items of intelligence, for the purposes of cyber warfare can allow us to plan attacks, perhaps down to the point of specific vulnerabilities that can be exploited on individual systems.

Using some of the tools that we discussed in Chapter 6, we can begin to construct a very specific picture of our target environment, in preparation for Computer Network Attack (CNA), or even as a basis to plan refinements to our Computer Network Defense (CND) strategies. We will discuss CNA further in Chapter 10 and CND in more depth in Chapter 11.

INTELLIGENCE AND COUNTER-INTELLIGENCE

Identifying who exactly the enemy is for purposes of CNE can be a bit of a tricky proposition. In the virtual world, when we refer to an enemy or threat, we may actually be referring to what are really the second- or third-order effects of the actual activity of our enemy. In other words, when we see a Distributed Denial of Service (DDoS) attack coming from a group of machines in China, it is important to understand that the Chinese may not be related to the attack at all, other than in the sense of being an endpoint. To truly identify the enemy, we need to look at the targets, sources, attackers, and sponsors of the activity that we are monitoring.

Sources of Cyber Attacks

Attack sources can be a bit of a vague notion in the world of logical attacks. In this particular case, we use the term source to indicate the endpoint from which the actual attack arrived. For example, systems in China are frequently theorized to be used as a stepping stone to attack other systems. Although such a system certainly can seem to be the actual source of the attack, this may not be the case at all, due to the relative ease of compromising a system and using it as a proxy to attack another target. In fact many times both nation-states and criminals will route their attacks through countries that will not cooperate with an investigation. We can generally classify attacks as either direct attacks or proxy attacks.

Direct attacks, as they sound, are attacks conducted directly from the system that is directly controlled by the attacker, i.e., the attacker is not attached to the system remotely from another system. Although direct attacks certainly have the benefit of not spreading the route that the attacker is taking out over a series of potentially unstable connections, they do nothing to disguise the origin of the attacks.

Depending on where a direct attack is originating from, being able to trace the origin of the attack may or may not cause problems for the attacker. In many countries, a serious attack reported to an Internet Service Provider (ISP) may result in the connection that the attacker is using to be shut down. Additionally, an attacker working directly from their own system runs the risk of the target retaliating against and disabling the attacking system, or worse yet, retrieving information regarding the attacker.

Proxy attacks, those attacks that are run through one or more intervening systems, are a safer type of attack to use from the standpoint of disguising attribution. Although using a single machine as a proxy for an attack may not provide much in the way of indirection to keep the actual attacker from being discovered, this protection increases greatly with each additional step along the way. By the time an attacker has proxied through several machines, each located in a different geographical area, the attacker has created a virtual morass of networks, system, and legal structures to hide behind.

On the other side of the proxy attack situation, a consideration is also the potential set of technical issues caused by connecting through a series of systems. An attacker has not only potential technical and stability problems with the network connections and systems that they are utilizing, but with each additional layer that an attacker has in place, the attacker greatly increases the chances that the administrators or users of the system will notice the unusual activity and that the attacker will be detected.

Attackers and Sponsors of Attacks

As we discussed in Chapter 2, we will see threats from a variety of angles, and from many different types of attackers. We can generally categorize these groups into state and nonstate actors, i.e., those that do and do not have the sponsorship of, or act directly on behalf of a nation-state and those that do.

Most nation-states, and the parties that they sponsor directly, have certain sets of laws that they are generally bound to follow when conducting warfare, including warfare of a cyber variety. Although how exactly these laws apply to cyber warfare is still being sorted out, we will discuss them at some length in Chapters 12 and 13.

Additionally, we may see attack from nongovernment sponsored organizations, or nonstate actors, such as corporations, political or activist organizations, criminal groups, individuals, or any combination or variation of these. We will discuss such attackers in considerably more detail in Chapter 12.

RECONNAISSANCE

Cyber reconnaissance can be divided into three major categories, Open Source Intelligence (OSINT), passive reconnaissance, and Advanced Persistent Threat (APT). Although these three methods of reconnaissance are, for the most part, diametrically opposed, they all have their place in cyber warfare. An attacker often will want to start with the use of OSINT to gather as much information as they can without directly indicating their interest, then proceed to passive reconnaissance when they need to gather more specific information that they have not been able to gain through the passive route.

Open Source Intelligence

OSINT involves the use of methods that are designed to not alert a target to the fact that they are under observation. Many of the tools that we discussed in the reconnaissance tools section of Chapter 6 fall squarely into this category. Investigating Domain Name System (DNS) information, Google hacking, information gathered from websites, investigation of document metadata, and other similar methods can all be excellent means of executing OSINT operations, as long as they are careful to not expose their interests in the process of conducting them. In OSINT they will likely start with public information, then job-related information, then Google hacking, then DNS information, then metadata gathering, as shown

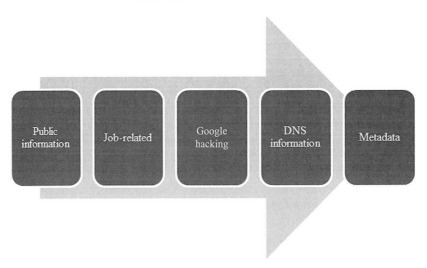

FIGURE 9.1 OSINT process.

in Figure 9.1. When conducting reconnaissance against a target the attacker will generally start with OSINT, and then move to passive.

Primarily, when taking an OSINT approach to reconnaissance, an attacker will want to use information sources that do not leak information about our interests, or at least minimize such leakage. For instance, although they may use a public web-based whois query tool to conduct research against a target, the administrators of such an application may find it interesting that the IP address block of a known government contract organization had a suddenly high level of interest in the DNS information of systems related to the Chinese government. In such cases, it is often best to use a network masking technology such as The Onion Router (Tor) and to spread such queries out over many different sources.

> **TIP**
>
> Tor, which can be found at www.torproject.org, is a tool that provides network anonymization by routing the traffic from a client through a variety of intermediate systems and out through one of many possible endpoints. Although Tor does indeed provide some measure of protection against a target or application being able to trace back the source of the network traffic in question, there are several attacks and configuration issues, including endpoints set up specifically to sniff traffic, that may make it possible to do exactly this.

To a certain extent, attackers can also use some network monitoring techniques for OSINT purposes. Although attackers are very limited in what they can do for sniffing on a wireless network when bound by the requirement of stealth, there are packet sniffing tools that are entirely passive in nature and are very difficult to detect without taking specific measures to do so.

NOTE

The battle between passive network sniffers and the systems that can pick them out is an ongoing one. As we note, if we put a passive sniffer on the network, it is difficult to detect, but we can do so with a properly configured Intrusion Detection System (IDS). We can also adjust our sniffers to avoid such IDSs, and tune our IDSs to ferret out such avoidance measures, and so on ad infinitum.

There are also network sniffing tools that work through induction rather than direct interface with the network that are, in theory, truly impossible to detect without physically finding the inductive tap itself [2]. Even fiber optic cables, often considered to not be passively tappable, in fact are exactly that. Low cost devices are available to read the light leakage through the jacket of a fiber cable without actually needing to cut it to insert a tap [3].

Additionally, we can eavesdrop on wireless network traffic in relative safety, as long as we are careful not to interact with the network itself. Even encrypted wireless traffic can reveal information about the devices that are connecting to it and, based off names and Media Access Control (MAC) addresses of such devices, we can often infer quite a bit of information about the environment.

A technique that we cannot discount in cyber warfare scenarios is that of passive physical observation, which is part of Human Intelligence, or HUMINT. Such techniques, as they generally require, at least at some point, the physical presence of an observer, do have the opportunity to alert the target in question that they are being watched, but when carried out carefully can be invaluable. Physical observations of traffic patterns at facilities, movement of vendors, arrival of equipment, and other similar factors can allow us to infer much about the goings on at our target location. We discussed this and some of the other intelligence gathering methods in more depth in Chapter 2.

Passive Reconnaissance

Passive reconnaissance takes more direct steps to extract information on our target environment that OSINT does, but is passive in relation to our actual target. A good example of an attack being passive relative to the specific target might be compromising a router used by the target, then disrupting or degrading other paths in order to channel packets to the compromised router where we might more easily eavesdrop on the traffic. In such a case, we have altered the environment to aid in our reconnaissance, but have not touched the target itself.

Passive reconnaissance will often involve many of the tools that we discussed in Chapter 6 that involve directly interrogating a network or system, in order to discover its particulars. Passive reconnaissance will often be, as we discussed, the next step after OSINT gathering and may be partially based on the information gathered during that activity. During passive reconnaissance, an attacker may unintentionally expose information to a target from the nodes that are active in these tasks. In this way passive reconnaissance may differ greatly in cyber warfare activity than in penetration testing.

In penetration testing, presuming that we are performing it in the recommended and legal fashion, we have permission to attack the target environment, and any attempt to gain information from our attacking systems is likely to be short lived and shallow, at best. We will also

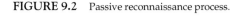

FIGURE 9.2   Passive reconnaissance process.

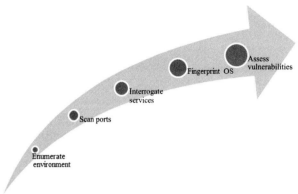

be unlikely to see any attempt at counter-attack or retaliation in such a scenario. In a true cyber warfare or cyber conflict, these are situations that we are likely to run into, and should take into account when planning. We can mitigate the likelihood of being noticed in our activities and, to a certain extent, retaliatory efforts by ensuring that our reconnaissance tasks are carried out from a variety of different sources, preferably from separated network blocks, at the very least, if not from geographically disparate locations. We can also mask such activities by performing them in a fashion that spreads them out over a much longer period of time that what we would normally examine when attempting to detect such attacks.

In the tools that we are likely to see used in passive reconnaissance, we will find various scanning tools, such as network sniffers for both wired and wireless networks, port scanners, vulnerability analysis tools, operating system fingerprinting tools, banner grabbing tools, and other similar utilities. We will be looking to enumerate the infrastructure devices, networks, and systems in place in the environment; assess the ports open and services operating on those ports; fingerprint operating systems; and assess vulnerabilities, as shown in Figure 9.2. This process is certainly not set in stone and is intended as a general guideline. There will be times when a chain of interesting information will lead us to one step sooner than another and there is absolutely nothing wrong with varying the approach.

We will often find our future actions or attacks will enjoy a much greater degree of success if we take the time to carefully document the information discovered regarding the specifics of our target environment. This documentation will not only ease the planning of future attacks or more detailed reconnaissance, but will also ensure that all of those involved in the operation are working from the same set of information. It is also important to keep this documentation up to date as new information is gained, or as changes in the environment are noted.

SURVEILLANCE

The major difference between reconnaissance and surveillance is that reconnaissance tends to imply a single observation of a given environment, whereas surveillance implies an ongoing observation [4]. It is certainly true that any of the tools and methods that we have discussed for conducting reconnaissance could be used in an ongoing manner as surveillance tools, and indeed some of them are, though extended operation of such tools would result in a very high likelihood of being discovered. Some of the same general techniques are still useful, but can be adapted to more long-term eavesdropping on communications of voice and data, or emissions into the electromagnetic spectrum.

Justifications for Surveillance

Although we can certainly justify the use of reconnaissance in advance of an attack, surveillance as a long-term measure is an entirely different case. Constant surveillance of voice and data communications implies the insertion of hardware, software, or both into the target environment in order to report the desired data out to a location from where it can be retrieved. In the case of surveillance being conducted by a nation-state, most countries are subject to various laws and treaties, both international and domestic, which strictly regulate such practices. In this case, any surveillance that is conducted is considered an act of espionage, which, although frowned upon, is still practiced by modern nations around the world, even allies.

WARNING

Conducting surveillance is fairly universally regulated by one or more wiretap laws in most countries around the globe. In most cases, conducting surveillance without following very specific rules, even on privately owned systems, may very well violate such laws and result in stiff penalties. In cases where such surveillance is required, consulting legal advice beforehand is strongly advised.

There is also the consideration that the target of surveillance may be internal to our nation or organization. Such cases are certainly more common in recent years, largely as a result of several large terrorist attacks having taken place. In the face of such activities, governments can often make a case, sometimes without consulting the public in the matter, for ongoing surveillance. Such programs are often implemented in the name of combating terrorism, drug trafficking, and other similar situations. Although there are also commonly laws that regulate domestic surveillance, such laws are not always followed to the letter, and in fact, are sometimes bent in the name of the public good. We will discuss some of these issues in greater depth later in this section.

Advanced Persistent Threat

Advanced Persistent Threat (APT) actors make use of organized and long-term attacks, designed specifically to access and exfiltrate information from the target systems and imply a more active role in gathering information than any that we have discussed previously. APT operations are more direct, and may have more in common with the CNA process that we will discuss in this chapter, closely matching some of the activities, but differing somewhat in intent and motivation. In APT, the steps that we might take are attack, escalate, and exfiltrate.

Attack activities in APT are motivated by getting us onto the system in order to extract the intelligence that is our main goal. Although an outright and obvious attack is certainly not necessarily out of scope here, this may not be conducive to our intelligence gathering activities. In this case, we may want to slowly and carefully infiltrate the system in order to pass unnoticed as we attack. A good example of this might be to use a client-side attack or low-impact custom malware to enter the environment quietly.

Once we have compromised the target system in order to gain access, we may need to escalate our access level in order to gain the desired information. As we are conducting an APT operation, we will likely be concerned more with gaining just enough access to carry out our task than we will be with owning the entire system. In some cases, if our attack phase has been very successful, we may be able to directly access the system with the credentials that we need, and not need to take this additional step.

Once we are on the system and we have the appropriate level of access, we will need to exfiltrate our target information. Depending on the system and the environment in question, there are a wide variety of ways we might be able to carry this out. In many commercial environments, we will often find several commonly open channels to the outside world. It may be possible to exfiltrate our data over such a channel by doing something along the lines of moving data over port 80 along with the normally large load of web traffic. In areas with higher levels of security, we may need to be more creative in our exfiltration attempts, and perhaps use an out of band method to communicate our data to the outside world one bit at a time. In either case, it may pay to move our data quietly and slowly so we do not burn the system as a source of information if we think that we might want to return again in the future.

Voice Surveillance

On voice communication systems built on older analog technologies, conducting voice surveillance was literally a matter of wiring a device into the phone line at some point, called a wire tap. As we move forward into newer systems, such tasks become increasingly easier to carry out and easier to execute from a distance as well, but we continue to use the same term. In digital phone systems, such surveillance may be as easy as activating a feature in the systems controlling the voice traffic for a particular location, rendering a once manual task into a few clicks in an administrative tool.

In recent years, Voice over IP (VoIP) traffic has begun to make large inroads toward replacing the common telephone service as the standard for voice-based communications. For those that intend to conduct surveillance on such communications, this is actually good thing, as VoIP traffic is considerably easier to eavesdrop on from a distance, and, depending on the implementation may have considerably less inherent security.

In essence, eavesdropping on unencrypted VoIP conversations, which may include many commercial and consumer services, is just a matter of having access to the network traffic in order to apply a sniffing device. Both sides of a voice conversation can be recorded in this manner and can easily be decoded and played back using a tool such as Wireshark or Cain and Abel, both of which have a simple point-and-click interface which will play back an audio version of the conversation in a given packet capture file.

Data Surveillance

Data surveillance is a longer term, and often more pervasive, version of some of the tools and techniques that we have discussed in the reconnaissance sections of this chapter and

Chapter 6. Data surveillance is often conducted by monitoring infrastructure devices that have been permanently or semipermanently installed with the express purpose of listening to the traffic going over the network or networks in question.

In smaller scale installations, such as those that we might find in a corporation wishing to conduct such surveillance, this is often carried out through the installation of specialized surveillance devices, such as those produced by NIKSUN, at key areas in the network infrastructure. Such devices can allow traffic to be captured as it goes over the network in order to allow for later analysis of attacks, application usage, communications, and any number of network-oriented activities. Although such solutions work very well for small- to medium-scale monitoring, they do not scale well when we wish to monitor much larger sets of data, such as monitoring of traffic or traffic patterns for an entire nation. For such purposes, the organizations, generally governments, that wish to do so generally implement their own solutions or have solutions custom built for them.

Large-Scale Surveillance Programs

The U.S. government provides us with several good examples of government-scale surveillance systems. One of the earlier such attempts at enabling voice and data surveillance on a large scale was seen in Echelon. Echelon is the popular term used to refer to the network of signals intelligence collection and analysis operated by the parties to the U.S.-UK Security Agreement, namely, the United States, Canada, United Kingdom, Australia, and New Zealand. Echelon is large-scale eavesdropping on international voice traffic over satellite, phone networks, microwave links, and even data sources such as fax transmissions and email. The original intent of Echelon was to monitor the communications of the Soviet Union and the countries allied with it in the 1960s. At present, it is believed to be used for monitoring of activities more along the lines of terrorism and drug trafficking, as well as to collect general intelligence information.

The Carnivore program was implemented by the U.S. Federal Bureau of Investigation (FBI) in the late 1990s. Carnivore was a device that when attached at the ISP of the target intended to be monitored could filter out and record all traffic going to and from the target. Carnivore was not contextually aware and could only filter traffic by the sending and receiving destinations [5]. After much public controversy, the Carnivore program was abandoned in 2001, and commercial replacements were put in place [6].

Another attempt at large-scale data monitoring, once more from the FBI, was Magic Lantern, first publically disclosed in 2001 [7]. Magic Lantern worked on a somewhat different principle. The tactic for this application was to implement keystroke logging on a remote machine through the use of a Trojan horse or exploit delivered via email [8]. Once the target had successfully executed the email attachment bearing Magic Lantern, it would install and presumably begin to send logged data to a monitoring station. In 2002, the FBI confirmed the existence of Magic Lantern, but stated that it had never been deployed [9].

Einstein, as discussed in Chapter 1, is a government-oriented data surveillance program. It began in 2002 as a program to monitor the network gateways of the U.S. government for unauthorized traffic and intrusions [10]. Through several revisions it became a wider reaching program until in 2008, it became mandatory for federal agencies with the exception of the Department of Defense (DoD) and certain intelligence agencies. Although intended primarily as a measure to protect the systems of the U.S. government, Einstein also collects a nontrivial amount of data as it traverses these networks [10]. The main goal of Einstein is "to identify and characterize malicious network traffic to enhance cybersecurity analysis, situational awareness and security response" [11].

Perfect Citizen, as discussed in Chapter 1, is a National Security Agency (NSA) program, designed to detect vulnerabilities in both public and privately run critical infrastructure systems and networks [12]. Although not a mandatory program, significant incentives in the form of government contracts have been offered to those that are willing to participate. Concerns have been raised over government entry into monitoring of private companies, such as utility companies.

Uses of Surveillance Data

Aside from the direct uses of surveillance data, we can also, given a sufficient amount of data, use it as a basis for detecting patterns of behavior among those being surveilled. The U.S. government, and likely other governments as well, have been searching for exactly such patterns in voice and data communications for some time.

Since the terrorist attacks that took place on September 11, 2001, the U.S. government, more specifically the NSA, has been conducting pattern analysis on voice conversations in order to detect the patterns that might presage a terrorist attack [13]. Such technologies and the policies that govern their use are continually updating and evolving. Using these types of techniques, we can infer that certain patterns of voice traffic, for example, a call from a known terrorist friendly country to a location in the United States, then sequential calls from the number in the United States to six other numbers, may very well be an indicator of unusual activity. Of course, this assumes foreknowledge of which phone numbers to watch for such patterns occurring, or an extremely powerful computing capability, likely beyond what currently exists.

SUMMARY

In this chapter, we discussed the basics of CNE. As we covered, CNE is a military term that does not use the term exploit in the way that it is typically used in the information security community, but instead uses it in the sense of exploiting data that we have gained through reconnaissance or surveillance to our own good.

We covered identifying our targets, in the sense of both gleaning information from targets of attacks, and in the sense of identifying targets to be surveilled. We discussed potential sources for attacks, and how the endpoint of the attack may only be distantly related to the identity and location of the actual attacker. We also provided historical examples of surveillance programs.

We talked about reconnaissance and how it might be used to conduct planning operations for future attacks, including CNA and CND. We covered the three major divisions of reconnaissance, OSINT, passive, and APT and the differences between them.

Lastly, we went over surveillance. We talked about the difference between reconnaissance and surveillance, this largely being a matter of scale in both the sense of time and implementation. We talked about the justifications for conducting surveillance, as well as some of the particulars of voice and data surveillance. We also covered large-scale implementations of surveillance and went over some of the programs that have been used over the years by the U.S. government. We also discussed some of the uses of data collected through surveillance methods.

References

[1] Joint Publication 1-02 Department of Defense Dictionary of Military and Associated Terms, http://ra.defense. gov/documents/rtm/jp1_02.pdf; 2011 [accessed 05.05.13].
[2] Leong P. Ethernet 10/100/1000 copper taps, passive or active? lovemytool.com, http://www.lovemytool.com/ blog/2007/10/copper-tap.html; 2007 [accessed 03.04.13].
[3] Olzak T. Protect your network against fiber hacks. IT security, http://www.techrepublic.com/blog/security/ protect-your-network-against-fiber-hacks/222; 2007 [accessed 03.04.13].
[4] U.S. Marine Corps. Imagery intelligence. s.l.: U.S. Marine Corps; 2002. MCWP 2-15.4.
[5] Tschabitscher H. How carnivore email surveillance worked. About.com, http://email.about.com/od/ staysecureandprivate/a/carnivore.htm; 2010 [accessed 03.04.13].
[6] Associated Press. FBI Ditches carnivore surveillance system. FoxNews.com, http://www.foxnews.com/story/ 0,2933,144809,00.html; 2005 [accessed 03.04.13].
[7] Bradner S. The FBI as an ethical hacker? NetworkWorld, http://www.networkworld.com/columnists/2009/ 042309bradner.html; 2009 [accessed 03.04.13].
[8] Sposato I. The FBI's magic lantern. WorldNetDaily, http://www.wnd.com/2001/11/11812/; 2001 [accessed 03.03.13].
[9] Hentoff N. The FBI's magic lantern. The Village Voice, http://www.villagevoice.com/2002-05-28/news/the-fbi-s-magic-lantern/; 2002 [accessed 03.03.13].
[10] Department of Homeland Security. Department of homeland security united states computer emergency readiness team. Privacy impact assessment EINSTEIN program. s.l.: Department of Homeland Security Department of Homeland Security United States Computer Emergency Readiness Team, http://www.dhs.gov/xlibrary/as sets/privacy/privacy_pia_eisntein.pdf; 2004 [accessed 03.04.13].
[11] US-CERT (United States Computer Emergency Readiness Team). Privacy Impact Assessment for the Initiative Three Exercise. s.l.: Department of Homeland Security; 2010.
[12] Gorman S. U.S. plans cyber shield for utilities, companies. The Wall Street J, http://online.wsj.com/article/ SB10001424052748704545004575352983850463108.html [accessed 03.04.13].
[13] Singel R. Top secret: we're wiretapping you. Wired.com, http://www.wired.com/science/discoveries/news/ 2007/03/72811?currentPage=all; 2007 [accessed 03.04.13].

Computer Network Attack

Computer Network Attack (CNA) is a military term defined as, "Actions taken through the use of computer networks to disrupt, deny, degrade, or destroy information resident in computers and computer networks, or the computers and networks themselves" [1]. Although this term meshes well with the common viewpoint of basements full of hackers bringing cyber war to the enemy, or individual attackers conducting similar activities, there is a large difference in how such activities are conducted by nation-states and non-nation-states.

It is entirely true that, in a purely cyber war sense, small groups or individual attackers can potentially wield similar weapons to a similar level of effectiveness as a nation-state, but the similarity will often end there. An individual hacker with access to the command and control system of a large botnet can certainly wreak havoc, but the capability to take the attack into conventional warfare, or to use the cyber attack as an accompaniment or complement to other attacks is often reserved for those with much greater resources.

Another common confusion when discussing CNA is differentiating it from the common attacks carried out by blackhat hackers and other similar groups that are not being actively sponsored by a nation-state, or even in the attacks that we carry out against ourselves in the penetration testing process. The difference, primarily, is a matter of scale in capabilities and completeness of the attack process.

Attacks conducted in the name of penetration testing and by random hackers do not usually "go for the throat" as we might in a conventional attack. Many such attackers work to compromise the target environment in order to own it, but do not take the destructive steps beyond that which might be required in actual warfare. In full-blown cyber warfare, where we have a presumably greater intent to significantly impact our target, such steps might lead to the wholesale destruction or disabling of critical infrastructure through a purely cyber attack, or might be used to disable systems that provide protection against a conventional attack, such as missile tracking systems, in order to facilitate such an attack.

WAGING WAR IN THE CYBER ERA

Cyber warfare capabilities are not only relatively new, when discussing them on their own merits, but they change the way conventional warfare is carried out as well. When we look at any of the traditional methods of warfare, cyber capabilities add new dimensions to them. In cyber warfare, we must consider the physical, electronic, and logical elements of warfare as major factors, as well as the reasons for our actions and the factor of time.

Physically

Cyber warfare can have great impact on the way physical war is waged. Given that even strictly physical warfare, in the sense of boots on the ground, depends a great deal on technologies, these things are vulnerable to cyber attack. Support for physical operations depends on supplies being delivered properly, soldiers being moved from one place to another on a tight schedule, communications functioning, and any number of other factors, e.g., the Army's six warfighting functions. If one or more of these activities does not take place, or, worse yet, is intentionally altered in order to engineer a weakness, solely physical warfare can quickly degenerate into chaos.

On the other side of the coin, cyber warfare activities are very vulnerable to physical effects. If communications lines are severed, power is unavailable, environmental conditions cannot be maintained, or any of a number of other conditions cannot be met, our relatively fragile computer systems and infrastructure become so much dead weight.

In either case, physical warfare can affect or be affected by cyber warfare attacks. When the physical component is ignored in cyber warfare, we potentially lose a large portion of the entire picture. Cyber warfare is indeed a distinct dimension of warfare, but isolating it from the other dimensions renders its capabilities incomplete, at best.

Electronically

Although often considered a subset of conventional or physical warfare, electronic warfare can have a profound effect on cyber warfare and vice versa. Electronic warfare is largely concerned with attacks that take place in the electromagnetic spectrum, an area which the systems that are used to carry out cyber warfare make great use of, and from which they are very sensitive to interference. Using the tactics of electronic warfare, we can potentially render the systems and infrastructure that make up the cyber warfare capabilities of our opponents useless without landing a single physical blow.

Likewise, the systems that allow electronic warfare to be carried out are generally of a highly technological nature and are potentially susceptible to attack on a cyber level. One can envision an exchange where a nation-state would attempt to remove the cyber capability from an opponent via electronic warfare attack, only to find that its electronic warfare capability had been nullified by a cyber attack.

Logically

Of course, as we discussed in the introduction to this chapter, we also have strictly cyber oriented attacks to consider. Such attacks can be used for reconnaissance and surveillance, as we discussed in Chapter 9, but they can also be used to conduct outright attacks against other systems and infrastructure. Such attacks are the meat of CNA and we will spend a considerable amount of time discussing them later in this chapter.

Purely logical attacks in isolation are very much lacking in their potential to be effective in an overall war effort. Although it is very easy for nearly any party to obtain and utilize such weapons to great effect, not being able to follow up with other attacks is extremely limiting. If we consider conflicts of a conventional nature as an example, using cyber warfare tactics in isolation might be the equivalent of conducting conventional warfare without the use of air support; definitely possible, but very limiting.

Reactively Versus Proactively

In considering cyber warfare attacks, we can act reactively, in the sense of defending against an attack or responding to the actions of our opponents. We can also act proactively, in the sense of anticipating activities stemming from threats or courses of action on the part of our opponents that would seem to indicate progress toward an undesirable state. Given cyber capabilities, we have the possibility of using tactics that are not immediately physical or overtly harmful, and do not require physical movement of troops or resources to carry out such activities.

When responding reactively, we will likely continue in the paradigm of traditional warfare. Although we do not necessarily need to move resources into the area, we still need to conduct many of the staging operations that are required to ramp up for such a conflict. In all likelihood, this will include conducting many of the reconnaissance activities that we discussed in Chapter 9 when discussing Computer Network Exploitation (CNE), and may be able to benefit from any ongoing surveillance that was already in place against our target. Once such activities are completed to the extent that we have sufficient information to conduct attacks, we can then move on to CNA.

If we are to conduct cyber warfare proactively, we have a very large range of options that are technically open for use, up to and including an all-out attack. At present many countries limit the use of such options via internal legislation and international treaty. Of great potential usefulness, however, are attacks that are put in place in advance, but not triggered until conditions are the most appropriate and advantageous for us to do so. Such tactics can be staged years in advance and may even be insinuated into the systems of our opponent at a hardware level. We discussed such activities in greater depth in the Supply Chain Concerns section of Chapter 7. In such situations, carefully planned proactive activity can be used to render the opponent entirely impotent at the exact time in which they are most dependent on their tools and weapons to function properly.

Time as a Factor

When conducting cyber warfare, we have the capacity to unleash an attack at speeds which are far above the reaction times of mere humans, presuming that humans are not a requirement in the decision-making loop. We may see actions take place on such a time scale in the operation of Intrusion Detection Systems (IDS) that are defending our systems, or in the autonomous or semiautonomous strikes from attack tools, which we will discuss at greater length in Chapter 12. Although such attacks are entirely possible to carry out in very short periods of time, they do not accurately represent the entirety of cyber warfare and Computer Network Operations (CNO), any more than an individual soldier firing a weapon represents an entire war.

Pure cyber warfare on a grand scale, which we have not yet witnessed, will, in the opinion of the authors, likely be a relatively slow operation. It will be prefaced by similar reconnaissance and surveillance activities that we see in conventional warfare, and, in fact, will probably be accompanied by conventional warfare activities. In small-scale skirmishes, such as the force of a major botnet being directed against government systems, we may not see the full engine of warfare brought to bear against the attackers, and in this particular case, we may see a swift and cyber only attack. In all likelihood, the speed at which entire conflicts are fought will closely model that of conventional war.

THE ATTACK PROCESS

The attack process is usually focused on a particular system or set of systems. In this process, as shown in Figure 10.1, we will likely conduct additional and more detailed reconnaissance and scanning oriented toward gaining yet more specific information from the system. At this level, we can potentially conduct reconnaissance in greater depth, as our need for secrecy and stealth may not be as great as it was while we were conducting CNE. We will then attempt to access the system, either through the use of an outright attack or using credentials that we have managed to gather from somewhere in the environment, through social

FIGURE 10.1   Attack process.

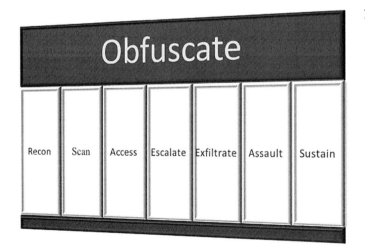

engineering, or other means. Once we have an account on the system, we may need to escalate the level of access that we have in order to accomplish our goals. The target for such privilege escalation is often root or administrator level access, giving us relative freedom on the system. Given the needed level of access to the system, we can then exfiltrate any information that we wish to, cause damage to the environment in any way that benefits us, then install any measures that we need to in order to ensure future access.

Throughout the entire attack process, we will also seek to cover or obfuscate our activities. We may want to appear to be attacking from a different location than where we are physically located or take other steps to ensure that our attacks are not traced back to us. We will also likely wish to remove any traces of our activities on the system when we intend to leave it.

Recon

We spent a good deal of time discussing reconnaissance and surveillance in Chapter 9 in the context of CNE. In that case, the reconnaissance that we would conduct would be done in a general sense, in order to map out and discover information on our target environment. As reconnaissance done in support of CNA and of the attack process, we may already have such general information already from the CNE and will be hunting for information on a much more specific level, given our potentially greater level of access and reduced need for stealth.

Another tool that may become useful during this more specific stage of reconnaissance is social engineering. Using some of the social engineering tactics that we discussed in Chapter 8, we may very well be able to gain specific information that will allow us to access the systems in question without needing to resort to the full spectrum of attacks that we might need otherwise. Through social engineering we may be able to discover shared passwords used in other services or applications, may be able to find account names through searching the physical surroundings of those that work in the environment or through dumpster diving, or any number of similar tactics.

Given the task of long-term reconnaissance at a more specific level, we may also want to plant the tools that would allow such monitoring on a particular system. Even on this scale, software such as a keystroke logger can produce enormous amounts of information, only a very small portion of which will generally have any great value; however, it may still be worth the effort. In environments where good password hygiene is not strictly enforced with technical controls, we can often find passwords that are manually synchronized between multiple systems, a great boon when attempting to gain access. We may also be able to sniff credentials from network traffic if less secure protocols such as telnet, File Transfer Protocol (FTP), or Post Office Protocol (POP) are allowed in the environment.

TIP

We should be prepared, at any step in the attack process, for our attacks to fail utterly and/or to be discovered. Particularly when our target is a highly secured environment, and we are facing stronger measures, such as multifactor authentication, this may very well be the case. It is always wise to have contingency plans that will allow us to still achieve our goals when we encounter such obstacles.

Scan

During the scanning portion of CNA, instead of the general port scans, fingerprinting, service versioning, and so on that we performed in our general reconnaissance, we will likely more closely examine the system for potential vulnerabilities during reconnaissance in CNA. In general, we will be scanning for further detailed information from applications and potentially more specific information from the operating system itself.

When attempting to collect more information from applications, beyond cursory checks for versions, we will often focus on finding an exposed application that might be particularly talkative, such as a web interface to a database, and drilling down from there. This is often a manual process and can be time consuming, but can be very useful. We can often discover very specific information in this manner, such as database versions from error messages, potential usernames from conducting SQL injection attacks through the web interface, and any number of other bits and pieces of information.

> **NOTE**
>
> Not only can applications provide us an opportunity to surveil a remote system, but they can also potentially provide us an open doorway into the operating system itself. Improperly secured web applications are one of the main vectors that allow such attacks to take place.

We may also want to collect additional information regarding the operating system such as specific patching information, uptime, or any of a number of other items that could potentially allow us to gain information through inference. Such additional small details may aid us in our attacks when we get to the attack and escalation steps of our process. As we discussed in the more general information collection sections of Chapter 9, documenting this information carefully can be very helpful through the entire process.

Access

Gaining access to a system can take place using a variety of tools and methods. If we have been successful in any of our previous attempts at social engineering, dumpster diving, stealing, or cloning access cards, such as Common Access Cards (CACs) mandated by Homeland Security Presidential Directive 12: Policy for a Common Identification Standard for Federal Employees and Contractors or have managed to find accounts with synchronized passwords on other systems that we have been able to access, we may very well have legitimate credentials with which we can simply log in. Slightly more complicated than this, although more likely, is that we will be able to find usernames that exist on the system and either crack or guess passwords, using some of the tools that we discussed in Chapter 6, in order to access them.

Another potential path that may gain us easy access would be to use client-side attacks against individual systems that belong to the users of our target system. Such attacks utilize vulnerabilities in software running on the client, such as a web browser, as an attack vector. We stand a much greater chance of being able to access individual workstations in order to gain access to credentials than we do when attempting to access a server that is carefully maintained and patched. Client-side attacks can be web-based, use email as a delivery method, ride in on a USB drive, or any of a number of other methods. One example of this that is commonly known today is the 2008 cyber attack on U.S. military computers in history named "Operation Buckshot Yankee." The case involves USB flash drives infected by a foreign intelligence agency and prompted the military to ban the use of them [2]. Particularly in nontechnical working environments, such attacks enjoy a high degree of success, although we may not find as much success in highly secured environments.

TIP

Client-side attacks are often some of the most effective attacks that we can carry out. Such attacks, when combined with a certain element of social engineering, as we discussed in Chapter 8, are very difficult to defend against. When we use human carelessness or ignorance as an attack vector, we will often enjoy success.

We can also attempt to use common operating system or application exploits in order to access a system. We have likely, at some point in the process, already used one or more of a variety of vulnerability scanning tools, either during the more general reconnaissance process, or during the more specific examination during the attack process.

NOTE

In the case of a cyber attack, we will likely not use exploits that are available to the general public. Such vulnerabilities are likely to already be patched or mitigated in some fashion, and easily rebuffed. Instead, we will use zero-day exploits which stand a much greater chance of success, due to not being commonly known.

Many common vulnerability analysis tools, such as Nessus, which we discussed in Chapter 6, can be used to locate vulnerabilities that we might use to access a system. Although it is unlikely that we will gain access in such a fashion on a fully patched system running a recent operating system, there are plenty of systems that are likely not in such a well-maintained state to which we may easily be able to gain access. It is also important to test our attacks in an environment as close as possible to the actual target as we can create. This will allow us to not only test our exploits, but to also help develop contingency plans to potentially compensate for issues that we might encounter when attacking.

Escalate

Once we have gained some sort of access to a given system, we may need to gain additional or upgraded privileges than those that we presently have, commonly known as privilege escalation. When we are attempting to gain access to accounts that have a higher level of privilege than those that we presently have, this is known as vertical privilege escalation. When we are attempting to gain access to different accounts that what we have access to, but are at the same level as the account that we already have access to, this is known as horizontal privilege escalation.

Privilege escalation of either variety can be accomplished through a variety of methods. We may be able to use a different set of exploits than we used previously, as we now have access to the system as a user. We may also be able to take advantage of misconfigurations or insecurely set configurations. It is entirely possible that, on some systems, the standard user account that we have managed to access may have the ability to act as an administrator directly or may be able to escalate privilege level as normal functionality of the operating system.

We may also be able to utilize the privileges of applications that are operating with heightened permissions. Applications such as those that run backups, various servers or daemons, or other processes that require privileges that are higher than the level of a general user are often vulnerable to attack. Various application flaws such as buffer overflows or race conditions can allow us to execute arbitrary code through these already running applications. We may also be able to access and modify interpreted scripts or shell scripts that are not secured properly, in order to pass operating system commands through them or gain direct access to an operating system shell.

Exfiltrate

Once we have gained the needed access to the environment, one of our primary concerns is to find any data that may be valuable to us, and exfiltrate it to a location that is accessible to us from another location, or to move it directly to our own systems. Exfiltration, in terms of Confidentiality, Integrity, and Availability (CIA), is an attack primarily against confidentiality, and potentially against availability.

We have a very wide variety of tools that we can use to exfiltrate data, from purpose-built tools and protocols that exist for the specific purpose of moving data around, to more general tools that can be bent to such a purpose, to out-of-band methods that might allow us to subvert security measures designed to specifically prevent such efforts.

In simple cases, we may be able to easily use common applications and protocols to move our files or data. File transfers can be accomplished with FTP, Secure Copy Protocol (SCP), Extensible Messaging and Presence Protocol (XMPP), or any of a number of other common protocols. In many environments we may find these particular transfer protocols blocked as outgoing traffic, but we will often find Hypertext Transfer Protocol (HTTP) traffic allowed, which will suit our purposes nicely. It is a rare and highly secure environment indeed where we will not be able to find some sort of outgoing protocol on which we can piggyback information.

In some cases, we need to create more specifically tuned tools in order to move our data out of the target environment in which we are operating. In such a case, netcat can be a very powerful tool for moving data around in a customized manner. The netcat tunnel setup that we discussed in multipurpose tools section of Chapter 6 would allow us to configure specific ports on each end of the connection and even relay the data through multiple systems in order to exfiltrate it from a hostile environment.

Assault

Assault is a step typically not included in the penetration testing process, which, in general, closely mirrors our attack process. In the case of actual cyber warfare, it is likely that once we have managed to gain access to a machine, escalate to the privilege level that we need, and exfiltrate any interesting data, we may want to use the system to sow chaos in the environment. In military terms, we have the five Ds to describe the effect of such activities: deception, disruption, denial, degradation, and destruction [3], as shown in Figure 10.2. In a CIA sense, the attacks in this section will mainly be against availability and integrity.

Deception is a somewhat more subtle tactic that carrying out a forthright attack, such as simply taking down a given system. If we can take over a system responsible for the control of communications, such as an email or Voice over IP (VoIP) server, we have the potential to falsify communications, alter those that are in transit, or simply make such traffic disappear while en route. The potential for internal manipulation in this way is relatively endless, as we, as a society, are highly dependent on such tools for communication and generally very trusting of them. Rendering them untrustworthy can be very psychologically destabilizing for the users of the target systems. In very high security environments, we may be hampered in such efforts by encryption or other similar verification systems, but, in such a case, we may merely need to insinuate ourselves into other sources of information. In the modern world, the computer is king and is not often questioned.

Causing disruption in systems that are on or connected to a computer is often a relatively easy proposition. On the systems themselves, processes can be interrupted, resources can be over-utilized, files can be moved or manipulated, or any number of other similar tasks. Particularly when timed to coincide with predictably scheduled tasks, such a system patching, quarter or year end financial closing, or large-scale military operations, system disruptions can cause panic and disruption among users and system administrators that is far out of proportion with the actual events.

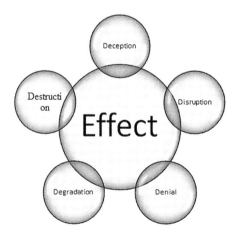

FIGURE 10.2   Five Ds.

WARNING

Carrying out an assault on a computer system may have implications far beyond the actual act itself. Particularly in the case of an attack launched by or attributed to a nation-state, such activities can lead to outright war, potentially including conventional warfare as a component.

Denial attacks of a certain variety are common enough in the world of information security. Denial of Service (DoS) and Distributed Denial of Service (DDoS) attacks are a frequent occurrence, largely due to the ease with which they can be executed. Such attacks are commonly launched against web servers, mail servers, FTP servers, and other public-facing components of a company or an organizational infrastructure. We can also launch such attacks against the technological components of physical access control systems, transportation systems, such as air traffic control, or any number of other critical components. In many complex systems, there are similar points at which failure can bring an entire process or facility to a swift halt.

Degradation in computing or industrial environments can be a virtual plague on those that use and maintain the environment. We can attack the performance of the system and networks, making portions of it function poorly in a sporadic manner, in order to cause those troubleshooting the issues to spend an inordinate amount of time on them. We can, in industrial systems, cause the output of the system to vary from its baseline, thus providing goods that are not produced to specification or are damaging to the infrastructure through which they move. We can also cause subtle degradation of data that is produced by a system, causing the results of medical tests to change, financial decisions to be altered, targeting systems to select incorrect locations, and no other end of harm that would be difficult to detect.

The term *destruction* can cover a wide variety of actions. We can destroy data, applications, or the operating system of the system in a software sense, which could potentially be very damaging in the case of valuable data or critical systems. We can attempt to physically damage the hardware that the system itself runs on, although this is a relatively limited tactic. Even in the case that we manage to destroy computing hardware, such equipment is often cheaply and easily replaced.

Sustain

Once we have gained sufficient access to a system, we may wish to reconfigure it to ensure our future ability to access it again. Although we may have used a specific exploit to gain access to the system and escalate our privileges when we were first able to do so, we may not be able to count on the same points of entry being available in the future. Against this eventuality, we will likely want to secure additional access by creating new accounts, opening services on additional ports, installing command and control software, placing backdoors in applications, and so on.

The most successful such efforts will likely be those that are the least obvious and the least prone to being accidentally discovered by a system administrator. Some of the more blatant methods, such as opening a new listening port on the system may very well be found in short order, particularly on an Internet-facing system. Additionally, we may want to be careful of leaving behind such measures in places where they might be found by another attacker. Many of the prebuilt backdoors that are available will use a standard port by default, which could render our backdoor very easily located if we do not change it.

In addition to leaving backdoors in place, we may also want to consider, as an attacker, patching or fixing the vulnerabilities through which we were able to gain access. If such systems are left in their original state, we may find that another attacker has used the same methods and that we are now sharing control of the system. Worse yet, future attackers may not be as careful as we have been, thus revealing that the system has been compromised, triggering a further investigation and potentially severing our access in the process.

Obfuscate

Our likely first and last step on a system that we have compromised or intend to compromise is obfuscating, largely with the goal of anonymity or deniability. Obfuscate means "to confuse, bewilder, or stupefy" [4]. We use this term to cover not only the methods that we might use to cover up or erase evidence of our intrusion, but also to potentially point any potential investigators to another source entirely. Obfuscation is really a layer that runs under all of the activities that we will take in the attack process. Some such obfuscatory actions take place even before our first recon, some take place during our various attacks, and some take place as our very last step before permanently vacating the system in question.

The simplest and earliest obfuscation measures that we might take are those that will prevent our attacks from being traced back to our actual physical location. Such tools might be various proxies or intervening machines that we use as an intermediary connection before attacking, IP spoofing, or any of a number of other methods that we might use to disguise our point of origination. Although some such tools may not be perfect in nature, they do provide an additional layer of protection in case our activities in the target environment are noticed.

We will also likely take steps to ensure that we do not leave digital forensic evidence behind on the target system. In such cases, we might change timestamps so that they reflect the original time before we modified any files, clean up any tools that we have moved to the system, remove or alter log entries, and generally ensure that we have not accidentally left any traces behind. On the other side of this same process, we may very well want to intentionally leave such traces behind but alter them so that they point to another source. If we can falsely attribute an attack to another source, this may not only cover our tracks, but cause significant confusion and consternation as well.

SUMMARY

In this chapter we discussed CNA. We covered the different factors involved in cyber warfare, including the physical, logical, and electronic elements of warfare. We also covered reactive and proactive actions in warfare, and how these prompt a rather different set of actions in cyber warfare. Additionally, we must concern ourselves with the factor of time, and consider that although cyber attacks can be conducted very quickly, cyber warfare cannot be conducted at such speeds.

We also discussed the different phases of the attack process: reconnaissance, scanning, accessing systems, escalating privileges, exfiltrating data, assaulting the system, sustaining our access, and obfuscating any traces that might be left behind. We covered the specifics of each step in the process, and how some of the tools that we covered in Chapter 6 might be applied to each of them.

These processes and the tools that we have discussed outline some of the major strategies and tactics that are used to conduct CNA. These tools are not unique, nor are many of them difficult to access, and the process is simple, but to carry out warfare at the level of a nation-state requires a great deal more resources, effort, and knowledge.

References

[1] Joint Publication 1-02 Department of Defense Dictionary of Military and Associated Terms, http://ra.defense.gov/documents/rtm/jp1_02.pdf; 2011 [accessed 5.5.13].

[2] Lynn W. Defending a new domain: the Pentagon's cyberstrategy. Foreign affairs, http://www.foreignaffairs.com/articles/66552/william-j-lynn-iii/defending-a-new-domain; 2010 [accessed 20.05.13].

[3] U.S. Air Force. AFDD 2-5 information operations. s.l.: U.S. Air Force. Air Force Doctrine Document 2-5, http://www.globalsecurity.org/military/library/policy/usaf/afdd/2-5/afdd2-5.pdf; 1998 [accessed 18.03.13].

[4] Dictionary.com. Obfuscate. Dictionary.com, http://dictionary.reference.com/browse/obfuscate; 2013 [accessed 18.03.13].

11

Computer Network Defense

Computer Network Defense (CND) is defined by the U.S. Department of Defense (DoD) as, "Actions taken to protect, monitor, analyze, detect, and respond to unauthorized activity within the Department of Defense information systems and computer networks" [1]. The broad scope of these CND activities may very well include components that would be considered Computer Network Exploitation (CNE) and Computer Network Attack (CNA), as we discussed in Chapters 9 and 10, respectively. Additionally, the strategies and tactics developed and utilized in conducting CNE and CNA against our opponents can be used to strengthen our own defenses. CND is also one of the few places in Computer Network Operations (CNO) where we will find military and civilian approaches to be very similar due to the use of the same tactics and equipment.

In the military sense, CND may very well parallel the strategies and tactics that are used for conventional defense. The cyber equivalent of defensive emplacements, listening posts, patrols, and so on can be formulated, and the defensive strategies of conventional warfare can be adapted to cyber warfare by mapping the concepts across. Although this may not always be the most efficient means for us to use the tools of cyber warfare, it does allow time tested concepts to be applied to the new dimension of warfare. Given that the military leadership that is likely to presently be planning and carrying out CNE and CNA will often have been educated in the affairs of war before the advent of cyber warfare, this is the approach that we will most likely find in CND when executed by a nation-state. This may also pose a possible weakness in CNO in general, as it does tend to add a certain element of inflexibility. Although it would be a gross generalization to call this a universal problem, we may find that some portion of military leadership will be hindered by conventional thinking on defense in the area of CND.

As we discussed in the introduction to Chapter 10 when we talked about CNA, being able to execute the complete cycle of CND will more than likely require resources similar to those of a nation-state. In a pure cyber attack sense, a non-nation-state can certainly be capable of defending against an attack. In the attacks that occurred against many US financial institutions in early 2013 [2], we can see a number of good examples of large commercial organizations defending against attacks of a purely cyber nature.

The collective financial industry response to these attacks was, in addition to the normal increases in hardening and redundancy in their infrastructure and architecture, highly focused in the area of defense against denial of service [3]. In a pure cyber attack sense, such a response is completely acceptable and likely to be successful in most cases. In the complete form of CNA, as we discussed in the Waging War in the Cyber Era section of Chapter 10, we would likely see a nation-state include elements of conventional warfare. Although many such institutions are very large, they are not operating at the level of even smaller nation-states just yet, and would be ill-prepared to fend off an attack that included physical attacks as a component.

WHAT WE PROTECT

When we look to defend against cyber attacks, it is often useful to examine what exactly it is that we are defending. In a very general sense, we are almost always concerned with the protection of information in one form or another.

Sensitive information, in the eye of the general public, is often categorized as Personally Identifiable Information (PII) or Patient Healthcare Information (PHI), and involves names, addresses, social security numbers, medical records, financial records, and a multitude of similar information. Such information, when compromised can lead to a variety of fraudulent activities, commonly gathered under the umbrella term of identity theft. Such activities can range from credit accounts being opened with stolen credentials to real estate being sold without the authorization of the legitimate owner, to simple theft of funds from bank accounts.

In the world of the military and government, information of a sensitive nature being exposed can have far greater consequences than mere financial loss. Information is categorized as Unclassified (U), Unclassified For Official Use Only (U//FOUO), Confidential (C), Secret (S), and Top Secret (TS). There can also be special clearances above TS. These are sometimes referred to as Sensitive Compartmented Information (SCI) or Special Access Program (SAP). Information housed by such agencies can include Operations Orders (OPORDERS), war plans, troop movements, technical specifications for weapons or intelligence collection systems, identities of undercover intelligence agents, and any number of other items critical to the functioning of military and government. When such information is accessed in an unauthorized fashion, lives can be lost on a large scale and the balance of power can be shifted significantly. The government also worries about data aggregation where multiple lower classified documents when combined produce information that should be at a higher level of classification.

Laws do exist to protect these types of information, but they are, in many cases, still a work in progress. In the United States, as far as personal data regarding individuals, laws at this point are fairly weak on a federal level. Individual states have gradually begun to enact more stringent data protection and privacy laws, such as SB 1386 in California, in order to compensate for this weakness. Regarding the data held by governments, the military, and some industries, the custodians of such information generally have very strict laws and regulations regarding specifically how the information is handled and controlled, thus putting them in a much better position to protect the data for which they are responsible. We will discuss some of the legal issues surrounding the protection and privacy of data in greater depth in Chapter 13.

Confidentiality, Integrity, Availability

The measures we take to protect our information assets can generally be described in terms of the classic CIA triad of Confidentiality, Integrity and Availability, as shown in Figure 11.1. The confidentiality of data refers to keeping it out of the hands of those that are not authorized to see it. The integrity of data refers to preventing unauthorized modifications to data or system functions. The availability of data refers to being able to access it when needed. These basic principles govern how we go about securing the data with which we are concerned.

Integrity

When protecting the confidentiality of data, we are concerned with keeping it out of the hands of those that should not be seeing it. In terms of specific security implementations, this often means access controls and encryption in order to provide such protections. When

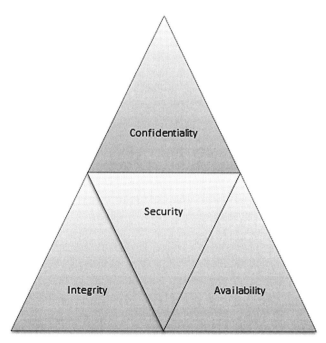

FIGURE 11.1   CIA triad.

applying these measures, we need to consider both data at rest and data in motion. Depending on where the data is at any given point in time, we may need to use different security controls, or different methods within a given control. We can see the results of lapses in confidentiality with the large breaches of PII that seem to occur with disturbing frequency in recent years, such as the breach of the U.S. Department of Energy in February of 2013, resulting in the loss of PII related to several hundred employees and contractors [4].

TIP

A lesser known alternative to the CIA triad, referred to as the Parkerian hexad, exists as well. The Parkerian hexad, developed by Donn Parker, breaks the same general concepts down into the categories of confidentiality, possession, integrity, authenticity, availability, and utility, allowing for a more detailed discussion of the relevant security concepts in a given situation [5]. The use of the Parkerian hexad allows us to be more specific when discussing security scenarios or situations without having to bend the rules of our model.

When we look to protect the integrity of data, or of the party sending the data, we are trying to prevent it from being manipulated in an unauthorized manner. Similarly to the measures that we use to provide confidentiality, we can use encryption to help provide integrity by making the data difficult to successfully manipulate without the proper authorization. In particular, hashes or message digests, such as MD5 and SHA1, are often used to ensure that messages or files have not been altered from the original by creating a fingerprint of the original data that can be tracked over time. Failures in integrity can have serious effects if we are not aware that they have happened, as data in the form of communications or files can be freely altered to reverse their meaning or to alter the outcome of decisions based on the data in question.

Availability

The availability of data simply means that we can access it when we need to do so. Ensuring availability means that we must be resilient in the face of attacks that might corrupt or delete our data or deny us access to it by attacking the environment in which it rests. It also means that we need to have a sufficiently robust environment in order to cope with system outages, communication problems, power issues, and any number of issues that might prevent us from accessing our data. Availability is often accomplished through the use of redundancy and backups for our data and for our environments.

Authenticate, Authorize, and Audit

Authentication, authorization, and auditing are commonly known as AAA (shown in Figure 11.2). These are the principles that allow us to practically carry out the securing of data. These are the means through which we can control and track how our data is being accessed, and by who, thus enabling us to enforce the policies that we have created to keep the data secure.

FIGURE 11.2   AAA.

Authentication is the means by which we verify the identity of an individual or system against a presented set of credentials. A very common implementation of an authentication scheme is the combination of login and password. In this particular case, the user's login name is the identity presented, and it is verified against a stored form of the password that the user has given. A common implementation of authentication used by the U.S. DoD is the Common Access Card (CAC). The CAC, sometimes redundantly referred to as a CAC card, has storage areas that can be used to store credentials, such as a certificate, and may also be used with additional forms of authentication such as a Personal Identification Number (PIN). Other hardware-based tokens are now in common use as well, one of the better known being the RSA SecureID. One of the main keys to the future of authentication is the use of biometric identifiers, such as fingerprints, iris scans, and other means based on physical attributes. Such identifiers are ubiquitous, portable, and difficult to forge, given properly designed authentication systems.

Once we have authenticated an identity, we can then check to see what activities that particular identity is allowed to carry out, known as authorization. We can see a common example of authorization in the different levels of account functionality that are defined in many operating systems. Where a root or administrator level account might be authorized to create additional accounts on a system, a general user will likely not be able to do so.

NOTE

The Principle of Least Privilege states that for any given layer in a computing environment, such as a person, process, or a system, that layer be given only the minimum level of privilege that is needed for it to operate properly. Following this principle negates many of the common security issues that we might face.

Auditing gives us the capability to monitor what activities have taken place on a given system or in an environment. While authentication and authorization allow us to control and set limits on user access to our assets, we also need to keep a record of what these authorized individuals have done. This allows us to balance system and network loads properly, as well as monitor for authorized but inappropriate or unwanted activities.

SECURITY AWARENESS AND TRAINING

People pose what is likely the single largest security vulnerability that we have, or will ever have, in any given system or environment. With most other security problems we can apply a patch, change a configuration, or pile on additional security infrastructure in order to fix the problem. With people, we unfortunately cannot do this. People can be lazy, careless, or simply make honest mistakes, all the while circumventing our carefully planned security measures from the inside and leaving us wide open to attack.

Although we can attempt to apply technical measures to keep untoward activity from taking place, and we can create policy that clearly points out correct and incorrect behavior, such measures will be for naught if we do not impress upon people some small measure of awareness regarding the issues surrounding security, and train them in the proper behaviors that will keep them and the organization in which they operate on a better security footing.

Awareness

Security awareness can be a difficult mode of thinking to those that do not already have some acquaintance with the basic concept. Bruce Schneier wrote a piece on this for *Wired* magazine in 2008, and called this sort of awareness the security mind-set. Schneier said "Security requires a particular mindset. Security professionals—at least the good ones—see the world differently. They can't walk into a store without noticing how they might shoplift. They can't use a computer without wondering about the security vulnerabilities. They can't vote without trying to figure out how to vote twice. They just can't help it [6]."

This security-aware mind-set is not only critical for security professionals, system administrators, network engineers, and others employed in technical fields, but it is also important for secretaries, doctors, teachers, soldiers, stay-at-home parents, and anyone else who handles information that could in any way be considered important or sensitive. To exacerbate the situation, evaluating which data may or may not be sensitive, and in what situations we need to be aware of the security implications of our actions is a function of security awareness, and needs to be taught as well.

To illustrate the consequences of such failures in both judgment and in the proper mind-set, we need only to look at the near daily security breaches that appear in the media. One good example of such a failure occurred during the time before the 2008 U.S. presidential election. Workers at the U.S. Department of State were discovered to have repeatedly accessed the passport records in an unauthorized fashion for three people who were, at the time, presidential candidates: Barrack Obama, Hillary Clinton, and John McCain. The systems containing this information are configured to alert a supervisor when the record of a high profile individual, such as a presidential candidate, is accessed without a legitimate reason.

As a result of this incident, several workers were fired or reprimanded, and those that remained had limitations placed on their access [7]. A modicum of security awareness might have alerted these individuals to the idea that unauthorized access to records containing the personal information of presidential candidates including name, address, date of birth, social security number, travel records, and a variety of other information, might have unwanted consequences for them on a personal level. The unintended consequence of accessing senior government officials' personal data could have a national impact.

Our example, while an apt illustration of lack of security awareness, unfortunately falls toward the relatively tame end of the spectrum, as far as incidents of this type can end. Numerous such cases, such as the VA laptop loss that we mentioned when we discussed CIA earlier in this chapter, can be found;from PII, such as social security numbers, being broadcast to large email distribution lists to unencrypted medical records of U.S. military veterans being lost, and virtually limitless other cases. While technical security measures can be put in place to help prevent such occurrences, as long as we continue to fail in the aspect of security awareness we will continue to have these issues.

When we attempt to teach these concepts to our users, the main point is simple: try to think like an attacker. In any given situation, whether it is a phishing email, social engineering attack, policy violation, or most any other issue that we may be confronted with, such guidance will usually steer us to the proper path. If we are able to instill a certain amount of constructive suspicion in our user base, we will often find ourselves on the proper side of such incidents. The training must result in changes to attitude and behavior to be effective. Although we may find that we tend to receive the occasional false positive from training our users in such a fashion, this is a far more desirable result than dealing with the security breaches that come from lack of care in such matters.

Training

In addition to the concepts of security awareness that we wish to instill, there is also the matter of general security training. In most organizations, such training for end users will consist of more specific direction to accompany our general security awareness efforts. In many governmental organizations, such training is mandatory on a reoccurring basis. Such training will often consist of instruction in properly secure behavior for use of various means of communication such as email, Instant Messenger (IM), and phone. These communications media are often used to scam or attempt to elicit information through social engineering, and are an important focus of our security training efforts. Additionally, depending on the environment in question, we may also wish to add additional items to our security training efforts, such as physical security, proper handling of sensitive information, and so on. For those who work in secure facilities these physical security measures often give a false sense of security—they are a key part of CND; however, they often are not funded to the same levels depending on the culture of the organization or experience of the leadership.

When conducting training for the more technical members of an organization, such as system administrators, network engineers, developers, security personnel, and the like, it is still important to go over the basics of our security training program, but we will likely need to compose additional training to address the specifics of such categories of specialization. For our system administrators and network engineers we will need to address the security of our operating systems and network infrastructure, for our developers we will need to address secure coding standards and practices, and for our security personnel we will need to make them aware of both the internal and external security practices of the organization. For all of these members, we need to stress the appropriate use and safeguarding of any privileged accounts to which they may have access.

DEFENDING AGAINST CYBER ATTACKS

When defending against cyber attacks, many of the steps that we will take will be proactive in nature and involve hardening our environments and monitoring the activities that take place in them. This is an easy statement to make, and is relatively simple to accomplish in a small- or medium-sized network environment, relatively speaking, such as what we might find in a business or corporation. When we look to perform such activities in the much larger environment that we might find when operating on a national or a global scale, this becomes a considerably more difficult prospect.

At present, we have the capability to perform a certain amount of monitoring on a large scale, as we discussed in the Surveillance section of Chapter 9. When we begin to look to more specific activities, such as intrusion detection or vulnerability assessment, the scale of environment within which we can cope shrinks to a much smaller set due to the sheer mass of data to be monitored. Presently, strategies are being developed in an attempt to monitor and address large-scale cyber attacks, but these are still in their infancy. Currently, much of the effort being put into CND is in the areas of policy and compliance, particularly in governmental circles.

In July of 2012, President Obama signed an executive order that many say constitutes, among other items, the long-discussed Internet kill-switch for the United States [8]. In the face of a concerted attack on critical infrastructure, some say that such measures may be preferable to potential destruction and loss of life that could accompany an attack on Supervisory Control and Data Acquisition (SCADA) systems and the environments they control. This may not be an ideal solution and will likely be exceedingly difficult to carry out. Although not necessarily a viable plan, this does serve as a good indicator of the present state of nationwide CND in the United States.

Policy and Compliance

One of the major keys to a successful defense lies in the area of security policy. Through the use of policies we can set the expectations for those that develop and use the environments that we expect to keep secured. Security policy defines the behavior of our users, the configuration of our software, systems, and networks, and innumerable other items. Ultimately our security policies define what exactly we mean when we say secure. Additionally, it is important to note that policy implemented without the proper authority to enforce it is utterly useless and often ignored.

In addition to defining our security through policy, we also need to ensure that the policy is followed, this being done through our compliance efforts. In government, compliance is verified against such bodies such as the Federal Information Security Management Act (FISMA), the Department of Defense Information Assurance Certification and Accreditation Process (DIACAP), the National Industrial Security Program Operating Manual (NISPOM), Director of Central Intelligence Directive (DCID) 6/3, and innumerable others. In the civilian world, we find the focus more in the direction of the Health Insurance Portability and Accountability Act (HIPAA), North American Electric Reliability Corporation's (NERC) Critical Infrastructure Protection (CIP) regulations, the Payment Card Industry Data Security Standard (PCI DSS), Sarbanes-Oxley (SOX), and many others. Without compliance, our policies are not worth the paper on which they are printed, or the bits in which they are stored.

Surveillance, Data Mining, and Pattern Matching

As we discussed in the Surveillance section of Chapter 9 many large governments presently have some sort of monitoring on the various means of communications moving in and out of their borders. While this is by no means a complete coverage, and gaps in such monitoring can, in many cases, be found or created, it does provide a measure of security. The ability to track communications with those in other countries can potentially give us a warning when coordinated activities, such as attacks may be taking place in the immediate future, possibly including cyber attacks, through data mining and pattern matching performed on the communications records we collect.

WARNING

Surveillance and reconnaissance activities, if not conducted properly, can often violate the relevant wiretap laws of the country in which they are carried out. It is important to secure the proper legal advice before proceeding with such efforts.

If we examine the systems that are used to perform large-scale communications monitoring, we can see many parallels to the familiar Intrusion Detection Systems (IDS) that we can commonly find in operation on smaller networks. In essence, these systems are IDS operating on a much more gross scale. Such systems may very well serve as the basis or technological precursors for large-scale IDS that is capable of the detailed examination of electronic communications that we are familiar with on a small scale. Although the level of technical sophistication needed to perform such activities is lacking at present, we are almost certain to see such capabilities in the near future.

Intrusion Detection and Prevention

Intrusion detection and intrusion prevention on a nationwide scale, as we discussed in the previous section, is a difficult prospect. At present, the networks that comprise the Internet are not segmented along national boundaries, for the most part. Additionally, we have a wide variety of media that can be used to carry network communications, including: copper and fiber optic cables, satellite communications, purpose-built wireless networks, packet radio, and any number of other means. This lack of network segmentation along physical borders and wide variety of communications methods makes IDS/IPS a technically challenging prospect to implement.

Two main strategies exist for accomplishing intrusion detection and/or prevention on this scale; we can either structure networks to provide a limited number of connections outside of the area that we wish to protect and monitor, or we implement massively distributed IDS/IPS; either method has its inherent issues. Restructuring our networks to provide only a few choke points is most certainly the cleanest route to take, and may be workable when building new networks, but would likely be prohibitively expensive for existing networks. Likewise, massively distributed IDS/IPS, although having the benefit of not requiring us to alter our networks, is likely to miss some of the traffic entering and exiting said networks. In either case, at present, conducting such operations is likely to prove difficult in a variety of ways.

An example where this has been deployed as part of national defense in the Department of Homeland security Network Security Deployment National Cybersecurity Protection System (operationally known as EINSTIEN). EINSTEIN was deployed in accordance with Comprehensive National Cybersecurity Initiative directive 5—Connect current cyber ops centers to enhance situational awareness. There are multiple blocks but the first was built around IDS [9].

Vulnerability Assessment and Penetration Testing

Vulnerability Assessment and Penetration Testing are two of the main tools of CND. These methods allow us to discover the weaknesses in our systems and networks that allow attackers to conduct reconnaissance and surveillance, gain entry, or other attacks. Vulnerability assessment and pen testing are just a few aspects of something called a Red Team assessment. Red teaming is used by both government and commercial entities alike.

Vulnerability Assessment allows us to, generally using scanning tools such as those that we discussed in Chapter 6, discover surface vulnerabilities in our systems. Typically such assessments involve iterating through the complete catalog of our systems and scanning for vulnerabilities on each, using known signatures for those vulnerabilities. Although this can indeed expose some of the means of entry that attackers can use, it is not a complete picture of how our systems might be vulnerable. In order to get a more complete picture of the holes in our systems, we need to be much more thorough in our efforts and conduct penetration tests.

Penetration Testing, when conducted properly, can much more closely mirror the activities of an attacker attempting to compromise our environment. Penetration Testing can be performed from a white box perspective, in which we are provided with information on the environment to be attacked, or can be done from a black box perspective, in which we have no additional information that an attacker would normally have. Many arguments can be made for either approach, but generally white box testing is less costly and black box testing more closely represents an outside attack. We may also wish to consider additional elements in our Penetration Testing efforts, such as social engineering, which we discussed in Chapter 8, and physical security, which we discussed in Chapter 7.

One of the dangers in planning and in trusting the results of penetration tests is to insure that the tests are not hampered to the point of not being useful. If we put restrictions on our penetration tests that disallow specific attacks, environments, or even legacy systems, then we are no longer accomplishing the goal of using the same methods that potential attackers will be using. Such restrictions are all too common in penetration testing scenarios and can not only render our efforts useless, but can provide us with a false sense of security.

Disaster Recovery Planning

Disaster Recovery Planning (DRP), as a defensive measure, can allow us to withstand or recover from the attacks, outages, and disasters that we were not able to prevent outright. Such measures are usually accomplished through the use of backups for our data and through the use of varying degrees of redundant systems and infrastructure. Although, in the case of CND, properly stored backups will certainly allow us to recover in the case of an attack, it is more likely that we will find greater utility in redundant infrastructure to resist an attack. DRP differs from Continuity of Operations planning in that it focuses on the IT infrastructure vs sustaining business operations.

In the case of a large-scale cyber attack, it is entirely possible that we will find ourselves unable to operate from certain network blocks, domains, systems, and so on. Unlike the disaster recover planning that most organizations undertake, when undertaking such planning for CND, it will more than likely pay to ensure that our backup locations from which we can operate are distributed widely in both a geographical and a logical sense. In this way, when we are under attack or need to operate from a logically separated location, we are likely to have one which has not been affected by the attack.

Defense in Depth

One of the more important principles of a successful defensive strategy is defense in depth. Defense in depth proposes a layered approach to security, as shown in Figure 11.3. In this

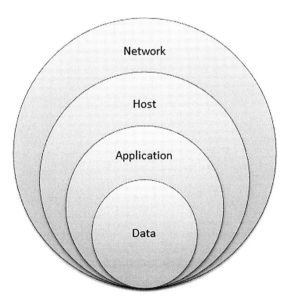

FIGURE 11.3   Defense in depth.

particular case we have defenses at the network level, the host level, the application level, and the data level. We might have, as an example, firewalls and IDS/IPS at the network level, software firewalls and antimalware tools at the host level, access controls at the application level, and encryption at the data level. In addition, the user awareness training we talked about in the security awareness section of this chapter, as well as physical security layers like badge access control, checkpoints, and guards, could easily be integrated into our layers of security. At the center of all these layers of defense lies our critical information. The layers and security measures at each layer may vary according to the environment in question, but the basic principles will remain the same.

NOTE

Defense in depth is actually an ancient military concept. One of the first recorded uses of such a strategy was carried out by Hannibal against the Romans during the Battle of Cannae in 216 B.C [10].

The principle behind defense in depth is, through the multiple layers of security measures, to hinder our attackers sufficiently so that our elements of detection will discover their activities or so that they will decide that our security measures are too great and give up on their attacks.

We may like to think that we can create an environment that is impenetrable to attack and can successfully fend off any attacker for an indefinite period of time, but this is an unrealistic expectation. Instead, we should configure our layered defenses so that we can slow an attacker as much as we can in order to have time to detect and deal with their attacks. Additionally, if we segment the information on the network, and restrict access to each segment based on need, we can help mitigate some of the risk of an attacker being able to get in, get everything, and get back out again.

SUMMARY

In this chapter, we discussed CND. CND is the defensive and largely proactive component of CNO. We discussed how CND fits into the overall category of defensive actions and how non-nation-states might not have sufficient resources to be able to defend against a complete attack by a nation-state.

We covered what exactly it is that we attempt to secure, in the sense of data and information. We also covered some of the key principles of security such as the CIA triad of confidentiality, integrity, and availability, as well as AAA, covering authentication, authorization, and auditing. These basic principles are the foundations on which we base the defense of our information assets.

We talked about security awareness and training efforts in order to secure what is likely to be the weakest link in our defenses: people. We covered the security mind-set, and what we can try to do to impart some of this mind-set to the users for which we are responsible. We also covered security training for our users, so that we might educate them as to the proper responses for some of the situations in which they might potentially damage our security footing. We also discussed the need for differing security training for the different levels of technical ability that we might need to address.

In defending against cyber attacks, we talked about some of the different strategies that we might use to defend ourselves against attack. We covered some of the uses that surveillance tactics from CNE might be used and how data mining and pattern matching might be used on such collected data. We also covered intrusion detection and intrusion prevention and how implementing these on a very large scale might be difficult. We discussed the uses of vulnerability assessment and penetration testing in discovering the security holes in our environments, and some of the ways in which such tactics might provide us a false sense of security. We went over DRP and how we might need to customize such plans to cope with the realities of cyber warfare. Lastly, we covered defense in depth and discussed how we might employ many layered security measures in our defensive implementations.

In CND we have to be successful all the time and every time. Our opponents can attack at any time, using any method at their disposal, and only need to be successful once. We have to be alert and react to every attack. This applies to every system, network, and organization equally. As a part of the military, critical infrastructure or even corporate systems, we are part of the ongoing fight.

References

[1] Director for Joint Force Development. Joint Publication 1-02 Department of Defense Dictionary of Military and Associated Terms, http://ra.defense.gov/documents/rtm/jp1_02.pdf; 2011 [accessed 05.05.13].

[2] Perlroth N, Sanger D. Cyberattacks seem meant to destroy, not just disrupt. The New York Times 2013; http://www.nytimes.com/2013/03/29/technology/corporate-cyberattackers-possibly-state-backed-now-seek-to-destroy-data.html?pagewanted=all&_r=0 [accessed 05.05.2013].

[3] Smith G. Banks fight cyber attacks by hiring outside help. Huff Post 2013; http://www.huffingtonpost.com/2013/01/10/bank-cyber-attacks_n_2441870.html [accessed 18.03.13].

[4] Schwartz M. Department of Energy Confirms Data Breach. Information Week 2013; http://www.informationweek.com/security/attacks/department-of-energy-confirms-data-breac/240147877 [accessed 18.03.13].

[5] Parker D. Fighting computer crime. s.l. New York: Wiley; 1998.

[6] Schneier B. Inside the twisted mind of the security professional. Wired.com, http://www.wired.com/politics/security/commentary/securitymatters/2008/03/securitymatters_0320; 2008 [accessed 18.03.13].

[7] Associated Press. Passport files of candidates breached. MSNBC.com, http://www.msnbc.msn.com/id/23736254/; 2008 [accessed 18.03.13].

[8] Obama B. Executive Order – Assignment of National Security and Emergency Preparedness Communications Functions. The White House, http://www.whitehouse.gov/the-press-office/2012/07/06/executive-order-assignment-national-security-and-emergency-preparedness; 2013 [accessed 18.03.13].

[9] U.S. Department of Homeland Security. Network Security Deployment. Homeland Security, http://www.dhs.gov/network-security-deployment; 2013 [accessed 05.05.2013].

[10] Flaherty K. Verifying your defense in depth strategy: from Hannibal to today. BreakingPoint, http://www.breakingpointsystems.com/community/blog/verifying-your-defense-in-depth-strategy-from-hannibal-to-today/; 2009 [accessed 18.03.13].

12

Non-State Actors in Computer Network Operations

INFORMATION IN THIS CHAPTER

- Individual Actors
- Corporations
- Cyber Terrorism

- Organized Cyber Crime
- Autonomous Actors

We have spent a great deal of time discussing the activities of nation-states in cyber warfare. Nation-states have the advantage in warfare, cyber or otherwise, of being on the formally accepted legal and ethical side of things, as we will discuss in Chapters 13 and 14. They also have the potential advantages of having greater access to resources and materials. They do, however, have the considerable disadvantage of being bound by the rules and morals that are imposed on such entities and are to a great extent restricted in their actions.

Non-state actors, logically, are those that take actions of a cyber nature, but are not directly part of a nation-state. States may certainly directly or indirectly employ or support such agents, particularly when they wish their activities to be clandestine. Non-state actors may include, to name just a few, script kiddies, scammers, hacktivists, blackhat hackers, criminal organizations, or any of a number of other individuals or groups. We will talk about these actors more in this chapter.

Also under consideration when we look at non-state actors are the activities of terrorist groups. While such organizations once depended solely on physical activities, largely revolving around the use of explosives to destroy people and resources, they too have been able to make use of the tools of modern technology. Terrorists can now make use of systems and networks to not only plan and coordinate their attacks, but potentially to carry out the attacks themselves.

Many non-state actors rightly fit into the same category as any other cyber criminal. One possible exception in this group is the corporation. Although we would like to think that most corporations generally follow the rules and regulations that bind such entities, we can see many illustrative examples in the media of this not being the case, the Enron scandal presenting an excellent example.[a] Corporations are, in many cases, entities with access to a great deal of resources and should certainly not be discounted as a factor in a cyber conflict.

Another category with the potential to carry out cyber operations to great effect are criminal organizations. Such groups not only have a great deal of resources with which to back cyber attacks on a large scale, but also have the organizational elements needed to manage them on such a scale as well. Criminal organizations can operate in a similar organizational manner to corporations, although they do not have the same compunctions to follow the rules, nor the same penalties for not doing so, and are often not bound by physical or national borders.

INDIVIDUAL ACTORS

In cyber warfare, many of the actions that we presently see taking place on a daily basis are presumed to not be the actions of nation-states, due to their potential conflict with the laws of war, as we will discuss further in Chapter 14. We see an innumerable host of small attacks: port scans, SQL injection attacks, cross-site scripting, and click fraud, as we discussed in Chapter 6, just to name a few. These activities are mainly the work of individuals and small groups who are acting to gain notoriety, steal Personally Identifiable Information (PII) to be used in identity theft, and even doing so just for the illicit thrill.

Such attackers range greatly in skill level, from the lowliest script kiddie who can only run automated tools, although often to great success, to the most highly skilled hacker, who can penetrate a system with disturbing ease and leave no trace for the owners of the system to detect. As with many professions, there are a great number of those operating at the lowest levels of skill, and only a rarefied few at the opposite end of the skill spectrum. As with ordinary criminals, those that are caught and prosecuted by law enforcement are often those that lack the skill to properly hide the traces of their activities, thus allowing them to be discovered.

As we covered briefly in the threatscape section of Chapter 2, the general list of non-state attackers can include actors such as script kiddies, malware authors, scammers, blackhats, hacktivists, and patriotic hackers. This is by no means an exhaustive list, but it does cover the main groups of such attackers. These groups are not mutually exclusive, and a given attacker may indeed fit in more than one group. Additionally, the terms used to describe such individuals or groups are rather arbitrary and tend to vary wildly from one source to another. A mapping of the terms used in this chapter to some of the alternative terms that may be used is presented in Table 12.1.

Script Kiddies

Script kiddies are often the least skilled, but most common, of the non-state attackers. The term script kiddie, often used in a derogatory sense, is used to describe someone of no

[a]http://www.time.com/time/2002/enron/

TABLE 12.1 Mapping of Terms for Non-State Actors

Terms Used in This Chapter	Alternative Terms
Script kiddies	Newb, hacker, cyber gang, criminal
Malware authors	Criminal, coder
Scammers	Criminal, phisher, identity thief
Blackhats	Hacker, hacker group, greyhat, cracker
Hacktivists	Environmental hacker, activist group
Patriot hackers	Political hacker, religious hacker, hacktivist

particular skill at attacking systems. Script kiddies generally use scripts and tools that have been written by others in order to conduct their attacks, but have no great skill or ability beyond the use of such tools. Even so, such attackers are often successful owing largely to the poor state of security in the systems being attacked and the very large number of Internet-facing systems that are available to be attacked. The large number of easy to use system penetration tools that are available also contributes to the sheer number of attacks that come from this set of attackers.

Malware Authors

Malware authors can be, but are not always, a very specialized type of attacker and may be independent or work for an organization. For those that actually write original items of malware, some certain amount of skill at programming and knowledge of the target operating systems is required. Such talented developers of malware are capable of developing the malware that botnets utilize, complex tools such as rootkits, and other similarly crafted tools.

The other source of malware, and the source of much of the malware that is loose in the wild, is in variations that are created from already existing sources. When we examine any item of common malware, we will likely find variants of it ranging into the dozens, if not far more. Often, the reason for so many variations of a particular item of malware existing is the use of malware creation kits. Such software packages allow malware to be created by choosing from a set of options allowing the user to vary delivery methods, payload, means of propagation, and other similar factors; the one from column A, one from column B, one from column C approach. Those that create malware using such tools are often grouped into the same category as script kiddies, as creating malware by such means requires no particular skill at programming. Again, as with the tools used by script kiddies, this renders them no less effective.

Scammers

Scammers are often considered to be the lowest of the low when it comes to attackers. They use many of the same techniques con artists have used for decades. The scammers that are caught and discussed publically often do not have the technical skill with attack tools of even the worst of script kiddies, as they prefer other methods of gaining their target information. Such scammers instead use tools that are of a social engineering nature, such as phishing or pharming attacks, in order to trick their victims into willingly parting with the information that they wish to obtain.

> **NOTE**
>
> Scammers, like other criminals in general, are often largely represented in the public eye by the least skilled members of their profession. When law enforcement parades such people in front of the media after their arrests, it is easy for us to think that they are representative of the level of skill present among the entire group of people. It is good to bear in mind that the highly skilled scammer will be considerably more careful and subtle, and we may not even realize that anything has happened until after they are long gone.

The goal of scammers is to separate their unwitting victims, often those that are not technically savvy, from their PII, including names, addresses, social security numbers, financial data, and other such information. Given this information scammers will seek to drain the victim's bank accounts and run their credit cards up to the limit, often moving such funds out of the country where they cannot be recovered easily.

The motivations of scammers are almost universally financial in nature. Scammers exist to, in one fashion or another, separate their victims from whatever items of value that they might have. This might mean actual currency, information, physical objects, or any number of other means of storing value.

Blackhats

Blackhat hackers, often known simply by the term blackhats (think cowboy movies), are the bad guys of the hacker world. Such hackers often have no particular care for the rule of law, the systems that they disrupt, or what ill effects that they cause. Blackhats are distinguished from whitehats, the good guys, who are often found working to foil the efforts of the blackhats, and grayhats, who ride the line between the two, often crossing from one side to the other.

Identifying an attacker as a blackhat often implies that they possess a certain level of skill at attacking and exploiting systems and networks, at least in excess of the average script kiddie. Blackhats may attack a system or network with a variety of motivations in mind. They may be doing so just for the thrill of exploiting a system, may be after specific information on the system, may be using the system as a "pivot" to attack other systems on the same network, or any of a number of other reasons.

Hacktivists

Hacktivists are, in essence, hackers that use their skills to support a particular point of view. One relatively well-known work on the subject, *Hacktivism and the Future of Political*

Participation, defines hactivism as "the nonviolent use of illegal or legally ambiguous digital tools in pursuit of political ends" [1]. The tools of the hacktivist can include website deface-ment, mass emailing, Denial of Service (DoS) or Distributed Denial of Service (DDoS) attacks, Domain Name Service (DNS) hijacking, or any of a number of other methods.

In February of 2010, a group known as Anonymous, well known for similar attacks, launched a DDoS attack against the website of an Australian senator, as well as the Australian Parliament House. Anonymous claimed to have launched the attack due to the attempts of the Australian government to introduce a mandatory Internet filtering service for the entire country [2].

The motivation of the hacktivist is almost entirely politically or religiously oriented in some fashion, and focused on influencing opinions on the particular issue in question. Causes that are supported by hacktivists can be nearly endless, but may include such topics as free speech, civil rights, religious rights, and so on. Nearly any issue that we can find supported or attacked by activist groups, protesters, and the like will have some element of hacktivist support, even if it is not an overt one.

Patriotic Hackers

Patriotic hackers may actually be reasonably argued to be a subset of hacktivists but are generally tied to national conflicts and can even join into cyber wars as independent players. They use many of the same tools and methods: Web site defacement, DDoS, attacks, and so on but generally act in support of a particular country, or an effort on the part of a country, although not in any officially sponsored sense.

There have also been occasions where such patriot hackers have been rumored to have actually been in the employ of a state and have been paid to carry out their activities. One such occasion in December of 2009 involved the theft and public posting of thousands of emails from the University of East Anglia Climatic research unit. It is believed that the patriot hackers involved in the incident were acting on behalf of Russia in order to discredit the need for reduction in carbon emissions to help fight global warming [3].

Patriot hackers will likely have many of the same motivations as hacktivists, although with a much more nationalistic focus. The activities of patriot hackers may additionally be of a somewhat more sharp and directed nature than those of a hacktivist.

CORPORATIONS

Large corporations can be possessors of great power and resources, often rivaling those of small countries. Corporations in the technical industry are often well organized, staffed with highly trained employees, and have access to the latest technologies and equipment, including those with which cyber warfare can be carried out.

Outside of organizations that are taking part in regular criminal activities, which we would define as organized criminal organizations and will discuss later in this chapter in the section on organized cyber crime, many corporations do not engage in overt cyber warfare activity. In general, we are more likely to find, with some exceptions, activities along the lines of espionage and intelligence gathering, which we discussed in Chapter 9. There is a long tradition of organized commercial and industrial espionage in business and politics, dating back to at least the height of the ninja of Japan in the fourteenth century [4].

Motivation for Corporations to Act in Cyber Warfare

The activities of corporations acting in cyber conflicts can be broken down into two primary areas: legal actions and illegal actions. Corporations carrying out acts in support of cyber war in a legal fashion will typically be doing so in the employ of a nation-state. In the United States, we can see many examples of corporations performing such roles on behalf of the U.S. government. Large defense contractors such as Northrop Grumman, General Dynamics, Lockheed Martin, TASC, and Raytheon provide expertise and resources to the government, enabling it to carry out the required cyber activities [5]. Another set of companies that support these efforts are think tanks and Federally Funded Research and Development Centers (FFRDCs). In such situations, the cyber warfare activities of these corporations are allowed and legally blessed, and the corporations are well paid for their efforts.

On the other side of corporate activities, we could potentially find similar actions taking place without the legal authorization of the powers that be. In such cases, we might see any number of activities taking place to benefit the corporation. Depending on the country in which the corporation is operating, it may have great flexibility in the cyber operations that it is legally allowed to carry out. As we will discuss in Chapter 13 when we talk about legal issues, the laws regarding cyber warfare, hacking, espionage, and similar activities can vary greatly from one country to another. By strategically placing equipment, resources, and subsidiaries of the corporation in various countries, it may be possible for the corporation to take certain activities with relative impunity, as long as it is careful in matters of scale during such activities. Certain outright attacks might be sufficient to draw international attention and cause difficulty for the host country, which would likely not be desirable for the corporation.

CYBER TERRORISM

Cyber terrorists are a rather emotionally charged category of attacker, subject to much debate and discussion. Cyber terrorism has been defined as "a criminal act perpetrated by the use of computers and telecommunications capabilities, resulting in violence, destruction and/or disruption of services to create fear by causing confusion and uncertainty within a given population, with the goal of influencing a government or population to conform to a particular political, social, or ideological agenda" [6]. Ultimately cyber terrorism can surely be seen as being related to both hacktivists and patriotic hackers, differing largely in both the scale and the intensity of their actions.

Cyber terrorists, as with conventional terrorists, are likely to choose targets that are highly disruptive and publicly obvious. One of the commonly supposed targets for cyber terrorism is the many large-scale electrical grids that provide power in various countries. The 2003 blackout that we discussed in Chapter 7 was, at first, investigated for signs of terrorist activity due to the nature of the attack [7].

Reasons for Cyber Terrorist Attacks

The motivation of cyber terrorists, as with any other branch of terrorism, is ultimately to influence the victim or victims of the attack into a particular line of activity or thinking. Cyber terrorists are also much more likely to resort to attacks that cause large-scale damage or destruction than hacktivists or patriot hackers.

Supervisory Control and Data Acquisition (SCADA) systems are often considered to be a prime target for cyber terrorist attacks. As we discussed in Chapter 7, such systems are responsible for control and monitoring of many processes that make life in an industrialized world possible, such as the distribution of power, flow of oil, communications, and many others.

TIP

As we discussed in Chapter 6, there are tools on the market that allow SCADA systems to be tested from a security perspective to help mitigate such threats. Nessus, for instance, has a whole section in its professional feed dedicated to finding vulnerabilities in SCADA systems. Use the tools that are out there, security through obscurity is not good enough!

Due to the nature of such systems, it would be possible to cause great physical disruption or damage by manipulating the devices such SCADA systems control in order to cause them to fail or behave erratically. Given that the nature of terror attacks is to evoke feelings of unrest, anxiety, and others of a similar nature in the target populace, highly visible and highly effective targets such as these present a great source of opportunity to terrorists.

What will Happen When we see a Cyber Terrorist Attack?

As we have not seen, at the time of this writing, what would be considered a terrorist attack of a cyber nature, it is difficult to say exactly what will happen when one does occur, but we can speculate. If we look at the activities surrounding the 9/11 attack in the United States, we can see a quick series of activities that took place. We saw great changes in the intelligence apparatus of the government, some good, some bad, but all designed to collect and share information in manner that would obviate the stovepiping of intelligence that allowed the attack to go unmitigated. New laws and new powers were enacted to allow more and greater amounts of information to be collected to feed the intelligence agencies as well. In general, a great deal more monitoring was put in place in an attempt to halt future attacks of a similar nature.

We also saw a great deal of military build-up, some directly within the branches of the U.S. military, but a great deal within defense contractors as well. Much of this was in support of the conventional war that was swiftly taken to the area of the world that was deemed responsible for the attacks. Whether this was reasonable or effective is a matter of much debate and largely inconsequential to this discussion.

Within the borders of the United States, we saw greatly tightened security for a period of time, with armed soldiers standing in airports and places of public interest. Directly after the event, such controls were very tight for a period of time, but relaxed considerably as more time passed without another large attack getting through. Generally, we saw a huge spike in security for a period of a year or two, then things relaxed but we can definitely still see some of the changes resulting from the attacks that were made permanent.

Given that response to a cyber terrorist attack is likely to be led by the same military thinking and leadership that responded to the last attack, it is fair to assume that the response will be of a similar nature. The 9/11 attack was a new attack, in both the sense of scale and technique, that the United States had not faced before and did not have hard experience in dealing with. Some mistakes were surely made in the process, but the end result was an overall heightened security posture in order to prevent a repeat of this type of attack and retaliatory action against those that we thought supported it.

In the cyber world, at present, our defenses are in a poor state to withstand such an attack. The virtual world has no borders to speak of, and, even if it did, the attack could very well come from within them, and we have no good way to prevent such a thing from happening. In the physical world, we can attempt to detect and prevent the entry of materials that might be used to cause mass casualties, but we have a considerably more difficult task in preventing the entry of or use of weapons of cyber terrorism. At present, our systems and defenses for dealing with such an attack are reactive only.

In the event of a large cyber terrorist attack, we would likely begin to see the development of borders and security in a virtual sense. This would be a difficult task indeed, due to the myriad of communications methods that can be used to move data in and out of a given country, and we would likely never be able to police them all, but it is something that could eventually be made to work, although with a great deal of pain being involved in the process. To say that the technical challenges involved in such an undertaking would be great and would be a massive understatement, but we would likely see an attempt made in such a direction.

A possible alternative would be to create a secure network for the specific use of critical infrastructure systems. Such a network could be considerably more restrictive than anything that needed to carry public traffic, as it would serve a more specialized set of needs. Although such a network, in and of itself, would not be technically challenging to create, standardizing the environments that might connect to it certainly would be. In addition, as with 9/11, we would likely see military action of a conventional warfare nature taken to the attacker if we could apply some sort of attribution to the source of the attack. While such attribution is very difficult to prove from a technical standpoint, when faced with a cyber terrorist attack that caused a great deal of physical damage, we would likely be able to track it back, to a certain extent, through the intelligence channels, presuming that it did come from a terrorist organization. Due to the nature of such organizations, such an attack is unlikely to be carried out without an increase in chatter, a term often used to describe the volume of communications among suspected or known terrorist organizations [8].

ORGANIZED CYBER CRIME

Although many of the different types of attackers that we have discussed in this chapter can clearly be considered cyber criminals, those that participate in organized crime can be considered to be in a different category entirely. Organized crime has existed since time immemorial, but cyber crime is a much more recent invention, and one that has been taken up wholeheartedly by such organizations. Those involved in the efforts of organized crime make use of malware, DDoS attacks, identity theft, phishing, outright cyber warfare, and any number of other tactics that might be the means to the particular end they wish to accomplish.

When looking to obtain identities for fraudulent use, financial or otherwise (but largely financial), organized cyber criminals have begun to target the organizations where large amounts of such data are warehoused, often credit card processing centers and other financial institutions. In some cases, the same criminal organizations have been implicated in breaches spanning multiple companies. Such efforts prove to be extremely lucrative, with one Ukrainian criminal organization that had been taken down shown to have made $900 million in a single month [9].

Motivations for Criminal Organizations

The motivations of those in organized crime are twofold: money and power. Given the tools, cyber and otherwise, that are at their disposal, and the resources that they can bring to bear against an enemy, such organizations are truly to be reckoned with. Of all of the non-state actors that we have discussed in this chapter, organized criminals have the most potential to be on an even footing with a nation-state in the areas of resources and effectiveness.

Cyber criminals, in the course of their activities, often develop real world skills in penetrating the defenses of their targets. Some of these attackers, whose activities have later been uncovered, have been found to have been operating inside the networks and systems of their targets for extended periods of time without discovery. Evidence has also been shown regarding cooperation between cyber criminal organizations and coordination in selecting targets so as not to interfere with the activities of other such groups [9].

AUTONOMOUS ACTORS

Another type of actor that we are just beginning to see on any large scale is the autonomous actor. We presently see such actors almost entirely in the form of malware. When malware is released into the wild, or is disconnected from its command and control structure, certain forms of it will continue to carry out their functions independent of any outside control. This has been the case in a primitive sense since the very first pieces of malware were seen outside of controlled environments.

In cyber warfare, the speed of actions, whether offensive or defensive in nature, is limited only by the speed of the networks and systems on which they take place, and primarily by the speed of the networks. As both of these factors are, in most cases, no longer particularly limiting, this means that engagements in cyber warfare can take place at speeds far in excess of the capabilities of humans to keep pace, as long as said humans do not interject themselves in the process and slow it down with human speed monitoring, approvals, and other activities. We are already at a place where the defenses of our systems and networks, through the use of tools such as firewalls and Intrusion Prevention Systems (IPSs), are allowed to act in a largely autonomous fashion, with human oversight in the areas of monitoring and, in some cases, configuration.

Exploratory Systems

As we discussed in Chapter 9, the first step in the attack process is to gather intelligence on the systems against which we intend to pursue further action. We need to map out border devices and networks, fingerprint systems, and gather as much information on our targets as we can. At present, there are tools that serve such exploratory functions, such as the famous tool Nmap, although they generally do so with very heavy interaction with the user of the tool, and are not very adaptive to the information that is gathered as they move along through the mapping process.

A good example of a tool designed with an exploratory purpose in mind, implemented as an item of malware, is the infamous Morris worm. The Morris worm, one of the first worms ever created, was written in 1988 by a Cornell University student named Robert Morris. Morris created the worm as a tool to gauge the size of the Internet. He took steps to disguise its point of origin, and used flaws in sendmail, finger, and rsh, as well as a process to break weak passwords, in order to propagate it from one machine to another [10]. Ultimately, due to a flaw in the worm's design, the result of its propagation was actually a DoS attack against the infected machines. The Morris worm ended up infecting an estimated 6000 systems, about 10% of the systems on the Internet at that time [11].

The potential for autonomous exploration systems is great, from the standpoint of automating a somewhat laborious task, particularly for large networks, and freeing up resources for activities that require more direct human interaction. Of course, depending on how such tools were implemented, they also have the potential to go disastrously wrong, as did the Morris worm. Particularly during the intelligence gathering phase of a cyber warfare attack, accidentally launching a DoS attack on our target would certainly ruin an element of stealth or surprise that we hoped to gain by quietly mapping out the systems and networks of our opponents.

Attack Systems

At present there are a wide variety of attack tools that are available to those wishing to conduct cyber attacks, ranging widely in toolsets and utility. Some such tools, such as the Metasploit Framework, provide an excellent library of attacks, but only a certain level of automation, and surely not autonomy. Other tools (such as those that we discussed in Chapter 6) combine multiple different applications into tool chains in order to add some level of automation to the process. Although such tools are not usually autonomous we can presently see autonomous or semiautonomous examples of attacks tools that are already functioning.

Much of the malware that exists in the wild can be considered autonomous to a certain degree. Such tools are constructed with a certain goal in mind, whether this is simple replication, information retrieval, or any of a number of other goals, and let loose into the world. We have seen numerous examples of malware over the years that have been, at least briefly, successful enough to infect millions of machines in the process of carrying out their programming.

In addition to simple items of malware, we can also look at greater structures that are built using malware, called botnets. Botnets are networks of systems running malware that have been recruited without the authorization of the system owners and connected to command

and control networks that allow the systems to then be remotely operated en masse. Such botnets can consist of millions of machines, and can be used to conduct DDoS attacks, crack encryption, or almost any task that can benefit from the application of distributed computing. Botnets are generally under the direct control of their operators, but they are also certainly capable of carrying out their tasks without such interaction, presuming that they have been assigned some task to carry out. The malware that recruits new nodes into botnets will generally continue to spread and grow the network in size, even if no commands are being given to the machines.

In 2008 and 2009, the Conficker worm was a regular news item in security and malware circles. The worm, in a variety of revisions, ultimately infected machines in the millions, with estimates generally ranging between 5 and 10 million devices. Regardless of the variety of interesting attack, propagation, and defense measures that were used by the worm, one item of interest for many researchers was that the worm was also recruiting devices into a botnet. As we mentioned earlier, such botnets are generally in the control of an operator or set of operators, who use them for various tasks. In the case of the Conficker botnet, no such operator appeared to be guiding its actions. The botnet continued, through the propagation of the worm, to recruit new devices until it grew to be one of the largest botnets that had ever been recorded at the time. One of the later and more prevalent variants of the Conficker network, Conficker E, quietly self-destructed in May of 2009, taking the control connections to a large number of botnet nodes with it. While a number of theories abound as to the reason behind the apparent inactivity of this botnet and its later self-destruction, one possibility is that it was created as a proof of concept for a cyber weapon, and had simply served its purpose and was then deactivated. Other variants of Conficker still continue working as of this writing.

WARNING

Experimenting with automated attack or counterattack tools is likely to be a fairly dicey proposition, potentially leading to a trip to prison, even when we have the best intention. In many countries, such tools operating outside of a very controlled environment will likely violate a variety of laws. Additionally, autonomous tools, no matter how well crafted, will likely not be possessed of any great deal of judgment in whom exactly they choose to fire upon. Yes, these are cool ideas, but they have great potential to burn the wielder.

Autonomous attack systems have great potential to change the face of cyber warfare, as long as we are not terribly picky about the results. Such tools would, in theory, be an offshoot of malware, and would exist with the express purpose of attacking a particular target or targets. Although we can go to great lengths to ensure that we control and limit the attacks of such tools, this is an area in which there are many examples of bugs in existing malware. In addition, the botnets that are active in the world today do not demonstrate aggressive behaviors, instead waiting for the command of the botnet operators. If such tools were created for the express purpose of attack, there is no reason that they could not be made to be sneakier, carry out their own attacks, and generally operate without human guidance. We could potentially, after the release of such an autonomous tool, find ourselves on the receiving end of its attacks, unable to call it off.

Defensive Systems

As we mentioned earlier in this section, we are already at a place where we have defensive systems that verge on autonomy. When we look at the standard Intrusion Detection System (IDS) and IPS in combination, what we essentially have is a system that will, based on its configuration settings, take automatic action to protect the application, system, or network that it is charged with monitoring. Such measures can be at a gross level, for instance dropping all traffic from a target or network that appears to be launching an attack; they can be very granular, in the case of dropping only specific packets that are part of a carefully crafted attack, or at any level of specificity in between. Systems such as these that can react without the express permission of an administrator are necessary in order to be able to handle cyber-related issues in a sufficiently short period of time.

As a variation on the traditional IDS/IPS usage, we could also consider a slight variation on the idea and include some facility for counterattack. We might call such a system, to slightly overload a term, an Intrusion Response System (IRS). An IRS (yes, we could aim the IRS on someone) might go slightly further than the traditionally defensive measures taken by an IPS, and actually launch an attack in return, perhaps using a somewhat "safe" attack such as a DDoS from a botnet built for the purpose. Such a solution is absolutely rife with problems, to include collateral damage and attribution, but might very well be implemented by a non-state actor that felt less restricted legally. We can certainly envision a scenario where multiple IRSs attacking each other created a chain reaction, resulting in a DDoS of truly monumental proportions.

Issues such as these could potentially create the need for new and, as of yet unimagined, defensive scenarios in order to maintain functionality in such a chaotic environment. As cyber warfare and its associated logical weapons begin to reach maturity, we may see the landscape of the Internet change dramatically in order to cope with such situations.

SUMMARY

In this chapter, we discussed the various non-state actors that might take part in cyber warfare. We covered a variety of actors that might take part in such activity on an individual scale or in smaller groups, such as script kiddies, malware authors, scammers, blackhats, hacktivists, and patriot hackers.

We covered the place of corporations in cyber warfare. Corporations not in the employ of nation-states may be involved in cyber warfare from a largely espionage-oriented standpoint. Other corporations may take place in cyber warfare to a more full degree, as they are providing such services to a nation-state and actually supplying the technical expertise for the state to carry out such operations.

We talked about the place of cyber terrorists in cyber warfare activities. The motivation behind cyber terrorism, as with other varieties of terrorism is to strike fear into targets and to influence the thoughts and actions of victims. The likely targets for such activities are those that are very publicly visible, or those that are capable of causing large-scale physical disruption, such as SCADA systems.

Organized cyber criminal groups are another major consideration in cyber warfare. Such organizations can be very powerful and well coordinated, and they often have access to highly skilled individuals and copious technology resources. Organized crime groups are largely motivated by gain of money and power, the increase of both are easily enhanced through the use of cyber techniques.

Lastly, we covered the participation of autonomous actors in cyber activities. We commonly see the use of such tools, at present, implemented in malware and defensive tools. We are likely to see the use of such tools become more commonly used in cyber warfare, as the speeds at which such activities take place preclude the use of waiting for human authorization at every step. Additionally, we discussed the potential use of autonomous attack tools and some of the dangers inherent in using them.

References

[1] Samuel A. Hacktivism and the future of political participation, http://www.alexandrasamuel.com/disserta tion/pdfs/index.html; 2006 [accessed 26.04.13].
[2] Staff W. Australian Government websites blitzed by DDoS attack. SC Magazine Australia/NZ, http://www. securecomputing.net.au/News/166860, australian-government-websites-blitzed-by-ddos-attack.aspx; 2010 [accessed 26.04.13].
[3] Telegraph.co.uk. Climategate: was Russian secret service behind email hacking plot? Telegraph.co.uk, http:// www.telegraph.co.uk/earth/copenhagen-climate-change-confe/6746370/Climategate-was-Russian-secret-ser vice-behind-email-hacking-plot.html; 2009 [accessed 26.04.13].
[4] Crowdy T. The enemy within: a history of espionage. s.l. Osprey Publishing; 2006, 978-1841769332.
[5] Drew C, Markoff J. Contractors Vie for Plum work, hacking for U.S. The New York Times 2009; http://www. nytimes.com/2009/05/31/us/31cyber.html [accessed 26.04.13].
[6] Hendershot H. CyberCrime 2003 – terrorists' activity in cyberspace, http://www.slideworld.com/slideshows. aspx/Cyberterrorism-ppt-713859; 2003 [accessed 26.04.13].
[7] Red Star Cafe. The Northeast blackout of 2003. Red star cafe. March 29, 2008, http://redstarcafe.wordpress. com/2008/03/29/the-northeast-blackout-of-2003/; 2010 [accessed 26.04.13].
[8] Barbara S, et al. Plots, evidence and chatter put U.S. on alert. CNN.com, http://archives.cnn.com/2002/ WORLD/meast/10/10/terror.roundup/; 2002 [accessed 16.04.13].
[9] Flack E. Experts: cyber crime now a billion dollar business. Wave3, http://www.wave3.com/story/13184652/ cyber-crime-a-billion-dollar-business-say-computer-experts; 2010 [accessed 26.04.13].
[10] Lowell B. A report on the internet worm, http://www.ee.ryerson.ca/elf/hack/iworm.html; 1998 [accessed 26.04.13].
[11] Graham P. Breaking news: the suit is back! The submarine, http://www.paulgraham.com/submarine.html#f4n; 2005 [accessed 26.04.13].

13

Legal System Impacts

The legal aspects of cyber warfare have been woven throughout this book as they are integral to the discussion of doctrine, ethics, and legal precedence based on similar circumstances. We covered the challenges with defining what a cyber war is and the changing definition of war in Chapter 1. We talked about how the cyber domain compares and contrasts to sea and space issues in Chapter 3. We reviewed aspects of attack versus exploit (espionage) versus defense and the many national policy issues in Chapter 4. This chapter will address the ubiquitous challenges of cyber across both warfare and commercial issues. Then in Chapter 14 we will address the ethical concepts we have codified into law such as the idea of "humane war" or "law of armed conflict" and Bellum Iustum (Just War Theory) that have come out of the lessons from the world wars in Europe. This chapter will address these concepts briefly and discuss how they are impacted and implemented in cyberspace.

First, we must analyze how the current laws, the foundation of which is the Law of Armed Conflict (LOAC), impact cyber warfare. The LOAC arises from a desire among civilized nations to prevent unnecessary suffering and destruction while not impeding the effective waging of war. A part of public international law, LOAC regulates the conduct of armed hostilities. It also aims to protect civilians, prisoners of war, the wounded, sick, and shipwrecked. LOAC applies to international armed conflicts and in the conduct of military operations and related activities in armed conflict; however such conflicts are characterized [1]. Conflicts or wars are divided into two categories: *jus ad bellum* (justification for going to war) and *jus in bello* (how war is fought). The latter, governed by United Nations Charters, the Geneva conventions, and the Hague conventions, has codified many of the existing customary international legal principles for warfare.

Next, we need to understand what an act of war and *use of force* are. Within the United States act of war is determined by the president. Use of force has different meanings for governments at war and law enforcement agencies (LEAs)—both center on actions taken whose impact forces the target to do something. This is often measured on a graduated scale or continuum. These acts must be carried out by lawful combatants (someone authorized by a sovereign nation) to fall under these guidelines. There are also noncombatants/bystanders and unlawful combatants/terrorists. These are much easier to identify in a traditional conflict but in an insurgency or in cyberspace they can become illusive.

Because the language used to develop these rules does not easily translate into cyberspace, there is no commonly accepted international understanding on how they will apply to this new war fighting domain. With that said, there have been two recent documents and one speech that have contributed greatly to national and international understanding. The first document is from the NATO Cooperative Cyber Defence Centre of Excellence: *The Tallinn Manual on the International Law Applicable to Cyber Warfare*, published in 2013 and written at the invitation of the Centre by an independent "International Group of Experts." It is the result of a 3-year effort to examine how extant international law norms apply to this "new" form of warfare. The Tallinn Manual consists of "rules" adopted unanimously by the International Group of Experts that are meant to reflect customary international law, accompanied by "commentary" that delineates their legal basis and highlights any differences of opinion among the Experts as to their interpretation in the cyber context [2].

Following are the key conclusions from the manual:

- States may not knowingly allow cyber infrastructure located in their territory to be used for acts that adversely affect other States.
- States may be responsible for cyber operations directed against other States, even though those operations were not conducted by the security agencies. In particular, the State itself will be responsible under international law for any actions of individuals or groups who act under its direction. For instance, a State that calls on hacktivists to conduct cyber operations against other States will be responsible for those actions as if it had conducted them itself.
- The prohibition on the use of force in international law applies fully to cyber operations. Though international law has no well-defined threshold for determining when a cyber operation is a use of force, the International Group of Experts agreed that, at a minimum, any cyber operation that caused harm to individuals or damage to objects qualified as a use of force.
- The International Group of Experts agreed that cyber operations that merely cause inconvenience or irritation do not qualify as uses of force.
- States may respond to unlawful cyber operations that do not rise to the level of a use of force with countermeasures. Countermeasures are actions that would otherwise be unlawful were they not in response to the unlawful actions of another State. As an example, if one State disrupts communications in another, it would be lawful for the target State to respond by conducting disruptive cyber operations of its own.
- A State that is the victim of a cyber "armed attack" may respond by using force. The force may be either cyber or kinetic. In international law, an "armed attack" is a "grave" use of force. Any cyber operation that results in death or significant damage to property qualifies as an armed attack.

- The majority of the International Group of Experts agreed that non-State actors, such as cyber terrorists, are capable of conducting armed attacks, to which the victim State could respond in self-defense. In other words, the matter is not solely one of law enforcement. In certain circumstances, it would be permissible to use force against those cyber terrorists when they are located in other States.
- Under international law, it is possible that a conflict consisting entirely of cyber operations would qualify as an "armed conflict" to which international humanitarian law would apply. This is important because not only does international humanitarian law contain certain protections for individuals and objects during an armed conflict, but it also gives immunity to combatants for certain actions, such as intentionally killing the enemy, which would otherwise be unlawful.
- During an armed conflict, commanders and other superiors may be criminally responsible for ordering cyber operations that constitute war crimes or for failing to stop such operations when committed by their subordinates.
- Although there is no prohibition in international humanitarian law on civilians—such as hacktivists—conducting cyber operations during an armed conflict, if they do so, they sometimes become legitimate targets.
- Not all cyber operations directed against civilians and civilian objects are prohibited during an armed conflict. Instead, international humanitarian law primarily addresses operations that qualify as an "attack."
- The majority agreed that an attack is a cyber operation that causes injury or death to individuals or damage or destruction to objects or which interferes with the functionality of cyber infrastructure in a manner that requires repair. Therefore, these experts would conclude that cyber operations directed against the civilian population or civilian objects are not prohibited by international humanitarian law when they merely cause disruption, irritation, and inconvenience.
- Directing a cyber operation against a civilian is a war crime if it injures the civilian or was likely to do so.
- It is unlawful to use cyber attacks to spread terror among the civilian population.
- Cyber weapons must be the subject of a legal review before they can be fielded on the battlefield.
- It is unlawful to launch a cyber attack that is not directed at a lawful target and which therefore would indiscriminately cause damage to civilians and civilian objects.
- During armed conflict, cyber operations must be employed against a target if they are militarily feasible in the circumstances and would result in less harm to civilians and civilian objects than the use of conventional weaponry.
- The special protections that medical and religious personnel, medical units, and medical transports have under international humanitarian law apply fully with respect to cyber operations directed against them. The same is true with regard to "objects indispensable to the survival of the civilian population" like medical supplies, food stores, and water treatment facilities.

In general, these conclusions show that cyber operations could qualify as use of force but the same rules apply to cyber operations in the physical world. They detail the different aspects of the law and apply it to cyber operations. The first two bullets are important to many countries as it ties responsibility for cyber operations back to the nation-state.

The next influential document is the Department of Defense Cyberspace Policy Report A *Report to Congress Pursuant to the National Defense Authorization Act for Fiscal Year 2011, Section 934* November 2011 [3]. Following are extracts from answers to the thirteen specific questions on cyber policy for both DoD and the U.S. Government posed in Senate Report 111-201.

1. The development of a declaratory deterrence posture for cyberspace, including the relationship between military operations in cyberspace and kinetic operations. The Committee believes that this deterrence posture needs to consider the current vulnerability of the U.S. economy and government institutions to attack, the relatively lower vulnerability of potential adversaries, and the advantage currently enjoyed by the offense in cyberwarfare.

   Answer: The President's May 2011 International Strategy for Cyberspace states that the United States will, along with other nations, encourage responsible behavior and oppose those who would seek to disrupt networks and systems, dissuading and deterring malicious actors, and reserving the right to defend these national security and vital national assets as necessary and appropriate.

   Deterrence in cyberspace, as with other domains, relies on two principal mechanisms: denying an adversary's objectives and, if necessary, imposing costs on an adversary for aggression.

   This will be done with like-minded nations.

   Deterrence is a whole-of-government proposition. DoD supports the White House Cybersecurity legislative proposal to protect the American people, U.S. critical infrastructure, and our government's networks and systems more effectively.

2. The necessity of preserving the President's freedom of action in crises and confrontations involving nations which may pose a manageable conventional threat to the United States but which in theory could pose a serious threat to the U.S. economy, government, or military through cyber attacks.

   Answer: The Department recognizes that a nation possessing sophisticated and powerful cyber capabilities could attempt to affect the strategic calculus of the United States. Any state attempting such a strategy would be taking a grave risk. Our efforts focus on the following three areas:

   - First, the Department, in conjunction with the Intelligence Community and Law Enforcement agencies, strives to secure the best possible intelligence about potential adversaries' cyber capabilities.
   - Second, the Department recognizes that strong cyber defenses and resilient information architectures, particularly those connected to critical infrastructure, mitigate the ability of a future adversary to constrain the President's freedom of action. If future adversaries are unable to cripple our centers of gravity, they will be more likely to understand that the President has the full menu of national security options available.
   - Finally, the President reserves the right to respond using all necessary means to defend our Nation, our Allies, our partners, and our interests from hostile acts in cyberspace. Hostile acts may include significant cyber attacks directed against the U.S. economy, government or military. As directed by the President, response options may include using cyber and/or kinetic capabilities provided by DoD.

3. How deterrence or effective retaliation can be achieved in light of attribution limitations.

Answer: The same technical protocols of the Internet that have facilitated the explosive growth of cyberspace also provide some measure of anonymity. Our potential adversaries, both nations and non-state actors, clearly understand this dynamic and seek to use the challenge of attribution to their strategic advantage. DoD actively seeks to limit the ability of such potential actors to exploit or attack the United States anonymously in three ways:

- First, the Department seeks to increase our attribution capabilities by supporting innovative research and development in both DoD and the private sector. This research focuses on two primary areas: developing new ways to trace the physical source of an attack, and seeking to assess the identity of the attacker via behavior-based algorithms.
- Second, the Department has significantly improved its cyber forensics capabilities over the past several years. The Intelligence Community and U.S. Cyber Command continue to develop a highly skilled cadre of forensics experts.
- Third, in partnership with the Department of Homeland Security, DoD is expanding its international partnerships to increase shared situational awareness, warning capabilities and forensics efforts.

4. To the extent that deterrence depends upon demonstrated capabilities or at least declarations about capabilities and retaliatory plans, how and when the Department intends to declassify information about U.S. cyber capabilities and plans to demonstrate capabilities.

Answer: Effective deterrence in cyberspace is founded upon both the security and resilience of U.S. networks and systems, and ensuring that the United States has the capability to respond to hostile acts with a proportional and justified response. The International Strategy for Cyberspace provides a clear statement that the United States reserves the right to use all necessary means—diplomatic, informational, military, and economic—to defend our Nation, our Allies, our partners, and our interests in cyberspace.

5. How to maintain control of or manage escalation in cyberwarfare, through, for example, such measures as refraining from attacking certain targets (such as command and control and critical infrastructure).

Answer: The unique characteristics of cyberspace can make the danger of escalation especially acute. For instance, the speed of action and dynamism inherent in cyberspace, challenges of anonymity, and the widespread availability of malicious tools can compound communications and increase opportunities for misinterpretation. As a result, DoD recognizes the clear importance of steps such as the development of transparency and confidence building measures, in addition to further development of international cyberspace norms, to avoid escalation and misperception in cyberspace. The Department also seeks to prevent dangerous escalatory situations by following the same policy principles and legal regimes in its cyberspace operations that govern actions in the physical world, including the law of armed conflict. Finally, the Department believes that increased transparency minimizes the likelihood that a cyber incident will escalate to a dangerous or unintended level.

6. The rules of engagement for commanders at various command echelons for responding to threats to operational missions and in normal peacetime operating environments, including for situations in which the immediate sources of an attack are computers based in the United States.

    Answer: DoD has implemented rules of engagement for the operation and defense of its networks. In current operations that occur in designated Areas of Hostilities, specific rules of engagement have been approved to govern and guide DoD operations in all domains. DoD's cyber capabilities are integrated into planning and operations under existing policy and legal regimes.
    DoD will continue to work closely with its interagency partners, including the Departments of Justice and Homeland Security, to address threats to the United States from wherever they originate, through a whole-of-government approach. The Department is dedicated to the protection of the Nation, and to the privacy and the civil liberties of its citizens.

7. How the administration will evaluate the risks and consequences attendant to penetrations of foreign networks for intelligence gathering in situations where the discovery of the penetration could cause the targeted nation to interpret the penetration as a serious hostile act.

    Answer: Espionage has a long history and is nearly always practiced in both directions. For the U.S. and many other states, traditional espionage has been a state-sponsored intelligence-gathering function focused on national security, defense, and foreign policy issues. The United States Government collects foreign intelligence via cyberspace, and does so in compliance with all applicable laws, policies, and procedures. The conduct of all U.S. intelligence operations is governed by long-standing and well-established considerations, to include the possibility those operations could be interpreted as a hostile act.

8. How DoD shall keep Congress fully informed of significant cyberspace accesses acquired for any purpose that could serve as preparation of the environment for military action.

    Answer: The Department has been working closely with Congress to improve the reporting schemes for cyberspace operations. DoD will provide quarterly cyber briefings to appropriate Members of Congress and their congressional staff in fulfillment of notification requirements. For sensitive operations that may require out-of-cycle reporting, DoD will ensure that appropriate Members of Congress and their congressional staff receive any necessary additional briefings.

9. The potential benefit of engaging allies in common approaches to cyberspace deterrence, mutual and collective defense, and working to establish norms of acceptable behavior in cyberspace.

    Answer: The President's International Strategy for Cyberspace makes clear that hostile acts conducted through cyberspace could compel actions under the commitments we have with our military treaty partners, and DoD has been working actively to clarify those expectations within our alliances.
    To implement that vision, the Department of Defense Strategy for Operating in Cyberspace emphasizes the importance of building robust relationships with U.S. Allies and partners to strengthen the deterrence of malicious cyberspace activity and to build collective cyber defenses.

10. The issue of third-party sovereignty to determine what to do when the U.S. military is attacked, or U.S. military operations and forces are at risk in some other respect, by actions taking place on or through computers or other infrastructure located in a neutral third country.

    Answer: The nature of the DoD response to a hostile act or threat is based upon a multitude of factors, but always adheres to the principles of the law of armed conflict. These responses include taking actions short of the use of force as understood in international law.

    DoD adheres to well-established processes for determining whether a third country is aware of malicious cyber activity originating from within its borders. In doing so, DoD works closely with its interagency and international partners to determine:
    - The nature of the malicious cyber activity;
    - The role, if any, of the third country;
    - The ability and willingness of the third country to respond effectively to the malicious cyber activity; and
    - The appropriate course of action for the U.S. Government to address potential issues of third-party sovereignty depending upon the particular circumstances.

11. The issue of the legality of transporting cyber "weapons" across the Internet through the infrastructure owned and/or located in neutral third countries without obtaining the equivalent of "overflight rights."

    Answer: There is currently no international consensus regarding the definition of a "cyber weapon." The often low cost of developing malicious code and the high number and variety of actors in cyberspace make the discovery and tracking of malicious cyber tools difficult. The interconnected nature of cyberspace poses significant challenges for applying some of the legal frameworks developed for specific physical domains. The law of armed conflict and customary international law, however, provide a strong basis to apply such norms to cyberspace governing responsible state behavior. As the President recognized in the International Strategy for Cyberspace, the development of norms for state conduct does not require a reinvention of customary international law nor render existing norms obsolete.

12. The definition or the parameters of what would constitute an act of war in cyberspace and how the laws of war should be applied to military operations in cyberspace.

    Answer: The phrase "act of war" is frequently used as shorthand to refer to an act that may permit a state to use force in self-defense, but more appropriately, it refers to an act that may lead to a state of ongoing hostilities or armed conflict. Contemporary international law addresses the concept of "act of war" in terms of a "threat or use of force," as that phrase is used in the United Nations (UN) Charter. Article 2(4) of the UN Charter provides: "All Members shall refrain in their international relations from the threat or use of force against the territorial integrity or political independence of any state." International legal norms, such as those found in the UN Charter and the law of armed conflict, which apply to the physical domains (i.e., sea, air, land, and space), also apply to the cyberspace domain.

13. What constitutes use of force in cyberspace for the purpose of complying with the War Powers Act (Public Law 93-148).

    Answer: The requirements of the War Powers Resolution apply to "the introduction of United States Armed Forces into hostilities or into situations where imminent involvement in hostilities is clearly indicated by the circumstances, and to the continued use of such forces in hostilities or in such situations."

Cyber operations might not include the introduction of armed forces personnel into the area of hostilities. Cyber operations may, however, be a component of larger operations that could trigger notification and reporting in accordance with the War Powers Resolution.

These answers to Congress show a progression of formal and public declarations from both political and military sources. We have Congress formally ask the military a series of questions around what the rules and policies are for cyber warfare. Similar to Tallinn Manual conclusions most of the answers tie to current policies for kinetic warfare. The answers to three, five, eleven and thirteen have specific cyber connotations.

Finally we have the Legal Adviser for the U.S. Department of State Harold Hongju Koh's speech at the USCYBERCOM Inter-Agency Legal Conference at Ft. Meade, MD on September 18, 2012 where he answered some fundamental questions around cyber [4].

Following are extracts from his answers:

Question 1: Do established principles of international law apply to cyberspace? Answer: Yes, international law principles do apply in cyberspace.

Question 2: Is cyberspace a law-free zone, where anything goes? Answer: Emphatically no. Cyberspace is not a "law-free" zone where anyone can conduct hostile activities without rules or restraint.

Question 3: Do cyber activities ever constitute a use of force? Answer: Yes. Cyber activities may in certain circumstances constitute uses of force within the meaning of Article 2(4) of the UN Charter and customary international law.

Question 4: May a State ever respond to a computer network attack by exercising a right of national self-defense? Answer: Yes. A State's national right of self-defense, recognized in Article 51 of the UN Charter, may be triggered by computer network activities that amount to an armed attack or imminent threat thereof.

Question 5: Do jus in bello rules apply to computer network attacks? Answer: Yes. In the context of an armed conflict, the law of armed conflict applies to regulate the use of cyber tools in hostilities, just as it does other tools. The principles of necessity and proportionality limit uses of force in self-defense and would regulate what may constitute a lawful response under the circumstances.

Question 6: Must attacks distinguish between military and nonmilitary objectives? Answer: Yes. The *jus in bello* principle of *distinction* applies to computer network attacks undertaken in the context of an armed conflict.

Question 7: Must attacks adhere to the principle of proportionality? Answer: Yes. The *jus in bello* principle of *proportionality* applies to computer network attacks undertaken in the context of an armed conflict.

Question 8: How should States assess their cyber weapons? Answer: States should undertake a legal review of weapons, including those that employ a cyber capability.

Question 9: In this analysis, what role does State sovereignty play? Answer: States conducting activities in cyberspace must take into account the sovereignty of other States, including outside the context of armed conflict.

Question 10: Are States responsible when cyber acts are undertaken through proxies? Answer: Yes. States are legally responsible for activities undertaken through "proxy actors," who act on the State's instructions or under its direction or control.

Final Question: Is international humanitarian law the only body of international law that applies in cyberspace? Final Answer: No. As important as international humanitarian law is, it is not the only international law that applies in cyberspace.

Unresolved Questions

- 1: How can a use of force regime take into account all of the novel kinds of *effects* that States can produce through the click of a button?
- 2: What do we do about *"dual-use* infrastructure" in cyberspace?
- 3: How do we address the problem of *attribution* in cyberspace?

Similar to the previous two statements we see most of the legal review focuses on how current law covers most of the questions around cyber warfare. Koh's statement was unique in two aspects. First he did not address the need for international cooperation but rather referred to current international laws. Second he listed unresolved issues. So we have looked at official statements from international, U.S. military and U.S state department and in overall find them to agree on the fact that many of the issues around cyber warfare are covered by current laws. This is easier in broad theoretical statements than when applied to the realities of specific cyber conflicts.

As cyber warfare will be conducted over public or commercial networks by actors from both nation-states and independent parties it is important to understand the laws that impact general Internet interactions. First there are some laws that may be applied to impact how cyber conflicts are resolved. One is the concept of due care and/or due diligence. This relates to how much care someone should take to protect their systems. The average person would not leave a handgun unprotected sitting where anyone could take it because they understand their responsibility to secure the gun so it will not be used inappropriately. In many cases today that same person would leave their computer unprotected and not feel responsible if it was used to electronically rob a bank. Responsibility may need to be regulated like the automobile seatbelt law; it might require basic firewall and antivirus protection or the owner of the computer may be liable.

Another legal principle that may be applied to cyber conflicts is the Nuisance Law. There are two types: public and private. A private nuisance is something (such as an activity) that constitutes an unreasonable interference in the right to the use and enjoyment of one's property and that may be a cause of action in civil litigation. A public nuisance is something that unreasonably interferes with the health, safety, comfort, morals, or convenience of the community and that is treated as a criminal violation [5]. If we look at reactive or even proactive attacks, this rule could be applied if governments or individuals took action against that person who left their system unprotected. This concept is tied to the right to self-defense. The challenge is that the computer actually attacking the victim might be a third party system that was compromised and is being used by the attack. In this case a reactive attack could take out a system in a critical system for a hospital or one that manages an energy grid. It has not been determined how these legal concepts will be applied to cyberspace or if they will be used to address cyber events rather than the traditional systems used to adjudicate LOACs.

Finally, there is the Principle of Neutrality which aims to maintain the confidence of all by not allowing cyberspace to be used to engage at controversies of a political, racial, religious, or ideological nature due to the reliance of all on it. This concept is usually used for peacekeeping or humanitarian missions to support organization like the International Red Cross and Red Crescent Movement.

Looking at how the law will impact the cyber domain is further challenged because of the ubiquitous nature of computer systems today. The infrastructure is commercially owned, the systems being used to build botnets can be both privately owned and government systems, every industry is dependent to some degree on the Internet and a typical transaction could span multiple legal jurisdictions. This chapter will look at the legal systems, some U.S. laws that will impact how the government responds, privacy issues, and digital forensics because they are enmeshed with cyber warfare issues.

> ## NOTE
>
> This chapter is not intended as legal advice. We will discuss the laws that exist today and how they relate to cyber warfare to help understand the impacts but it is not intended as guidance or advice. The authors would like to thank Robert Clark for his advice and insight on legal issues throughout the book.

LEGAL SYSTEMS

When examining today's legal systems we have international and nation based law which has four general types of systems: civil law, common law, customary law, and religious law (plus those with a mix, called pluralistic).

International Law has three separate disciplines: (1) public international law, which governs the relationship between provinces and international entities and includes treaty law, law of the sea, international criminal law, and international humanitarian law; (2) private international law, which addresses legal jurisdiction; and (3) supranational law, a legal framework wherein countries are bound by regional agreements in which the laws of the member countries are held inapplicable when in conflict with supranational laws. The sources of international laws are set out in Article 38-1 of the Statute of the International Court of Justice within the UN Charter [5].

Under national system law we have civil law, which is the most widespread type of legal system in the world and has laws that are organized into systematic written codes. In civil law, the sources recognized as authoritative are principally legislation and secondarily, customs. Next is common law. The foundation of common law is "legal precedent"—referred to as "stare decisions," meaning "to stand by things decided." The United States uses a variation of common law which has a several layers, possibly more than in most other countries, and is due in part to the division between federal and state law. Then we have customary law (also referred to as "primitive law," "unwritten law," "indigenous law," or "folk law") that embodies an organized set of rules regulating social relations that are agreed upon by members of the community. Although customary law includes sanctions for legal infractions, resolution tends to be reconciliatory rather than punitive. Finally we have religious law. The main types of religious legal systems are *sharia* under Islam, *halakha* under Judaism, and canon law under some Christian groups. Islamic law is the most common law governing religious legal systems in use today. It is embodied in the *sharia*, an Arabic word meaning "the right path." *Sharia* covers all aspects of public and private life and organizes them into five categories: obligatory, recommended, permitted, disliked, and forbidden. There are some systems that have mixed or pluralistic law, mixed law consists of elements of some or all of the other main types of legal systems—civil, common, customary, and religious [6]. Each of these systems deals with warfare and the Internet in different ways so it creates a complex situation when one country tries to prosecute a crime with a suspect in a different legal system.

All of these systems base their foundational principles on geography to determine what laws the incident will fall under. For example, if someone trespasses on our property in Texas we can shoot them, in Colorado we cannot shoot them until they break into our house, in California we cannot shoot them unless we feel in danger of losing our life and have no way to escape.

The second issue is that laws are written at a very deliberate pace over years while Internet issues develop at the speed of technological innovation. A prime example is the "I love you" worm in 2000. The investigation tracked the programmer to an individual in the Philippines, but as there were no laws about releasing malware on the Internet no charges were brought against him [7]. There is natural pressure to enact laws based on these events but without careful study laws could be signed that have unintended consequences that are worse than the original problem. The challenge is how do we determine what laws apply to technology that are not addressed in the current set of laws and are not tied to geography?

International

The United Nations is considered by many to be the foundation for international law but there are many treaties, agreements, conventions, charters, protocols, declarations, memoranda of understanding, or on the military side, coalitions that govern how nations interact. The most formal are treaties that are ratified by all sovereign nations involved. Some of these come after major events like the establishment of the North American Treaty Organization (NATO) while others develop over time like Admiral or Maritime Law. Still others are driven by technology like nuclear weapons, biological weapons, and satellites. There are some key lessons that can be learned from maritime law and space law. Let's look at the parallels they have to the cyber warfare.

Maritime Law

Maritime or admiralty law is a system of law concerning navigation and overseas commerce. Because ships sail from nation to nation over seas that no one nation owns, nations need to seek agreement over customs related to shipping. Though maritime law is general in character, only those parts that determine the relations among nations—particularly those that deal with problems arising on the seas in wartime, such as questions of belligerency and neutrality—are part of the international law proper [7]. Much like the Internet where traffic needs to flow over circuits not owned by the parties sending and receiving the messages, there need to be some rules on how nations act and react to each other and to non-State actors launching attacks from sovereign territory. The responsibility to help ships in trouble could become the Internet responsibility to both protect and prevent hostile cyber actions in their country. Some will argue that most countries don't control the systems we are talking about but that is also true for the shipping industry. Privateering (state sponsorship of privately owned ships used to attack enemy shipping) is not a problem on the high seas today, but as we look at the many cyber incidents that have indicators of state sponsorship, we should examine how Privateering was addressed to make sure we take advantage of lessons learned over history. Piracy is another age-old issue and there are many customs and laws on how they can be dealt with; these principles should be considered as precedents for how to react to criminals on the Internet.

Space Law

Space law is defined as the agreements governing the exploration and use of outer space, developed since the first launching (1957) by humans of a satellite into space. Space law, an aspect of international law, has grown under the aegis of the United Nations. A 1963 UN declaration stated that the exploration and use of outer space would be for the benefit and in the interest of all people; that no sovereignty could be claimed in space; that objects and persons launched into space would be returned promptly and safely if they landed in a foreign country; and that nations launching objects would be responsible for damages caused by them. In 1967, a general treaty went into effect embodying these principles and adding a prohibition on the military use of space and a provision for the inspection of installations on celestial bodies [8]. Like the Internet, space is an area where technology is changing rapidly and geography is difficult to define, so is a good template to look to for methods to develop mutually beneficial treaties. The biggest difference is the cost of entry to this domain is very high so the group of nations is small, while cyberspace has little if any cost barrier. It is imperative we draw from all areas that parallel cyberspace if we want to accelerate the development of cyber law.

The lessons drawn from nuclear and biological were addressed in Chapter 1 and also have some basic principles that can help develop the international legal framework to address cyber warfare issues.

United States Laws

In the United States, cyber incidents can be handled under Criminal Law (Penal Codes, Statutory, and Case Law), Civil Law (Tort, Contract, and Property Law), or Tribunal Law (Industrial, Labor, and Arbitration Law) depending on the circumstances. Penal codes are laws concerning crimes and their punishments and can be used to prosecute malicious cyber acts. Torts are wrongful acts, other than a breach of contract, that injures another and for which the law imposes civil liability. A serious issue related to national cybersecurity is whether or not our critical infrastructure companies are practicing due care/due diligence for computer security. If they were found to not be compliant then they would assume liability (the accountability and responsibility to another enforceable by civil remedies or criminal sanctions). Finally, tribunal law is a court or forum of justice where a person or body of persons (such as village elders) hear and decide disputes so as to bind the parties [9]. These different systems show the complexity within the United States when it comes to deciding jurisdiction for cyber attacks.

These legal systems need to be modified and enforced to raise the level of defense for the commercial sector today. This raises the argument about whether the government should be using "the carrot or the stick" to motivate industry. Some feel each industry (e.g., energy or finance) should self-regulate as they understand the risks to their business better than the government. Others feel the industries judge risk based on revenue and not on national security so they cannot be expected to implement the appropriate level of security. If the government is to incentivize industry they can offer either something like a tax break for good security practices or penalties for poor practices. Either would require a standard to be followed and audits to validate. If any country hopes to raise their national level of computer network defense they will need to start to impose standards of practice on key industries.

Criminal Law

Generally criminal law is the government against an individual, while civil and tribunal laws are a person against another person. When we look at some of the issues surrounding cyber conflicts we see some actions will be tried in civil court as economic issues, while other attacks can be prosecuted as criminal acts and still others will be moved into foreign or international legal systems. Each of these systems requires a different level of proof. Burden of proof is when the prosecutor must produce sufficient evidence in support of a fact or issue and favorably persuade a judge or jury; it encompasses both the burdens of production and persuasion. The proof is usually offered as evidence. There are three types of evidence: physical evidence, intangible evidence, and direct evidence. Evidence can be obtained by LEA as part of the investigation but often requires some type of court order (mandate from a superior authority) such as a warrant (writ issued by a judicial official authorizing an LEA to perform a specified act required for the administration of justice) or a subpoena (a command for the production of artifact or person).

An example would be to subpoena a hard drive, log files, emails, or documents (note it is not unusual to have a warrant for email files but not the rest of the information on the hard drive). This process is imperative for computer security practitioners to understand, as to take any retaliatory action they will need to be able to defend their actions in a court of law. For many of us this is a foreign concept; the military is not used to collecting evidence—they collect intelligence (which requires different processes and burden of proof), and in the commercial sector the key is detection then mitigation and recovery (focus is fixing the vulnerability and getting back into production—not prosecution). To change the cycle of defenders reacting to each new attack there will need to be a change in how defenders react and start to counteract, use of the legal system is one such method.

Electronic Discovery

The collection of evidence is known as Electronic Discovery (or e-discovery); it is the method used by parties to a civil or criminal action to obtain information held by the other party that is relevant to the action. E-discovery costs are spiraling ever higher, posing a significant challenge for companies faced with litigation and regulatory investigations that require extensive data collection and review. A sample scenario could be when the prosecution requests the email, web traffic, and Microsoft Office documents for 10 key people involved in a case for the last seven years. This would require the IT staff to get the backup tapes (assuming they have them), load them (understanding they may no longer run the same hardware), unencrypt them (if they still have the passwords on file), and extract just the required records under evidentiary process rules (i.e., tagging and tracking who has had access to them). See Figure 13.1, the Electronic Discovery Reference Model, for a general flow chart of the process. It is easy to see how labor intensive this is if everything goes right. For companies which have not developed policies and processes to facilitate this, it never does. These processes are necessary for countries as well as companies who want to track where the threat has been in their network and most government agencies are not funded or required to be able to facilitate this kind of an investigation.

While e-discovery is essentially a narrowed focus of digital forensic investigations, it is important to understand that it must be done by trained personnel who understand both how to conduct an investigation and the technology involved. That said, a good forensic investigator will not limit their investigation to just examination of the technology. They should also use the following techniques:

- Depositions: Sometimes referred to as witness interviews, it is the primary method for interviewing individuals to uncover important concepts and facts.
- Interrogatories: Similar to depositions, but in written form. Instead of a live interview, written questions are presented to a target.
- Document Requests: Sometimes referred to as a Discovery Request or a Subpoena, this is the primary method for obtaining documents and other items.

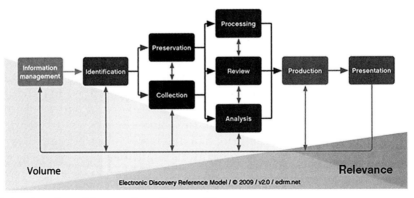

FIGURE 13.1   Flow chart of the steps for e-discovery [7].

Once the case is complete and a verdict of guilt has been issued, it is time to determine punishment (such as a fine or imprisonment) inflicted on an offender through the judicial process. These can serve as a deterrent for other attackers as they see the cost of cyber crime or warfare is higher than the benefits they gain.

KEY U.S. LAWS

In Chapter 4 we touched on the United States Codes that impact cyber warfare: Title 50—Intelligence/Counter Intelligence (DNI), Title 10—War (DoD), and Title 18—Legal (DOJ) which need to be integrated into one process (sometimes referred to as Title 78). We also mentioned the use of Title 32 (National Guard) and Title 14 (Coast Guard) as they have different regulations governing them and can fill different missions the active military forces can't. One major restriction is the Posse Comitatus Act which prohibits search, seizure, or arrest powers to be used by U.S. military personnel. This law states that the U.S. military cannot collect information on U.S. citizens. This has created quite a challenge as it is often difficult to determine which IP addresses and other network/cyberspace information belong to U.S. citizens. The National Guard and Coast Guard don't fall under the same rules and in some cases can facilitate that collection.

> **TIP**
>
> Words matter, and the legal landscape for all things cyber is rapidly changing so finding the right resource is vital to developing a sound strategy or argument. This includes tracking events from sources like United Nations documents, national military doctrine (for the United States it is being updated almost monthly), international organizations (e.g., Internet Engineering Task Force's Request for Comments) as well as recent court cases and new laws. It is important to develop a set of references or news feeds to keep up to date.

International Trafficking in Arms Regulations

Another often overlooked tool is the International Trafficking in Arms Regulations (ITAR) Title 22—Foreign Relations; Chapter I—Department of State; Subchapter M—International Traffic in Arms Regulations which authorizes the president to control the export and import of defense articles and defense services. The fact that an article or service may be used for both military and civilian purposes does not in and of itself determine whether it is subject to the export controls. This includes sending or taking technical data, articles, or equipment related to computers specifically designed or developed for military application, cryptographic techniques, software designed or modified to protect against malicious computer damage, and electronic equipment which has substantial military applicability. There is a very involved process to determine if something falls under ITAR regulations. This can be used to restrict what technology developed in the United States can be sold to potential adversaries. This is not necessarily an effective technique and has had some unintended consequences in the past but can be a useful part of a larger integrated plan.

U.S. Cyber Related Laws

For the U.S. military the foundation of military law is the Uniform Code of Military Justice (UCMJ). The UCMJ applies to all members of the uniformed services of the United States: the Air Force, Army, Coast Guard, Marine Corps, Navy, National Oceanic and Atmospheric Administration Commissioned Corps, and Public Health Service Commissioned Corps. The current version is printed in the latest version of the Manual for Courts-Martial (2008), incorporating changes made by the President (executive orders) and National Defense Authorization Acts of 2006 and 2007 [10]. These are implemented through a number of regulations and in many cases limit what the military can do by policy rather than technological issues. We will not get into the details in this book but a simple example is that the U.S. Cyber Command may have the resources to help defend against an attack on the U.S. energy grid but they are prevented by law/policy from helping. These issues are being addressed through work between NSA/Cyber Command/Northern Command and Department of Homeland Security but are far from resolved.

There are a number of U.S. Acts and institutions that relate to cyberspace such as the Radio Act of 1912 which regulates private communications, the Computer Fraud and Abuse Act of 1984, the Computer Security Act of 1987, the Foreign Intelligence Surveillance Act of 1978 known for its support of warrantless surveillance and the Amendments of 2008 and the Obstruct Terrorism Act of 2001 (known as the Patriot Act), the Federal Information Security Management Act of 2002, and the 1965 establishment of National Institute of Standards & Technology (NIST) which has responsibility for IT standards and technical assistance. Others that are well known, such as Health Insurance Portably and Accountably Act (HIPPA), Digital Millennium Copyright Act (DCMA), Gramm Leach Bliley Act (GLB) and Sarbanes—Oxley Act (SOX), don't have a direct impact on cyber warfare but are crucial to overall cybersecurity [11]. This is just a sampling of the current laws to understand how they impact cyberspace. There are a larger number of bills in Congress today related to the Internet so this subject matter will be under constant change.

Computer Fraud and Abuse Act

Let's examine a few to see how they can impact cyber warfare. First is the Computer Fraud and Abuse Act of 1984 (18 U.S.C. § 1030: U.S. Code—Section 1030). It states fraud and related activity in connection with computers by someone who has knowingly accessed a computer without authorization or exceeding authorized access, and by means of such conduct having obtained information that has been determined by the U.S. government pursuant to an executive order or statute to require protection against unauthorized disclosure for reasons of national defense or foreign relations, or any restricted data can be fined under this title or imprisoned for not more than 20 years, or both [11]. This allows the federal government to take legal action against hackers/attackers. This is complicated by the fact that many of the systems or people involved may not reside inside the U.S. borders but it is a useful tool when it can be applied.

Cyber Security Enhancement Act

The Cyber Security Enhancement Act allows service providers to disclose the contents of communications to "federal, state, or local government entities" in the event that the provider has a "good faith" belief that "an emergency involving immediate danger of death or serious physical injury to any person requires disclosure of the information without delay." These changes effectively expanded the scope of disclosures possible under the law and lowered the standard by which such disclosures could take place [12]. This allows for both LEA and Intelligence Community (IC) to gather and analyze data to determine who and what is involved in a cyber incident in a timely manner.

The Uniting and Strengthening America by Providing Appropriate Tools Required to Intercept and Obstruct Terrorism Act (Patriot Act), passed in the wake of the 9/11 terrorist attacks, is the controversial Act that expands the type of information to which law enforcement officials may obtain access and permits service providers to divulge the contents of communications in emergencies. Some sample sections that cause debate are [12]:

- Section 212 of the Act permits service providers to voluntarily release the contents of communications if they reasonably believe that "an emergency involving immediate danger of death or serious physical injury to any person requires disclosure of the information without delay." This provision was further modified by the Homeland Security Act to increase the number of governmental agencies to which service providers may disclose communications and to soften the standard by which communications can be disclosed to a "good faith" belief from a "reasonable belief."
- Section 214 of the Act significantly expands the FBI's electronic surveillance powers under the Foreign Intelligence Surveillance Act (FISA), as well as lowering the standards under which the secret FISA court can authorize the FBI to spy on our phone and Internet communications. In particular, Section 214 makes it easier for the FBI to install "pen registers" and "trap-and-trace devices" (collectively, "pen-traps") in order to monitor the communications of citizens who are not suspected of any terrorism or espionage activities.
- Section 215 allows the FBI to secretly order anyone to turn over business records or any other "tangible things," so long as the FBI tells the secret FISA court that the information sought is "for an authorized investigation. . .to protect against international terrorism or clandestine intelligence activities." These demands for records come with a "gag order" prohibiting the recipient from telling anyone, ever, that they received a Section 215 order.
- Section 217 permits service providers to "invite" law enforcement to assist in tracking and intercepting a computer trespasser's communications.

These amendments make it easier for LEA and the IC to conduct investigations into suspected threat activity.

Federal Information Security Management Act

Finally, under the E-Government Act, the Federal Information Security Management Act (FISMA) was designed to require that all federal agencies conduct a "privacy impact assessment" (PIA) for all new or substantially changed technology that collects, maintains, or disseminates personally identifiable information (PII), designate a Chief Information Officer (CIO), implement an information security program, report on the program's adequacy and effectiveness, participate in annual independent evaluations of the information security program and practices, and develop and maintain an inventory of the agency's major information systems [13]. The first federal CIO, Vivek Kundra, produces an annual FISMA report card under the Office of Management and Budget. In the past it has not been unusual for agencies to receive a failing grade. In 2003, he told the House Committee on Oversight and Government Reform—"when FISMA was enacted, the Internet and the mobile computing revolution were not as pervasive as they are now. Today, agencies are leveraging technologies and business models such as cloud computing, mobile platforms, social media, and third-party platforms to increase efficiency and effectiveness. For example, the Department of Veterans Affairs contracts with mortgage services to service VA-owned home loans. These new models increase efficiency but leave agencies struggling with the question of how to apply FISMA's requirements in an environment where system and enterprise boundaries no longer define the security points. There are a number of issues that contribute to our vulnerabilities, including: lack of coordination, culture of compliance, lack of an enterprise approach and need to energize national agenda for cybersecurity research and development" [14]. To fix these, the Federal CTO plans to overhaul how FISMA is enacted, moving more authority to the National Institute of Standards and Technology (U.S.) (NIST), developing metrics and real-time situational awareness (moving away from the current static document based Certification and Accreditation programs) as well as tracking return on security investments, increasing cyber skill set, and improving response to attacks. These are foundational to computer network defense of the government.

NOTE

When talking about the value of regulations, a good analogy is the local fire department. They have two roles. The firefighters react to fires that are going on in real time while the fire marshal conducts inspections to make sure fires don't get started. The fire codes are pivotal to keeping the number of fires down and the amount of damage done to a minimum. So the value of implementing cybersecurity standards is preventive and will save money in the long run.

Standards to Support Cybersecurity

We will briefly touch on some enabling standards that organizations can use to quantify and measure their security posture. To develop a solid security system, we can look to the International Organization for Standardization (ISO) 27,000 family of Information Security Management System (ISMS) standards and the Information Technology Infrastructure Library (ITIL) model. These can be supported by Capability Maturity Model Integration (CMMI) for documentation and Six Sigma for cost effectiveness. Operationally Critical Threat, Asset and Vulnerability Evaluation (OCTAVE) by Software Engineering Institute, Carnegie Mellon University is a set of tools and processes for risk-based cyber strategic assessment and planning. Control Objectives for Information and Related Technology (COBIT) by Information Systems Audit and Control Association (ISACA) is a good auditing system. Some industries like North American Electric Reliability Corporation have developed a set of best practices like Industrial Automation and Control System Security Committee of the Instrumentation, Systems, and Automation Society (ISA) SP 99. When looking at systems we can see if they have been through Common Criteria evaluation. These are just a sampling of the resources that are available to organizations today.

PRIVACY IMPACTS

Privacy can have a major impact on cyber warfare: the government must balance national security against the rights of the citizens. There are issues of expectation of privacy in the home and workplace, generational attitudes, constant technological advancements not covered by current laws, and basic human rights of freedom that cyber warfare tactics, techniques, and procedures must take into account. Examples are the move to state/national identity badges, and the use and tracking of biometrics that could enable aspects of national security but impinge on individual privacy rights.

The United States has a number of laws related to privacy. There are indirect references throughout in the Constitution but no declaration of a right to privacy. When we look at congressional statutes we have the Privacy Protection Act, Telecommunications Act, Health Insurance Portability and Accountability Act (HIPAA), Right to Financial Privacy Act, Identity Theft and Assumption and Deterrence Act, and Children's Online Privacy Protection Act. On the other side of the coin, we have Freedom of Information Act and Patriot Act that start to curtail privacy rights in the name of national security. These laws must be kept in constant tension to achieve the right equilibrium between security and freedom.

Electronic Communications Privacy Act

A good example of this balance is the Electronic Communications Privacy Act (EPCA) of 1986 (18 U.S.C. § 2510-22) which as amended protects wire, oral, and electronic communications while those communications are being made, are in transit, and when they are stored on computers. The Act applies to email, telephone conversations, and data stored electronically. ECPA has three titles: Title I which is often referred to as the Wiretap Act, prohibits the intentional actual or attempted interception, use, disclosure, or "procurement of any other person to intercept or endeavor to intercept any wire, oral, or electronic communication." Title II, which is called the Stored Communications Act (SCA), protects the privacy of the contents of files stored by service providers and of records held about the subscriber by service providers, such as subscriber name, billing records, or IP addresses. Title III, which is called the Pen Register and Trap and Trace Statute, requires government entities to obtain a warrant before collecting real-time information, such as dialing, routing, and addressing information related to communications. The ECPA was significantly amended by the Communications Assistance to Law Enforcement Act (CALEA) and the Patriot Act to facilitate national security investigations [11].

DIGITAL FORENSICS

Forensics is the discipline of science dedicated to the systematic gathering and analysis of evidence to establish facts that can be presented in court. The key to forensics is understanding exactly what happened (not why) and determining who did it. Digital forensics is applying this discipline to computer devices and networks. The most difficult goal in this field is determining attribution (ascribing the actions of an incident to a specific person or organization). This discipline is key to national security for Computer Network Defense. Although the evidence may not end up in a court of law it may be what is needed to authorize a counterattack (virtual or physical).

Let's start with an analogy. In America many places have a beat cop. These are the policemen who patrol a specific set of blocks; they may spend the morning working a traffic accident and an armed robbery investigation, then in the afternoon take care of a domestic disturbance call and write up a vandalism incident. Their job is to enforce the laws within their neighborhood. If one day while walking along they see a man in the alleyway lying on the ground bleeding from a knife stuck in his chest they would immediately call for an ambulance and start basic life saving procedures. If these failed and the man died they would change their priority to preserving evidence to support a criminal investigation. They would call for homicide detectives who would bring along the Crime Scene Investigation (CSI) team. These folks are trained in collecting and analyzing evidence to support the investigation and be able to present it in a court of law. The beat cop could help the detectives with simple tasks like canvassing the area for witnesses but generally they go back to their normal duties. In the virtual world system, administrators are the beat cops for the local network. They ensure the normal operation of the systems and monitor for abnormalities. If they detect a problem they will work to fix it until they determine it is an intrusion. In most organizations the sys admins will work with management to determine if they want to rebuild the system or investigate to facilitate a prosecution.

The problem with just rebuilding is the threat will simply use the same method to regain entry so some analysis is normally warranted but it may not be in accordance with evidentiary rules. If the decision is to investigate then a determination needs to be made if the organization's leadership just wants to know what happened or if it could end up in court. With the possibility of going to court comes the need for specialized skills and qualifications (often in the form of certifications). The systems involved must be treated as evidence. The investigation must be documented and the conclusion must stand up to legal standards. The tools and methodologies used must be able to stand up to review by the opposition. The investigator must be able to present the findings in an understandable way and justify their conclusions. Much like the cop trying to save a life the sys admin can damage evidence if they go too far before calling for help. Also like the beat cop they are not well equipped to testify in a court of law.

WARNING

One note for those who watch the *CSI* TV show, the last thing a digital forensic investigator would do is log into the computer. That is actually destroying evidence.

Digital forensics is similar to physical forensics but there are some key differences: first, it is a much newer discipline and in many cases both the judge and jury have difficulty understanding it (compared to something like DNA evidence which is in the common public understanding today); second, it is very transitory (it is important to baseline the evidence as computer systems are in a constant state of change); and finally, it is not a skill set that many LEA officers have (compared to the amount of training they get in handling and analyzing physical evidence). This brings up the challenge of live vs. static analysis. There will be times when the system cannot be pulled offline to analyze so it must be done live, which requires unique tools and procedures.

There are four basic steps to the computer forensics:

1. Preparation—this is where Tactics, Techniques, and Procedures (TTPs), tools, and documentation methodology are developed
2. Acquisition—this is where the collection, preservation, and review of the evidence is done
3. Analysis—this is where the investigator constructs the events into facts about what was done and if possible who did it
4. Reporting—this is where all the documentation is presented in a format that facilitates the decision needed (this is different in court vs. intelligence activities)

These very simple steps do not reflect the complexity of most investigations. A simple investigation of a laptop could involve network devices it communicated with and mobile devices (e.g., external hard drive, memory sticks, or a Blackberry) that were attached to it. Each of these requires different forensic knowledge and tools.

For physical acquisition here are some tips: first create a cryptographic hash digest of the original media (MD5/SHA-1). A hash is a one-way mathematical algorithm that when run against a file or hard drive creates a bit string signature or message digest. If anything in the file or on the hard drive changes, the message digest changes. This allows copies of files to be used in court as authentic original evidence. The investigator can keep one copy and work on others and never change the original. Next comes the collection of the relevant specimens, which must be validated with the hash digest.

Then using forensics tools like Encase, Forensic Tool Kit, or Helix, analyze the evidence and document everything done and found. These tools will do much of the discovery but in every investigation there may be specific issues that call for unique tools such as developing scripts. Cell phones are a good example of when a new tool may need to be added to the investigator's tool kit. There are open source tools but be careful as they may not stand up in court as well.

Finally, develop a report of the findings based on a standard template which can facilitate the ability to accurately testify months or years later on the findings. It is important to keep all notes and logs of the investigation as cases can go from analytical to a court case years later and you will need to be able to recall specifics based on your records.

WARNING

There is no program that will act as a dummy or wizard program to facilitate an untrained individual conducting a digital forensic investigation both because every investigation is unique and because only a trained and certified investigator should be in charge. An investigation done by unqualified personnel will result in compromised results and be unusable.

Certification

There are a number of computer forensics certifications. Generally they are broken out by vendor sponsored or LEA supported. Under vendor certifications the major certifications are by the vendor who sells the tool like the EnCase Certified Examiner Program for those who have mastered their software, AccessData Certified Examiner (ACE) by AccessData for their software, the Forensic Toolkit and GIAC Certified Forensic Analyst (GCFA) by the SANS (not tool based). For the LEA sponsored certifications the major certifications are: International Association for Computer Investigative Specialists (IACIS) which has the Certified Forensic Computer examiner (CFCE) and the Certified Electronic Evidence Collection Specialist Certification (CEECS). The International Society of Forensic Computer Examiners which has the Certified Computer Examiner (CCE). DoD has the Cyber Crime Center which has the Certified Digital Media Collector (CDMC), Certified Digital Forensic Examiner (CDFE), and Certified Computer Crime Investigator (CCCI) certifications. There are a number of other vendors, training programs, certifications, and organizations. This was just meant to be a sampling of what is being done.

One interesting trend in this area is the development of laws governing the field. Some states require certifications while others are moving to require a Private Investigators license. At issue here is the standard for an Expert Witness Qualification where a witness (such as a medical specialist) who by virtue of special knowledge, skill, training, or experience is qualified to provide testimony in a court of law. For many areas it is easy to determine what an expert is, but in the digital investigation world there are very few people with law enforcement training to understand due process and digital forensic skills to understand how to extract and analyze data and no common standard to determine what the qualifications are for an expert.

SUMMARY

The president must determine whether a particular cyber attack against the United States is of such scope, duration, or intensity that it is an "armed attack" and whether the initiation of hostilities is an appropriate exercise of our right of self-defense [14]. This will require a clear standard to be measured against and these standards need to be established now so they become the standard we can use.

This chapter has reviewed the different legal systems and some of the current laws that can impact how cyber warfare is conducted. The importance of these can be found in the overlap with Chapter 1 and definitions, Chapter 3 on the cyber battlefield, Chapter 4 on doctrine, and Chapter 14's coverage of ethics. We discussed the need to balance methods to fight the interconnected cyber crime, espionage, and warfare with the right to privacy. Finally, we dove into the need for digital forensics to support cyber warfare. The goal was to show that cyber is ubiquitous and cannot be divided into clean areas of nation-state, commercial, and military. They use the same infrastructure, involve many of the same systems, and the second and third order effects bleed over into what for a traditional armed conflict would be unrelated areas of the law.

Finally at the time of publishing there were a number of laws being proposed. Most centered on information sharing and protecting privacy. While many of these bills stand little chance of being passed there is another option—relook at the way current laws are being enforced and/or interpreted.

References

[1] Force, US Air. AFPAM36–2241 professional development guide. Air Force e-Publishing, http://www.e-publish ing.af.mil/?rdoFormPub=rdoPub&txtSearchWord=36-2241&client=AFPW_EPubs&proxystylesheet=AFPW_ EPubs&ie=UTF-8&oe=UTF-8&output=xml_no_dtd&site=AFPW_EPubs&btnG.x=14&btnG.y=10; 2009.

[2] Tallinn Manual on the International Law Applicable to Cyber Warfare by the NATO Cooperative Cyber Defence Centre of Excellence, http://www.ccdcoe.org/249.html; 2013 [accessed 17.02.13].

[3] Department of Defense Cyberspace Policy Report A Report to Congress Pursuant to the National Defense Authorization Act for Fiscal Year 2011, Section 934 November 2011, http://www.defense.gov/home/features/ 2011/0411_cyberstrategy/docs/NDAA%20Section%20934%20Report_For%20webpage.pdf [accessed 17.02.13].

[4] Harold Hongju Koh the Legal Adviser, U.S. Department of State speech to USCYBERCOM Inter-Agency Legal Conference 2012, http://opiniojuris.org/2012/09/19/harold-koh-on-international-law-in-cyberspace/?utm_ source=rss&utm_medium=rss&utm_campaign=harold-koh-on-international-law-incyberspace [accessed 17.02.13].

[5] Agency, Central Intelligence. Field listing – legal system. Fact book, https://www.cia.gov/library/publica tions/the-world-factbook/fields/2100.html; 2010 [accessed 17.02.13].

[6] Burke L. Love bug case dead in manila. Wired, http://www.wired.com/politics/law/news/2000/08/38342? currentPage=all; 2010 [accessed 17.02.13].

[7] Encyclopedia, Columbia. Library, http://www.answers.com/; 2010 [accessed 17.02.13].

[8] N/A. Law dictionary. Find law, http://dictionary.lp.findlaw.com/; 2010 [accessed 17.02.13].

[9] The electronic discovery reference model, http://edrm.net/ [accessed 17.02.13].

[10] DoD. Uniform code of military justice, http://www.ucmj.us/; 2010 [accessed 17.02.13].

[11] U.S. Department of Justice. Information sharing. Federal statutes, http://it.ojp.gov/default.aspx.

[12] Foundation, Electronic Frontier. Statutory protections. Internet law treatise, http://ilt.eff.org/index.php/Pri vacy:_Statutory_Protections#The_Cyber_Security_Enhancement_Act; 2010 [accessed 17.02.13].

[13] U.S. Department of Justice. Information Sharing. Federal Statutes, http://it.ojp.gov/default.aspx [accessed 17.02.13].

[14] Kundra V. Federal information security testimony. CIO.Gov, http://www.cio.gov/pages.cfm/page/Vivek-Kundra-Testimony-Federal-Information-Security; 2010 [accessed 17.02.13].

Ethics

Ethics is defined as "a system of accepted beliefs which control behavior, especially such a system based on morals [1]." Ethics is highly subjective, and can vary between cultures, businesses, or even individual upbringing. Many of the systems of ethics that are in place are of religious or cultural origin, and may present completely different concepts of what is right and what is wrong.

In the business world, we can see repeated failures of ethics in the form of one calamity after another being broadcast in the media. One of the more famous incidents is the Enron scandal of 2001, in which the company conspired to hide billions of dollars in debt from its shareholders and eventually went bankrupt [2]. The Sarbanes-Oxley Act of 2002 was passed in a large extent due to the Enron scandal, and actually specifies that corporations must publish a code of ethics for their senior officers, or disclose their reason for not having one [3].

When considering activities that might be classified as cyber warfare, we also need to consider the ethics of the situation. Cyber operations are a new dimension in warfare, and do not have all of the same attributes that traditional warfare does. We need to take into consideration that some of the items that may be very clear in conventional warfare such as deciding if we are really being attacked, who is attacking, whose infrastructure we are using to conduct the attack, who we are attacking, and that both the immediate and sec- ondary consequences of such attacks, may not actually be as simple as they seem during planning.

Additionally, in cyber warfare, the right to go to ware, in both a legal and moral sense may be a line not as cleanly drawn as we find in conventional warfare. We may not only have problems distinguishing who our attackers are, but we may also have issues in limiting our response to those that we think are attacking. As networks are not necessarily geographically bounded, we may cause considerable collateral damage in the process of carrying out our operations.

We can see an example of a questionable basis to conduct cyber war activities in the hacktivist attacks that took place as a direct result of Julian Assange (of Wikileaks fame) being arrested in late 2010 [4]. A variety of attacks, many of them Denial of Service (DoS) oriented, were launched against organizations that were thought to have taken action against, or to not have supported, Wikileaks or Assange, with a few of the larger being Amazon, Mastercard, and PayPal.

ETHICS IN CYBER WARFARE

In cyber warfare, there are certain concepts that have the possibility to change the way that the laws of war are interpreted. When we look at cyber warfare-related issues we may diverge somewhat from the more clean-cut situations that we come across in conventional warfare. For instance, the question of whether cyber warfare attacks constitute use of force and the lack of clarity in attribution for such attacks are problems with no easy solution.

Use of Force

An excellent question, and one that commonly comes up during discussions of cyber warfare, is the question of the *use of force*. In conventional warfare, *use of force* is generally an obvious occurrence, accompanied by the arrival of troops, fighter jets overhead, and things exploding.

> **TIP**
>
> When talking about the legal authority to conduct warfare, cyber attacks are judged by their effects. The consequences of a cyber attack are considered to be generally equivalent to a kinetic attack producing the same results. If a cyber attack causes system outages in a hospital and results in a number of deaths, it may very well be considered to be a violation of the laws of war, and therefore possible a war crime.

In the *use of force* in conventional warfare, we might bomb a portion of our opponent's infrastructure in order to disrupt their electrical grid. In cyber warfare, *use of force* could mean the sabotage of a Supervisory Control and Data Acquisition (SCADA) or Industrial Control System (ICS) system controlling a portion of the electrical grid, and the subsequent failure of the grid. Although we might never have moved a single combatant, or, in fact, moved from our desk, we have still achieved our goal of disrupting the infrastructure of our opponent. This tends to imply that the term *use of force* is inadequate, or needs to be redefined, in order to include attacks of a cyber nature.

Although it has yet to be specifically quantified in a particular law, case law, or treaty, there is a common understanding regarding the qualification of a cyber attack as a *use of force*. In essence, if the cyber attack causes the equivalent amount of damage that would be rendered by a kinetic attack [5], i.e., a conventional warfare attack, then it would be considered an equivalent *use of force*. For example, if a cyber attack were used to cause an airliner to crash, the attack would be considered the equivalent of a kinetic attack, such as shooting it down with a missile, causing the plane to crash.

As mentioned, the definition of *use of force* is still somewhat of a state of flux. More recently, the Tallinn Manual on the International Law Applicable to Cyber Warfare states "a cyber operation constitutes a use of force when its scale and effects are comparable to non-cyber operations rising to the level of a use of force" [6]. While this definition may sounds very similar overall, the Tallin Manual goes on to provide additional details on use of force, including "providing an organized group with malware and the training necessary to use it to carry out cyber attacks against other States" [6], would qualify as such.

Intent

When dealing with network, system, infrastructure, or other issues that are causing us a great deal of trouble, it is easy to imagine that they are the intended actions of a malicious attacker.

Given the broad arsenal available for cyber attacks, such an attack could look like a random occurrence; a service crashing, files being altered or deleted, unusual traffic to a particular port or ports, accounts being locked out repeatedly, or any number of similar problems.

Problematically, such problems can also be caused by any number of legitimate issues. Services may crash due to faulty operating system or application patches, files may be altered or deleted on accident by legitimate users, unusual traffic to ports may be due to application configuration issues, and accounts may be locked out repeatedly due to login attempts by maintenance processes. Any number of such issues may appear to be an attack and, without taking the time to determine the actual intent of the "attacker" we may jump to the wrong conclusion and take rash actions.

Attribution

Beyond intentionally obscuring the source of an attack, steps can be taken to cause the attack to be attributed to another source. Using another country or organization to mask the source of an attack can lead to tensions, or outright attacks on the systems behind which we are hiding, potentially drawing our unwitting shield into a conflict. Although such tactics are used in the intelligence world for exactly these purposes, they are not a component of outright warfare, and may be considered to be "bad form" by some parties.

Military Laws Based on Ethical Systems

When conducting warfare, in either a conventional or cyber sense, nation states, but not necessarily non-state actors, generally follow certain sets of rules in order to prevent truly horrific weapons from being used, civilians from being attacked, hospitals from being bombed, and other similar actions that are generally considered to be morally reprehensible. At present, this set of rules is known as the law of armed conflict, a set of laws and treaties with a basis in ancient Rome.

Law of Armed Conflict

The law of armed conflict, at present, comprises the Geneva Conventions, the Hague Conventions, and a number of other treaties and laws. These laws are considered to be binding for the countries that are signatories to the treaties of which they are composed [7], although it is important to note that not all countries are party to such treaties. The laws specify what countries are and are not permitted to do in times of war, as well as the applicability to those that are non-state actors and those that are not signatories to the treaties. The Hague Conventions are somewhat more focused on the actual conduct of war, while the Geneva Conventions are more oriented in a humanitarian direction.

There were two Hague Conventions, one in 1899 and one in 1907, both conducted at The Hague in the Netherlands [8]. The first Hague Convention produced four major sections and three declarations related to the general conduct of war and the use of projectiles. The second Hague Convention, consisting of thirteen sections, established voluntary arbitration, set conventions on the collection of debts, expanded upon the rules of war, and laid out the rights and obligations of neutral parties.

The Geneva Conventions are composed of four conventions and three protocols, developed between 1864 and 1949 [9] and are the standards in international law for the humanitarian treatment of victims of war. These conventions cover the treatment of the sick and wounded, prisoners of war, civilians, and medical and religious personnel.

The law of armed conflict was developed in an attempt to mitigate the atrocities of war. It was also developed to deal with issues of warfare that take place on an entirely mental and physical level. Since we have added cyber warfare as an additional dimension, we need to either adapt or reinterpret the existing laws of war to fit, or create new laws to fit some of the special situations that cyber warfare creates, as we discussed earlier in this chapter in the section on the ethics of cyber warfare.

It is also important to note that the law of armed conflict is primarily intended to govern the conduct of war between states. In cyber warfare, it is entirely possible that we will find ourselves facing an opponent that is fully capable of carrying out attacks that would be considered an act of war if launched by a state, but are in fact sourced to an individual or a small group. This situation is specifically covered in the following section on *jus ad bellum*.

When we look into the specifics of the laws of warfare, we find that they are constructed on an older set of concepts called *bellum iustum*, or just war theory.

BELLUM IUSTUM (JUST WAR THEORY)

Just war theory gives us a good framework on which to discuss the ethics of warfare in general and more specifically, of cyber warfare. In just war theory, we look at conduct during three different phases of warfare; beginning a war (*jus ad bellum*; the right to wage war), during a war (*jus in bello*; conduct during war), and ending a war (*jus post bellum*; ending a war).

When discussing just war theory, the right to wage war, and the proper conduct during war, are universally included. These principles find their origin in ancient Rome, often first attributed to Cicero, and have been the basis of the rules of warfare from then into modern

FIGURE 14.1 Immanuel Kant, from the painting by Döbler.

times. Justice after war is a newer concept, and has its basis with Immanuel Kant in the eighteenth century [10] (shown in Figure 14.1) [11].

Each major section of *just war theory, jus ad bellum, jus in bello*, and *jus post bellum*, contains a number of principles that provide more specific guidance. As some of these principles have been modified, removed, added, and argued over for thousands of years, the specific principles and their meaning vary greatly from one source to another. With sufficient research, it is possible to find two entirely different sets of principles for a given concept, but the general ideas remain the same for each.

Jus ad Bellum (The Right to Wage War)

Jus ad bellum discusses the right to wage war. The five principles of *jus ad bellum* are: right authority, right intention, probability of success, last resort, and proportionality [12]. The right to wage war is a concept that is largely tied to states, which are much more bound to the laws of war than individuals or organizations, criminal or otherwise. In the case of such non-state attackers, the concept of the right to wage war may be reduced to more of a question of having the capability to do so. For those who have no intention of obeying domestic or international laws in the first place, the legal and moral barriers posed by the laws of warfare are likely no impediment at all.

Right Authority

The legal authority that allows us to carry out attacks comes from a combination of laws, on a national and international level, treaties, and various other institutions. How exactly such laws relate to issues of cyber warfare is still in the process of being worked out and could definitely be an issue. We discussed this at length in Chapter 13.

Of particular note for applicability in cyber warfare is the fact that only the legitimate authorities of a state have the legal authority to wage warfare. In effect, this means that a state, generally the equivalent of a country, is the only entity that can legally wage war. For conventional warfare, the legal authority to wage war, on an international scale, and the capability to do so, generally match up fairly closely.

When we look at cyber warfare, the capability to conduct warfare differs greatly in the sense of resources required. A trip to a local computer store and a small amount of coding ability can be sufficient to arm a group or individual for cyber war. In such cases, the laws of war may not apply to criminal organizations, hacktivists, individual hackers, and the like, as they may be considered unlawful combatants. Unlawful combatants do not enjoy the protections of the laws of war and can be prosecuted under the laws of the state in which they are detained. Similar laws apply to corporations that conduct such unlawful cyber operations, although the consequences to them may be somewhat different from a legal standpoint.

> **NOTE**
>
> The laws that govern cyber crime and attacks vary quite a bit from one country to the next. Certain countries with laws that are more lax on such points, Bolivia for instance [13], can provide a good home, or at least a good place for collocating servers, for those non-state actors that conduct cyber attacks. As they are not bound by the laws of war, this can provide them with a certain measure of safety from a legal perspective.

In order for a non-state actor to be detained or prosecuted as an unlawful combatant, they would need to have committed an act that would be considered to be a *use of force* if they had been a nation state. If we look back to our discussion on the *use of force* earlier in this chapter, the common understanding is that, at present, *use of force* in cyber attacks is decided by the results of the attack. Unlike conventional warfare, a cyber operation of sufficient effect to be classified as *use of force* can very easily be carried out by an individual or small group.

Right Intention

Right intention in warfare specifies that we may only use or threaten force against another state for a truly just cause. It is understood by the signatories to the United Nations (UN) Charter that this specifically refers to a response to the *use of force*, and not other actions of an unfriendly nature, such as "unfavorable trade decisions, space-based surveillance, boycotts, severance of diplomatic relations, denial of communications, espionage, economic competition or sanctions, and economic and political coercion [5]," regardless of the way in which such attacks are used. Such unfriendly acts would include many attacks of a cyber nature, excluding an attack that had an effect qualifying it as a *use of force*. While these may not be classified as actual acts of war, the results can still be devastating.

Probability of Success

The principle of probability of success dictates that force may not be used in a futile war effort. As we have already discussed, the distinction between what does and does not constitute *use of force* depends on the ultimate effect of the action in question. In the case where a cyber attack did not result in an outcome of a physical nature, it would likely not be considered a *use of force*. This leaves the possibility of a state using lesser attacks that are of a harassing or disruptive nature without violating this particular tenant of jus ad bellum. It does seem likely that the definition of use of force will need to be changed at some point, specifically to avoid parties using this as a loophole through which to conduct cyber attacks with impunity.

Last Resort

The principle of last resort stipulates that force may be used only after diplomacy fails, or is considered to not be practical. As is the case in the principle of probability of success, the definition of *use of force* in cyber warfare is an issue of importance. Although the actual issue of *use of force* might be problematic, there are many cyber attacks that could be used short of the *use of force*. In the case of attacks that do equate to *use of force*, for UN signatories, approval by the UN Security Council would likely be required in most cases [5].

Proportionality

The principle of proportionality states that the benefits of warfare must outweigh the harms that are caused by it. In cyber warfare, due to the potential unpredictable results of our attacks, judging proportionality may be a somewhat difficult prospect. While we can launch a cyber attack with the intent and relative surety that it will have a limited set of effects, the possibility always exists that we will do a far greater amount of harm than was originally planned.

Jus in Bello (Proper Conduct in War)

The idea of *jus in bello* specifies how a state must act in times of war. The two principles of jus in bello are distinction and proportionality [14]. Distinction covers the way that we carry out the war itself, in the sense of which targets are and are not legitimate. The concept of proportionality means that we cannot attack a legitimate target and cause a great deal of collateral damage in the surrounding area without cause to do so.

Distinction

The concept of distinction specifies that war should not be directed at noncombatants and neutral parties. In conventional warfare, while this concept is not always easy to carry out, it is rather clear-cut; we should not attack civilian targets without affecting a sufficiently valuable military goal as the end goal. In the logical world, where cyber operations are carried out, this distinction is more difficult to make, due to the intermingled nature of military and civilian networks and systems. When we attempt to make the distinction between such targets, there may actually not be a separation, as many such targets will be dual use.

We also have some difficulty when it comes to the matter of neutral parties in cyber warfare. Given the nature of cyber operations, attack traffic can traverse a wide variety of networks and systems in order to reach its intended target. We may be routing packets through the networks of multiple different countries, some of them neutral, some of them not; and many of them completely unaware that the traffic is even going through their infrastructure. We also have the possibility of a target not actually being located in the state that is being attacked. Our opponent could have systems located in a multiple different geographical locations in order to render such systems more difficult to attack physically, and such a system might be physically located in a neutral country. This also brings up the question of whether there are obligations for a neutral party to take steps to stop attacks coming from or routing through their country. Such questions will likely not be resolved until sufficient cyber incidents have occurred that new laws are created to deal with them, or the present ones are given new interpretations to include them.

Noncombatants

Noncombatants are a particular issue in cyber war. In conventional warfare, the issue of not attacking noncombatants is somewhat clear-cut. In general, we do not want to bomb orphanages, hospitals, and other similar areas that are considered to be of a non-military nature. Although such rules do not always hold true, accidental strikes do happen and opponents do sometimes use such facilities as shields, but the rules are relatively clear.

When considering a cyber operation, the boundaries between what is acceptable and not acceptable are not as clear. At present, such activities are carried out almost universally over public networks, as these same networks are used by civilians and military equally. We cannot presently attack one group without affecting the other in an equal measure. When we destroy infrastructure in order to remove the capability for communications and propaganda from the hands of our opponents, we also disable such services for the civilian and noncombatant populace.

While it is easy to say that we cause no true or permanent harm by taking out the Internet connectivity in an area, we may be causing more of a significant impact than we might think. We may be disabling connectivity for those working for companies from remote locations, people who operate stores over the Internet, or schools that access educational materials online. Worse yet, we may be disabling the systems that enable the distribution of food and supplies, SCADA systems that monitor and control utilities, and other critical components. Removing the ability to run heating or air conditioning systems at certain times of year may indeed result in loss of life.

Destroying or disabling network systems or infrastructure in an area of poorer economic status may leave a considerable barrier toward the local populace being able to restore such functionality within any reasonable amount of time. Permanently removing such systems may have a profound effect indeed, even without shedding a drop of blood with the weapons of conventional warfare.

Proportionality

The concept of proportionality covers the effects of the attack in relation to the type of target being attacked. If we attack a target that is a military objective, we cannot cause harm to targets that are civilian, noncombatants, or neutral parties while carrying out this attack that is in excess of the value of the original target.

Problematically, the effects of cyber attacks can be difficult to detect or quantify. Whether such attacks do physical damage or not, the estimated amount of damage done would need to come from the party being attacked, without any direct way of verifying such a claim by the attacker or any interested third parties. Since, other than any obvious physical components to the attack, there is no immediately and publically visible effect, such estimates can prove to be guesswork at best.

Additionally, some cyber attacks are reversible, and some are not. If we use something along the lines of a DoS or Distributed Denial of Service (DDoS) attack, the first order effects should be relatively reversible. When we stop the attack, a few systems may need to be rebooted or restored, but this should largely be the extent of any material damage. If we use a cyber attack to take control of the systems managing the water level in a dam and the dam breaches, then we have caused a great deal of physical damage that cannot be undone.

Collateral Damage

As with conventional warfare, we need to be concerned with our cyber attacks affecting people and facilities that are not considered to be part of the conflict. Considering that the systems and networks that provide the basis for such operations are the same systems and networks that public services operate over, achieving this separation can be rather difficult.

Given the present structuring of our networks, being able to direct our attacks so as to avoid impacting noncombatants, as is specified in the Hague and Geneva conventions that we discussed earlier in this chapter, may be very difficult, if possible at all. In the future, we may see changes to systems and networks in order to separate civilian networks from military networks in order to make such distinctions easier to arrive at in times of war or crisis.

Limiting Attacks

When we look at attempting to limit attacks in cyber warfare, we encounter a rather technically difficult proposition. As the Internet is not geographically bounded, attacks of a logical nature, even when carried out with the greatest care and planning, are very likely to have impacts that we do not anticipate.

WARNING

In the context of using malware as a tool of cyber warfare, limiting such attacks may prove to be very difficult indeed. We can certainly implement features in such tools in an attempt to limit them to a particular network, geographical area, or any of a number of factors, but such efforts will not always be successful. Even if we were to code our attack tools in such a way as to be limited to a particular IP address range, in order to only target a given organization, we would also be likely to infect geographically distant machines that were connected over Virtual Private Network (VPN) connections, and other similar cases. In effect, we would very likely spread a tool of cyber warfare into personally owned systems, other countries, and support organizations in very short order.

One potential solution to such issues is the implementation of logical borders to match our physical borders. In areas that are largely physically separate from other land masses,

Australia for instance, such an implementation may be somewhat easier to carry out, at least from a wired perspective. If we were to attempt the same in one of the countries in Western Europe, the task becomes considerably more difficult. Although challenging to implement, such divisions may be beneficial in the near future.

Jus Post Bellum (Justice After War)

Jus post bellum defines justice after war; basically how to properly shut down and handle the aftermath of the war. The principles of jus post bellum are: seek a lasting peace, hold morally culpable individuals accountable, and extract reparations [15].

Seek a Lasting Peace

As we discussed earlier in the chapter in the section on *jus ad bellum* when we covered the need for a legitimate authority for a state to wage war, peace must also be offered and accepted by a legitimate authority. While this is the normal state in conventional warfare, in cyber warfare, our opponent may very well be a non-state actor such as a hacker, hacktivist, criminal, or a corporation. In such a case, these non-state actors are likely to be considered an unlawful combatant.

Hold Morally Culpable Individuals Accountable

Holding morally culpable individuals accountable for actions under cyber warfare may be a difficult prospect. As we have discussed several times in this chapter, many cyber operations fall outside of the bounds of the *use of force*. For such activities, it is unlikely that there will be anything substantial for which someone might be held to account. For attacks that do qualify as *use of force*, finding a specific individual upon which to pin responsibility might be difficult.

For example, in the case where a malware infection caused the system responsible for formulating a particular medication to produce an improperly mixed batch, we have several points at which we could assign blame. We could blame the author of the malware, although proving that they had this particular intent in mind when writing it would likely prove difficult, if we could identify them at all. We could blame the worker at the facility that carried the malware in on a thumb drive and infected the system, although this was likely done completely by accident. We could blame the system administrator for not having sufficient controls in place to catch the malware, and so on.

In some cases, we may have sufficient evidence to attribute such attacks to individuals, if they indeed were attacks at all, but these are likely to be few and far between. Even in such cases, the possibility of being able to prosecute such actions will, in all probability, be limited to state-sponsored activities.

Extract Reparations

The process of extracting reparations for an act of war runs into many of the same difficulties that we find in attempting to hold individuals accountable for such actions. We may be able to link a cyber attack to a particular individual or state, but outside of an officially declared war, reparations seem unlikely. As is the case in many interactions that take place in the world of the logical, attacks of a cyber nature will probably be of a less forthright and formal nature than conventional warfare.

SUMMARY

In this chapter, we discussed the ethical issue surrounding cyber warfare. Such issues differ significantly from those in conventional warfare due to the potential for cyber attacks to be misattributed. We discussed attacking ethically in cyber war, including issues such as secrecy in attacks, noncombatant immunity, and what constitutes use of force in cyber warfare.

We covered issues that may arise to the determination or improper determination regarding the specifics of an attack. It is entirely possible that due to configuration issues, hardware problems, application misbehaviors, or any number of other issues, that we might mistake a technical problem for an attack. There is also the matter of the intent behind the attack. Attacks may be malicious in nature, intended to draw attention, legitimate security testing, or prompted by any of a variety of other motivations. Being able to respond appropriately to the intent of the attack is important.

Just war theory provided us with a good framework in which to discuss certain aspects of cyber warfare. We covered the authority under which we conduct such operations, from both a legal and moral standpoint. We also talked about proper conduct during war, including properly proportional responses to attack, the legitimacy of attack and response, and the international laws of war, including the Geneva and Hague conventions.

Lastly, we covered collateral damage issues as relates to cyber warfare. We went over problems of limiting attacks in the virtual world, and the technical issues involved in trying to do so. Due to the intermingled nature of governmental and civilian networks, it may not always be possible to restrict our attacks to targets of a military nature. Despite taking steps to confine our attacks to certain areas, we may become the target of a great deal of public frustration due to the impact on non-military targets.

References

[1] Cambridge Advanced Learner's Dictionary. Definition of ethic noun from Cambridge dictionary online. Cambridge dictionary online, http://dictionary.cambridge.org/ictionary/british/ethic?q=ethic; 2013 [accessed 03.03.13].

[2] BBC News. Enron scandal at-a-glance. BBC News, http://news.bbc.co.uk/2/hi/business/1780075.stm; 2002 [accessed 03.03.13].

[3] Competence Software. Section 406 – Code of ethics for senior financial officers. Sarbanes Oxley simplified, http://www.sarbanesoxleysimplified.com/sarbox/compact/htmlact/sec406.html; 2013 [accessed 03.03.13].

[4] Vinograd C. Julian Assange arrested: Wikileaks founder taken into custody in London on Swedish warrant. The Huffington Post, http://www.huffingtonpost.com/2010/12/07/julian-assange-arrested-w_n_792956.html; 2010 [accessed 03.03.13].

[5] Owens WA, Dam KW, Lin HS. Technology, policy, law, and ethics regarding U.S. acquisition and use of cyber attack capabilities. Washington, DC: National Academies Press; 2009.

[6] Schmitt M. Tallinn manual on the international law applicable to cyber warfare. New York: Cambridge University Press; 2013.

[7] Solis G. The law of armed conflict: international humanitarian law in war. New York: Cambridge University Press; 2010.

[8] Yale Law School. The laws of war. Avalon project, http://avalon.law.yale.edu/subject_menus/lawwar.asp; 2008 [accessed 03.03.13].

[9] International Committee of the Red Cross. International humanitarian law – treaties and documents. International committee of the Red Cross, http://www.icrc.org/ihl.nsf/INTRO?OpenView; 2005 [accessed 03.03.13].

[10] Orend B. War and international justice: a Kantian perspective. Waterloo, ON: Wilfrid Laurier University Press; 2000.

[11] Anonymous. The project Gutenberg EBook of picturesque Germany, http://www.gutenberg.org/files/23446/23446-h/23446-h.htm; 2007.

[12] Maiese M. Jus ad Bellum. Beyond intractability, http://www.beyondintractability.org/essay/jus_ad_bellum/; 2003 [accessed 03.03.13].

[13] Lovet G. out-law.com. How cybercrime operations work – and why they make money, http://www.out-law.com/default.aspx?page=7791; 2007 [accessed 03.03.13].

[14] Moseley A. Just war theory. Internet encyclopedia of philosophy, http://www.iep.utm.edu/justwar/; 2009 [accessed 03.03.13].

[15] Dimeglio RP. The evolution of the just war tradition: defining Jus Post Bellum. Military law review, http://www.citadel.edu/smll/Seminar/Additional%20Resources/DiMeglio,%20The%20Evolution%20of%20the%20Just%20War%20Tradition,%20Military%20Law%20Review,%20Winter%202005.pdf; 2005.

15

Cyberspace Challenges

INFORMATION IN THIS CHAPTER

- Cybersecurity Issues Defined
- Interrelationship of Cybersecurity Challenges
- Way Ahead

This chapter is based on research conducted for a white paper developed by the company TASC under the CTO's office CyberAssure™ program. The study was designed to help customers understand the entire set of cyber challenges facing them today so they could determine where resources would best be used. It was done in conjunction with University of Virginia Applied Research Institute. The original authors were Steve Winterfeld, Anthony Gadient, Kent Schlussel, and Alfred Weaver. It is used here with their permission.

While updating this chapter, it has been somewhat discouraging that not much has been accomplished to change the disposition of these challenges. With the current state of the economy, there are not many funded research efforts going today so nobody should expect any dramatic improvements on the near term horizon.

Currently, the United States, Western Europe, and much of Asia have integrated the Internet into both their economy and military to the point they are dependent on it for daily operations. For the United States, these digital capabilities have become a strategic center of gravity. Additionally, most other nations are quickly moving in this direction. The number of systems (computers, mobile devices, infrastructure devices) and applications (stand alone, networked, and web-based) that support this cyber capability are growing exponentially. Due to this explosive growth, nations struggle with systems that are plagued with vulnerabilities that could easily impact our ability to maintain confidentiality, validate integrity, and ensure availability. This increasing reliance on technology has created significant national cybersecurity challenges.

At the same time, advanced technologies and tools for computer network operations have become widely available at low cost, resulting in a basic, but operationally significant, technical capability for U.S. adversaries of all types, including hackers (anyone conducting unauthorized activities on a system), insider threats hacktivists (cause-based hackers), industrial spies, organized crime, terrorists, and national governments (often called Advanced Persistent Threat or APT). In 2012 President Barack Obama said, "It's now clear that this cyber threat is one of the most serious economic and national security challenges we face as a nation. It's also clear that we're not as prepared as we should be, as a government or as a country" [1]. A comment echoed in his 2013 State of the Union address.

There is no single document that succinctly and comprehensively identifies the cyber challenges facing the United States and other nations, and then organizes these issues so that senior leaders can develop a comprehensive plan to address the challenges facing their organizations while the technical staff can identify which challenges most impact their organization. This chapter addresses this gap in three ways. First, it provides a concise review and taxonomy of the principal cyber challenges we face today. Next it lays out who should allocate resources to the different challenges. Finally it provides a look at the way ahead. It is not designed to provide the answers but rather to start a discussion about the next steps to prepare for success in cyberspace. While this chapter will focus on how the United States is impacted by these challenges they are uniform for all nations.

CYBERSECURITY ISSUES DEFINED

These challenges were selected based on customer feedback, Senior System Security Engineer input, and review of studies like: Institute for Information Infrastructure Protection's (I3P) National Cyber security R&D Challenges [2], Networking and Information Technology Research and Development's (NITRD) National Cyber Leap Year [3], InfoSec's Hard Problem List [4], Computing Research Association's Four Grand Challenges in Trustworthy Computing [5], Department of Energy's A scientific R&D approach to Cybersecurity [6], Center for Strategic and International Studies' (CSIS) Securing Cyberspace for 44th president report [7], Bush's National Cybersecurity Strategy [8], HSPD 54's Comprehensive National Cybersecurity Initiative (CNCI) focus areas [9], and Obama's Cyberspace Policy Review [10]. The authors picked the final list based on the major pain points they think our nation is facing. They acknowledge there are subjects that could be argued to be added, while some of the ones included are not applicable to every organization as well as they could be grouped differently.

The authors have categorized each challenge by level of complexity. The rankings are: Extremely Difficult (ED), Very Difficult (VD), Difficult (D), and Not Cost Effective (NCE). There is no clean way to rank them, as the types of resources are different for each challenge, so we have tried to quantify/qualify the complexity and types of resources needed. The term resources is not restricted to financial. In some cases it is classic research and development for new technology, for others it is political will, while others require new or changes to regulation. Some are dependent on external forces, others need financial investments and finally they all need some level of leadership focus.

We have also categorized the challenges by resources required, while we have stated that there are a number of types of resources this metric will focus on overall financial investment required. We have used the following designations to show the level of effort needed for each challenge: Very Significant = $$$, Significant = $$, Less Significant = $. While it is difficult to address how to categorize levels of resources, as different challenges require different methods to solve in general, we will use the initial unclassified CNCI budget of $18 billion as very significant, less than $9 billion as significant and less than $1 billion as less significant. These are very general estimates and each problem would need to be examined against a specific plan to determine resources required.

The challenges are grouped to show their relationships. The major areas are Policy, Technology, and People. The areas of overlap between them are Policy and Technology have process in common, Technology and People have skills in common, and People and Policy have organizations in common. Then there is a core set that is common to all the challenges (the mapping is shown in Figure 15.1). They are not listed by order of importance as each organization would rank these issues differently based on their risks.

This graphic has been used to lead workshops for all types or companies or organizations trying to determine where they should allocate resources based on which challenge is causing them the most pain balanced with where the level of investment they can make will have the greatest impact. The workshop starts with eliminating those challenges that are not appropriate for the organization (i.e., most companies do not have a need for Rules of Engagement policy). It then goes into discussion on what is critical for them. After a while the discussion usually comes down to should the organization invest in more technology (often monitoring focused) or in training (people focused). General agreement is that there is a desire to invest in changing the behavior of the users but the level of resources required to truly make an impact on how they act is not practical so most organizations default to buying tools to monitor them.

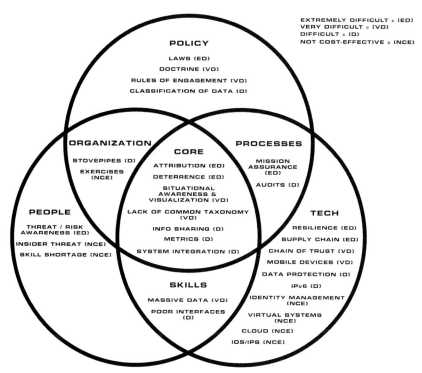

FIGURE 15.1   Categorization and relationships of the challenges.

Policy

Laws (ED $) encompass policy, legal issues, national security, and privacy. In the United States today, these issues tend to conflict with each other. Our culture and heritage influence the formation of our laws. Relatively speaking, cyber issues are new when compared to the backdrop of our legal system (dating from common English law and the Magna Carta in the year 1215). Our legal system lacks experience in setting boundaries for many of the technological advances today, to include cyber, medicine, and advances in communications. The legal issues are further complicated within the United States as each state sets its own laws that vary widely and even federal law is interpreted differently in various courts. There are a number of proposed regulations, statutes, and international agreements being worked today that will impact many of the issues discussed in this chapter.

Doctrine (VD $) suffers from a lack of consistency across the military services that address offense and defensive cyber strategy through tactics, techniques and procedures. This is not to say that there is a complete lack of doctrine or that it conflicts but rather there is no common unifying doctrine. The DoD has made progress by establishing a common set of terms [11]. Also each service has stood up commands and at the Joint level CYBERCOM has been stood up. Though much has been done the problem remains that there is no common vision of cyber operations and cyberspace warfighting doctrine.

Rules of Engagement (ROE) (VD $) are needed for local commanders who understand how to react to real world or kinetic attacks based on approved ROEs, but in cyberspace there is no common understanding of what constitutes a "use of force" or "act of war" on the Internet, hence, there is no agreed doctrine on how to fight a cyber war. If there is an attack, the response to the attacker (if attribution is accomplished) is not uniform. There need to be clear rules on what constitutes an incident or attack and what type of response (technical, legal, or diplomatic) should be conducted. One conundrum this challenge faces is where there is progress it is often classified.

Classification of data (D $$) issues is a result of each organization within the U.S. government utilizing different practices for classification of data, creating disconnects in the ability to work with non-DoD organizations. Even though there is one official set of rules, the implementation of the rules differs wildly among many agencies that handle classified documents. Coupling that with the different cultures in each organization, the sharing of data between agencies can often be difficult. Outside of the Intelligence Community (IC), the rest of the DoD and other non-IC agencies, people may not be able to discuss certain matters and properly collaborate due to lack of clearance. There is a move to increase the number of people with clearances but that will not address the issue as each crisis will require a unique set of experts to fix and there is no way to determine who will be needed beforehand. We need a system that can share information based on need, not background checks, while maintaining operational security.

Processes

Mission Assurance (ED $$) is the focus on protecting networks and information during operations. There is a need to fight through a contested cyber domain to make sure the operational tasks are accomplished to achieve the mission of the organization (this includes military systems, the Defense Industrial Base and the commercial backbone networks they use). What is needed is an understanding of which systems are critical to accomplishing the mission and how they can be used in a degraded mode (i.e., using a limited or alternate set of protocols) to continue to maintain maneuverability and basic capabilities in an environment that they may no longer control.

Audits (D $) are the regular, structured evaluation of an enterprise's IT systems, personnel, and processes. The audit process represents the measurement step in a continuous cybersecurity improvement program (implement ⇒ measure ⇒ correct). As such, regular cyber audits represent the keystone of any cybersecurity program. One key new collaborative resource is the "Twenty Critical Security Controls for Effective Cyber Defense: Consensus Audit Guidelines" by the Center for Strategic and International Studies. These top 20 Controls were agreed upon by a powerful consortium including NSA, US Cert, DoD JTF-GNO, the Department of Energy Nuclear Laboratories, Department of State, DoD Cyber Crime Center plus the top commercial forensics experts and pen testers that serve the banking and critical infrastructure communities [12].

NOTE

There are a number of complementary standards like Information Systems Audit and Control Association's (ISACA) Control Objectives for Information and related Technology (COBIT) or the International Organization for Standardization's Code of Practice for Information Security Management family of standards that can be very useful. These can be supported with processes like Information Technology Infrastructure Library (ITIL), Capability Maturity Model Integration (CMMI), and Six Sigma but there is no common industry-accepted practice today. Furthermore, today these audits are very manual and labor intensive; the trend needs to move to real time auditing via automation.

On a slightly different track we have the current set of Certification and Accreditation standards that are used today. The DOD Information Assurance Certification and Accreditation Process (DIACAP) and Director of Central Intelligence Directive (DCID) 6/3 processes as well as the Federal Information System Management Act (FISMA) process for all government agencies are undergoing change to be more focused on real-time monitoring. The NIST Special Publication 800-137 Information Security Continuous Monitoring for Federal Information Systems and Organizations (Sept 2011) [13] is a great example of where they are headed.

Technical

Resilience (ED $$$) is designed to have systems self-heal with no intervention from humans. In the cyber context, a resilient IT system must continue to operate (as intended) even if compromised. For example, if unauthorized access is achieved. It should be noted that this is different than Continuation of Operations Planning (COOP), Disaster Recovery Planning (DRP) or reconstitution. Given the highly distributed nature of IT systems today, an important aspect of resilience is the ability of a system to meet its specified function in the face of denial of service attacks which might compromise network access. Resilience is therefore an attribute we need our IT systems to process. The challenge is to develop a resilient system, and in particular to design an enterprise-level system to be resilient in a contested cyber conflict environment. Rapid recovery in a contested environment will be key for military cyber conflicts.

Supply Chain (ED $$$) relates to the development and manufacturing of both hardware and software which has increasingly been accomplished in foreign countries. Traditionally, the military would build Government Off the Shelf (GOTS) software to meet their needs but today there is a trend to leverage Commercial Off the Shelf (COTS) and/or Open Source software to save costs. This problem is becoming ubiquitous. There is very little hardware or software that does not contain foreign components. With the increasing complexity of hardware, the verification and validation of hardware has become very difficult. If we can authenticate all the interactions among the hardware components in a system, then we can verify that the hardware does what it claims to do.

How authentication of hardware and software is done is the challenge. Many hardware components come from many different (and sometime competing) manufacturers and the software/firmware is integrated at different stages of manufacture. Every interface and transaction must be authenticated to insure the device works as advertised and that there are no hidden capabilities that can cause harm to the overall system or create covert channels and unknown vulnerabilities that can be exploited by advisories (be they nation state or criminal).

An example of the type of challenges that could arise from a supply chain attack is the intentional inclusion of a logic bomb in a hardware implementation by a potential adversary. This is of particular concern given the significant number of integrated circuits that are fabricated in Taiwan and China. I would like to lay out a complex attack that is a nightmare scenario. Imagine that a silicon chip includes circuitry whose existence is only known to a potential adversary. Imagine further that this silicon chip has been included in a variety of missile systems—air to air, air to ground, sea to air, and so on. Finally, imagine that a conflict arises with this potential adversary and the logic bomb is activated disabling the most advanced systems available to our forces and allies. Out of necessity, the conflict ends almost as soon as it begins and we have lost.

Chain of trust (VD $$) comes from the need for increasing trustworthy computing in an enterprise setting which can occur if we can authenticate all interactions among enterprise hardware supporting the enterprise users' computing needs. Such an approach using hardware that can authenticate every connection prevents or makes much more difficult a man-in-the-middle type of attack. An example would be when a command and control system sends an order to a weapons system: how does the sender know it was received, how does the receiver know it was really from the command and control system, and how do both know the contents of the message were not modified? In the commercial world this is done by digital signatures and hashing messages to produce a digest which will enable detection of any changes but these are not used in everyday system to system transactions and can be compromised if the root certification database is hacked.

Mobile devices (VD $$) are a challenge as more and more devices connect to the grid (i.e., smart phones, thumb drives, iPads, and laptops). There is a need to both protect them and validate their security before they connect. In many cases these devices are being used to conduct sensitive business and connected to protected networks with little to no security monitoring. The younger generation of workers are bringing their technology from home to the work place and doing work on their personal devices. They are connecting to more sites like social media which encourages sharing digital identity, postings about work, location services and photos. It is becoming a challenge for the security team to keep up to date with what is going on at the enterprise level of the network. One of the ways the security team can mitigate risk is to train the users on the risks involved. As mobile devices become more prevalent on the physical battlefield, this will become a key component of military cyberspace.

NOTE

DHS program—"Stop.Think.Connect" emphasizes four key cyber issues: Identity Theft, Fraud and Phishing, Cyber Bullying and Ethics, Cyber Predators. This program is a good resource when talking about safety on the internet [14].

Data Protection (D $) is the focus on providing the core concepts of information security "confidentiality, integrity, and availability" to the data rather than protecting the network or operating system layers. Today, in a fortress mentality, many organizations focus their cybersecurity efforts on protecting the cyber perimeter using products such as firewalls. This "line in the sand" or "Maginot Line" approach fails to recognize that a significant portion of the value of an organization's information system assets lies in the data that is stored on their IT systems. These data include more than just documents; it also includes emails, web pages, web apps, and key executables such as operating systems. One obstacle many organizations would need to face first is categorizing their data by level or importance/value. Therefore, a comprehensive cyber strategy should place significant emphasis on data protection in addition to any efforts that are applied to perimeter defense. When viewed in this information-centric manner, critical questions arise. We must ask if a perimeter defense is the most appropriate approach to data protection, or is an asymmetric, decentralized, defense required [15]. The answer is no and the solution is that we need to move to a new model. Many of the military weapons systems depend on the validity of the data they are using so this is crucial for accuracy.

TIP

When looking for process to use to implement security NIST has a very wide set of policies and guidelines: Guide to Enterprise Telework and Remote Access Security, Minimum Security Requirements for Federal Information and Information Systems, Guide to Security for Full Virtualization Technologies, Guide to Protecting the Confidentiality of Personally Identifiable Information (PII) are a sample of the dozens of resources available at their web site [16].

IPv6 (D $$) presents a challenge because during the transition to the new protocol there will be new opportunities for both defenders and attackers. In 2013 the Internet Corporation for Assigned Names and Numbers (ICANN) is predicted to be out of IPv4 Internet Protocol

(IP) addresses. This will force implementation of IPv6 over the next couple of years. Most of the challenge will come from upgrading equipment and finding staff with IPv6 skills. With the new protocol comes new security changes like so many addresses that scanning all the network addresses for an organization will become resource prohibitive which will cause a shift in tactics and tools. So while it is still early in the implementation phase, there is more security built into the protocol which means it will provide better security than today's version.

Identity Management (IDM) (NCE $$) consists of three functions that need to be accomplished when allowing personnel to access the network: authenticate—they are who they say they are; authorize—what they have access to; and audit—what they do. The days of IDM being just an 8-12 character password are dead. Today most companies are moving to tokens or biometrics to help ensure they are authenticating the individual (preferably using multiple factors). They are also building rules that limit what each individual can do so they only have access to what they need to do their jobs. Finally, auditing what they have done to validate policies are being followed. The issue is that there is no common standard today. There are efforts like the DHS which runs the National Strategy for Trusted Identities in Cyberspace program [17] that could help at the national level. Every fort or base has security around them to control access, it is just as important for the network they are using.

TIP

When dealing with a vendor selling cloud services it is important to understand there are three primary cloud-based delivery models. Be sure you are getting the right one for your organization.

- Software as a Service (SaaS): The user accesses applications that are on the network. This type of access has no effect on the user's local environment or operating system.
- Platform as a Service (PaaS): The user uses the cloud as an environment for executing applications. This is the opposite approach from SaaS, because users control their applications but have no control over the operating system, network or hardware on which their applications execute.
- Infrastructure as a Service (IaaS): This is an even higher level of abstraction. Rather than purchasing servers, software, memory, or networking equipment, the user accesses its necessary resources as a fully outfitted service from a third party, typically on a pay-per-use basis.

Virtual Systems (NCE $)/Cloud (NCE $) may occur at many levels (e.g., hardware, memory, storage, software, data, desktop, network, or entire data centers). Virtualization at the level of the operating system (OS) permits the hosting of multiple virtualized environments within a single OS instance. Applications can be virtualized, allowing them to be hosted independently of the underlying OS. Cross-platform virtualization allows software written for a specific central processing unit (CPU) and OS to nevertheless operate on different CPUs and OSs. At the top level of abstraction, a Virtual Machine (VM) is a software implementation of an operating system or computer. At the network level, virtualization allows access to applications, data, and computing resources through the Internet (also known as "cloud computing"). Cloud computing allows the user to move from a desktop model of computation to a network-based model.

For reasons of security and governance, clouds can be deployed as public, private, or hybrid. Public clouds are those data centers outside a user's firewall and are provided by third parties. Private clouds remain within a user's firewall; hybrid clouds offer a mixture of both.

From a security point of view, virtualization has issues with configuration management, patching, cross platform attacks, and auditing. Cloud computing has issues with shifting applications, data management, and processes to a third party set of configuration standards, control/ownership over sensitive data, reliability of company hosting the data, applicable laws (i.e., U.S. vs. EU privacy laws are very different), and lack of physical control. Security and confidentiality are crucial issues for successful transition to these technologies. In addition, there are legitimate concerns over performance variability, reliability, and resilience of cloud-based services. This is where the market is moving and we need to build security in upfront. Cloud computing consolidates resources and can become a cyberspace "center of gravity" for military organizations.

Intrusion Detection Systems (IDS)/Intrusion Protection Systems (IPS) (NCE $$) are the monitoring of the network to detect signatures of known malware or patterns of activity that are unauthorized. Today, significant attention is paid to protecting our IT systems to prevent intrusion. The philosophy underlying this is that if only authorized individuals have access to the IT systems, those systems are to a large degree protected. The philosophy driving interest in intrusion detection is that if no intrusion is detected, then it can be inferred that only authorized individuals are accessing the system and the system is *de facto* safe (clearly, per our earlier discussions, insider threat does not go away). However, ignoring the challenges represented by insider threat, Intrusion Detection is in itself a challenging problem. Today most security detection systems are signature-based, yet signature-based defenses are inherently perimeter-focused and state-of-the-art cyber threats tunnel through or go around these defenses. Also, Intrusion Detection Systems only show what they catch, not what they are not catching, so if there is no signature in place, the attack may go completely unnoticed. Looking forward we must detect/protect against zero-day exploits and move away from signature-based systems. IDS technology is not good enough to fight the APT, the military needs to move to advanced defensive techniques.

Skills

Massive Data or as it is more commonly being called today *Big Data* (VD $$) is the result of so much data being collected that there needs to be a way to stop data mining and start real-time correlation. Today logging is a challenge; the classic debate is how much needs to be done because it raises costs. Most large networks (over 10,000 users) do not have the resources to log more than a few weeks worth of data and even that is not truly analyzed. We need systems and processes that allow us to do long-term trend analysis (over months not just days or weeks). The military must analyze and react to data faster than their enemy. This will require more automation and intelligence systems.

Poor Interfaces (D $) are problematic as most systems are not designed to allow a user to rapidly manipulate information at the rate it is coming into the database. Those who have ever been in a Security Operations Center know it is not unusual to see Intrusion Detection System (IDS) events scrolling off the screen. The analyst is not able to control the process and must depend on correlation rules that the vendor developed so they cannot tell their managers what events they are getting are based on. We need security systems that are intuitive and allow the analysts to develop and manage the investigations in a way that they provide an advantage rather than just a person to react to what they are provided.

People

Threat/Risk Awareness (ED $$) is a concern because most users today implicitly trust their computer system when they log on, they assume emails are from who the email names in the "from" line and they do not think attachments like word documents could contain malware. This behavior issue must be addressed. We need to change the mindset of the user to "trust but verify" when they log on. Users should understand how to validate their security and know what kind of indicators to look for in a compromised system. We do not expect everyone to become a cybersecurity expert but we do want them to have basic survival skills to keep their information secure. One simple example is to use encrypted email when discussing sensitive material. There needs to be a national program; for awareness it could be based on the "Smokey the Bear says: stop forest fires" or "This is your brain on drugs" campaigns.

Insider Threat (NCE $$) is quite possibly the greatest challenge. There is no clear definition of who is an insider is. Most people automatically think an insider is an employee, a student, or other member of the staff of a host institution that physically operates a computer system. These people have a legitimate reason to access the IT systems and can be considered insiders. However, it can be many other types of people:

- A contractor, associate, business partner, computer maintenance technician, computer supplier, or someone who has a formal (or even informal) legitimate business relationship with the institution that hosts the computer system.
- An authorized person that is allowed to perform limited operations (e.g., a bank's customer who uses the bank's system to access his/her account or a student who is allowed to access grades).
- A spoofed authorized user.
- A person who has been coerced or even duped by an outsider to perform certain operations on the outsider's behalf.
- A former insider using previously conferred access credentials that were not revoked when the insider status terminated.
- A former insider who created "secret" credentials while working as an insider to give his/her access at a later date.

There are many reasons why a person behaves in a malicious manner. Some of these are for ideological reasons: revenge, ego that proves the insider can just do it, and plain greed. While people have not significantly changed in the last 20 years, the technical and economic landscape of the U.S. has changed significantly. Technology advances and e-commerce have made it easier for the insider to gain access to critical information [18]. This problem will continue to get more complex as the world becomes more interconnected. We need to increase our ability to use role-based management and real-time auditing.

WARNING

The precedent setting WikiLeaks case involving U.S. diplomatic cables [19] is the act of an insider that poses a new kind of threat. In the past we had people who were disgruntled, or had criminal intent, but now whistleblowers and hacktivists pose a new danger. This new potential breach of confidentiality could impact political systems, financial systems, and average companies with sensitive material. It will require a new set of processes, skills, and tools to address.

Skill Shortage (NCE $$$) is influenced by the general lack of skilled cybersecurity engineers today and the poor pipeline for new talent coming out of the schools. In the report "Human Capital Crisis in Cybersecurity," Jim Glosler a NSA visiting scientist and founding director of the CIA's Clandestine Information Technology Office was quoted saying "There are only about 1000 security specialists in the United States who have the specialized skills to operate effectively in cyberspace: however the United States needs about 10,000-30,000 such individuals." There is a severe shortage of skilled cybersecurity professionals to address the needs of the force today, as many of the U.S.'s top cybersecurity minds are "unclearable" or have no interest in working for the government or the military. Also, educational programs focusing on cybersecurity at institutions of higher learning are still in their infancy. For the workforce challenge we should look at the Sputnik Moment the United States had when it realized they need a more Science, Technology, Engineering, and Mathematics (STEM) based workforce. There is some effort underway. In March of 2010 the U.S. administration did kick off the National Initiative for Cybersecurity Education (NICE) [20] and DHS/NSA have the Centers of Academic Excellence in Information Assurance Education [21] to help address this challenge.

Organization

Stovepipes (D $) are built around Computer Network Operations (CNO) functions of attack, defend, and exploit today. While it may be easy to separate different "disciplines" of cybersecurity for discussion points, they are all interrelated to one another in operational practice. These stovepipes are built around organizational structure, budgets or legal regulations. They are joking called "cylinders of excellence" by many in leadership positions who are trying to change the stovepipes but it very difficult to change as the organizational structure and budgets are built around them. When we look at Computer Network Operations, which consist of Computer Network Attack (CNA), Computer Network Defense (CND), and Computer Network Exploitation (CNE), we see them treated as separate disciplines and there is little to no cross-talk or collaboration. Part of the challenge is much of the information for each aspect of CNO is classified at different levels. All three disciplines need to integrate the offense lessons learned (CNA) with the defense (CND) and enable them with intelligence (CNE). The DoD does this today in the kinetic world and needs to apply the same processes to the virtual battle space across the different organizations that control these capabilities. There has been progress in the integration of CNO and the doctrine continues to evolve.

Exercises (D $$) are simulations designed to practice responses to cyber scenarios. When we look at the number and types of exercises today there is simply a lack of both focused and integrated exercises to understand the responses to a cyber event. One of the reasons cyber is not included in most current government national security and military exercises is that the exercises are very expensive and the goals are usually not centered on cyber issues; as a result, many leaders do not want to allow cyber events to have a huge impact on the exercise. Generally, the rules that limit current cyber exercises do not accurately reflect the level of impact cyber is expected to play in a real world conflict so organizations are not training as they expect to fight. So while cyber is considered to be another domain of warfare (others being land, sea, air, space), there has been no unifying doctrine to understand the various aspects of "cyberspace" or Tactics, Techniques, and Procedures (TTPs) that would come out of exercises. Note that there are some efforts like Cyber ShockWave and Cyber Storm but cyber needs to become a ubiquitous aspect of exercises.

Core (Impacting all Areas)

Attribution (ED $$$) for cyber is the process of determining who conducted an activity. There are three types of attribution in cyberspace: geolocation (used to facilitate kinetic strike or military attack), tracking a cyber identity (facilitates the intelligence community tracking activity of a specific person or group), or tie a person to the keyboard (facilitates law enforcement in criminal investigation). It is worth noting there are many technical attribution capabilities that are not used due to policy or legal restrictions.

The ability to identify, beyond a reasonable doubt, the originator of a cyber attack is essential to enable an effective and legal response. This is the key to deterrence or retaliatory policies. Given the virtual nature of the cyber challenge, collection of forensic evidence takes on a new life. What is the cyber equivalent of a fingerprint or DNA? What does the "reasonable doubt" threshold mean in a virtual world? To complicate things further, if investigators are able to trace an attack, what can be done with the results? For the military what level of intelligence is sufficient to authorize and attack? Fundamentally, today there exists no way to reliably identify the original attacker.

In his 2010 testimony before Congress, General Alexander stated that: "Conflict in cyberspace, moreover, is highly asymmetric. Minor actors can afford and deploy tools to magnify their effects; witness the recent press reports about arrests in Europe of several individuals charged with creating the so-called 'Mariposa botnet'—a collection of 13 million computers slaved together for criminal purposes. The tools these actors can employ are almost anonymous—a defender can sometimes learn where an attack came from, but can be time-consuming. That means 'attribution' in cyberspace is costly and comparatively rare. The 'price' an adversary pays for a capability—a tool or weapon—can be slight; the cost and impact borne by the victim of the attack can be very high" [22]. This comment is still relevant today.

Deterrence (ED $) is associated with what will happen if we launch a cyber attack or practice poor cyber behavior. Deterrence only occurs when there is something, such as a legal rule, cultural taboo, or consequence that makes us not "attack" a system, knowing full well what happens when we get "caught." The most critical aspect of deterrence is to make the cost/benefit ratio change from today's high benefits and low cost or risk to us to where the costs outweigh the benefits. This can be accomplished by making the cost of the attack too high by either increasing the barriers so that an effective attack requires significantly more resources to perpetrate, or by increasing chance of detection. In an economic example, deterrence could be preventing spam email by charging one-tenth of a cent for each email; this would not impact normal users but would make spam email too costly. A military example would be a counterattack (virtual or kinetic). A technical example would be to find and block the threat so quickly it is not practical try to maintain a persistent presence on the target network.

Situational Awareness and Visualization (ED $$) is the correlation and fusion of data from multiple sources that enables decision making. This is, at best, poorly understood today. Situational awareness allows leaders to make informed decisions. There are many Common Operational Picture (COP) tools and dashboards today, but they fail to facilitate true risk posture understanding and/or provide information in a format that enables decisions. If the data does not facilitate a decision it will soon be ignored. The types of data and their presentation should be driven by the types of decisions that must be made. It will vary at different levels of an organization and for different functions within any organizational level but today they are driven by the type of data available. First the roles need to be set, and then we must understand what decisions need to be supported. Finally the standards for implementing how we present information to the different audiences need to be established. This is a fundamental capability for command and control within the military.

Lack of Common Taxonomy (VD $) issues revolve around the need for a standard "language" for cyber topics. When we read or discuss computer security, network security, InfoSec, Information Assurance, cybersecurity or cyber war, we must be careful to understand the terms that are being used and that everyone is using the same definition. There is no governing industry standard, government regulation or international agreement on what is meant by simple terminology like "intrusion." This lack of a governing body establishing a common baseline of definitions makes interaction between organizations problematic. This can quickly lead to confusion when trying to have a diverse group of professionals analyze an incident. Within DoD there was so much confusion on what malware was called they hired MITRE to establish a Common Vulnerabilities and Exposures (CVE) [23] database. There needs to be an international body that determines the definitions for IT terms that will be used by the technical community, governments, and the legal authorities. The military is working to standardize this between U.S. service branches and internationally to allow clear communications.

Information Sharing (D $$) is a challenge in the sense that people like to share most information with the exception of what they believe to be private. However, this is not the case for governments and corporations. Corporations often do not share information simply due to competition, and governments do not share information for matters of national security. In the cyber world, the question arises whether corporations and governments should share information on cyber attacks. There are over 30 programs attempting to do this today as well as governmental and legislative efforts but they are challenged by concerns over liability, brand protection and value provided based on the cost of participating.

However, there are cases where we may want to keep cybersecurity issues limited to a few key personnel. Some examples of these cases are: do not want to expose a vulnerability, desire to protect reputation, need to limit liability or cost of participation in external investigation. Efforts in one area often do not share information with efforts in another despite being interrelated. Knowledge transfer in a large organization is more difficult due to the size and communications flow. There are also a number of public/private efforts that the government is trying to get industry to share information but these efforts are not coordinated and many of them are only achieving limited success.

Note that the WikiLeaks' release of hundreds of state department cables was not an Info Sharing issue, but rather an Insider Threat issue of someone motivated by what we would call hacktivism. Organizations often do not systematically review their processes to prevent internal cyber attacks. They need to review industry best practices, internal and external, in order to improve organizational performance. They need to conduct after action reports or lessons learned to conduct sharing with the appropriate level of risk.

Metrics (D $) revolve around the need to quantify the impact of malicious and suspicious cyber activity. Just as there is no common understanding of definitions for cyber topics, there also exists no set of predefined, industry standard metrics for cyber activities. Metrics for cyber are difficult to implement because of varying definitions of what is needed and important. For example, how we measure Return on Investment (ROI) is varied based on what organizations see as important. There are three basic types of metrics:

- Technical: Most organizations track how many intrusion attempts were stopped, how many viruses were detected, number of days/hours systems were up, communications exchanged (email, IM), number of incidents closed out.
- Security: If an organization introduced new processes to detect intrusions that increased detection by 20% or lowered cost by $50,000, or introduced a new tool in the Security Operations Center that cut time to accredit systems by 17 weeks. These goals must be set before the change and methods to track performance are established.
- Risk Posture: Examples include: when an organization is connected to new partner networks and it impacted our risk by 40% or our external router was compromised and it lowered our security posture to yellow because it forced us to change the access control list to block IP ranges that were attacking us without normal configuration control processes.

There are many groups working on this issue to include the Administration's CIO's IT Dashboard and the IT Workforce Committee's Importance of Effective Performance Metrics studies, but these are not getting the level of wide acceptance needed [24]. The solution may be regulatory, legislative, or industry best practices, but there needs to be a standard so we can measure the impact and benefits of our actions. A great resource that has been developed by MITRE is the "making security measurable" project. [25] They have a Common Weakness Risk Analysis Framework with supporting threat-based analytical programs.

System Integration (D $$) is the desire to overcome the common practice today of an organization purchasing multiple point security systems that do not work together and instead, get one system that coordinates and correlates protection activities. Most security systems used today have a specific function. For example, an organization may have a firewall, an intrusion detection system, anti-virus and anti-spyware tools, forensics tools to help with attribution, network management and monitoring systems including packet sniffers, encryption/decryption capabilities, virtual private networks, patch management systems, web activity filtering, password, and log activity correlation. Each of these systems produces logs which need to be correlated together to provide a view of the overall system health and risk posture. This type of correlation is only possible through the appropriate integration of our subsystems and is essential to address a variety of cyber threats including the ability to identify and track potential insider threats. However, too often today's subsystem act as a series of point tools that do not interact to achieve the synergistic effects integration can provide.

It should be noted that, while systems integration can provide numerous benefits, including enabling a more complete and integrated operational picture of the cyber threat, it also increases the risk that, like dominos, an effective cyber attack that brings down one subsystem causes the entire system to fail. This highlights the importance and need for resilience and represents an important challenge in architecting the cyber enterprise. Just as in insurgency warfare, there is a trade-off between pushing down control to the lowest levels to allow small units to act independently versus having more centralized control to enable larger coordinated efforts. Likewise, the architecting of a robust cyber enterprise faces similar challenges. We cannot continue to have multiple point solutions, we need a unified framework.

INTERRELATIONSHIP OF CYBERSECURITY CHALLENGES

Many of these issues are interdependent. We will follow some examples of how they are tied together. The following examples will highlight some of the interrelationships between the issues.

Deterrence is something the United States uses as a foundational part of their foreign relations policy. There have been many discussions about how this principle can be applied to cyberspace. Before we can begin to utilize deterrence we require attribution pointing to a specific individual, group or nation that is responsible. If we are able to solve this (through use of all our intelligence capabilities) we would still need clear policies on our reaction, military doctrine and ROE showing our responses. This would not be a simple if A then B equation like the Nuclear Mutually Assured Destruction (MAD) policy, as there is a wide range of factors that could come into play. It would be more like a complex matrix of options which is hard to use as deterrence because the response is often not clear.

Military ROE is complex for the same reasons deterrence is difficult. There would need to be a clear set of actions with easily understandable reactions preauthorized. National policy, supporting laws and doctrine would all need to be established. Finally standards of attribution would need to be determined so commanders could know when they had enough intelligence (military normally acts on intelligence and not the legal requirements required for evidence to be presented in a court of law) to act.

Mobile devices would require a set of common interfaces to allow system integration. There are so many proprietary systems using unique protocols and configuration that it is not practical or cost-efficient to have one network operations center or security operations center try and manage them all. Some advancement in systems integration is needed to allow the management of all the devices being introduced to networks every year.

Audits are becoming critical to risk management, but it depends on developing industry standards. Before these standards can be created we need to baseline the identity management systems, agree on what metrics will be analyzed and document the definitions of everything involved.

Stovepipes are tied to Classification of Data. Stovepipes are organization-based issues but the culture of classification of data is normally set inside the same stovepipe. Once a culture of sharing is established and the walls are broken down the culture of what can reasonably be declassified will allow the release of a lot of information. It is important to note that insider threat is also a key concern when establishing a functional system for sharing information. Auditing and good identity management (both authentication and authorization) are the foundation for building a system that allows safe sharing of information.

Situational Awareness is the "holy grail" for many large networks. It can mean understanding what the attacker's intent is, what they have done after they got in, how an event has changed the risk posture of the network, what the impact to mission capabilities or identifying who it was that penetrated the network. Each of these questions requires a slightly different set of data to answer the question. For some it is just correlation of the integrated systems, for others it is metrics, some require internal auditing, a number of them want attribution. The data must facilitate a decision and be presented visually in an intuitive manner.

Insider Threat needs policy support, auditing, and identity management. First, privacy issues need to be addressed. Then we have to find a cost-effective way to track activity of all users and be able to recognize malicious behavior. Finally, we have to be able to positively identify who took which actions. These must all be solved in a standardized and cost-effective way which requires solving the auditing set of issues and situational awareness issues.

Then there are the issues that involve multiple challenges. To some degree they are all impacted by lack of taxonomy, metrics, and the standard rules (doctrine, policy, regulations, procedures, standardization, laws, etc.). It is very difficult to have a discussion about the solution if there is not a common baseline on the meanings of terms and methods or measurement much less without common set of guidelines everyone will follow. Finally, supply chain underlies all of the technical issues. If we cannot have confidence in our hardware or software then nothing that happens can be believed.

WAY AHEAD

What should we focus on with limited resources? Some of these issues require national policy/legal guidance (if not international agreements) others are tactical in nature and can be fixed at lower levels while still others require technical innovations for new solutions. Let us look at what level the issues resides at.

At the international level we need agreements and processes to address attribution, supply chain and legal issues. At the national level the government needs to set a consistent and interconnected policy/legal strategy, set up governance for standardization of taxonomy and metrics, publish our policy on deterrence, doctrine (with ROE), and expand our development of the skilled work force we need through both training and exercises. To do this we have recommendations on organizations at the U.S. national level that should be the lead for specific missions:

- U.S. Congress should set the course for national policy and legal statutes and assign/resource many of the roles discussed here.

- NIST should focus on taxonomy, metrics, and auditing. They could establish standards for virtualization, cloud computing, data protection, insider threat protection, system integration, and mobile device management.
- DoD should develop doctrine with ROE. They would need to build ways to develop chain of trust and mission assurance for key command and control as well as weapon systems. They require a core of service members with cyber warrior skills through training and exercises. They are in a good position to address the classification processes and stovepipe issues.
- DHS should focus on situational awareness, identity management, IDS/IPS, IPv6 implementation, and dealing with massive data. They would also be the lead for national program to increase risk awareness and developing the skilled workforce we need.
- DoS should be the lead for developing deterrence strategy and building international agreements.
- DoJ should focus on policy and legal enforcement of the laws we have.
- Organizations like Federally Funded Research and Development Centers and Defense Advanced Research Projects Agency (DARPA) should focus on resilience, chain of trust, attribution, and supply chain.

This assignment of challenges is extremely basic and does not represent a clear mapping of missions of the different agencies/organizations. These organizations would all need to work closely together so they would not get stovepiped on their own solutions set. We have left out players like White House CIO, CTO, and Cyber Security Coordinator as they do not control significant resources. We did not include DoE who is working cybersecurity for smart grid technology. This list was just a sample but reflects some of the intricacy involved with these issues, a more detailed study would need to be done with specifics based on a scenario to get a more complete list. It is meant to be more of a starting point to allow everyone to weigh in on which issues belong to each organization. It is clear the current distributed and poorly coordinated efforts are not proving to be effective enough to position the U.S. to maintain their current level of influence in cyberspace. We need a national roadmap that assigns responsibility and resources to address these concerns.

Another way to categorize these challenges is to look at a rough timeline to solve them (understanding that resources determine if and when they will be solved). So, with no crystal ball, here is a prediction on some of the issues. In the next 5 years doctrine should be well established based on the current activity in DoD, though ROE may not be defined very well. There will also probably be new laws based on the number of bills in Congress. Many technical issues like virtualization, cloud computing, identity management, data protection, massive data analysis, and situational awareness are all being heavily invested in and will see major improvements. Expect to see cyber being included in more exercises and cyber centric exercises to become more common. IPv6 will force its way onto center stage and become a standard protocol—time will tell how much it solves. There are organizations, both inside the government and commercial industry that are working on metrics and auditing so we expect major improvements but it is doubtful there will be any global standards established.

Then there are issues that will be worked on over the next 10 years but it is doubtful there will be a clear solution without significant effort: taxonomy, attribution, deterrence, the shortage of a skilled cyber work force, risk awareness, and systems integration. These issues are so complex and today there is no clear champion to drive them to closure that it is hard to see them being worked out. Looking long range the level of research will determine which issues will be cracked but we would hope to see resilience, chain of trust, poor interfaces, and supply chain addressed.

For those cross walking all the issues we listed there are some we did not talk about because we are unclear where they could fit so did not try and make a prediction.

SUMMARY

The United States faces multiple security challenges today competing for limited resources. However, one of them is woven throughout the rest and is vulnerable to attack from everyone from a lone individual to a nation state: cyberspace. There are a number of organizations trying to solve or profit from these issues but there is no critical mass to enable real progress on any of the key issues we have covered in this chapter. The national and international debate on cyber needs to determine what we must address as many of these issues have a long lead time to solve. We need a leap ahead effort to introduce game changing technology or change the rules we play by with new policy or even morph the game board by a paradigm shift in the underlying infrastructure of the Internet.

References

[1] Obama B. Remarks by the President on securing our nations cyber infrastructure. The White House web page, http://www.whitehouse.gov/the_press_office/Remarks-by-the-President-on-Securing-Our-Nations-Cyber-Infrastructure; 2009.

[2] IP3 National Cyber security R&D Challenges. http://www.thei3p.org/docs/publications/i3pnationalcybersecurity.pdf.

[3] National cyber leap year, http://www.nitrd.gov/leapyear/RFI_LeapYear.pdf.

[4] InfoSec's hard problem list, http://www.cyber.st.dhs.gov/docs/IRC_Hard_Problem_List.pdf.

[5] Four grand challenges in trustworthy computing, http://cra.org/uploads/documents/resources/rissues/trustworthy.computing_.pdf.

[6] DoE A scientific R&D approach to cybersecurity, http://science.energy.gov//media/ascr/pdf/program-documents/docs/Cyber_security_science_dec_2008.pdf.

[7] Securing cyberspace for 44th president report, http://csis.org/files/media/csis/pubs/081208_securingcyberspace_44.pdf.

[8] President's Critical Infrastructure Protection Board. http://georgewbush-whitehouse.archives.gov/pcipb/ [accessed 17.12.10].

[9] Comprehensive National Cybersecurity Initiative (CNCI) focus areas, http://www.whitehouse.gov/cybersecurity/comprehensive-national-cybersecurity-initiative.

[10] Obama's Cyberspace Policy Review. http://www.whitehouse.gov/assets/documents/Cyberspace_Policy_Review_final.pdf [accessed 17.12.10].

[11] James E. Cartwright vice chairman joint chief of staff. Cyber reference library. National Security Cyberspace Institute, Inc. (NSCI), http://nsci-va.com/CyberReferenceLib/2010-11-Joint%20Terminology%20for%20Cyberspace%20Operations.pdf.

[12] CSIS: 20 critical security controls version 4.0, http://www.sans.org/critical-security-controls/.

[13] NIST. Special publications (800 series), http://csrc.nist.gov/publications/PubsSPs.html.

[14] DHS stop – think – connect program, http://www.dhs.gov/stopthinkconnect-key-cyber-issues.

[15] Wulf WA, Jones AK. s.l. Reflections on cybersecurity. Sci. Mag. 2009;326(5955):943–944.

[16] NIST publication site, http://csrc.nist.gov/publications/PubsSPs.html.

[17] DHS. http://www.nist.gov/nstic/.

[18] Stern-Dunyak A. Insider threats: countering cyber crime from within. MITRE, http://www.mitre.org/news/di
gest/homeland_security/10_09/cyber_crime.html.

[19] Shane S, Andrew WL. Leaked cables offer raw look at U.S. diplomacy. New York Times. http://www.nytimes.
com/2010/11/29/world/29cables.html?_r=4&bl=&adxnnl=1&adxnnlx=1292778173-
fMW1SzDCUGvclejwT3KnJA&pagewanted=all; 2010.

[20] NIST. National Initiative for Cybersecurity Education (NICE), http://csrc.nist.gov/nice/.

[21] NSA. National Centers of Academic Excellence, http://www.nsa.gov/ia/academic_outreach/nat_cae/index.
shtml.

[22] Alexander KB. Statement to house committee on armed services. DoD, http://www.defense.gov/home/fea
tures/2010/0410_cybersec/docs/USCC%20Command%20Posture%20Statement_HASC_22SEP10_FINAL%
20_OMB%20Approved_.pdf.

[23] MITRE. Common vulnerabilities and exposures (CVE), http://cve.mitre.org/ [accessed 01.01.13].

[24] CIO, Steven VanRoekel U.S. CIO homepage, http://www.cio.gov/; 2010 [accessed 02.01.13].

[25] MITRE 'making security measurable' project, http://makingsecuritymeasurable.mitre.org/index.html.

16

The Future of Cyber War

When we think of how the science fiction stories in the 1970s predicted one computer the size of Texas would control centrally everything it is easy to see how impractical predicting the future is. At the time it was a natural extension of how the mainframe computers of the day would evolve, but then came the personal computer and everything changed. However, now that the trend is shifting to cloud computing, where we leverage large data centers; who knows, maybe they had it right after all. Surprise is the enemy of national strategies, so how do we avoid or survive it. First, let us start by looking at a couple of theories that might help— the impact of Black Swan events and the Air Force study on how to minimize the impact of Capability Surprises, revelations in military affairs and catalysts events.

The Introduction of *The Black Swan: The Impact of the Highly Improbable* offers a great description:

> Before the discovery of Australia, people in the old world were convinced that all swans were white, an unassailable belief as it seemed completely confirmed by empirical evidence. One single observation can invalidate a general statement derived from millennia of confirmatory sightings of millions of white swans. All you need is one single black bird. What we call here a Black Swan (and capitalize it) is an event with the following three attributes. First, it is an outlier, as it lies outside the realm of regular expectations, because nothing in the past can convincingly point to its possibility. Second, it carries an extreme impact. Third, in spite of its outlier status, human nature makes us concoct explanations for its occurrence after the fact, making it explainable and predictable. I stop and summarize the triplet: rarity, extreme impact, and retrospective (though not prospective) predictability [1].

This section of the book points out the challenge of predicting cyber warfare from both long-term evolution and sudden paradigm shifts.

It is also worth looking at the condensed version of the ten principles for a Black Swan-proof world [2] based on our recent housing financial crisis. Following this philosophy will lead to an economic life closer to our biological environment: smaller companies, richer ecology, and no leverage. A world in which entrepreneurs, not bankers, take the risks and companies are born and die every day without making the news. In other words, an economy more resistant to Black Swans. These principles are built around a different problem but can be used as an example to develop similar rules for cyberspace. We need a framework that is resilient to Black Swans. Here are the areas epistemologist and author of the book *The Black Swan: The Impact of the Highly Improbable* Nassim Taleb suggests we focus on as we look at the economy:

1. What is fragile should break early while it is still small.
2. No socialization of losses and privatization of gains.
3. People who were driving a school bus blindfolded (and crashed it) should never be given a new bus.
4. Do not let someone making an "incentive" bonus manage a nuclear plant—or your financial risks.
5. Counter-balance complexity with simplicity.
6. Do not give children sticks of dynamite, even if they come with a warning.
7. Only Ponzi schemes should depend on confidence. Governments should never need to "restore confidence."
8. Do not give an addict more drugs if he has withdrawal pains.
9. Citizens should not depend on financial assets or fallible "expert" advice for their retirement.
10. Make an omelet with the broken eggs; do not try to patch them.

Next, we have the *Defense Science Board publication discussing Capability Surprise* report. This report was designed to address the need for our military to be prepared to deal with the shock of new abilities or technologies that could impact national power. Capability Surprise can spring from many sources: scientific breakthrough in the laboratory, rapid fielding of a known technology, or new operational use of an existing capability or technology. A review of many surprises that occurred over the past century suggests that surprises tend to fall into two major categories: (1) "Known" surprises—those few that the United States should have known were coming, but for which it did not adequately prepare. (2) "Surprising" surprises—those many that the nation might have known about or at least anticipated, but which were buried among hundreds or thousands of other possibilities [3]. The most recent examples would be the announcement of two jets: the Russia's stealthy PAK-FA [4] and China's fifth-generation J-20 stealth fighter [5]. These capabilities were not expected as soon as they were developed and could change the balance of air power.

As we look at the framework for handling cyber surprise in the context of strategy, plans, and preparations, we see it also provides an assessment of current readiness. Three cases are addressed (see Table 16.1 for details):

1. Prevent surprise (influence, uncover, eliminate)
2. Deal with surprise (stabilize, mitigate, recover)
3. Create surprise (adapt, reverse, reshape)

TABLE 16.1 Sample Managing Cyber Surprise Framework [3]

Strategy	Plans	Preparation
Prevent surprise (influence, uncover, eliminate)	Deal with surprise (stabilize, mitigate, recover)	Create surprise (adapt, reverse, reshape)
Understand adversary's capabilities and intentions	Detect attack	Support IO through cyber deception
Keep cyber assets and capabilities within the U.S.	Plan/exercise with varying degrees of degradation	Prevent enemy actions through cyber intervention
Assure hardware and software provenance throughout lifecycle	Reconfigure and reallocate resources	Co-opt cyber attacks
Deter attacks	Capture forensics data	
Defend the network		
Strengthen robustness		

Of the 16 capabilities examined during this report we used the traditional stoplight naming convention of green being in good shape, yellow having concerns, and red being broken. As the capabilities ranked two were considered "green" (satisfactory), five were "red" (unsatisfactory), and the rest "yellow" (not ready, but some progress being made).

So understanding there will be Black Swan events, and some of them can come in the form of surprises in our adversary's capabilities, it becomes more important to keep a close eye on how trends and new technology will impact cyberspace. The sooner we recognize the change and begin to respond, the easier it is to adjust strategies and reorient resources.

These changes are often driven by technology. Technical advancements have had impacts on tactics, policy and strategy of warfare throughout history. Some, like gunpowder, nuclear bombs, and space platforms, have caused a "Revolution in Military Affairs" (RMA), also known as "Military Technical Revolutions." Others have caused paradigm shifts in organizational structures and doctrine such as airplanes, submarines, and machine guns. Some innovations have been transformational like stirrups, precision strike munitions, and radios. Some inventions were designed for the military while others like internal combustion engines, railways and information technology advances were leveraged by it. Some of these technological changes were incremental, like the machine gun being a natural evolution to increase the rate of fire for rifles. Others reflect the concept of Black Swans [6] or the parallel idea—Dragon Kings [7] (when diverse elements on the internet self-organize their internal structure and their dynamics with novel and sometimes surprising macroscopic "emergent" properties disrupting current relationships of influence or power) where there is dramatic surprise about the change. Cyber warfare has undergone transformation under all these aspects of change.

Cyber warfare has undergone changes in what has been called, including Electronic Warfare, Information Superiority, Information Dominance, Network Centric Warfare, Information Warfare, Command, Control, Communications, Computers, Intelligence, Surveillance, and Reconnaissance (C4ISR), Hyperwar, Netwar, and Third Wave Warfare. These terms generally refer to conflicts in the cyber domain. Cyber is separate from other RMAs ongoing today in unmanned aerial vehicles or drones, nanotechnology, robotics, and biotechnology.

Cyber is built on a physical infrastructure but is unique in that it has a virtual component. It is also prone to more rapid shifts since software is developed at a much faster pace than hardware. Technology will continue to drive change in society, economies, and warfare. We will start by looking at some of the changes that have impacted the Internet in general.

As a baseline we have provided a timeline of the major events along the cyber timeline (see Appendix). This is a good format to look for paradigm shifts in both security and threats as well as where we seem to be stuck in a paradox experiencing the same issues year after year. We will see that while at the time of an event many of us believed it to be significant, many seem to have had no long-term impact. There are some major evolutionary events and a few with revolutionary impact. As a sample we would point to 1988 when the Morris worm should have been a wake-up call for security, but in 1999 we see the same thing when the Melissa virus hit, then again in 2004 when LoveLetter caused havoc. These show a pattern of the military and the IT industry ignoring the fundamental security issues that allowed these worms and viruses to spread. Some major (but still evolutionary) events in cyber conflicts are the 2004 Supervisory Control and Data Acquisition (SCADA) attack on the Russian pipeline [8], 2007 attacks on Estonia [9], the 2008 agent.btz intrusions which resulted in operation Buckshot Yankee [10] and the cyber attacks against Georgia during conflict with Russia [11]. In 2010 we had Operation Aurora against Google (which has both counter intelligence and intellectual property theft aspects) [12] and Stuxnet SCADA [13] attacks. These events show an increasing use of cyber attacks with overtones of state sponsorship. In the revolutionary category there is ARPANET being stood up and social media exploding onto the net. These were events that created paradigm shifts in how we use the Internet and open up net threat vectors at the same time.

As we look at the potential threats, one way to categorize them is by the level of resources they commit [14]. There are some tier one nations that are committing billions of dollars to cyber warfare like the United States, China, and Russia. In McAfee's report "In the Crossfire Critical Infrastructure in the Age of Cyber War" executives from many nations, including many U.S. allies, rank the United States as the country "of greatest concern" in the context of foreign cyber attacks, just ahead of China [15]. At the next level there are countries and non-nation state actors like criminal organizations investing millions of dollars in developing and employing cyber tools. Finally, there are individual hackers or groups like Anonymous only spending a few dollars. Unfortunately, unlike conventional weapons development the potential impact of these organizations cannot be based on their resources alone. That said we will continue to see rapid increases in attack capability, many of which are designed to be stealthily or are classified.

NOTE

Every year we have a number of reports on the issues with our Critical Infrastructure (CI) but there is nothing driving the commercial companies that run our CI to invest in cybersecurity. In defense of the CI leadership, a simple question on return on investment would go something like this:

CEO: If we give you all the money you want to build the best cybersecurity possible could you guarantee our systems would be secure?

CISO: Nope, there could be a zero day exploit that we cannot protect against.

CEO: Then why should we invest more than the absolute minimum?

Another way to categorize potential threats is how they impact aspects of national power. These would be based on evaluating impact of attack/defend/exploit capabilities across Diplomatic, Information, Military, and Economic (DIME) elements of national power. Typically discussions on warfare focus on armies, weapons, and leadership but in today's conflicts we are seeing more integration of all these capabilities. The U.S. Secretary of Defense is talking about both cyber and the national debt today. DIME presents a solid way to evaluate the multiple aspects of Internet-based activities that can be part of cyber warfare. The impact of intellectual property theft can be looked at as economic warfare when you consider the aggregated damage to a nation—but what about the impact of cybercrime? This chapter will review where cyber warfare is going based on these elements, but in the end we must devise a national formula that will ensure we are ready for the next conflict based on something like Aggregation of capabilities + Innovations + Resources + Leadership = Strategic Advantage.

Finally, we need to look at catalyst events like the Battle of Waterloo, Pearl Harbor, Hurricane Katrina, and 9/11. When many of us started out in security it was just the technicians talking about how the internet was going to enable Virtual Guerilla Warfare and create the parameters for an Electronic Waterloo, today it is the senior national leaders talking about a Cyber Pearl Harbor or 9/11. The terms we use to frame the discussion will to some degree determine the solution. If we are talking about a cyber Katrina or pandemic, it is very different than events that lead us into wars.

There are clearly two camps framing the argument over cyber warfare. On the "cyber-armageddon" side an unofficial spokesperson is Mike McConnell, former Director of National Intelligence, and currently a Senior Executive for a defense contractor, who wrote in Washington Post, "The United States is fighting a cyber-war today, and we are losing. It's that simple" [16]. On the "cyber war is hype" side there is Bruce Schneier who wrote a Cable News Network piece saying, "We surely need to improve our cybersecurity. But words have meaning, and metaphors matter. There's a power struggle going on for control of our nation's cybersecurity strategy, and the National Security Agency (NSA) and Department of Defense (DoD) are winning. If we frame the debate in terms of war, if we accept the military's expansive cyberspace definition of 'war,' we feed our fears. . . If, on the other hand, we use the more measured language of cybercrime, we change the debate. Crime fighting requires both resolve and resources, but it's done within the context of normal life. We willingly give our police extraordinary powers of investigation and arrest, but we temper these powers with a judicial system and legal protections for citizens" [17]. These statements still represent the general outline of the agreement today.

Are these positions diametrically opposed? One very interesting perspective and potential answer was from Lt. General Harry D. Raduege, USAF (Ret), Senior Counselor, The Cohen Group. He sees cyber warfare divided into war with a small "w" (think "war on drugs" or "global war on terror") and War with a capital "w" being a congressionally declared war (think back to WWII). This leads to the possibility on a strategic level of a "pure cyber War" or a War with major cyber implications. It would also break out today's "war on cybercrime" or "war on cyber espionage" as vital government operations involving all elements of national power but on a more operational or tactical level [18]. This would lead to clearly different levels of engagement and could bridge the gap between hype and Armageddon.

Another perspective is from Eugene Kaspersky, CEO and co-founder of Kaspersky Lab who provided the following statement:

> What is the difference between a full-scale war and a special-forces raid? The answer is obvious: the scope of the conflict. The same can be applied to the cyberworld. When I speak about cyberwar, I understand it as a permanent stand-off between states, with each country targeting the opposition's critical infrastructure in the form of cyberweapons. Luckily we haven't experienced a true cyberwar yet, and hopefully we never will. However, instances of cyber attacks that fall within the scope of a special-forces raid, such as Stuxnet, indicate the danger and inherent risks of these conflicts escalating into a full cyber war. A cyber war would be an extremely serious and critical event, with the potential to inflict significant damage to a country across all levels – national, corporate and civilian. An attack during a cyber war would be designed to cause physical damage to a country's critical infrastructure, including its energy, transportation and financial systems, telecommunications and government networks.
>
> Many countries understand the possibility of a cyber war and the capabilities of cyber weapons. The United States, China, United Kingdom, Germany, India and other countries have already implemented special units who are tasked with developing and protecting their country. However, it's extremely important to understand that a cyber war also introduces new risks and dangers that span beyond direct cyber-attacks targeted at opposing countries. Unlike traditional weapons, tools used in cyber warfare are very easy to clone and re-program by adversaries or other threat actors. For example, it would be extremely difficult for a cyber terrorist group to steal an intercontinental ballistic missile and locate a launch pad to fire it. Even if they succeeded in this scenario, they would not be able to duplicate the missile unless they stole another one. These physical barriers are nonexistent with cyber weapons – they can easily be hijacked, reprogrammed, duplicated and launched in a series of sustained strikes. It's imperative for countries to understand the consequences, dangers and potential damages that cyber war imposes before developing and possessing offensive cyber weapons.
>
> I believe that there is only one way to save the world from cyber war – a non-proliferation agreement, similar to nuclear weapons, must be signed. I see two ways in which the world can move forward in the next decade. The first is dark and apocalyptic – an uncontrolled arms race will continue, and sooner or later a global cyber war will start. I cannot estimate the results of such a war, but I can definitely say that it will be extremely serious. The second direction is more optimistic. International collaboration and information sharing among nation's leaders will increase, resulting in a peaceful meeting where an international agreement is signed. I believe that common sense will prevail, leaving the cyber world's Pandora's Box safely locked up.
>
> There is a good chance there will be a cyber-catalyst event. It is quite possible if the general population was aware of the amount of intellectual property theft it could cause popular demand for action – the type of action could be determined by whether we called it cyber-crime, cyber industrial espionage or economic warfare. How we react to a catalyst event could allow us to take actions quickly that causes more damage in the long run. We could establish treaties that put us at a disadvantage or impose restrictions that take away our competitive advantages. On the other side of the argument is that our inaction will result in technological atrophy and we will not have the cutting edge technology or skilled cyber engineers/warriors needed to maintain our cyber health much less than the cyber national power parity we currently have.

This statement covers the challenge of defining a cyber war, the players and the need for international agreement and concern there will be a cyber-catalyst event. As we look across cyber experts from many different nations, we see there are a lot of common themes you will find throughout this book driving home the point that it's a shared problem we all face.

EMERGING TRENDS

In this section, we will address some of the recent events that will lead to some natural evolutionary trends. This is based on logical progression ignorant of the many factors that will impact what happens over the next few years. First, we will look at three events and see what they may impart—Aurora, Stuxnet, and WikiLeaks. Aurora [19] was the breach of Google (among other companies) by Chinese hackers. This brought espionage into the headlines and ended in cooperation between a commercial company and NSA. These public/private partnerships will be key going forward, but the momentum seems to have fallen off quickly. An expansion of the number of companies that enter into a partnership with the federal government will help everyone. In the past, most companies have felt that it has been a one way street and the government has not been sharing much of what they have learned. The authors hope that this trend of sharing will increase and the government will address the need to share more. There are a number of programs and efforts working toward that end today. Next, we had Stuxnet [20], a piece of malcode that was reported by the New York Times to have been developed by the U.S. and Israel to attack a specific national capability to develop nuclear material in Iran. This brought cyber weapons into the headlines but, even though many of the news articles were worthy of a Hollywood action movie script, there seemed to be no national policy reaction to what could have been a targeted raid, show of force, or act of war. It did however create interest in how weaponized code could become rogueware, having unintended consequences, as some analysts believe it started attacking systems that were not part of the original target set. This trend will likely continue until some rules (official or unofficial) are developed to determine what level of cyber intrusion is acceptable. Finally, we have the WikiLeaks site exposing banking records and U.S. State Department cables [21] to name a couple of examples. This may be the first case of a new type of insider threat where whistleblowers now go straight to posting documents online. It will create a new need for data control management and insider threat programs. This form of exposing secrets could become a game changer if we see a sharp increase in the number of "authorized users" who start to post restricted, proprietary, or even classified information for altruistic reasons or because they have become disgruntled. These types of events seem to get a lot of play in the news but often do not turn into changes in how people, organizations or countries protect themselves.

NOTE

Moving at Cyber speed vs real world is an interesting problem. We know one human year is roughly equal to seven in a dog's lifespan. How do we measure cyber time? Some say we need to move at the speed of light (generally when talking about making decisions). Others that we need to move at the speed of need (mostly referring to acquisition). We have Moore's law that the number of transistors on a chip will double about every two years. For how quickly things are changing in social media it would seem one cyber month is equal to one human year. For legal or regulatory practices it might be more like one cyber minute is equal to one year of legislative activity. One concern we face is that we act like all these activities move at a constant speed rather than the relative speeds they really do. So do we take the human out of the loop and let machines react at cyber speed?

Some issues that seem to be on the radar with little progress despite their critical needed are: cybercrime, Critical Infrastructure Protection (CIP)/SCADA vulnerabilities, social networks, mobile devices (apps), information sharing and cloud computing.

Cybercrime is growing rapidly but still does not seem to have hit the level of pain needed to be addressed in a concerted way. There are a lot of agencies and companies fighting it but they are all isolated efforts and the crime wave is unbroken. The unanswered question is what will it take to make this an international issue? The most likely course of action is cybercrime will follow the "drug war" program which has a lot of resources but does not seem to be getting much better either.

CIP/SCADA vulnerabilities is in the news and often part of national security discussions but there has been little change in policy. There is some confusion on which government agency owns the cybersecurity-related issues for the different critical infrastructures and what the role of government should be. In the U.S. there is not likely to be any legislation impacting how they are regulated in the next couple of years so any changes will be driven by user demands.

Even if we do secure our networks we have "social networking" activities, which open attack vectors through our users that bypass our network security infrastructure. Most organizations are not putting the effort into training their staff on how to practice due care when on websites like Facebook and Twitter, so we believe this issue will continue to grow. This issue ties into the next one which is the number of mobile devices users that are connecting to an organization's networks so they can do their work and manage their personal life at the same time. People have laptops, smart phones, thumb drives, and tablets to be more productive, and they use them without thinking about security. They continue to download applications to all these devices with no concern about the security or validity of the programs. There are also a lot of devices that are not necessarily mobile but are now connected to the Internet. Our cars can be remotely tracked; our houses will soon be able to be monitored to track our activities and our heating system and refrigerators have become connected. While we think of the advantages, the threat is busy thinking of new "business models" to take advantage of them. If we are mad at our neighbor we can turn off their heating system when they leave for work in the winter. If we want to sell more tune-ups we can remotely turn on the check engine light on the cars that use our garage. If we want to sell information on the people who live in a particular city we can track their electricity usage and sell the information to companies that sell solar panels so they would know who their best potential sales targets would be. This could be a threat to privacy or in the case of military personnel attack on OPSEC.

TIP

When thinking about how to protect our systems first we must determine what information is truly critical (i.e., to lose or have it compromised could cause irreparable damage), what is vital (e.g., things like email, web access, and resource management applications) and what we can do without (e.g., Instant Messaging and access to file servers with historical data and corporate policies). Once we know what is critical, we can build a security plan that employs the right tools and focus resources appropriately. It is time to stop protecting all the systems at the same level and increase the monitoring and protection of the critical data.

Cloud computing is becoming more prevalent, which brings benefits and new attack vectors. For most companies, running a network is a distraction and at some point it is natural to outsource things that are not part of the core business. Looking at a historical example of this, when electricity was initially used, manufacturing companies would run their own electrical power plants but as a common power grid became more reliable manufactures eventually decided to move to the common power grid and so they could go back to focusing on their core business of building products. We are approaching that tipping point in the next few years with corporate networks and cloud computing. As the cost, security, and reliability continue to increase it will become standard to get rid of the distraction and outsource to the cloud. Use of the cloud still needs strong corporate governance and for some organizations (finance, military, Intelligence Community) it will never be an acceptable risk but for many it will. There are security advantages and disadvantages to hosting data in a cloud or outsourcing computing resources, but it is important to remember that the threat will target the place that it can gain the most from. Botnet builders love the idea of consolidating resources into one target. Compromising one cloud provider would give them an instant army. The Advanced Persistent Threat today has to break into multiple systems to find the information they are after; they also would love one target that has all the answers they are looking for.

A couple of technical trends cybersecurity needs to watch are biometric and nanotechnology. The trend toward biometrics is going to lead to new threats as their use grows. First, there are no governing statutes protecting our biometric data today. Second, biometrics are not a silver bullet—the threat will eventually find ways to compromise it. Finally, as we field these systems we will need to build analytics and security integrated into the design. If we use biometrics (perhaps to avoid someone voting multiple times or registering for government aid under multiple names), we need to ensure it has been reviewed by folks who can think like malicious hackers instead of engineers who think about how to make things work. The second is nanotechnology, where generally devices are sized from 1 to 100 nm. These devices can swarm to accomplish more complex tasks. The concerns revolve around building security into the devices upfront and losing control of the devices as they morph into new capabilities.

The legal landscape for cyber is moving in two parallel directions today. First is the idea that private lawsuits will drive public law. The second is that Congress will enact laws to protect aspects of national critical infrastructure, privacy, and intellectual property [22]. There are a number of lawsuits and legislative initiatives ongoing today and there is no clear trend on what guiding principles will come from them. At the same time there are commercial companies offering cyber services to support the military and Law Enforcement Agencies to the point many organizations are outsourcing what was traditionally thought of as government employee-only work because of the lack of skills within the military. At the end of the day this is an international issue. Because the United States and China have developed technological capabilities in the cyber arena, the nations must work together to avoid misperception that could lead to a crisis, according to Defense Secretary Leon E. Panetta [23].

Finally, public perception is that cyber is becoming ubiquitous. We see military strategy books like *7 Deadly Scenarios: A Military Futurist Explores War in the 21st Century* by Andrew Krepinevich which states "A terrorist war on the global economy, by means of attacking infrastructure and logistics chains, and through sophisticated cyber-attacks" as one of the scenarios. Twenty years ago Tom Clancy had his hero Jack Ryan stealing a submarine, today in his book *Threat Vector*, Jack Ryan is dealing with cyber-attacks. You see aspects of cyber talked about in the news and debated by politicians. That said the topic is so complex most of the public will tell you they have heard/read about cyber but they will not be able to tell you what it is.

TRENDS DRIVING WHERE WE WILL GO

We are on the brink of a new type of world—a virtual one. We talk about the cyber domain but we generally just mean the network devices. There is a growing part of the digital native generation that is living part of their life inside the grid. They have avatars that represent them in gaming environments like World of Warcraft, there are people who make a living running businesses in virtual worlds like Second Life and World of Warcraft, and we have technology driving us to devices that will provide us with augmented reality allowing us to overlay the virtual over the real world. Some of these virtual worlds are large enough and have big enough economies to be ranked against countries. This presents a new place to have a small "w" war—be it economic or political.

As we look at the leadership of most organizations today there is what we call the "wrist-watch syndrome." Most of the people making decisions today were not raised around computers and think of them as support devices—not as the primary means of accomplishing the mission. They still wear their watch even though they have the time available on their cell phone because they have always worn a watch and do not need to change. The younger generation has never worn a watch and many have never had a camera that used film or know how to use a paper map. In fact as we mentioned in Chapter 3 one of the authors was at a simulation exercise and asked a young airman what they would do if they lost the network in the command center and was told, "We couldn't fly anymore." For the generation of military personal who used grease pencils to track movement of entire divisions this attitude was unthinkable. So for the baby boomers who are in charge today they many times do not think in terms of risk to mission when talking about the network. When the digital native generation takes over leadership of the terror groups plotting to attack the west they will default to remote attacks trying to use our mission control systems and critical infrastructure to be the central point of attack rather than a supporting function. This lack of understanding by many of the current national level leaders has led to lack of decisive action. As we look at the near term trends, indecision seems to be a key concern; it could (should) put the countries and militaries at a disadvantage. Nation states and their militaries need to rank the issues facing their country and execute an action plan to address those they can, as well as develop contingency plans to deal with those they cannot afford to solve now.

Some say the problem is too big to solve because of how the internet works. An interesting insight is to look back in history and see we have faced similar problems in the past. Dale Meyerrose, Vice President & General Manager Cyber Integrated Solutions, Harris Corporation, told an interesting story at the 4th annual Homeland Security Conference.

> September 2, 1752 was Calendar Adjustment Day in Britain and the Colonies, correcting the Julian calendar which had gotten seriously out of whack. The day after Wednesday, September 2, was proclaimed to become Thursday, September 14, 1752. This caused some riots among people demanding the return of the 11 days they were cheated out of. The adjustment also moved New Year's Day to January 1 (formerly March 25), and resulted in there only being 282 days in 1751. Thomas Jefferson had his tombstone engraved with two dates for his birth (both Old Style and New Style) and left instructions that two more dates for his death were to be chiseled in [24].

Today this seems odd that folks would get that upset about a calendar change but it took a lot of political will to fix an issue that was growing out of control. The question for us today is will we act on the issues facing us or muddle along?

We have heard the term "Sputnik moment" [25] (when the USSR launched a satellite and the U.S. realized they were behind in the race to space) on the political stage lately. One of the institutions that came out of America's reaction to "losing the race to space" was Defense Advanced Research Projects Agency (DARPA) [26]. DARPA has a cyber thrust designed to enable military systems and infrastructure to operate effectively in the presence of cyber attacks. Technologies that eliminate entire classes of vulnerabilities, that adapt immediately to evolutions or novel developments of the cyber threat, and that raise the cost of employing cyber technologies against U.S. forces are the focus of this thrust. DHS has a National Initiative for Cybersecurity Education (NICE) program consisting of Highlights National Initiative for Cybersecurity Careers and Studies (NICCS) and the National Cybersecurity Workforce Framework. That said we need to look at our open education system—it is a national strength but also presents a threat vector. We do not teach other countries how to build atomic-bombs in our universities, but we do teach them everything we know about cyberspace. Most products related to cyber are not actively controlled by International Traffic in Arms Regulations (ITAR) as we do not have clear rules about what constitutes an export of a cyber capability that can be used as a weapon (classic example here is encryption which is covered by ITAR). As the government (to include the military) has moved from driving technology to buying it, they are now using standard commercial-off-the-shelf products many of which were programmed and built all around the world. Much of the research is now also being done overseas. So as we continue to realize and talk about how critical the cyber domain is to our national interests and what a central role it will play in any kind of conflict we are aggressively exporting everything about it.

The final driving concern is the Cyber Arms Race that is starting. With more and more countries becoming dependent on the Internet it becomes more dangerous for weapons of mass disruption to be built. The chance of a cyber war escalating into a traditional armed conflict is too high to risk; we need to establish rules and processes to ensure appropriate reactions.

There is no quick fix for the many issues we face that need to be addressed at the national level. We need to start making incremental steps on each issue starting with our allies and economic partners. There needs to be a national plan that lays out how we will engage a Computer Emergency Readiness Team (CERT), Law Enforcement Agency (LEA), Legal System and Military, and has incentives and punitive measures built in. It needs senior leadership sponsors and technical competence teamed together.

Finally, it is key to establish the roles and responsibilities for cyber conflicts. If this is a war then it belongs to the military, if it is espionage it belongs to the intelligence agencies, if it is a national security issue it belongs to Department of Homeland Security (DHS). "This is a turf war, The Constitution doesn't allow for idiocy. You either make DHS do their job or you find another way." said James Cartwright, the retired US Marine Corps general who stepped down as vice chairman of the Joint Chiefs of Staff in August and is now with the Center for Strategic and International Studies. The practice of DoD, in the form of US Cyber Command (CYBERCOM) or Northern Command (NORTHCOM), assisting when it comes to attacks against private entities runs into potential legal problems, said Dale Meyerrose, former associate Director of National Intelligence and founder of the Meyerrose Group. "It's against the law for the military to directly support commercial companies," he said. "We sometimes forget that the United States military does not protect the United States except in a very gross aggregate sense. The United States military does not operate within the borders of the United States. What people are calling for is a redefinition of that role [27]."

SUMMARY

So as we look at the ages—Stone Age, Bronze Age, Iron Age, Agricultural Age, Industrial Age, Information Age, Space Age, and now Digital Age—it is clear that technology has been a large driver in our progress. The pace of change has increased over time and continues to accelerate almost exponentially. The domains of war have gone from kinetic to analog to digital and are now enmeshed with our baseline society infrastructure. There are Evolutionary (WikiLeaks, Stuxnet) versus Revolutionary (social media) challenges coming and we need to have a process to address them at the speed of need.

One of the key aspects we have looked at is what a "cyber war" is. The Chatham House Report "On Cyber Warfare" said that, in order to understand whether a hostile action in cyberspace is warlike, it is necessary not just to observe the event but also to understand the actor's intent. Warfare, in the Clausewitzian view, is "an act of force to compel our enemy to do our will." It follows that the actor's intent or "will," on either side of the conflict, must be established before it can be stated that what is taking place is an act of war, or is something else altogether [28]. This traditional view is no longer practical; we cannot identify the intent of someone who steals national security secrets today. Others want to restrict the term to a Congressionally declared war. Again this is not practical today both because it is hard to see a situation where we will be in a declared "War" in the twenty-first century and the term "war" has been co-opted by slogans like "war on drugs." The answer lies not so much in what we call it but what tools we use to address it. We think we must accept the term since it is widely in use and "cyber warfare" is the standard bearer for the cyber conflict challenges we are facing daily. The key is determining and defining what tools do we use to address it: Research, Law Enforcement Agencies, Homeland Security Department, Cyber Command, National Security Agency, and Legislation all have a part but none of them are in charge today.

We must pull from adjacent disciplines such as cultural experts like Toffler (three key drivers of change that are powerfully shaping the future of businesses and governments are innovation, sustainability, and adaptability) [29] and change management experts like Dr. John Kotter (studies have proven that 70% of all major change efforts in organizations fail) [30] to help us organize the right answer. As we move forward into the cyber domain of warfare there will continue to be national and international issues around doctrine, legal principals and generally accepted use of cyberspace as a battle space. For now, regardless of what we call it, there are active cyber conflicts across the national elements of power and continued need for skilled practitioners and capabilities to deal with them.

References

[1] Taleb N. NY Times first chapters, http://www.nytimes.com/2007/04/22/books/chapters/0422-1st-tale.html; 2007.

[2] Taleb N. Ten principles for a black swan-proof world, http://www.fooledbyrandomness.com/tenprinciples.pdf; 2009.

[3] Defense Science Board Reports – Capability Surprise VI and VII, http://www.acq.osd.mil/dsb/reports2000s.htm; 2008.

[4] WG CDR Chris Mills, AM. PAK-FA, F-35, F-22 and "Capability Surprise", http://www.ausairpower.net/APA-NOTAM-230210-1.html; 2010.

[5] Joseph Farah's G2 Bulletin. U.S. failed to detect Chinese stealth fighter, http://www.wnd.com/index.php?fa=PAGE.view&pageId=252165; 2011.

[6] Taleb N. NY Times first chapters [online], http://www.nytimes.com/2007/04/22/books/chapters/0422-1st-tale.html; 2007.

[7] Didier Sornette Dragon-Kings, Black Swans and the Prediction of Crises [online], http://www.uvm.edu/pDoDds/files/papers/others/2009/sornette2009a.pdf; 2009.

[8] Reed TC. At the abyss: an insider's history of the cold war. New York: Ballantine; 2005.

[9] Davis J. Hackers take down the most wired country in Europe [online], http://www.wired.com/politics/security/magazine/15-09/ff_estonia?currentPage=all; 2007.

[10] Jackson W. The cyberattack that awakened the Pentagon [online], http://gcn.com/articles/2010/08/25/DoD-cyberdefense-strategy-082510.aspx; 2010.

[11] Krebs B. Russian Hacker Forums Fueled Georgia Cyber Attacks [online], http://voices.washingtonpost.com/securityfix/2008/10/report_russian_hacker_forums_f.html; 2008.

[12] Zetter K. Google Hack attack was ultra sophisticated, new details show [online], http://www.wired.com/threatlevel/2010/01/operation-aurora/; 2010.

[13] Zetter K. How digital detectives deciphered Stuxnet, the most menacing malware in History [online], http://www.wired.com/threatlevel/2011/07/how-digital-detectives-deciphered-Stuxnet/; 2011.

[14] Interview with James Gosler Sandia Fellow; May 26, 2012.

[15] McAfee in the crossfire-critical infrastructure in the age of cyber war [online], http://www.mcafee.com/us/resources/reports/rp-in-crossfire-critical-infrastructure-cyber-war.pdf; 2010.

[16] McMonnell M. Washington post. Outlook & opinions, http://www.washingtonpost.com/wp-dyn/content/article/2010/02/25/AR2010022502493.htm; 20l0.

[17] Schneier B. Threat of "Cyberwar" has been hugely hyped. CNN, http://edition.cnn.com/2010/OPINION/07/07/schneier.cyberwar.hyped/; 2010.

[18] Interview with Raduege H. January 25, 2011.

[19] Zetter K. Google hack attack was ultra sophisticated, new details show. Wired, http://www.wired.com/threatlevel/2010/01/operation-aurora/; 2010.

[20] Carr J. Dragons, tigers, pearls, and yellowcake: 4 Stuxnet targeting scenarios, http://blogs.forbes.com/firewall/2010/11/22/dragons-tigers-pearls-and-yellowcake-4-Stuxnet-targeting-scenarios/; 2010.

[21] Calabresi M. WikiLeaks' war on secrecy: truth's consequences. Times, http://www.time.com/time/world/article/0,8599,2034276,00.html; 2010.

[22] Interview with Douglas DePeppe Principal at i2IS Cyberspace, Solutions June 1, 2012.

[23] Cheryl Pellerin US, China Must Work Together on Cyber, Panetta Says [online], http://www.defense.gov/news/newsarticle.aspx?id=116235; 2012.

[24] Meyerrose D. GM of cyber integrated solutions. In: Presentation at 4th annual homeland security conference: s.n.; 2010.

[25] Wilson S. What's a 'Sputnik moment'? washingtonpost.com, http://voices.washingtonpost.com/44/2011/01/whats-a-sputnik-moment.html; 2011.

[26] DARPA History. http://www.darpa.mil/history.html; 2011 [accessed 17.01.11].

[27] Fryer-Biggs Z. Debate slows new US cyber rules [online], http://www.defensenews.com/article/20120507/DEFREG02/305070004/Debate-Slows-New-U-S-Cyber-Rules; 2012.

[28] Cornish P, David L. Dave clemente and claire yorke. On cyber warfare. A chatham house report, www.chathamhouse.org.uk; 2010.

[29] Associates T. Technology and innovation 2025, http://www.toffler.com/our-thinking/other-publications.html; 2010 [accessed 17.01.10].

[30] Kotter Dr J. The 8 step process, http://www.kotterinternational.com/KotterPrinciples/ChangeSteps.aspx; 2011 [accessed 17.01.11].

Appendix

CYBER TIMELINE

When anyone thinks about a recent event or tries to remember a historical incident in context, it is very difficult. We have provided this timeline of some of the significant events that have shaped or impacted cybersecurity to help you understand the relationship of what has happened.

- 1912 Radio Act Regulates private communications
- 1945 Rear Admiral Grace Murray Hopper discovers a moth trapped between relays in a Navy computer. She calls it a "bug," a term used since the late nineteenth century to refer to problems with electrical devices.
- 1946 ENIAC was the first general-purpose computer
- 1960 AT&T introduces its Dataphone, the first commercial modem
- 1962 First computer game invented—Spacewar Computer Game
- 1965 Established NIST responsibility for IT standards and technical assistance
- 1969 Department of Defense (DOD) Advanced Research Projects Agency (DARPA) established Advanced Research Projects Agency Network (ARPANET)
- 1970 Creeper worm and reaper virus are seen on ARPANET. (Reaper is created to delete creeper)
- 1971 The Floppy disk is created. This is the first instance of removable media
- 1972 Draper discovers a toy whistle from Cap'n Crunch could emit a 2600-Hz tone to get free phone calls from pay phones
- 1973 First encrypted message sent over ARPANET
- 1974 Institute of Electrical and Electronic Engineers (IEEE) proposed TCP/IP
- 1974 Rabbit virus was seen outside of the closed ARPANET
- 1977 PC Modem developed
- 1977 Data Encryption Standard (DES) encryption program is approved by National Bureau of Standards
- 1978 First SPAM e-mail sent (sent to 393 recipients on ARPANET)—becomes rampant by mid-1990s
- 1981 Chaos Computer Club (CCC) founded. It was the first hacker organization, striving for "freedom of information"
- 1981 First IBM PCs sold
- 1982 The 414 group broke into 60 computer systems and the incident appeared as the cover story of Newsweek with the title "Beware, Hackers at play"
- 1982 Movie TRON came out
- 1983 Internet Protocol Suite (TCP/IP) became standardized, and became the only approved protocol on ARPANET. The U.S. Military portion of ARPANET broke off to

become MILNET (later known as NIPRNET). ARPANET with MILNET was foundation for what became the Internet.

- 1983 The movie WarGames introduces the wider public to the phenomenon of hacking
- 1983 The FBI busts the "414s," a group of young hackers who break into several U.S. government networks, in some cases using only an Apple II+ computer and a modem.
- 1984 Computer Fraud and Abuse Act passed
- 1984 Domain Name System (DNS) was initiated
- 1984 The hacker magazine 2600 begins regular publication
- 1985 Elk Cloner was the first large-scale virus outbreak
- 1986 The first PC virus, "The Brain," is released by programmers in Pakistan
- 1986 Electronic Communications Privacy Act passed
- 1987 The number of network hosts reaches 10,000
- 1987 Computer Security Act passed
- 1988 Robert Morris created the first "worm"
- 1989 The number of network hosts surpasses 100,000
- 1989 Clifford Stoll discovers USSR cyber spies on Berkeley mainframe—becomes book "The Cuckoo's Egg"
- 1990 Secret Service launches Operation Sun Devil to hunt down hackers
- 1991 First digital cell phones sold
- 1992 The number of network hosts surpasses 1,000,000
- 1992 The first SMS (text message) is sent. It uses the control channel of a cellular connection
- 1992 Movie Sneakers came out
- 1993 The first DEFCON hacking conference takes place in Las Vegas
- 1994 First publicly known major cybercrime—Russian Vladimir Levin leads a group of hackers that steals millions of dollars from Citibank though its dial-up wire transfer service
- 1995 Time magazine has cover on "Cyber War"
- 1995 Hacker with handle "Hobbit" released Netcat (army knife of hacker tools)
- 1995 Kevin Mitnick arrested and eventually gets a five-and-a-half-year prison term
- 1996 The number of network hosts surpasses 10,000,000
- 1996 President Clinton Executive Order 13010, President's Commission on Critical Infrastructure Protection (PCCIP). "Examine physical and cyber threats to the critical infrastructures"
- 1996 Term Phishing Attacks becomes common as identity theft becomes bigger issue
- 1996 Health Insurance Portability and Accountability Act passed
- 1997 Nmap published as an article in Phrack magazine with source-code
- 1997 Eligible Receiver exercise tests the government's readiness for cyber attacks, results immediately classified
- 1998 Google search engine established
- 1998 Solar Sunrise incident hits the news as Pentagon gets hacked, ends up being two kids from California mentored by Israel hacker
- 1998 Martin Roesch starts open source called Snort—free Intrusion Detection System
- Wireshark (formally Ethereal) open source project starts—free sniffer/protocol analyzer

- 1998 Renaud Deraison started open source project called Nessus—free security scanner
- 1998 Digital Millennium Copyright Act (DMCA)
- 1998 Internet Corporation for Assigned Names and Numbers (ICANN) stood up
- 1998 Moonlight Maze incident DoD found intrusion from systems in Soviet Union but the sponsor of the attacks is unknown and Russia denies any involvement
- 1999 60 Minutes starts regular stories covering "Waging War With Computers"
- 1999 DES encryption broken due to small 56-bit key size
- 1999 Melissa virus unleashed; the first self-replicating worm
- 1999 Hackers in Serbia attack NATO systems in retaliation for NATO's military intervention in Kosovo
- 1999 Gramm Leach Bliley Act passed
- 1999 NATO accidentally bombs the Chinese embassy in Belgrade, spawning a wave of cyber attacks from China against U.S. government Web sites
- 2000 The number of network hosts surpasses 100,000,000
- 2000 Y2K bug hype ends up with little impact
- 2000 Mafiaboy shuts down major commercial Web sites
- 2000 First Top Officials (TOPOFF) exercise
- 2001 NIMDA (Admin spelled backward) hit
- 2001 USA Patriot Act passed
- 2001 Code Red worm hit—designed to conduct DDoS against White House
- 2001 Kournikova virus hit, malware embedded in an image
- 2001 AES, Advanced Encryption Standard, is published, and the standard becomes effective in 2002. Its key sizes range from 128-bits up.
- 2002 Bill Gates decrees that Microsoft will secure its products and services, and kicks off a massive internal training and quality control campaign
- 2002 Federal Information Security Management Act passed
- 2002 Solo (Gary McKinnon) hacked into government computers looking for UFOs
- 2002 Sarbanes–Oxley Act passed
- 2003 Titan Rain attacks identified, believed to be from China; it spawns new term "Advance Persistent Threat"
- 2003 SQL Slammer worm reached its peak within three minutes
- 2003 Metasploit Framework project started
- 2004 ILOVEYOU, aka LoveLetter, e-mail attack hit
- 2006 MySpace becomes main social networking site
- 2006 First Cyber Storm Exercise
- 2006 BackTrack, a forensics/penetration-testing-focused Knoppix build was released based on WHAX/Whoppix and Auditor Security Collection
- 2007 The number of network hosts surpasses 500,000,000
- 2007 Hackers believed to be linked to the Russian government bring down the Web sites of Estonia's parliament, banks, ministries, newspapers, and broadcasters—NATO reacts
- 2007 Storm Worm (one of the first BotNets) began infecting thousands of (mostly private) computers in Europe and the United States
- 2007 British Security Service, French Prime Minister's Office, and Office of German Chancellor all complained to China about intrusion on their government networks

- 2008 Facebook takes over from MySpace as main social networking site
- 2008 Operation Buckshot Yankee in reaction to Agent.btz forcing U.S. military to stop using thumb drives
- 2008 Databases of both the Republican and Democratic presidential campaigns were hacked and downloaded by unknown foreign intruders
- 2008 The networks of several Congressional offices were hacked by unknown foreign intruders (some incidents involved offices with an interest in human rights or Tibet)
- 2008 Cyber attackers hijack government and commercial Web sites in Georgia during a military conflict with Russia
- 2008 FBI conducts Dark Market sting on cyber identity theft ring
- 2009 Twitter Revolution occurs in Iran over election unrest
- 2009 FAA computer systems were hacked
- 2009 Ghost Net report released by Canadian researchers who found espionage tools they attributed to China implanted on government networks of 103 countries
- 2009 Reports in the press suggest that the plans for Marine Corps 1, the new presidential helicopter, were found on a file-sharing network in Iran
- 2009 Conficker worm infiltrated millions of PCs worldwide including many government-level top-security computer networks
- 2009 Reports reveal that hackers downloaded data about the F-35 Joint Strike Fighter, a multibillion-dollar high-tech fighter jet
- 2009 Zeus banking Trojan Horse released
- 2010 TRON Legacy hits theaters (28 years after original movie)
- 2010 First Cyber Shockwave exercise
- 2010 Operation Aurora in which Google publicly reveals being hacked (China blamed)
- 2010 October U.S. Cyber Command begins overseeing the protection of military networks from cyber threats
- 2010 WikiLeaks released U.S. embassy cables, Anonymous attacks MasterCard for stopping accepting donations for them
- 2010 Stuxnet worm attacks SCADA devices in Iran causing physical damage, eventually reveled as part of operation code-named Olympic Games by the United States and Israel in the book "Confront and Conceal Obama's Secret Wars and Surprising Use of American Power"
- 2010 China Redirect of 15% of internet traffic through its country (claimed it was an accident), this showed the DNS weaknesses
- 2011 The number of network hosts surpasses 883,000,000
- 2011 RSA attack allowed their security tokens to be compromised (used by Gov, DoD contractors, and financial organizations to name a few), China suspected
- 2011 Duqu (son of Stuxnet) released
- 2011 Tehran Bomb—Comodo Certificate Authority (CA) compromised allowing access to e-mail accounts of Iranian citizens and showing weakness of CAs
- 2011 saw an spike of Android threats as the phones started to outsell the iPhone
- 2011 Global Energy Cyberattacks "Night Dragon" report released showing systematic economic espionage against energy sector companies, China suspected
- 2011 Operation Shady RAT Report
- 2012 Anonymous attacks Sony multiple times causing impact on gamers
- 2012 Stop Online Piracy Act (SOPA) defeated when major vendors held webpage blackout

- 2012 Mac Defender and Flashback malware attacks Apple systems
- 2012 Flame and Gauss state-sponsored cyber exploit discovered—tied to Stuxnet
- 2012 Thunderstruck Atomic Energy Organization of Iran was attacked. The attackers played the AC/DC Thunderstruck song
- 2012 LinkedIn password leaks impact over 6 million users
- 2012 Shamoon attack against Saudi Aramco, one of the world's largest oil conglomerates, resulted in more than 30,000 computer systems wiped of all data
- 2013 President Obama signed Executive Order for Improving Critical Infrastructure Cybersecurity
- 2013 The Spamhaus Project—CyberBunker feud
- 2013 Mandiant Intelligence Center Report—APT1 Exposing One of China's Cyber Espionage Units
- 2013 South Korean banks and media report large number of computer network crashes causing speculation of North Korea cyberattack
- 2013 Kaspersky Lab releases reports on "Operation Red October" and "Operation NetTraveler"

Index

Note: Page numbers followed by *b* indicate boxes, *f* indicate figures and *t* indicate tables.